D0898451

JUST BECAUSE

JUST BECAUSE

*the story of the national movement
of Church Women United in the U.S.A.*
1941 through 1975

by

Margaret Shannon

Omega Books
Corte Madera, California

Library of Congress Catalog Card Number 77-0404

ISBN 0-89353-027-1

Cover Design by George Ivan Smith

All designs appearing in Section and chapter title pages in this volume are from *Handbook of Designs and Devices* by Clarence P. Hornung. Dover Publications, Inc., New York, 1946. Reprinted through the permission of the publisher.

Printed in the U.S.A.

JUST BECAUSE . . . .

the story of the national movement
of Church Women United in the
U.S.A. from 1941 through 1975.

To The Reader . . .   1941 through 1975

This book was written mostly for those who, by reason
of a birthdate or other circumstances, did not share in the
earlier years of our history. Just because they are at ease with
our tradition and purpose their vision will hearten onward the
company of Protestant, Orthodox, and Roman Catholic
women traveling together the venture-filled way ahead.

. . . Margaret Shannon

A living movement

CHURCH WOMEN UNITED IN THE U.S.A.

In encounter with the times
1941 to 1975

Acknowledgments

Margaret Sonnenday and Margaret W. Driscoll initiated this project out of the conviction that the experience of Church Women United since 1941 would be of historic value. A great deal of freedom was offered for me to reflect my own understanding of the dynamic nature and human aspects of the national movement.

This book is written now partly because two earlier publications are out of print. With deep appreciation I have used material from FOLLOW THOSE WOMEN by Gladys Gilkey Calkins. Published in 1961, this volume contained valuable material on the cooperative efforts among Protestant women between 1900 and 1940 in addition to the story of the first 20 years of United Church Women. Marjorie Terrell wrote a short sequel covering the years from 1961 to 1965 entitled THIS IS OUR HERITAGE.

I have borrowed freely from *The Church Woman* magazine. The fact that each issue is a current history in itself is a tribute to three editors: Mabelle LeGrand (1942-51); Helen Baker (1951-65); and Ruth Weber, the present editor.

In addition I have depended on the archives, memories, and good judgment of many others, particularly Mrs. Emory Ross, but also Mrs. Percy Rex, Mrs. Leo Marsh, Mrs. J.C. Piper, Mrs. John Minsker, Mrs. George Martin, Dr. Lillian O'Conner and the former national presidents and staff.

I am especially grateful for those who wrote contributions for the last section inasmuch as a variety of perspectives was needed in that fast moving decade when the forest and the trees really were the same. I am indebted to Anna Harrison and Nina Boswell who delved into files to secure or correct dates to make the appendices a compendium for quick referral.

Most especially it was a privilege to work with C'Lee Fogg during the last stages of shaping up an over extended manuscript to a more acceptable size. Her spirit heartened me onward and her editorial skill made a book come out of the discouraging period of reconstruction.

—M.S.

Preface

Church Women United was never as good as our claims for it. On the other hand it was always better than we could prove! The national movement is unique in ecumenical history in that it began with women who already were experienced in working together across a wide spectrum of denominations in their local communities. Rooted in many ethnic and ecclesiastical traditions, church women found in unity the freedom to respond in their own way to a God-given calling. It was this authentic core that held them together. Although its jurisdiction remains American based, this movement from its beginning was a channel of worldwide interest and involvement.

Writing about a living movement has its problems. It seemed simple enough to begin by cranking up its Constituting Convention in 1941 only to discover that I had to back up 40 years to get started. As for stopping this omnibus book, I slammed on the brakes to bring it to a halt in 1975, only to watch the movement rush past me into the future before the book came off the press.

To be on our way together for thirty-five years may not seem a very long time. However, it is long enough to indicate that this movement will outlive its founders which is a prime test of any social or religious movement.

History is only punctuated by the calendar. In cycles of related events, the earthshaking forces are perceived. In the midst of them, we express our faith. It would have violated the real achievements of Church Women United if we had attempted to contain its spirit in a series of happenings year by year, for linear is only one dimension in the living of these years. Moreover, there is the broadening which comes from experience and encounter. There is the depth that comes from reflection.

So I have partially resolved this predicament by gathering the substance of this story within three time cycles, the boundaries of which are determined by a basic change in the national movement calling for a new phrasing of purpose, new bylaws, a more suitable structure and a more descriptive name.

The change of the name in itself is not as significant as the reason for making a change. Bylaws are only the frame after the picture has been taken. Each set of bylaws contains in words how church women see themselves coping with their times and how the movement adjusted its relationships with church structures as a whole.

The three sections of this volume are as follows:

I. The *Seeds of Hope Sprouting,* Chapters 1 and 2, covers the period when we were The United Council of Church Women (1941-1950).

II. The *Circle of the Possible,* Chapters 3 through 6, is of the time when we were The General Department of United Church Women of the National Council of Churches of Christ (1950-1966).

III. *Hand Touches Hand,* Chapters 7 through 12, is of our time as Church Women United, again a national autonomous movement (1966-1975).

Let me say that these rapidly changing cycles also created a semantic problem of style and substance. Particularly I was caught by the transitions of the liberating movements. The old words were forced to carry all the shame of the former oppressed condition. The new words were charged with emotion that cut off communication. I was advised to use the word that was most commonly accepted in the particular period being described, but those were not even themselves commonly accepted matters.

Seeking the forbearance of all concerned, I shall use the word "Negro" in Sections I and II, and the word "black" in Section III; the word "chairman" until the early 1970's and then "chairperson" in the rest of the narrative.

Likewise, as was the accepted custom during most of this period, I shall identify a woman by her husband's name in Sections I and II—at least the first time she is mentioned. In Section III I shall use her given name. In the index you will find both forms for each person, whenever that information is available.

Within each time cycle, there are certain recurring patterns, designed to describe the way in which church women coped with certain issues of the time. This topical approach on a background of a repeated span of years may make the pattern seem too busy. But actually that is the way it was. "We came into being on the swing," wrote one national president, "and have been at it ever since . . . meeting each crisis as it comes with little time to analyze—leaping from crag to crag."

In other words our program was not determined by professional planners. Even though it might have been better, the result would have been different. What national officers attempted to do was to capture the trends and concerns of their large constituency and give them some shape and impetus.

Purposely I have written in detail about some events and some people more than the occasion itself justifies. I hoped thus to convey the mood and manner which pervaded many similar situations at the time. Even then I can only describe what the problem was and what we did about it at the beginning. The final impact can never be determined and that is our hope of spiritual maturity and human humility.

The choice of the title, JUST BECAUSE, came out of a lifetime interest in WHY church women initiated certain efforts.

In an effort not to deal only in vague generalities, I included with each story even the actual names of women connected with it. If I had chosen another set of stories, there would have been others equally worthy of being named. The frustrations and foibles, the minor skirmishes and victories of a particular person are included not because they are unique but because her words and experience could be echoed by hundreds of women who lived in the same generation. Just because church women believe that being one in spirit is more important than individual credit lines, Church Women United has grown through the years.

I shall always hurt because I did not have the words to describe the quality and contribution of each of the national officers and professional staff whose names are listed in the valuable compendium in the closing pages. I knew and worked with all of them personally. For them the movement was more

important than anything they did for it. Some of their assign-
ments were newsworthy while others were working just as
persistently on sustaining the whole program in ongoing
administrative operations.

If only I had words that could sing and groan as I write
about the dreams which grew and blossomed and died and
rose again through the lives of all these women. But I do not.
Church Women United is an experience. It is living in the
company of the longings of many other women.

If at any given time, you had asked "WHY" or "HOW
COME", any one of them might have answered in terms of
sensing and doing the will of God. However, more likely, she
would have flashed a knowing smile and made a modest
response: JUST BECAUSE—

Margaret Shannon
January 1977

Let the new idea speak
unafraid, its meaning to us.
And let us speak to it, also without fear
And give us the humility and power
to hear quickly
the *little green seed of hope sprouting*
lest we trample it not knowing it is here.

(from the poem "Teach Us To Listen"
by Lillian Smith)

TABLE OF CONTENTS

Acknowledgments
Preface

SECTION ONE: SEEDS OF HOPE

United Council of Church Women 1941-1950

A seed of hope
SECTION TWO: CIRCLE OF THE POSSIBLE
General Department of United Church Women 1950-1965

chapter 3   Circle of the possible

chapter 4 **A friend-filled circle**

chapter 5 **Encircling all with human rights**

SECTION THREE: HAND TOUCHES HAND

Church Women United 1966 through 1975

Explore units; Listening teams, p. 171; Committee on New Dimensions in a Continuing Commitment, p. 173; National Goals, p. 174; Program elements: Visible Fellowship to affirm Jesus Christ and responsible action in our own time, p. 175; Spiritual renewal (the Wells), p. 177.

chapter 9 **God-given gifts . . . . .**

Context: from their position of relative freedom, American women became less satisfied with superficial values; realized that their potential gifts were not being used, nor were they fully participating in the social and political process. Why? p. 270;

Liberating voices come from many sources; confrontation at the NCCC Assembly, p. 272; revelance of era with several simultaneous breakthroughs and resulting rapid social changes, p. 275.

Commission on Women in Today's World, p. 278; pilot workshops with interracial team, p. 280; Board statements on ERA and abortion, p. 280;

chapter 10 **Integrity in relationships . . . . .**

.

Section 1: See

s of Hope

JUST BECAUSE

from the beginning

its roots were in mission;

the United Council of Church Women

was like .... A SEED OF HOPE SPROUTING

SECTION I

1941-1950

**United Council of
Church Women
1941-1950**

chapter 1

A seed of hope sprouting

The damp, wintry weather added to the murkiness of my usual Sunday afternoon drowsiness. I was wide awake instantly however when the symphony coming in over the radio was interrupted with emergency announcements:

PEARL HARBOR BOMBED BY JAPANESE AIRFORCE
SURPRISE ATTACK CRIPPLES AMERICAN FLEET IN PACIFIC
PRESIDENT CALLS EMERGENCY SESSION OF CONGRESS
MOUNTING CRIES FOR U.S. ENTRANCE INTO WAR

Like many other Americans on December 7, 1941, I felt the shock across the miles. Jumping out from behind the academic bushes of my mind, the fragmented events of the two previous years were screaming, "So? So? I told you so."

Franklin D. Roosevelt had won his third term on a platform of keeping us out of war. University students whom I had coached for peace teams the year before were now commissioned officers in the armed services. The fascist tentacles strangled many aspects of life in Germany and Italy with its satellite holdings; the peoples in the colonies of Africa were being used as supply lines for different European powers; Generalissimo Chiang Kai-shek, beset by millions of poverty-ridden peasants and competitive war lords, was now challenged by the Communist uprising as well as the Japanese military; the German army was invading Russia, consolidating a people once divided by ideological discussions. And now, inevitably, the United States!

Despair and loneliness overcame me. I knew no one in my apartment house. I walked over to the office hoping that people would be gathering to decide what to do about the emergency. But the doors locked the dark silence in and the bewildered me out. Doubtless my colleagues were in their suburban homes where their families and neighbors could all talk at once without feeling the necessity of standing by what they said or felt at that moment. I walked back to the apartment to call my family in the middle west. The lines were busy.

COMMITTEE ON COOPERATION The next week found me on the train bound for Atlantic City where the Constituting Convention of the United Council of Church Women was scheduled to convene. Something about the rhythmic clank of the wheels as they passed over the joined sections of the track made me recall the final meeting of the Committee on Cooperation which had met in Swarthmore in June 1940 to complete the final plans for the proposed new movement. A few weeks previously I had moved to New York to begin work for the Presbyterian Board of Foreign Missions. Gertrude Schultz, who had been influential in the causes of unity among women since 1920, decided to yield her place on that committee to her young associate: "This is a movement you will have to live with, Margaret," she said prophetically. "You might as well take responsibility for its proposed constitution."

And so it happened that my first interdenominational assignment was to attend the meeting that considered the proposed framework of the United Council of Church Women.

The formation of a constitution is not exactly the place to develop enthusiasm for a women's movement. At the meeting were representatives of three national interdenominational committees: The National Council of Church Women, the Council of Women for Home Missions, and the

Committee on Women's Work of the Foreign Missions Conference. For a number of years these national groups had been trying to come to terms with each other and their overlapping influence with the growing number of "united" groups in local communities.

In 1937 there had been created a Committee on Cooperation, charged with bringing into harmony the various interests and with formulating the constitution of one movement in which all could agree. Under the leadership of Miss Daisy Trout from Indiana (a member of the Disciples of Christ), Mrs. Katherine Silverthorn (a Presbyterian), and Miss Mary Smith of Minnesota (an Episcopalian), the Committee was ready to report in 1940 to a representative meeting held in a guest house on the Swarthmore College campus.

Even if I had been briefed, I would not have had enough organizational experience to appreciate the anxiety and the hopes of those whose lives had been invested in the merging organizations and their constituencies.

At the time I did not catch the innuendoes introduced as amendments, polite opposition, or compromises. Sitting on the outer edge near the door, I did not feel the thrill of group triumph when the plan of union was unanimously adopted as a basis for the calling of the 1941 Atlantic City Constituting Convention. As the entire Committee on Cooperation rose spontaneously and sang the Doxology, I slipped out to walk alone in the garden—somewhat annoyed at the fuss. "Praise God from whom the blessing of a constitution flows" thought I, remembering the dull document over which there had seemed to me to be much "nit-picking." Do these women know where the action is? Do they know there is a world out there?

I was 29 at the time and did not realize I had witnessed the last birthpang of a movement about to be born. In the years that followed, this movement was to demonstrate that women could initiate programs of corporate significance; it was to prove that women could mobilize an affirmative response to the challenge of the times and bear the pain and changes of a world in turmoil.

Let me offer a belated word of appreciation for this

*negotiating committee and its proposed constitution. In later years I was to struggle through several revisions in these bylaws, each of which defined the movement of church women for a particular time in history. The threads of such agreements are almost invisible to the majority of women who approve these legal documents; yet together they form the cord binding together intentions with responsibility, enabling church women to become an organized point of force—**just because** they do care about the world out there! Confronted by the rapid and radical social changes of the 60's and 70's, we would not have had the time nor the available leadership to have formed the basic structure. An opportunity would have been missed; the future would have gone another way.*

After three years of negotiations, the Committee on Cooperation was ready to issue its call for a Constituting Convention to meet in December 1941. It was agreed that the Convention would be composed of 100 delegates, half of whom would be representatives of local interdenominational organizations and the others appointed in equal proportion by the Council of Women for Home Missions and the Committee on Women's Work of the Foreign Missions Conference.

It did not seem strange to me at the time that nothing was said about denominational representation. The Convention was to be made up of women both on a local and national level who had already demonstrated their willingness and eagerness to work together for mission and unity.

This was an important base for women to discover. Christian women were free as individuals to express their own convictions in the company of others who shared their driving purpose.

It was living faith in God and each other which bound them together as a movement.

The plan was completed on a Saturday. It was proposed that we spend Sunday morning through lunch together in silence, as a preparation for the service of dedication. Silence was a new group experience for this committee. Already victims of semantic smog, a few registered nervous reactions.

Others breathed a prayer of gratitude out of deep satisfaction knowing that the future of a beloved Cause would be in safe hands. Within all of us there rose a lively hope that this document would lace with reality our dreams of a movement of Christ's women working together to the glory of God.

AN EXCURSION INTO THE PAST What the women of 1941 had going for them was the foundation work of others during the previous 40 years. For a better understanding of many traditions which were to endure for decades, we need to detour around the present story via the by-paths of its past.

In 1941 there already existed hundreds of united organizations in local communities. They had come into being on their own momentum and had a variety of forms and names such as missionary unions, federations of church women, local councils of church women. Some of them were at least 50 years old at the time the new national organization was being proposed. There is some evidence that some of them went as far back as 1868. The Women's Missionary Union of Springfield, Missouri, for example, dates from a day in 1887 when its constitution was adopted at an all day meeting where 300 women from 11 churches were in attendance. A survey of the Federal Council of Churches around 1926 reported a total of 1900 of these local united groups. There was no understanding that most of them were interested in conforming to one national pattern, at least as an auxillary to the Federal Council!

Possibilities within this healthy grassroot constituency gave the proposed UCCW its lease on a future. It was fairly certain that all of them utilized material produced by the National Committee of the World Day of Prayer. In 1940 this material was used by 7,000 local World Day of Prayer committees. Many of the organizations looked to one or more of the national bodies for guidance, but were free to make decisions on their own activities. "It was an intangible sort of freedom," wrote Mrs. Calkins, "but real enough to women who had not previously experienced it within their own churches."

So it was true, as was claimed later, that the national movement grew out of the vibrant life of local units. But it is equally true that national leadership played an important part in the development of the nature and achievement of these interdenominational groups in local communities. Until about 1920 these national leaders were members of Women's Boards of Home or Foreign Missions related to one of several denominations. These Boards were able to command the services of women of unusual calibre who gave freely of their time as volunteers carrying on administrative functions as well as promotion of educational activities among the women of their churches. (Later when their Boards merged with the general missionary boards of their churches, these same tasks were assigned to paid staff, not all of whom were women!) For these remarkable women the Cause was of supreme importance and they readily associated with women in other denominations who shared their enthusiasm.

It was from these women that the calls for Days of Prayer were issued in 1887 and 1890. Mrs. Darwin James, the mother of seven children, who grew up in the aftermath of a nation divided over slavery, was concerned for the poor immigrants from Europe and the Orient who had come to these shores seeking a new life. She was president of the Women's Board of Home Missions (Presbyterian Church U.S.A.) which seemed to be making only a dent in the problems of these helpless newcomers. Believing that those who prayed persistently would become advocates of the powerless, she issued a call to set aside a day of prayer for Home Missions in 1887.

In 1890 Mrs. Henry Peabody of Boston and Mrs. Helen Barrett Montgomery of Rochester, N.Y., both outstanding Baptist women, made an appeal for a Day of Prayer for Foreign Missions. The response was immediate for both days. Prayer for one cause was in addition to, and not in lieu of, the other.

This was the beginning of an exciting era for women and it was highlighted by several dramatic achievements between 1900 and 1920. In 1900 the World Ecumenical Missionary Conference spearheaded by Dr. John R. Mott brought Christian leaders from all over the world to New York. The American women in attendance were inspired to share the vision of a world Christian movement with other women. The idea came to prepare and issue jointly materials for mission study which up to this time had been done separately by each of the denominational women's boards of missions.

"This eminently sensible idea resulted in the first truly interdenominational undertaking by women," wrote Mrs. Calkins in *Follow These Women.*

A Central Committee on the United Study of Foreign Missions was set up in 1901; two years later a similar one for home missions was formed, and a few years later they merged. The Committee insisted that the manuscripts be of high quality and took the responsibility for editing, publishing and widely promoting their use. Thousands of volumes were published during the next 30 years. Their experience proved valuable in 1938 when the Missionary Education Movement was created.

It was only natural that a training program for leaders of mission study would follow. The first in 1907 was established at Winona Lake, Indiana and twelve such regional schools were in operation by 1920. There was a mystique about these experiences that was hard to explain. The 'Northfield spirit' (or that of Silver Bay or Asilomar or Lake Geneva) had to be experienced, for no one could really describe how inspiration and serious study created fast friends across denominational lines in a week.

JUBILEE - 1911   Their success in the publication program through the Central Committee encouraged the women's boards to plan together for a Jubilee program celebrating 50 years of women's work for missions (1860-1910). Thousands of women from every denomination were reached in series of meetings held across the country. There was a special program featuring a pageant written by Helen Barrett Montgomery, a New Testament scholar and author of many books. Mrs. Peabody and Mrs. Montgomery, both dynamic speakers, presented the world mission cause as central to the message of the Church and not a matter to be handled by a few dedicated women in a small society. A Jubilee gift amounting to a million dollars was received by the sponsoring committee. In order to administer these funds there was established the Federation of Women's Boards of Foreign Missions. The Women's Council for Home

Missions had already organized in 1906. Stimulated by the association of women working together across denominational lines on the Jubilee, many new missionary unions were formed.

In 1914 the Federation of Women's Boards launched another cooperative effort that was to continue on through the years ahead. It rose out of a concern that Christian women, many newly literate, in Asia, Africa and Latin America needed literature written in their own language and cultural patterns which conveyed the basic information that every adult needs. Of course one of the tools which mothers wanted was good general reading material for children. So the committee for Christian Literature for Women and Children in Mission Lands was formed. Periodicals and books in many languages were thus subsidized. Training programs for writers and editors were also undertaken.

In 1921 under the leadership of a national committee, the church women of America raised over two million dollars, mostly in small amounts, for housing facilities and staff of the Union Christian Colleges for Women in the Orient. The fund was augmented by another million from the Laura Spelman Rockefeller Trust Fund, so that initial investments could be made in several new women's colleges in India and Japan and China.

Stewardship of the ongoing programs of the Women's Colleges as well as those of the Committee on Christian Literature became a continuing commitment after 1928 by church women united in the World Day of Prayer.

This need for a National Committee for the World Day of Prayer was readily seen by this time, and such a committee was organized in 1919 by the two interdenominational mission bodies to prepare worship materials and to correspond with local communities. Already there was pressure to establish a single day of prayer for both home and foreign missions and to have a uniform date for this annual occasion.

Recognizing its coordinating function, the national committee promptly responded with a call for all church women to come together on the first Friday of Lent in 1920 to pray together for the mission of the Church in the United

States and other countries. That same year Mrs. S. S. Hough, the President of the Women's Mission Association of the United Brethren Church and also chairman of the World Day of Prayer Committee, corresponded with interested women in Canada to encourage them to form their own national committee.

Soon after, other Committees were formed in Great Britain, Australia, New Zealand and South Africa. Missionaries from each of these centers were part of the company who carried the story of the Day of Prayer in other countries. In 1927 the Day of Prayer became in name what it already was in fact—a World Day of Prayer for Missions.

In 1927 the first offering of 70 dollars came spontaneously from one community. However the amount grew rapidly even during the depression and was divided equally between the Council of Women for Home Missions and the Committee on Women's Work of the Foreign Missions Conference. Four major projects were named to receive support: the ministry among migrant workers and their families, a religious educational program for Indian youth in the United States, the united christian colleges for women in Asia, and the Committee for Christian Literature for Women and Children in Mission Lands.

At the time of the Constituting Convention, Margaret Applegarth had been chairman of the National Committee on the World Day of Prayer for several years. A nationally known author and speaker, Miss Applegarth utilized her extraordinary skill to enrich the worship material. Her insights into and love of the Bible, her sensitive interpretation of women in other areas of the world, and her high regard for the four approved projects were combined to give breadth and depth to the meaning of the World Day of Prayer.

Involvement in specific projects was the secret of interdenominational work. Since national leaders with a single minded purpose were not so readily available in later years, the achievements of these two decades were never equalled. This was not primarily due to the fact that the Women's Boards were merged with the general missionary boards of the denomina-

tions with the consequent loss of leadership in initiating program and mobilizing response.

Just because the next 20 years were different times there was another dimension of ecumenical growth. From 1920 to 1940 our times compelled us to live in the midst of: . . . *the aftermath of World War I* (A generation, expressing revulsion of the costly war 'to make the world safe for democracy', indulged themselves in wild sprees, 'speakeasies' and cheap commercial entertainment. A mood of national isolationism rejected the League of Nations.)

. . .*an awakening among women as citizens* (The 18th Amendment gave voting rights, and increasing awareness). discrimination in industry.)

. . .*a battle of Fundamentalism vs. Liberalism* waged from pulpits and political platforms, and in courtrooms.

. . .*a major economic depression* with the federal government assuming a new role in massive welfare and recovery programs.

MAY It was during the bank moratorium in March 1933 **LUNCHEONS** that the Administrative Committee of the Women's Council for Home Missions was holding its annual meeting. Realizing that they were being gripped by the same fear as the people who stood in long lines for food in downtown New York, they began to plan to turn their despondent mood into a "festive party to prove the life that is in us." Six weeks later a May Day Luncheon was held on Monday, May 1, 1933 at 12 o'clock at the George Washington Hotel in New York City. A program was presented on two topics: "Child Health" and "Children of Migrant Families". A report later showed a balance of 33 cents to be returned to the treasurer after all the expenses were paid!

For four successive years the annual luncheon prospered, growing in interest and in attendance. One report says that among those present were "a number of clergy and Mrs. Calvin Coolidge."

In 1937, Mrs. Augusta Trowbridge, chairman of the Administrative Committee, suggested that the May luncheon in New York take the form of enlarged luncheons open to all Protestant women in the city. The luncheon was a great success with 670 women attending. Dr. Mary Ely Lyman and Dr. Joseph Sizoo spoke on unity. Said Dr. Sizoo, "We want a world without slums and without sweatshops."

In 1938 a letter went out calling Protestant women all over this land to gather in their respective communities simultaneously to consider "Unity in Christian Service." Excitement must have run high as requests for the program material came pouring in from 44 states and Canada.

Quite independently the National Council of Federated Church Women began a series of Dedication Days in 1933 for the purpose of encouraging community interest in local councils of church women and their social concerns. In 1935 it was proposed that local councils celebrate Dedication Day on Ascension Day because "it was then that the church received her mandate to evangelize all of life." For the first time programs were printed in advance—"free to all groups affiliated with the NCFCW, 3 cents per copy to other groups."

In 1939, probably as a result of the work of the National Committee on Cooperation, as well as a recognition that some local communities were being approached from two sources, the Home Missions Council proposed that the appeal be combined and invitations be issued only in the name of the National Council of Church Women. In 1940 the minutes of this organization noted the three-fold purpose of this annual occasion: "To strengthen a growing sense of unity, the joy of Christian fellowship, and the power of Christianity in the day of need."

The fact that women in more than a thousand communities were meeting around these purposes was one of the unifying forces at the Constitutional Convention. The new United Council of Church Women was glad to continue the tradition which in 1945, was officially called May Fellowship Day.

Christian women working unitedly were not thrown by these circumstances even though as individuals every one of them was affected. They were bound to do something about this obvious need in their own communities. They were pragmatic rather than doctrinaire in their approach to social action.

If those who had so eagerly promoted the major mission projects displayed some sensitivity that social action was competitive to their primary interest, likewise those who were undertaking community centered projects did not hide their concern that too much energy and money was going through the established channels.

The staff of the Women's Boards were now enmeshed in the 'total church' program which was hurting badly from depletion of funds. Noting the drive, as well as the restlessness, of local organizations with more comprehensive programs, Mrs. Silverthorn and Mrs. Ferguson, the chairmen of the interdenominational women's committees of Foreign and Home Missions, began deliberately to explore other options.

And of course there was a further point. What help could a mission board executive in New York be to the women in the local Missionary Union of San Diego, California who listed as their objectives "to work for a new jail, improvement in children's tubercular wards, and the installation of a Rock Pile for drunken drivers?"

Some staff of the Federal Council had received letters making inquiry as to the possibilities of this more general group forming some linkage with the FCC. In 1924 they sought an interview with representatives of the two mission bodies. Meetings with the Association of Council Secretaries over the next several years obviously were not getting the answer.

At the Association meeting in Buffalo on May 30, 1928, it was proposed that a National Commission of Protestant Church Women be formed as an advisory body to local groups. The Associated Press gave ample coverage and the *New York Times* carried the news on the front page. An office was set up at 1123 Broadway in New York, and Mrs. Josephine M. Stearns of Indianapolis was appointed as the new executive.

NATIONAL COUNCIL OF FEDERATED CHURCH WOMEN Within a year the Commission was being challenged by a division of opinion from within as to its autonomy and from without by the onset of the economic depression.

At the first annual meeting of the National Commission at the Hotel Bellevue in Boston, internal tension was generated. Feeling that there was too much domination by the mission boards, the representatives of some of the local councils got together, organized themselves, adopted a name "The National Council of Federated Church Women" and elected Mrs. James T. Ferguson, a very able woman from Kansas City, as their president. In 1930, the National Commission on Church Women merged its interest and dissolved.

In 1932 the NCFCW moved its offices to Kansas City to be close to the heart of their constituency. These were tough depression years and the officers did most of their own work with the help of a halftime secretary.

The program adopted by the NCFCW covered a wide spectrum of interests: Bible Study, Christian family life, personal faith and experience, community issues, major social relations, the Church—its life and outreach, and world relations. These seven areas were the same as those offered in the general adult curriculum of the International Council of Religious Education. However, without adequate staff to provide services, this attempt to merge the women's program into the Christian Adult Movement was more of an experiment in cooperation than a permanently useful plan.

Although never able to claim more than 250 local councils as affiliate members, the NCFCW became a channel of productive volunteer efforts. A concern for more wholesome movies appropriately had begun from a local effort of previewing films in Southern California. The state council president in Indiana toured the state to get signatures of 100,000 people including young people to pledge to be on the alert in their communities for the choice of movies and to boycott those with "unwholesome advertizing appeal." One of the vice presidents, Mrs. Jesse M. Bader of New York, developed a national committee to review and evaluate films. Her work led directly to the establishment of the Protestant Motion Picture Council in the next decade.

Each of the annual meetings generated enthusiasm and,

according to Mrs. Calkins, the turning point in the fortunes of NCFCW was in 1935 marked by the meeting in Rochester, New York. With the return of better times there was a good attendance. Mrs. Harper Sibley, president of the local council, was prominent in the city and planned a program around the theme: "Frontiers of a Christian Social Order" as well as a series of social events in lilac time, which gave prestige and publicity to this self-propelled movement. State councils were encouraged: Texas and Georgia had been organized in 1934, Nebraska and Iowa in 1935, and others in succeeding years.

There was nothing limiting about the ideas lifted up by this group of women. The next year in Dayton the theme was "Exploring and Possessing the Unclaimed Areas of Life in Citizenship, Personal Living, World Peace and Economics." A social creed dealing with these issues was debated and adopted. One man observer, Dr. Harry C. Munroe, General Secretary of the ICRE in attendance at this meeting, wrote in admiration of the dynamics at work among them:

> Non-ecclesiastical agencies or movements have a spontaneity, a freedom, a vitality, which enables them to make a distinctive contribution to the Christian movement . . . *Watch these women!* Here we see a power, a radiance, a dedication of talents and service, a social idealism, and a passion which are sorely needed by our Christian movement.

THE CHURCH WOMAN   In 1937 the national office was moved to Chicago where more space was available and its name shortened to the National Council of Church Women. Its offical magazine, *The Church Woman,* which had come into being as a 12-page journal the year before was naturally moved also.[1] The president, Miss Daisy Trout, who had succeeded Mrs. J. N. McEachern of Atlanta as national president, showed her versatility by becoming the executive secretary and temporarily editor of *The Church Woman.* From its inception the magazine was a voice for justice and peace. As the war clouds gathered, an article was prepared by Muriel Lester, a pacifist, advocating "love of enemies" and a program of feeding women and children affected by hostilities in

Europe. Mrs. Herbert Crowe, of Peoria, Illinois, remembers the
reaction and she recounts it in a letter to Mrs. LeGrand on June
18, 1948:

> Some of the leading churchmen in the nation wrote tele-
> grams begging us to take no such stand since to do so
> would sever the unity of the church and certainly ruin
> the circulation of the magazine. But the committee
> decided that that was a Christian principle and we dare
> not be false to it. Finally, we presented both sides of the
> question. Having Muriel Lester write that article was a
> scoop for us editorially.
>
> Later other far better known magazines came out
> advocating the same thing but it was *The Church
> Woman* which fearlessly led out in an unpopular cause.
> Instead of hurting the circulation, we had dozens and
> dozens of letters from women across the country who
> said in effect "Thank God that one magazine dares to
> stand for the right. I want to take that kind of magazine,
> here is my subscription and one for a friend!"

Mrs. Crowe was connected with *The Church Woman*
from its beginning (as a committee chairman, business
manager, or editor) and she tells of Daisy Trout returning from
a meeting of the Committee on Cooperation in 1937. Waving a
copy of *The Church Woman* in the air, she made a surprising
announcement, her voice giving away her excitement, "Ladies,
I offered *The Church Woman* to the committee as the next
opportunity in cooperation for our three groups!" She then
went on to describe the further planning of the Committee on
Cooperation to the startled women.

The December, 1937, issue launched *The Church
Woman* as a joint publication. Daisy Trout continued editing it
and each organization sent material and promoted
subscriptions. In reality this did not change the policy of the
magazine which had been designed several years before in the
format of a religious *Reader's Digest,* containing information
of what was going on in the areas of concern to all church
women.

A joint committee was named and Susannah Crowe became its chairman. Almost unbelievable obstacles were overcome. Harriet Harmon Dexter edited the magazine from her home in Springfield, Illinois, where she was close to Susannah Crowe who was handling the whole business operation from her home—including addressing all subscription labels. When Mrs. Dexter moved to Wisconsin, Mrs. Percy Hayward became the editor until the United Council of Church Women came into being and the operation was moved to New York.

The Church Woman became the official organ of all three parent bodies in 1938. "This magazine exists," its chairman, Mrs. C. Burns Craig, wrote in 1939, "to show what adventures the women of the church have already started and more they may well begin . . . "

Thus *The Church Woman* became a unifying force in itself as well as a powerful instrument in interpreting the issues which would be before the Constituting Convention of the UCCW in 1941. The potential contribution of women both to make and to carry out decisions was emphasized in a time when the "voice of the official church is largely a male voice," wrote the editor of *The Church Woman* (September 1939). The tensions between home and foreign missions and between social actions and "missions" which had plagued the national leadership were interpreted as various aspects of the same Christian mandate finding expression in every neighborhood and nation.

As you soar over these events from some future present, perhaps you will recognize that some of the paths of pioneer women have become major highways over which many women are traveling in today's movement.

Because I am old enough to review the whole era with bifocal perspective, I discovered that many of the innovations of more recent years were not so new after all. But I also became aware of a stratospheric layer of values which was pervasive of this whole period. The atmosphere which gives breath and life is as important as the vehicle or the road if we are to arrive in faith at some up-to-then unknown destination in the future.

Therefore let me ventilate some of the elements which it is our obligation to conserve as a wholesome environment for any living moment:

* *Prayer and planning together, as well as patience with one another are more important than offices or committees when it comes to the ultimate satisfaction of most Christian women.*

* *Women with genuine aspirations and convictions can usually find for themselves simple flexible organizing relationships to carry out those convictions where they live.*

* *A happening which glitters for the first time in any generation is genuinely new. No generation is likely to U-turn to handle it the way it was done earlier.*

* *The size of her town and her income does not limit the concern of a woman for the whole world.*

* *Changing an attitude is uncomfortable for all concerned but it is an accepted part of the reality of growing relationships.*

* *A national movement becomes a roadblock if it is unwilling or unable to clear the path for the highest and best of its constituents.*

* *JUST BECAUSE Christ's women believe in unexpected acts of God through people, they have a lively hope; JUST BECAUSE Christ's women do all that is possible for them to do, they faithfully give evidence of things hoped for. JUST BECAUSE Christ's women keep in touch with one another, and all of the earth's peoples, love binds them together in a Kingdom of God's own making.*

The above are my convictions and the rest of this book affirms them.

The upcoming constituting convention was not called to be an all time answer to every need. Its intention was to face the fact that growth had reached an awkward stage, and there needed to be ˙a thinning out of complex and confusing superstructures. The constitution to be proposed was like one set of lockgates on a canal. It would form, for the time being, a single channel where the waters could deepen enough, God willing, to float a larger vessel. When the lockgates wear out they will be replaced.

CONSTITUTING CONVENTION   Every one of the women who arrived at Atlantic City was aware of the national crisis.

Threatening war clouds swirled across two oceans ready to destroy dreams of a movement of peace and good will. Telegrams awaited some that their menfolk had been called into military service. The windows of the local Japanese shops had been shattered by embittered local citizens. The shock which shook the nation punctuated every affirmative proposal with a question mark.

How would these events affect the planning for this new national organization? It was expected that the recommendations of the Committee on Cooperation would be accepted in principle. But at such a time in history, the tenuous shoot of a new organization would be buffeted by blustery winds outside the control of any organizing convention!

After the first round of commiserations of how the news of Pearl Harbor affected each person, the women settled down and worked hard at the task in their hands. Thus they kept their sanity in a national crisis in much the same manner as any one of them would have in a crisis within her own family.

The worship services were led by Margaret Applegarth, whose gentle greatness was in the intimate way she breathed life into the ecumenical movement.

One of the participants, Mary Lediard Doan, comments about the opening session in an article entitled "Church Women Unite" published in the *World Call,* February 1941.

Growth is always interesting, even though at times it seems slow. Its persistence was evident as Mrs. Katherine Silverthorn, quoting Bunyan's character who said, "Keep that light in your eye", led us in recollection along the tortuous path toward union. The journey ran from 1860 and the first women's union missionary organization, through a fiftieth anniversary in 1911 when $1,500,000 was raised as a special offering, through the formation of a National Council of Church Women in 1938, and through the first steps toward union of the NCW with the two national missionary groups of Protestant women, and on to the formation of one inclusive organization in 1941. Great personalities have given years of committee meetings, anxious planning, searching thought to the formation of this united group of church women which looks forward and pledges itself to larger service that will, in turn, demand greater wisdom, vision, courage, and strength . . ."

Miss Mable Head of Cleveland, Ohio, presented the proposed Constitution and Bylaws.

When approved, the Constitution of UCCW stated its purpose:

The purpose of the United Council of Church Women shall be to unite church women in their allegiance to their Lord and Savior, Jesus Christ, through a program looking to their integration in the total life and work of the church and to the building of a world Christian community.

The Bylaws called for a national Board which would include fifteen members appointed by each of the two inter-denominational mission agencies, forty-five members elected by the National Assembly to represent state and local units, appointees of other national interdenominational agencies, some members-at-large selected by the National Board, and the officers and committee chairmen.

Mrs. Emory Ross of New York City, chairman of the Nominating Committee, had anticipated the adoption of the proposed Constitution and Bylaws and was ready to present nominees for officers and members of the Board for election by the Convention. The nomination of the first president had been left open as a matter which the new board would want to determine. With three merging organizations, care and tact were called for; Myrta Ross had an abundance of both.

After the election, Mrs. Ross telephoned Miss Amy

Ogden Welcher of Connecticut to inform her that she had been elected first vice president. She urged her to come to Atlantic City to preside over the remainder of the Convention. Miss Welcher was surprised by what she found. "They thought of me," she later modestly said, "because I was both 'home' and 'foreign'—involved in home missions and in the China College Board. In Atlantic City I discovered a whole group from the grassroots, a movement already begun that was pushing me into leadership."

Her ability to conciliate all forces made her an ideal leader for the new UCCW. In her statement to the new Executive Committee she expressed the confident hope that "each of the very able and devoted women who has been serving the former organizations so splendidly . . . will feel the same sense of responsibility and a freedom for creative initiative in the advancement of the great work for which the United Council of Church Women is formed." In lieu of blueprints she challenged her co-workers: "When in doubt, let's accelerate!"

The Convention agreed to carry on the traditions of the uniting groups. Miss Margaret Applegarth of New York City reminded the women that the most precious treasure to be turned over to the new organization was the World Day of Prayer. Although its cultivation was assigned to UCCW, the national World Day of Prayer Committee was continued to plan the worship services. It was agreed that the offerings were to be turned over to the two interdenominational women's missions committees for administration; the overseas correspondence would be carried by an executive of the Foreign Missions Conference.

The Convention also agreed to carry forward the tradition of the May Fellowship Luncheons which were to become a strong rallying point of local councils under UCCW. Mrs. Eleanor Roosevelt had written to Mrs. Silverthorn regarding this occasion:

> I am glad that the May Luncheons are being held to bring church women together. Christians should exert to the full their influence on this troubled world, and cooperation is the way in which we can do this.

NATIONAL CRISIS The delegates, sensitive to the fact that feelings were running high during the week following the declaration of war, made their own declaration in a statement:

> We, the women members of the Constituting Convention called at Atlantic City, December 11-13, 1941, to unite the three interdenominational bodies of church women in the United Council of Church Women, meeting at the hour of our country's involvement in a war and at the time of the world's greatest tragedy, still believe individually and collectively that God reigns and that ultimately His will shall prevail. In deep penitence for our share in the world's guilt and woe, we call upon the women of the churches to enter with us into the suffering and sacrifices of the human family.
>
> To combat the rising tide of hatred caused by war;
> To minister to those suffering from the ravages of war;
> To show friendship and understanding to the men and women in service for the defense of our country;
> To maintain the integrity of the home;
> To continue to its fullest degree the ongoing ministry of the church, even to the uttermost parts of the earth;
> To consecrate ourselves to the task of building a democracy at home which recognizes individual worth and strives for justice to all the people;
> Finally, to dedicate ourselves to the task of demanding of our country that it assumes its full responsibility in the days to come in helping to build a World Order based on love and justice without which there can be no durable peace.

On December 13th the convention sent the following telegram to President Franklin D. Roosevelt:

> The newly constituted United Council of Church Women in session at Atlantic City, December 11-13, 1941, representing ten million women of seventy communions, pledges its loyalty to the highest ideals of our nation in this hour of grave crisis and assures you of

its prayers for wisdom, strength, and divine guidance as you carry your heavy responsibilities.

In the years that followed much was made over the fact that the United Council of Church Women came into being during the week of Pearl Harbor. The timing of the two events was, of course, a coincidence. The declaration of war struck a blow against any illusion of comfortable provincialism so that a national movement was all the more needed. Yet its destiny would have been different if the women gathered in Atlantic City in the name of the United Council of Church Women had failed to realize who they were, or had wavered before the opportunity of stating clearly their position in a time of crisis in the nation's history.

American women did not have to suffer the raw effects of an invaded territory. Never was their worship blacked out. They did not have to scrounge for food among the rubbish cast off by occupying armies or look for some precious heirloom in the ashes of their homes as did the women of Europe and Asia. Their sisters overseas spent the war years preoccupied with the daily necessities related to the survival of family. It seems God gave to American church women the special privilege of holding the world in their hearts with the prayerful hope that the time might come when all the earth's peoples could live together in peace.

The United Council of Church Women was born for such a stewardship as this. The tough roots would stand them well, but this green seed of hope must be held tenderly and humbly until it sprouted into a new corporate being in its own time.

**United Council
of Church Women
1941-1950**

chapter 2

An ever growing spiral

They might have busied themselves with pat little projects that could have been checked off as finished. Instead, United Church Women tackled frontiers of world peace, human rights and Christian unity. So there was always ahead of them more than they could do. They were engaged in the same issues but always under different circumstances. And so their encounter with their times was an ever growing spiral.

Yet there was a recurring rhythm in their destiny which might have been described as the ceaseless work of the Holy Spirit. Their hope lay in a movement where Christ's women would continue to be empowered to fulfill their God given tasks in larger and larger spheres.

The executive board of the United Council of Church Women lost no time in meeting for business. The Nominating Committee presented the name of Amy Welcher for president and she was enthusiastically elected. Fortunate indeed was our Board to have the competent leadership of Amy Welcher, a woman with the pilgrim spirit of her native New England. In her unassuming manner she agreed, because it was necessary she said, to "get on with the work." The first Assembly meeting in Cleveland in December, 1942 re-elected her for another term because they likewise wanted to "get on with the work."

And there was a lot of work to be done. The Board had to find the way to carry forward the ongoing commitments, to make into concrete proposals the bold claims of the Constituting Convention, to communicate with the various constituent groups of the three merging organizations, to begin to speak on behalf of the whole, and to cooperate with other national and civic bodies having similar goals.

The setting up of a national office would require both faith and finance. The agreement had been reached that the office would be located in the New York City area, and therefore the Chicago office of the NCCW was closed and the process of producing *The Church Woman,* which at that time had 2,235 subscribers, was transferred to New York.[1]

A friend of the movement, Dr. William Bancroft Hill, gave $5,000 in honor of his wife, Elise Weyerhauser Hill. This $5,000 was put into a revolving fund to finance the output of the World Day of Prayer material and to help open the modest office of UCCW. Dr. Hill was a Reformed minister and a professor of Bible at Vassar College. One of his students was Peggy Weyerhauser, a favorite niece of Dr. and Mrs. Hill who themselves had no children. It was to be one of God's planned coincidences that twenty-six years later this niece, then Mrs. Walter Driscoll, agreed to be the chairman of the Finance Committee of Church Women United. No person has given more of her time, experience and substance to stabilize the renewal of the movement. Although she did not know who gave the first gift until it came to light in the writing of this history, the connection across the generation shows how deep are the roots in the Church which nourish seeds of hope to bear fruit in their own time.

Office space was obtained at 156 Fifth Avenue in New York City. Furniture was scarce but there was an abundance of good will among the crew of volunteers who handled the mail, counted the offerings, and began the public relations. An office secretary was hired and a committee appointed to search for the first executive.

The woman of their choice, Ruth Mougey Worrell, was able to leave her job as executive of the Ohio Council of Church Women to come to New York by the end of 1942. Mrs.

Worrell brought with her vast experience in the development of strong local and state councils of church women. She also possessed an imaginative approach to both writing and programming, and a vision of the unlimited possibilities for the women of the churches. Her enthusiasm was contagious and church women across the country began to find the will and the way to combine their efforts to reach achievement.

These national undertakings depended on the responsiveness of the growing constituency. No one knows the hours of travel, letter writing, woman-to-woman talk that went into the inception of every local and state organization. In addition this was a decade of growth for the denominational women's societies, an ecumenical dimension of which was provided by UCCW. This vigorous focus on the grassroots continued to be the genius of UCCW and accounts for its growth to 1,432 local councils of church women during its first six years. The national office also provided services to thousands of local committees on the World Day of Prayer.

1942 ASSEMBLY CLEVELAND, OHIO The first biennial Assembly of UCCW occurred at Cleveland in December 1942, only a few months after Mrs. Worrell's arrival as executive secretary. It was not large in numbers due to difficult war-time transportation, but it fulfilled its promise "courageously to survey the church woman's place in the war crisis and point up her alertness to the kind of peace that must follow." Its program illustrates the subjects that especially concerned UCCW during the war period: problems arising in camp and defense communities, the war-time problems of families, the spiritual implications of racial problems, and sacrificial living.

WORLD COMMUNITY DAY Having received a report from their seven delegates who had participated in the Study Conference of the Churches on "A Just and Durable Peace" held in Dayton in April 1942, the Assembly was pleased when Mrs. Albert Palmer, the president of the Chicago Council of Church Women, made a motion that a day be set aside in the fall of 1943 for the study of peace by church women. This proposal turned out to be of great significance to the future of the movement.

The national presidents and executive secretaries of the denominational organizations met the next June. Each denomination had previously printed its own study on the new world order; they now realized that in unity lay strength and so they determined to call for one day of united study on November 11th, to be called "World Community Day" (the name itself seemed to be an inspiration) on the theme—"The Price of an Enduring Peace."

They turned to UCCW for the preparation of the material and agreed to alert their local organizations to seek the company of other church women in pursuing the study. The material contained a worship service written by Margaret Applegarth; four topics for discussion with background material prepared; a suggestion that instead of luncheon, each woman bring something to "break her fast," and consider together the task of the church in overseas relief.

During the last ten minutes of their time together everyone was asked to cast a ballot, registering a response to two questions:

1) Should we urge the United States to join and take its full responsibility in a world organization?

2) Are you willing to continue rationing of food, gasoline and other wartime restrictions in order that the needs of victims of the war overseas be met?

The new office sent out 90,000 leaflets, but even so, many orders could not be filled.

The excitement in the national office began within twenty-four hours of the meetings. The December 1943 issue of *The Church Woman* was just going to press. Myrta Ross, who had joined the staff as the public relations officer, wrote a diary-like account on what happened in the New York office on the day after the first World Community Day:

Today is November 12th. Already reports have come in from meetings in 36 states and the District of Columbia. Telegrams and postcards are piled, giving the first quick report in necessarily concise words. The full story will come in the days ahead. We know that the day was observed in every state in the union.

Early the first day we can record that 83,134 women voted that the United States should join and take its full responsibility in a world organization. 630 voted against. On the second question, 80,395 women voted a willingness to continue for a period after the war such wartime regulations as rationing of food, gasoline, restriction of travel, etc. More women were uncertain of willingness for this than on the first question—897 have already this first day been reported as voting "No." This indicates perhaps two things—the need of continued study of the needs of the world and our responsibilities toward them, and the assurance that those needs will be met honestly by our government. Perhaps even more it indicates America's need of learning the spirit of sacrifice.

Ere the sun had set on November 11, women had come into the national office from nearby towns to ask for suggestions and help on follow-up courses for five or six weeks study. There were reports of discussions running an hour beyond the time set—and couldn't be stopped! Offerings for world relief have already begun to come in.

United and Associated Press have called periodically throughout the day for the ballot totals. A photographer came to take a picture of the office group working on the tabulation of votes. This picture, incidentally, tells a story of world community across racial lines in our office of national headquarters.

In the air is a feeling of something significant happening. There is evidence that at least many eyes are turned on church women to see what they really believe and how far they are determined to go to obtain it. There is further evidence that church women united can move in a powerful stream of influence.

At the close of this really great day, as our beloved executive secretary left the office for several weeks of enforced hospital leave she turned in the doorway and said, "Isn't it thrilling what the church can do together?"

By November 24th, 1350 communities in 46 states had reported to the UCCW office. On the first question on the ballot, the women voted 58 to one "Yes"; on the second 43 to one in the affirmative. The press picked it up immediately and Eleanor Roosevelt wrote from the White House a note of congratulations.

UCCW was one of seventy-five organizations participating in a conference sponsored by Mrs. Roosevelt the next June (1944) at the White House on "How Women May Share in Post-War Policy Making."

WARTIME SERVICES UCCW set up a special committee on Religious Ministries to Women in the Services with Mrs. Samuel McCrea Cavert as chairman. Women serving as WACS and WAVES were making a contribution to the war effort, as well as to women's place in our national life.

One of the concerns of the Committee was a ministry among unwed mothers in the WACS and WAVES who were being returned to military hospitals in the United States. It was felt that sensitive women chaplains could offer their spiritual help to lonely women at this time of personal crisis. There would be opportunity to interpret Christ as the physician who could heal broken lives, and to celebrate this wonder-filling fact with the Holy Communion.

I was asked to explore with the ranking chaplain in the training center for the WAVES the possibilities of making provisions for ordination of qualified women. We discovered what we already knew: women would be welcome as social workers, but generally the Church was not ready for women ordained to the full gospel ministry.

Recalling this experience since, I remember that my host seemed to give a high sign to his fellow chaplains as we passed them in the corridors. When I asked what the sign meant, his explanation was a friendly male compliment. "It's a signal that you are a 'brother elk.'" My lack of success with the "brother elks" on this particular mission gave clear indication that the long struggle for women's ordination would largely be left to the "sister dears."

A War Emergency Committee was set up by the national church bodies where women as volunteer workers in defense areas were particularly welcome. They served as special counselors in camp and defense communities, and established child care centers and daily vacation Bible schools, and other projects which met needs among families in transition.

In 1945, church women made thousands of layettes for shipment overseas. In 1946, they sent half a million useful "Kiddie Kits" and 500,000 bundles of clothing to Europe through Church World Service. In 1947, emphasis was placed on the collecting of hundreds of thousands of *Pack-a-Towel* bundles of necessities destined especially for the older boys and girls in camps for displaced persons. The *Pieces for Peace* project of 1949 resulted in over 700,000 pounds of new materials which would give useful employment as well as new clothes to the women in refugee camps.

It should never be thought these undertakings were as simple as they sound. With a small staff and with communications costly, it took all the ingenuity Ruth Worrell could muster. She once asked me to represent UCCW in an emergency meeting of a committee on overseas relief composed of men executives of the denominational agencies. The problem was how to respond to a cable from relief workers in Czechoslovakia urgently requesting a million diapers as the early winter approached. The chairman had already phoned several yardage concerns and learned that due to wartime shortages, so much cloth could not be bought. After utterly exhausting the subject in discussion, all eyes rolled my way and the inevitable final question was asked: "Can't the women do something about this?"

An hour later I reported to Ruth Worrell the result of the Committee meeting: that UCCW was to deliver one million diapers to Czechoslovakia. She was not a bit non-plussed. "Every grandmother can swipe one. Every mother can spare one! It is possible," she said. It was.

HUMAN RIGHTS The war hysteria brought on what seemed an impetuous government action against the first and second generations of Japanese living in this country. With only a 48-hour notice, these Japanese-American families were ordered to sell their household possessions and move into relocation centers for the duration of the war.

Church women lifted their voices in protest and did what they could to ameliorate the conditions in the restricted camps and aid in resettlement in new communities. This dislocation involving thousands of persons of Asian extraction indicated clearly a racial bias since Europeans who had been born in 'enemy' countries did not suffer the indignity of losing homes and livelihood.

The traumatic experience of the war in general also seemed to call attention to the discrimination in this democracy against the millions of Negro citizens. Although the first UCCW Board of Managers had a token representation of Negro members, one of the vice presidents, Mrs. Christine S. Smith of Detroit ably articulated the issue at the 1942 Assembly. She spoke for a revision of the bylaws which would explicitly establish the interracial character of UCCW. The reply was that since the UCCW included women who were members of churches belonging to the Federal Council of Churches, some of whom were Negro denominations, the interracial fellowship would come about naturally. Later learnings have supported Mrs. Smith's original concern!

In 1944 while UCCW was supporting the establishment of a Fair Employment Practices Committee in our national government, Myrta Ross went to Washington to testify on behalf of UCCW before the Senate Committee considering the bill. At noontime she and Dr. Anna Arnold Hedgman were refused lunch in the cafeteria of both the Senate building and the Senate office building because of Dr. Hedgman's race. That evening Mrs. Ross sent a letter to President Roosevelt and released its contents to the Associated Press. It said, in part:

If you are to save our nation from civil war more horrible than the horrors that now engulf us, you cannot permit conditions that give rise to such an incident to exist in our nation's capital. We have built these buildings. They are ours, those of us who are Americans, no matter what the color of our skin. We have built them to serve in carrying out the justice and freedom promised to all citizens by the constitution of the United States. That freedom must not be denied within their very walls.

During the next days, clippings of the AP release came

to the office of UCCW from many parts of the USA. It was just one bit in the struggle for the right.

Another distinguished member of an early Board was Abbie Clement Jackson of Louisville, Kentucky who was appointed as one of the representatives of the Home Missions Council. (Her mother, Mrs. Henry Clement, was named American Mother of the Year in 1945). When the announcement of Mrs. Jackson's Board membership was printed in a Louisville newspaper, the local Council, at that time composed entirely of white women, was greatly upset. The president of that Council tried to resolve the embarrassment by suggesting that there be organized a Council of Negro Church Women in Louisville.

Abbie Jackson saw it another way. She called the key women from all the Negro churches in town. Out of a possible 100, ninety women came together to decide what to do, and after discussion the Negroes decided to wait until they were accepted as part of the central body.

Prior planning was one of Mrs. Jackson's assets. With the help of local ministers, she set about selecting a competent Negro woman to serve on each Council committee. For instance, a social worker was selected to serve on the committee pertaining to health and welfare; an assistant high school principal was asked to serve on the committee related to education, and so on. Abbie Jackson recommended such well qualified women that all but one committee became interracial within a short time.

Another instance followed a special meeting of UCCW held at Fisk University in Nashville, Tennessee; Ruth Worrell and Abbie Jackson rode to the train station together. When Mrs. Jackson had to go into the "Jim Crow" coach, she looked back to see Ruth Worrell crying!

These individual instances could, of course, be multiplied in kind by hundreds of Negro women in every walk of life. Many white women were unconscious of the deep-seated nature of the problem in their own communities, yet it was clear enough that race relations must become a priority program of this new movement. UCCW was an appropriate channel for both Negro and white women to work on this problem together. Although individual congregations were almost universally segregated at this time, the United Council of Church Women declared its intention to make its fellowship open to all Christian women. Their commitment in racial justice remained an ever-growing spiral of involvement.

Mrs. Worrell's gift of involving a high calibre of lay leadership brought Dr. Louise Young of Scarrett College to New York during her sabbatical in 1945 to act as executive of the Committee on Race Relations. Mrs. Theodore Wedel of Washington, D.C., who had been a member of the Committee since its beginning in 1942, was persuaded to take the chairmanship. She and Louise Young made a fine team—often called twins, not just because they both had reddish brown hair but because they possessed a similar personality trait—a well tempered openness toward other human beings.

In a conversation years later, Louise Young spoke of the working basis of the Committee: "We didn't want to browbeat anyone East or West, black or white or put anybody up against the corner. We wanted everybody to do things gladly and freely. We lived out the Congregational term 'Freedom and Fellowship.' We didn't want anyone to do anything she couldn't do from the heart. Many Southern women couldn't have a May Fellowship Luncheon from the heart, so we changed the name to May Fellowship Day because they could have a 'tea' from the heart!"

The program got a big boost when, through the help of Mrs. Charles Johnson, a member of the national board, the Rosenwald Foundation made a grant of $25,000 to be spent over a three year period for race relations.

It was decided that UCCW would recognize only state councils which were open to all races. Practice lagged behind policy, but even if the meeting was nearly 100% white, women felt they could speak freely on the issue. Cynthia Wedel reminisced about this period, "At that time there were local and state laws that forbade interracial meetings, and yet we used to get around it. Several times I can remember there would be black and white women at state Board meetings from the same town—and they had not met each other at home. We were able to welcome all women into these illegal meetings all across the South."

In 1945, a survey was undertaken in thirty five communities to determine the degree and causes of discrimination. Interestingly enough, this rose out of a study of the United Nations Charter and its application locally. Louise Young summarized what UCCW learned from this survey:

> Study groups were asked to check each item as to whether there was segregation and whether it was by law or custom. Although there is considerable difference in the pattern in different communities, certain general conditions are outstanding from the reports.
>
> 1) There is widespread segregation on a national scope.
> 2) The greater part of segregation is by custom rather than by law.
> 3) The most consistently segregated patterns throughout the different regions are those of housing and the church.
> 4) The services in which there is the least segregation are the post office and labor unions and CIO.

The survey was evaluated according to geographical areas and concluded that:

> One can see where this leads. In some cases it leads to outstanding leadership among the black people in trying to right the wrongs to their race, but in the majority of cases it results in psychological injuries from which they never recover. After the rude awakenings of childhood, these wounds crusted over with bewilderment, frustration, and bitterness often lead to delinquency, violence and illegal activities. These millions of wounds are forming a hideous cancer in the society of our day which, if not cured by the power of God working through us, will either split asunder or destroy it altogether.

In the late forties when the Rosenwald Foundation was liquidated according to the terms of Mr. Rosenwald's will, UCCW was given a second grant of equal size. Mrs. Sibley recalled the occasion:

I went to Chicago for that final banquet to thank them for their generosity to the United Council of Church Women and had the privilege of sitting with some of the members of the family at the banquet. It is interesting that a Jewish Foundation should have seen and felt the value of our organization at such an early date.

1944 ASSEMBLY COLUMBUS, OHIO   Already evaluation had begun to take place when the Second National Assembly met in Columbus, Ohio, in 1944 with 600 delegates. With countless opportunities before it, UCCW might have been overwhelmed or its efforts scattered. It could become a superficial "good will" organization lacking skills and expertise in any chosen field. If it were really to help mold public opinion, it must give fresh thought to a distinctive function, its administration and its relationships.

Mrs. Harper Sibley was elected President at that Assembly and would be re-elected in 1946 and 1948. The statesmanship of Mrs. Sibley was an asset as the United Council of Church Women developed its plan for peace building and ecumenical expansion. She was gifted with the power to inspire large audiences with enthusiasm for causes with which she was aligned. She also could readily establish a comforting sense of intimacy with individuals. She was quickly sensitive to offer an encouraging word and used the weight of social prestige when support was needed. "Stay close to me," she muttered to Abbie Jackson when they entered a restaurant which would have barred one of her race.

In October 1945, 150 leaders, among them many state presidents, met in Washington for an expanded meeting of the Board. Although careful advance planning had been done, the reservation of the Negro participants was not honored at the hotel desk, whereupon all participants of the consultation left the hotel, receiving hospitality in the homes of Washington.

This action on the part of the members of the Board made an impact for open housing in the Capital city. The *Washington Post* reported on October 24, 1945:

The Council accepted an invitation from the Washington chapter to hold its conference here only on condition that there would be no racial segregation of members. A number of members are guests . . . at Negro residences, and some Negro delegates are being entertained in white homes. Mrs. Harper Sibley, president of the Council, is a guest at the residence headquarters of the National Council of Negro Women . . . Mrs. Emory Ross and Miss Jane Tiffany Wagner are guests of Judge and Mr. Armand Scott, Negroes. Dr. Paul Douglas, President of American University, is among white persons entertaining Negro delegates.[2]

The business for which they had come to Washington went on in one of the churches. In groups of ten, the women met with senators, representatives and scientists to discuss current issues and the atom bomb. They were received for tea by President and Mrs. Truman and for dinner in the home of the President of the American University. The findings were considered "the most important of any since the birth of the movement."

UNITED NATIONS CHARTER - 1947 Mr. and Mrs. Sibley attended the meeting in San Francisco in 1945 which brought into being the United Nations. She later describes her experience in *The Church Woman:*

It is memorable and exciting to be part of history making. One may not always appreciate the significance of the occasion until years later. But in this case no one could possibly have missed the importance of the event in the San Francisco Opera House as men and women from many nations gathered for one purpose: to save succeeding generations from the scourge of war and to create the international machinery to settle differences among nations peacefully.

My husband was there as a consultant to the Social and Economic Section of the UN. I was an Official Observer, representing what was then the United Council of Church Women. Invitations had been sent to every volunteer organization in the United States, urging them to be present so they could interpret the newly forming organization to their various constituencies and enlist their support.

It was a moving experience to be handed a mimeographed copy of the Preamble to the Charter and to read there these significant words: "That all should be treated alike without regard to race, sex, language, or religion."

At long last, the United Nations had affirmed not only justice for all men and women, but righteousness as well! It is a new platform on which the peoples of the earth can stand and move forward together into a new era—perhaps more like the "kingdom of God" on earth. This great document has now been signed and ratified by 135 nations—large and small.

Mrs. Sibley returned from this occasion to work hard in following months interpreting the event. Through a radio program in ninety-six cities and many workshops, UCCW built up a body of support within the churches for the United Nations.

The United Council of Church Women was one of the first non-government organizations to name an official observer to the United Nations. Miss Mable Head of Cleveland, Ohio, resigned her position as vice-president in order to accept this position at the UN. She traveled regularly by train coach with her sandwich in her bag to save money, but spent herself completely in establishing relationships with various international organizations and reporting the activities through a column in *The Church Woman.*

FRIENDS FROM OTHER LANDS   Church women used the opportunity provided by the whole program on exchange of persons to discover the points of view of new friends from other lands. There was a great influx of overseas students beginning to come to the United States for training in special fields. They were met and shepherded by the Committee on Friendly Relations Among Foreign Students. By 1946, there were 10,000 students from abroad. This became a world-stretching fact for many citizens.

During a government reception in Djakarta, Indonesia,

*in 1965, another American came up to introduce herself to me.
She was a United Church Woman from Colorado who had
been spending the previous six weeks as a guest in many
different homes in Java—all return visits with student guests in
her home a decade before! It was not uncommon to hear a
church woman refer to a "Brazilian daughter," or a "Japanese son" or an actual son-in-law from Hungary or Ghana!*

Under the auspices of the State Department in 1950, ten
Japanese women came on a cultural exchange from Japan.
After their briefing in Washington, their first stop was New
York City where the interdenominational women of the city
welcomed them. I was delighted to meet Michi Kawai, a
distinguished Christian educator who had done her graduate
study in the United States much earlier. By way of conversation, I asked what they had been told in Washington the
previous week. Without changing expression, Miss Kawai
replied, "We were taught American manners!" I did not know
whether to laugh or cry. I looked at her for a clue and noted the
well of mirth deep in the quiet eyes of this very cultured
woman. I responded with a genuine American grin. Knowing
that these Japanese women were to be received by church
women across the country, I had reason to assume that their
hostesses would outdo in practice what the State Department
preached!

American responsibility was different but not
diminished as the hostilities of World War II ceased.
Unquestionably a world power, the nation was confronted with
international obligations and opportunities.

Ahead of the nation were these tasks:
• reconciliation between nations whose political
philosophies now defined regional or cultural affinity;
• food and security for common people everywhere;
• rebuilding of homes, of industry, of social systems;
• the interplay between weaker and stronger nations;
• the living out of what the term "social and economic
development" means.

War-worn Europeans had tackled a big reconstruction
job in their own communities. The same was true of many
peoples in East Asia who, along with other Asians and

Africans, were also straining toward newly independent governments. The American hemispheres were sorely divided by gaping economic inequities. How could the United States respond to the unparalleled expectations of the rest of the world? What share would the churches take in their fulfillment?

1946 ASSEMBLY   Reflecting the general feeling of a new era,
GRAND RAPIDS   the third National Assembly meeting in Grand
                      Rapids, Michigan, in November, 1946, generated new energy around significant tasks. Looking forward to the postponed first Assembly of the World Council of Churches and the results of the study of the Committee on Closer Relationships among Interchurch Agencies, studies in faith and order were called for. The challenge of the formation of the United Nations called for local councils to plan programs of general interpretation, particularly of its many agencies of development, i.e., UNICEF, UNESCO, UNRRA.

MISSIONS OF   However, the sober reality of the war having
RECONCILIATION   been terminated by a nuclear bomb devasta-
                      ting Hiroshima forced church women to consider reconciliation as their primary responsibility. Both through their denominations and through UCCW, Fellowship Missions were planned to go into Germany and Japan as they could be received. However, the first encounter was destined to be in the United States when the Asian Women's Team of Reconciliation came to the U.S. in 1946, traveled extensively in communities, and was featured at the fourth Assembly in Grand Rapids, Michigan, in November of that year.

The team itself was a symbol of reconciliation within Asia since it was composed of Christian women whose nations were on different sides of the war: Hsiang Foh Mei, a teacher from Shanghai, China; Dr. Josefa Ilano, a doctor from the Philippines; and the Reverend Mrs. Tamaka Uemura, a pastor whose church had been reduced to rubble by American bombing in Tokyo, Japan.

Japan was at that time occupied by American forces who for two years enforced the regulation preventing letters leaving or entering the country. Marvelling that a civilian had received an invitation and also permission to enter the U.S.A., Mrs. Sibley, who had been one of the signers of the petition to the State Department, said to me: "How could this happen?"

"Prayer," I answered.

"I believe it!" was her quick response. So did we all.[3]

In 1947, Georgiana Sibley and Welthy Hossinger Fisher, the chairman of the World Day of Prayer, were permitted to go to Japan on a mission of reconciliation. They returned to interpret the new Japan. Mrs. Sibley worked with a foundation made up of both Japanese and Americans who raised the funds to create the Japan International Christian University.

The next year, together with Catherine Shaffer of the Catholic Relief Services, Mrs. Sibley traveled through Europe, restoring relationships or establishing new ones, particularly in Germany and Czechoslovakia.

What became abundantly clear was that the restoration of a shattered personality or reconciliation of a crumbling community were neither simple or speedy matters. The wounds of war were not healed by generous relief programs nor delegations to peace conferences. Reconciliation was more than formal apologies, statements of repentance or expressions of sympathy to the surviving family of war dead. Yet there was a longing of individuals on both sides to discover a supporting community that would continue, as one German woman expressed it, through "sick and sin." Human reconciliation is a daily affair, a heart-to-heart matter, a new style of learning to give and take, to stand alongside another until common understanding is reached.

Americans would need to grow considerably if they were to carry their share of the reconciliation. There were deep cultural differences which had to be understood—the defeat of an Emperor who had been generally venerated in Japan; the reactions of a population long under rigid controls of dictatorship whose heroes were now disgraced; the revulsion at the holocaust which sent millions of Jews to the gas chambers.

Some of the conditions are reflected in these sentences from letters received during these war years from both Asia and Europe!

Please don't try to understand me. I don't understand myself. I am sick and old, but it pleases God to use me as his tool and I just can't despair. It's not my personal self who is doing all this. I am just the cover of some secret Power who—as it seems—needs human packing to accomplish some of his deeds.

Those who deported us never knew what a real good deed they did. We lost all that is superfluous for happiness and gained all the simplicity, modesty that is indispensable.

Just at present I feel dead tired and sour all over my bones.

You keep asking us what we need most. We are like a stagnant pool which receives all the time without giving out. The greatest thing you could do for us is to tell us something we can do for you. Aren't your Navajos needing something?

I am geting tired, but when my friends say, "You have done enough," I know it is only my gentleman friend, the devil!

There is another voice saying, "Keep true!"

Reconciliation requires an act dealing with the root cause of the bitterness or alienation. Such an opportunity came following the visit of Mrs. Sibley to Germany after the war. While in Germany she met Dr. Nopitsch, a social worker who during the 1930 depression had become deeply concerned about the exhausted, overworked mothers.

We all know that there is a relationship between weariness and war; between the desperation of people in time of economic depression and the response to fanatic leaders of super-nationalism, between bitterness gnawing at the heart of people and the betterment of society.

Dr. Nopitsch was not the kind of person to leave the situation unchanged. She went to a conference of pastors who agreed that tired mothers might be the cause of family and neighborhood disintegration. But it was the way things were! They would have to accept their role as expressed in the 3 K's: Kinder (children), Kirche (church), and Kuche (kitchen). And who would organize a service for mothers? There were so many of them. She went to the meeting of the Committee of the Evangelical Women's Work in Bavaria. They thought it important, but it must be a united work. It would take a lot of money. But they might as well begin now! A hat went around to collect 80 Reich Marks.

It was a start to build mothers' rest homes.

As war came the usual consequences followed: homes and families were bombed; thousands of families were separated in the concentration camps and the long refugee lines; the ordinary housewife had to scrounge to get even potatoes to cook. The need for services for mothers was even greater. By its nature war leaves many men dead and maimed and the increasing burden of livelihood is upon the women.

Mrs. Sibley visited the leaders of the mothers' rest homes while in Germany on her postwar visit, meeting among others Mrs. Liselotte Nold who later became the remarkable administrator of this expanded work which still exists in a form adapted to the special needs of the modern woman.

SPIRAL OF COMPASSION We can see the spiral of Christian compassion at work if we look ahead thirty years to December 1971 and a follow up of this story. UCCW received a bank draft from the World Day of Prayer Committee of Germany and a letter from Dr. Nopitsch which read as follows:

It is a real pleasure for me to send you warm greetings from Stein for your Celebration. We shall always remember how much help we received from the American Christian women during the difficult days after the war. We would never have finished our mothers' rest home, where hundreds of tired mothers are getting rest and some kind of renewal, without the generous gift of the American women.

Now as we have overcome those times it is my sincere desire to assure you that we shall not forget the support. I am very happy about the possibility of expressing our gratitude with a gift of the World Day of Prayer for the farm workers who need physical and spiritual help.

I am especially thrilled to know that this work is corresponding somehow to the original idea of our mothers' recuperation work and that Spanish-Americans will benefit from it, for I had come to know myself the situation in Mexico during a travel to the United States.

The World Day of Prayer Committee of Germany designated the gift of several thousand dollars for the La Paz Retreat Center in California, where Cesar Chavez hoped to develop a place of renewal for workers and their families. Jessica Govea, the director of social services at that time for the United Farm Workers, came to Washington to receive the gift. A young German woman, Helga Day, presented the gift to her Mexican-American sister with these words:

> Many of us in Germany have heard of the hard and good work of Cesar Chavez and they hope their contribution will support his struggle for social justice . . . May the center of La Paz be a source of strength and peace for those people who enter it and leave to work and make the world of tomorrow.

Jessica replied in part: "On behalf of the many thousands of farm workers—men, women and children who want so desperately to see hope for their children and perhaps even some hope for themselves in their lifetime, I want to thank you for this gift today. Some of us are living at La Paz now and soon there will be many other people who will be coming there not only to rest but to gather strength to keep on. We have started. There are many, many years ahead of us that will be the same in terms of struggle. Whatever we do will be constructive and we will never be led away from the path of bringing about justice—not only for ourselves, not only for our children, but for farm workers of all races."

PROPOSED MERGER   The United Council of Church Women was not the only interdenominational body which was launched or which gained impetus during this decade. UCCW had a natural relationship with the programs of most of them. As early as 1940 there began a series of committee meetings among various cooperative organizations of the churches to consider a wider overall structure and representatives of UCCW were present in these discussions.

By the close of the decade an overall plan and tentative bylaws were drawn up calling for each organization to consider both its program and its resources in relation to the proposed National Council of Churches of Christ. The other interdenominational organizations were: the Federal Council of Churches, the Foreign Missions Conference of North America, the Home Missions Council, the International Council of Religious Education, the Missionary Education Movement, and the United Stewardship Council. In addition to the United Council of Church Women, there were certain constituency-centered movements such as: the Interseminary Movement, the United Christian Youth Movement, the Council of Higher Education.

Although each of these organizations was confronted with internal decisions to make, let me sketch here only some of the thinking which went on among church women about their own movement. All agreed that common approaches to the major issues of our time should result in greater Christian impact on the life of the nation.

Yet there were serious questions about which many who cared most about the future of the united work among women were troubled. Would this merger challenge a value that had proved to be important—women's independent action as a group? Why had there not been more efforts to include women in all policy-making in church bodies? Would active cooperation on a national level thwart initiative on the part of local units? Would UCCW be allowed to continue moving among its own constituency? Would the fact that the other agencies were by nature composed of national denominational representatives, most of them professionally employed for specific purposes of national or international administration, affect the unique nature of a grassroots movement such as UCCW?

The United Council of Church Women by now had assumed a form that gave promise for the future. The national organization was autonomous yet worked in close cooperation with more than forty other national organizations. A truly responsible administration had been set up responsive to the desires and interests of their local units. It was a structure sufficiently integrated to be coherent yet flexible enough to allow for diversity of interests.

The Executive Committee of UCCW gave continual attention to the developments of this merger. In October 1947, the national Board issued an important statement outlining conditions to preserve the identity of the women's movement should it join the proposed NCCC:

1) Full right to continue to organize, develop, and serve local and state councils of church women.

2) Full right to call a national assembly to review work, set goals, adopt a budget, and decide ways of securing it.

3) The right of local and state councils, either as entities or as parts of larger councils of churches, to select their own officers and committees, raise and disburse their own money, and draw into their fellowship any Christian women willing to subscribe to and help carry out the purpose of the organization.

4) Assurance of representation on the various sections and committees of the National Council, including representation on the governing board and the executive committee.

5) The name of the women's group in the National Council, while not of prime importance, must be one giving it sufficient identity.

FOURTH ASSEMBLY MILWAUKEE - 1948 At the fourth biennial Assembly at Milwaukee in 1948, Mrs. Worrell, the retiring executive, in summing up the movement from the vantage point of her six years of solid achievement, furnished creative clues to the UCCW's planning committee on the proposed merger:

Its (UCCW) values must be conserved not for the sake of an organization but for the sake of the contribution it has made and will make to the building of the kingdom ...

Its freedom from ecclesiastical control has proved to be one of its strengths.

It would be a tragic loss for UCCW to have no relation to the proposed merger. But the basic structure must not be destroyed in any way. Therefore, its identity must be conserved. There are several ways of merging: unity by absorption, by amalgamation or with diversity.

New leadership was chosen with the anticipation that there would need to be many adjustments during the years ahead. In 1948, Mrs. W. Murdock MacLeod succeeded Mrs. Worrell as the executive director with the knowledge that hers would be the task to work out the cooperative administration with the NCCC. Coming from the headquarters staff of the Presbyterian Church U.S. in Atlanta, Georgia, Dorothy MacLeod brought experience that put her in good stead for this assignment. Her devotion to the women of the churches gave her confidence as well as persistence in her tactful negotiations on their behalf. She carried the adjustments of several restructures in the NCCC over the next fifteen years with administrative skill without losing the graciousness which characterized her leadership.

GDUCW OF NCCC The leadership wisely carried on a program of information about the proposed merger among the local councils. Opinion surveys conducted by a committee headed by Mrs. William S. Terrell seemed to indicate that most local units were undertaking the study with the same spirit as their national officers. Since the national Board of Managers was meeting in Los Angeles in 1949, there was an opportunity for its members to travel through many states enroute and thus to ascertain what the general opinion locally might be.

Five hours had been set aside at the Board meeting for the discussion of all aspects before a vote was taken. The proposed bylaws of the National Council had been agreed upon in principle and it was on this basis that the vote was taken. In them UCCW was to become the General Department of United Church Women, which together with a General Department of United Church Men (yet to be set up) was directly related to central administration. The new General Department of United Church Women would maintain its own existing charter for legal purposes and the right to maintain its own department structure.

It seemed that the leadership had anticipated every guarantee that was necessary to preserve the nature and program of the women's movement. Their constituency was prepared. But, as in most of the significant decisions in life, they could not go both ways at the same time. Some decision had to be made.

"The position of the women was a positive, not a defensive one," wrote Mrs. Calkins. "They must not, in the name of protecting their organizational interests, be in fact an instrument of division. To hold out for the greater freedom of action and the greater degree of inclusiveness in membership which some still felt could only be achieved by complete independence, was of lesser value than to be a part of the life of the whole. The united work of the women of the churches in the service of the kingdom could be done within the larger framework of the whole. They were ready to take the step."

Mrs. LeGrand reported in *The Church Woman:*

For hours we talked, questioned, conferred and prayed. No haste. Every woman had full opportunity to ask about every word in the proposed bylaws for the integration of UCCW into the new NCCC. Then after prayer for guidance the first vote was taken. With only three dissenting votes the UCCW had decided to participate in the Constituting Convention, December 1950, of the new National Council of Churches. . . Then all rose and without any sense of division sang together, "Praise God from Whom all Blessings Flow."

The decision having been made, Mrs. Sibley took leadership in assuring that the women went into the new merger from a position of strength. They saw they were moving into a new league from the point of view of financial undergirding of the national movement. Each of the merging organizations was expected to pay for its own maintenance, staff salaries and program, as well as contribute proportionately toward the central services and administration. If, as they firmly believed, there would be even greater opportunity for Christian witness, then they should have funds which would allow women to take initiative in program ventures.

ECUMENICAL   The ambitious idea of an Ecumenical Register
REGISTER   was proposed. Every woman throughout the
                  churches would be invited to sign a register
and pay no more than one dollar. Under the leadership of Mrs.
J. Wallace Hamilton of New York, the campaign was launched
in December of the same year. "It is a moment in which
Christians need to stand and be counted," Mrs. Sibley wrote to
the women of the churches. "We will create a register of church
women, signed with their name, address and denominations,
and with a dedication of dollars. We will make 1950 a Year of
Jubilee."

*Be one of the first million women to sign the Ecumenical
Register* was a slogan that became familiar during the next
months. The goal of a million dollars was not reached by May
1951 when the Register was officially closed. However, the
very substantial amount (approximately $300,000) which had
come in one dollar gifts was significant. It was also a way of
informing women in local communities about the new
opportunities in the newly formed National Council of
Churches.

The Ecumenical Register enabled United Church
Women not only to make a contribution to the initial funding of
the NCCC, but also to contribute to the ongoing program of
several of its departments. A special grant was made to the
headquarters of the World Council of Churches and major
funds to assure staffing and program for its Department on
Cooperation of Men and Women in Church and Society. In
addition, the fund made possible some of the innovative
projects which were carried on during the next five years by
the General Department of United Church Women itself.

1950 ASSEMBLY   The fifth biennial Assembly held in Cincinnati
CINCINNATI   in November 1950 was the women's prologue
                     to the Constituting Convention of the
National Council of the Churches of Christ in the U.S.A. which
would be gathering the next week in Cleveland. An historical
drama, "This Noble Permanence," caught the mood of an
organization whose spirit continued even if name and
structure differed. Dr. Sarah Chakko, the first woman vice-

president of the World Council of Churches and also first executive of the Department of Cooperation of Men and Women, spoke. Dr. Samuel McCrea Cavert and Dr. Roy G. Ross were present to symbolize the new relationships with the National Council of Churches. Over 400 women traveled from Cincinnati to Cleveland as observers at the Constituting Assembly of the NCCC.

At the Assembly in Cincinnati, the delegates received warmly the suggestion of their nominating committee that the name of the Reverend Mrs. James D. Wyker be placed in nomination as the first chairman of the General Department of United Church Women at the Constituting Convention of the NCCC. (The rules required that the heads of all departments and divisions in the NCCC should be named by the nominating committee of the Council. Although the term *chairman* was required to be carried on the stationery for the next fifteen years, church women themselves held the practice of recognizing this person as the *president* of United Church Women.)

Mossie Wyker was admirably chosen for this role. As the president of the Ohio Council of Church Women, the state which first reached its goal in the Ecumenical Register, she had always offered a loving pastoral relationship to the women of the churches. At the same time she exercised rare judgment in developing strong relationships within the NCCC on their behalf. Under her leadership, and her successors, church women made an essential contribution to the National Council and at the same time opened up new vistas for achievement on their own. United Church Women was in a different position than any of the other merging organizations in its available channel to a rapidly growing organized constituency. From 1948 to 1950 several hundred new councils of church women were formed bringing the total number of local councils up to 1,724.

As a delegate of my own Church, I tramped through two feet of unprecedented snow in Cleveland in December 1950 to be among the 4,000 people gathered there to finalize the act which would bring into being the NCCC. We had high hopes that together the churches might make a contribution to better cope with the great problems confronting American society.

United Church Women shared in this commitment. Ahead was the ever growing spiral.

FOOTNOTES TO CHAPTER 2:

1. Files have revealed the interesting "Suggested Budget of $15,000 for Unified Organization, 1941":

Headquarters - Rent, Light, Heat, Cleaning	$1,000
Salaries	
Executive Secretary	3,000
Office Secretary	1,500
Extra Help	1,000
Operating Expenses	
Office Supplies - Stationery	900
Postage, Telephone, Telegraph	750
Printing and Publications	1,000
Travel	
Executive Secretary and President	1,000
Additional Travel	200
Meetings	
Assembly (1/3 each year)	150
National Board	25
Committee Expenses	
Program - Field and Promotion Publicity	1,500
Church Woman	1,000
Fees to Other Organizations	
Chautauqua	400
Cause and Cure of War	250
National Peace Conference	50
Miscellaneous	575
	$14,300
Office Equipment	700
Total	$15,000

In 1942 the national budget was $12,000; in 1943, $13,500; in 1944, $40,000, and by 1946 it had reached $60,000! Although only a part of the budget came from the local councils, the amount increased as they devoted nearly a third of their May Fellowship Day offerings to state and national support. In addition, the 134 members of the national board were carrying their own expenses. The World Day of Prayer offering leaped from $84,000 in 1942 to $145,000 in 1944 and to $148,000 in 1946.

2. This brought reaction from a Senator from Mississippi, Theodore G. Bilbo, in his book, *Take Your Choice—Separation or Mongrelization,* published in 1947. He wrote:

"There is in existence another religious organization operating under the name of the United Council of Church Women . . . this group is rendering a great disservice to the integrity of the white race in the United States. Some members . . . are not only preaching social equality between the white and black races, but they are brazenly practicing it."

Senator Bilbo continues, "Such 'stunts' . . . are not only disgraceful, unthinkable, and outlandish, but these practices are an open, brazen and defiant betrayal of the white race and an affront to every suggestion of the decent, cultural American ideals and aspirations of the Anglo-Saxon race . . . we do question the right of any white man or woman . . . to compromise, contaminate and do those things which will lead to miscegenation and the mongrelization of our white race . . .

"Mrs. Harper Sibley, who is head of this negrophilistic organization, went away from Washington fanatically exclaiming: 'We made Washington an inter-racial city for the moment.' May she and her kind never return! The one gratifying thing about the meeting was that this group vowed never to hold a session in any city in the United States where the people do not practice social equality of the races. Thank God that we will not be bothered with them below the Mason and Dixon Line!"

3. The circumstances of the first civilian to come from an enemy country are as follows: In 1945 a letter had come to me from a woman in Iowa suggesting we invite to the United States the Rev. Tamaki Uemura, a graduate of Vassar. Mrs. Uemura was encouraged by her father, himself a distinguished pastor, to get her theological training in Edinburgh after which she was ordained by the United Church of Japan. "I have started a prayer chain to bring her message to America," wrote my Iowa friend. "You do what you can."

I will never forget the incredible look on the face of my superior officer when I told him our dream. "It would take a woman to think a thing like this was possible," he said. However he immediately ordered a staff man to go to Washington to investigate. The unlikely chain of persons who were used both to get the message through and to arrange for some assurance that the military government would find the way to send her testified to the power of "prayer finesse."

She arrived at the Fountain Street Baptist Church in Grand Rapids after the beginning of the evening meeting the second day of the National Meeting of Presbyterian Women. A missionary friend had met her at the airport and came with her to a front pew. The national president, Mrs. Paul Moser of Kansas, was aware that this would be the signal that she had agreed to participate in the evening session in which the Restoration Fund was to be interpreted. She paused and then quietly announced to the 1400 women gathered: "The moment we have been praying for has arrived. The Rev. Tamaki Uemura has arrived from Tokyo. Mrs. Uemura, we await your ministry."

Fourteen hundred women rose spontaneously as the Japanese woman clad in the gray kimona walked softly to the pulpit. Her first words were a prayer; her prayer was a communion experience:

"O God, our Father, Father of Jesus Christ whose seamless garment we have torn, we come to thee, to the Cross of thy Son, and beseech thee for thy forgiveness . . . Thou bearest our infirmities. Thou bleedest for our souls. The torn garment is restored only when we become one in thee, all the peoples of the earth.

"Thou hast already begun restoring the unity of thy people. Thy work is to be carried on to its fulfillment . . . We intercede for those in other lands who are thinking of us in this gathering, and especially those who have been alienated by human devices from the beloved people of this land. Restore our unity, one with another . . . Now, we offer before thee a token of our dedication of ourselves to thine own work of restoration, of giving light and life and order to the world. In Christ's name we ask. Amen."

It was only later that we heard part of the miracle that occurred in Japan. A member of the church of which Mrs. Uemura was pastor was the lady-in-waiting to the Empress. When the Empress was told of the invitation that had come from an "enemy country," she was very moved. She took a jewel box from her dresser and said "Take this as a gift to whoever invited her." Later the Executive Committee of United Presbyterian Women met on the World Day of Prayer in 1947 to dedicate a beautifully bound Bible, "our most precious possession," and place it in Tamaki's hands to take back to the Empress.

In the meantime, I had gone to China in 1946 with a postwar deputation of my Church and carried a specially engraved formal thank you note for the Empress of Japan. However, I found out that it was no more possible to get a letter from China to Japan than to get it there from the United States. Aimie Millican in Shanghai proposed I try to send it with a Japanese pastor whom she had met through the Fellowship of Reconciliation. He was among the Japanese soldiers, the last of whom were just being evacuated. When I explained my mission, he responded: "I am being deported tomorrow and am not allowed to carry any piece of writing. However, I will memorize the message and deliver it to Her Imperial Highness."

"How will you get to her?" I asked skeptically.

"My mother is the lady-in-waiting who transferred the gift to Tamaki Uemura," he said.

Section 2: Circ

s of the Possible

JUST BECAUSE
the 50's and 60's were full of
anxiety and alienation,
it took a lot of living and
some scars of experience
to fill the ....CIRCLES OF THE POSSIBLE

**General Department
of United Church Women
of the
National Council of the Churches of Christ**

She had been warmly received at her first international conference and felt compelled to add a further statement as she introduced herself.

"Thank you for accepting me as a whole woman. At home I feel like half a person."

Little by little it all came out.
Just because she was born in South Africa, a black and a woman, she was restricted as to the

- place she could live
- job she could get
- dream she could offer her child
- right to share in nation-building
- care she might expect in old age.

"How do you find the will to struggle on," she was asked. She answered:

"Each day I fill the circle of the possible."

**General Department of
United Church Women
1950-1966**

chapter 3

Circle of the possible

The newly formed National Council of Churches of Christ was a highly complicated structure. Its organizing plan called for a General Assembly, meeting biennially, and a General Board, meeting bi-monthly. There were four divisions—Home Missions, Foreign Missions, Christian Education, Christian Life and Work—and each of these had from a dozen to a score of departments, commissions and committees dealing with special fields. There were the General Departments of United Church Women and United Church Men. There were the Joint Departments of Evangelism, Family Life, Religious Liberty, and Stewardship and Benevolence. There were Central Departments of Church World Service, Ecumenical Relations, Field Administration, Public Relations, Research, Publication, and Treasury and Business Management. A professional consultant in institutional administration who made an intensive study of the Council's structure after the first two years of experience expressed his amazement that it actually became a going concern.[1]

In addition to coordination of the work of the inter-denominational program agencies, the official representatives of the member communions were able to speak as one so that the General Board had become in fact a National Council of Churches.[2] The member churches as corporate entities established an endowment fund and pledged continual support to the general administration. Each department was expected to provide the ongoing support for its own staff and program and to take its fair share of the overhead of central business operations from its program funds.

All of this the Board of Managers of United Church Women knew when it voted to become one of the General Departments at which time it had also made clear the safeguards under which UCW would enter the proposed National Council. Mrs. Wyker entered confidently into the first meeting of the General Board, immediately after the Constituting Convention adjourned. Imagine her jolt then as she heard Franklin Clark Fry, president of the Lutheran Church in America and chairman of the Policy Committee of the National Council, enunciate the regulations concerning the appointment of board members of the various departments— all of whom must be approved by the Council's committee after clearance with their denominational officer. *"What are they doing to us?"* muttered Mrs. Wyker to the UCW general director, who sat at her side.

"They promised to leave our constituency free," whispered back Dorothy MacLeod, realizing full well that the four Unitarians in nomination for the Board of Managers of the General Department would never pass the theological requirements of the Council. Mrs. Wyker spoke her piece repeating again the understanding of the women prior to the merger. The NCCC officers promised that a committee would study the matter, but they were naturally preoccupied with the overall problems of many program departments. The women heard nothing for many weeks.

Just before the next meeting of the General Board, the president of the NCCC, Bishop Sherrill, asked to see Mrs. Wyker and Mrs. MacLeod. "A committee will not be necessary," he said. "I am ruling that Dr. Fry was correct in his inter- pretation of the bylaws of the Council."

For all the other departmental committees and boards it was a reasonable assumption; they were appointed by the appropriate officers of the member communions including the agencies for particular functions. Mrs. Wyker explained the need to maintain the UCW local constituency at full strength. She pointed out that the earlier agreements had stated that a loss of confidence in the national movement would affect program and funds.

However, the Bishop remained adamant. All must conform.

"Then you'll have to tell the women," said the indignant president of United Church Women. In the long run, it was the tactful letters of Dorothy MacLeod that explained the matter over and over again during the next fifteen years.

It had been a skirmish in which both sides held to values that were important. It was clear that the NCCC officials had little appreciation either of the nature of United Church Women or the value of making some adaptations to the reality of their position.

Associated with the NCCC at that time were councils of churches in 40 states and 875 local communities. They remained organizationally autonomous and, like the NCCC itself, their governing boards were largely professional people. In contrast, United Church Women had councils of church women in all 48 states and in nearly 1,800 local communities. The fact that the NCCC represented only 29 member churches was equally confusing to the constituency of the UCW. A survey had shown that the active membership came from 89 different denominations.

Across the country were women whose interest and conviction the new National Council needed. They were not specialists in bureaucratic practices or denominational polity, but they did have a lot of untroubled convictions.

Mrs. MacLeod and Mrs. Wyker had a real respect for the ordered structures of the church and for the officials who were the leaders. They also had enough good sense to know that a blueprint gives way once the available material, money, and future occupants of a household are taken into account! They knew that some of the favorable nods which had given them assurance had no legal standing once the "committee" was dismissed.

They were realists and were not upset that the content

and experience which crowded the box called General Depart-
ment of United Church Women could not be compared with
other "boxes" which still had to be filled. One of the favorite
mistakes made by architects of church organizations is to
draw the chart as they wish it were!

The staff of all the merging agencies began their arduous work of adjustment to the realities of coordination of program planning and administration as departments in the new Council. Each had its own financial system and restricted funds, each its own history and dynamics of operation. Their offices continued to be in eight separate buildings. The General Department of United Church Women moved to more adequate offices in 1955 in the old Flatiron Building at the intersection of Fifth Avenue, Broadway and 23rd Street in New York. Here they welcomed their out-of-town guests with views of both the Hudson and East Rivers and the skyline of mid-Manhattan. In 1959 all moved under the same roof on four floors of the new Interchurch Center at 475 Riverside Drive.

The coordination of budget planning and financial administration was naturally the most difficult. The finance director of GDUCW was the able Edith Groner who became the vigilant caretaker of all the restricted funds and provided the necessary oversight of income and expenditures as they went through the common accounting system. All of the formerly separate agencies kept their own financial records in order to feed in data, send out receipts, encourage income, control the budget—so the cost for general administration in the NCCC rose for all the cooperating departments. In order to avoid duplication of appeals to major donors and foundations, each department was required first to clear such appeals with the general finance office of the Council. The NCCC personnel policies applied to the employees of the merging organizations. Conformity seemed necessary to prevent confusion but it increased the overhead costs.

United Church Women should give giant credit lines to the resilient leaders of the next fifteen years: Mrs. James D. Wyker was followed by Mrs. Theodore O. Wedel, Mrs. William S. Terrell of Connecticut, Mrs. Theodore F. Wallace of Kansas, and Mrs. Stuart E. Sinclair of Massachusetts. Each was able to exercise the responsibilities of chairman of the General Department requiring tough decisions and hard committee work with their peers in other departments, and at the same time become the kind of dynamic president needed to command the loyalty of church women across the nation. This ambivalence had to be resolved within each person, else she could not have exercised leadership required in each capacity.

Take Mrs. Wyker for example—so delightfully disarming in manner and so doggedly determined in her convictions. The Department Board of Managers had acted on a number of things such as universal military training and the pollution of the Japanese fishing areas by occupation forces. Dr. Roswell Barnes was always sympathetic to the women, but dutifully reminded Mrs. Wyker that such public statements were to be cleared through the Council officers. Mrs. Wyker apologized profusely: "The women wouldn't embarrass the Council for anything. We promise not to do it again—well, not unless our conscience tells us to!" She explained carefully that the women felt the Holy Spirit moving through their meeting and were unanimous in their decision. "The men never know what to do or say when we talk about the Holy Spirit!" she told me once with a chuckle.

Church women knew who they were and what it was they were free to do in their own sphere. They had no property or ecclesiastical tradition to protect. Their destiny was not to bring the world into the walls of their divided churches, but to bring to bear their Christian convictions in the places where they lived. They were advocates for those persecuted for right-eousness sake. They kept the vision of the Kingdom of God on earth; yet in the times in which they lived, they steadily sought to fill the circle of the possible.

STATUS OF WOMEN IN THE CHURCHES Stimulated by special studies of the World Council of Churches—and perhaps also by the new context of their work within the NCCC—one area of exploration concerned cooperation between men and women in the church. Was it possible for women, who so long had remained on the periphery of the life of the churches, to share the privileges and responsibilities of the central circle?

Such a question must have crossed the mind of Mrs. Samuel McCrea Cavert as she sat in the reception area of the barracks which housed the World Council of Churches in-process-of-formation. Dr. Cavert was chairman of the committee of the Churches planning for the first Assembly of World Council which had been delayed due to the war until 1948. Day after day Mrs. Cavert waited for her husband to finish his conferences and noted that she saw only men coming in and out of the WCC offices.

Twila Lyton Cavert was a person who could make a contribution in her own right to any national or world meeting. She was an educator, having taught in the Women's College in Japan (where she was also a fellow in the Imperial University) and in Sarah Lawrence College, and had been a trustee on the boards of Yenching University and Mt. Holyoke. She had worked professionally for the leadership division of the national board of the YWCA and chaired committees for the Federal Council of Churches and United Church Women. To keep herself useful during the month in Geneva she was considering a request of the World YWCA to direct a study on the status of women in the churches.

Feeling that such a study would more appropriately be sponsored by the WCC itself, she approached Dr. Visser t'Hooft, the General Secretary, about the matter. Although he was unwilling that anything come into the Assembly in Amsterdam which was not thoroughly documented, he agreed that she could make a survey (as a volunteer) under the Study Department and that as material came in some consideration would be given to its use.

In the next two and a half years, Mrs. Cavert devised a questionnaire which covered five general areas: (1) the Biblical, psychological, and traditional aspects of the life and work of women in the church; (2) professional women in the church and problems surrounding the future; (3) volunteer activities; (4) trends in policy making groups and church boards; (5) comparison of the work of women of the church and the level of emancipation in their own country. Responses eventually came from 65 countries, some of which were composite reports of a number of denominations within the geographical area (as was true of the United States where Inez Cavert in the Federal Council compiled an extraordinary report).

The officials of the WCC felt the data was sufficient to call together a consultation of approximately 100 men and women in Baarn, Holland preceding the Assembly to offer some direction concerning further steps for member churches and for the WCC itself. A summary statement of substance was placed in the packet of each delegate to the Assembly. Among the recommendations for future study and action was the proposal to create a Commission on the Life and Work of Women in the Churches with adequate staff and budget to continue the studies and be of encouragement to women in the ecumenical movement.

With initial contributions from the Ecumenical Register of UCW, the WCC set up an office for women and selected Sarah Chakko as its executive. This delighted those who had been at the Assembly and had watched the running debate between this gifted Indian educator and the eminent theologian, Dr. Karl Barth.

At the meeting of the second Assembly of the WCC in Evanston, Illinois, a special commission brought in the recommendation to establish a Department of Cooperation Between Men and Women in Church and Society. As usual in long titles, each word means what it says and more. The accent on cooperation indicated that men and not only women, were involved.

The Department was fortunate in having Madeleine Barot as their first executive staff member. She was a member of the Reformed Church of France with doctoral training in anthropology and she was also a theologian to be reckoned with. She was the founder of CIMADE, a movement which offered special ministries on both sides during World War II and still works with rehabilitation and reconciliation teams in many parts of the world. Having the respect of the General Secretary of the World Council of Churches, Dr. Barot put in a word for women at important points.

Although there were conversations from time to time as

to whether the administration of the World Day of Prayer and the Fellowship of the Least Coin could be administered from her office, she always declined, partly because it would affect negatively the wholehearted participation of women in countries where the WCC was not accepted by the Churches (such as many in Latin America) and because the detail of correspondence and service would be too heavy a load on a staff with limited secretarial help.

She preferred to keep her department free to make selected theological studies in depth, to hold consultations on the integration of women into the life of the church, and to give concrete assistance to women in Asia and Africa where called for. Traveling widely, she often attended regional meetings on other continents and worked toward thoughtful involvement of the women in the churches there.

On one visit to the United States, she spent almost a week in the Wyker home trying to work out a way that theological studies might be introduced in the United States. European churchmen were heavy on theology and often considered the Americans working in the WCC to be practical administrators with very little competence in the theological area.

As president of UCW, Mrs. Wyker invited a small group of well known men and women to open the theological dialogue. The discussion was proceeding along the well worn passages of Genesis and Galatians, when suddenly Dr. Barot introduced a startling concept using the words, "the sexuality of God." Twenty years later the phrase was battered around frequently by feminist theologians, but in the 1950's credit must be given to the American clergymen for recovering quietly enough to discuss the semantic issue in relation to cultural patterns. The one layman present remained in a state of shock for the rest of the meeting!

Another issue which continually had to be in review by the Department of Cooperation was the relevance of separate women's organizations in the Church. The flexible style and scope of women's organizations in the United States always seemed to cause a certain bewilderment among sophisticated Europeans. There was somehow a feeling that church women's associations offered a sort of an 'alternative service plan' while women waited to become more fully involved in the decision making bodies. Actually when a proportionate number of women were appointed on boards, as trustees and in delegations, there still remained a majority of women who must discover some other way to give expression to their Christian faith. Not only the "polity of the Church" needed study, but also what was meant by the "life and work" of the Church.

When Madeleine Barot visited some of the large women's denominational meetings in the United States she commented on the sensitive nature of worship as developed by women and their prophetic interpretation of social problems. Church women were not just being used as tools to produce money for missions for their churches. They *were* in mission—a legitimate expression of their faith. No one was trying to export this particular expression, but neither were those who participated in this form of fellowship about to give it up.

Mrs. Wyker, in extensive speaking schedules, was instrumental in awakening women to their own part in this long range decision of the full partnership with men in all realms of church life. As she talked with women who had finished their seminary training, she recognized the bleakness of their futures since neither clergy nor laity were eager to open up opportunities for women.

A small volume entitled *Church Women in the Scheme of Things* by Mossie Wyker was published in 1953 and widely used as a basis for discussion. It opened up wide-ranging implications both in the lives of women and in the concern of the churches.

EMPLOYED WOMEN Early in 1958, the General Department of United Church Women and the Department of Church and Economic Life of the NCCC jointly convened a consultation of specialists from the churches and other areas on "Employed Women and the Church."

About six of every ten women working in 1958 were married and half of these were over 40 years of age. More important than the numbers was the new style of life which this meant for families, youth, and children. The economic and social level of jobs open to women, the changing relationships in the home, church and community—all were to remain of primary concern to the Church.

This Consultation explored the causes and extent of new developments and their meanings for the programs of the churches. The chairman of the consultation, Mrs. Theodore O. Wedel, was asked to write a study booklet on "Employed Women and the Church." Drawing from her vast experience in observing the changing currents in the life of women, both in the United States and around the world, she produced a guide well designed to bring this discussable subject to the attention of church people. The problems that this study raised and the answers called for could not be ignored by either men or women.

STRUGGLE FOR MUTUAL TRUST   In the early 50's, fear and suspicion were rampant in every community. Under the guise of rooting out communists, the powerful Committee on Un-American Activities headed by Senator Joseph McCarthy used tactics that threatened the nature of all democratic institutions.

A rural school teacher trying to explain the difference in governments to elementary school children lost his job without a hearing. A social worker collecting small amounts of money for the Republican Cause in Spain (those opposing the monarchy) was asked by the Committee on Un-American Activities for the list of donors. When she refused to submit her confidential list, she was put into federal prison on the charge of contempt of Congress. Some Church and Congressional leaders were openly accused.

The irritating part of the whole process of accusation was that there seemed to be no recourse. No one pointed out exactly what activity was being questioned. Parts of the pattern included those engaged in interracial or international activities. The most un-American thing about the Committee on Un-American Activities was its un-American procedures. There seemed to be hysterical fear of a "communist under every bed" as one national officer put it.

Mrs. Wyker tells of being at a small tea in New York when a German visitor said to Mrs. Roosevelt: "We do not understand you in this country. This happened in Germany. We saw it happen. We said it is ridiculous. This is a crackpot. But it happened! You too are going the same road and doing nothing about it."

And Mrs. Roosevelt answered: "You do not understand our form of government. We move slowly. It seems cumbersome. It takes us a long time. But give the American people time. We'll work this out."

The national Board of United Church Women was not about to let the situation go unchallenged. Not only did they wish to speak out in testimony for those leaders of the government and churches who were being attacked, but they must do something by way of interpretation to the nearly 2,000 local and state councils across the nation so they would not be afraid to speak up in the name of justice in the communities where they lived. The time of decision-making was May, 1953 at the meeting of the Board in Turkey Run National Park, Indiana. Carloads of Board women were driven from Indianapolis and Cincinnati, so one could be sure that many things had been discussed before they reached the meeting as a whole!

Under the leadership of the executive secretary of the Evangelical United Brethren, Florence Partridge, a special committee was asked to come up with a statement. The result was a "Declaration of Loyalty" which the Board approved. It had been printed as a red, white, and blue leaflet and widely distributed. It read as follows:

A CHRISTIAN DECLARATION OF LOYALTY

"As Christian Americans we are dedicated to maintaining the freedom of all Americans and their institutions. No body of citizens is more alert to the threat of communist thought and conspiracy both to the Christian faith and to freedom than the Christian churches . . . "

"At this moment when national unity based upon mutual confidence is of paramount importance to our security, men in responsible positions must not, through unsubstantiated charges and blanket indictments, destroy confidence in our American schools, colleges and universities."*

Men in responsible positions and self-appointed groups and individuals are even now spreading distrust of churches, of charitable foundations, and of loyal American citizens with whom they disagree.

The Board of Managers of United Church Women view these threats to American freedom as among the most serious dangers ever faced by our people.

As a witness to our Christian faith we therefore accept the following disciplines and responsibilities:

1. **A Christian Declaration of Loyalty**

   This is God's world and we are in His care . . .

   We do believe;

   Earth might be fair . . .

   We will strive to do our part in making it so;

   Fear comes of the unknown . . .

   We will know;

   The young and the uninformed are open to false teaching . . .

   We will share the truth;

   Forces of dissension would undermine the very institutions that can overcome communism . . .

   We will become aware of these forces and throw our strength with the superior force of Christianity;

   Many valiant defenders of God-given freedom are being wrongfully accused . . .

   We will uphold them;

   We ourselves may for our beliefs face disapproval, insinuation or slander . . .

   We will stand;

   It is our heritage from the Old Testament, from Greek knowledge, from the American founding fathers and from the Christian gospel of love, to think freely and to speak our thoughts . . .

   We do our own thinking;

   We are sovereign American citizens, followers of Christ, children of God . . .

   We dare to speak out.

2. **Dedication of ourselves as a disciplined group to study, pray and individually to take courageous stands.**

3. **Commitment as individuals to:**

   Maintain confidence and composure; do basic reading; confer with Congressmen (in home state); express basic beliefs to clergymen and laymen and to local school boards concerning personal and academic freedoms; contact and co-operate with community groups taking similar stands; encourage more accurate reporting and more careful interpretation of news; encourage the organization of study and discussion groups, for both men and women, through council and denominational channels.[3]

VISIT WITH EISENHOWER   Church women are never satisfied with just *"speaking."* They must *be heard.* They felt that the time had come for this point of view to be taken directly to President Eisenhower, with the hope that he would accept an invitation to the upcoming Assembly to be held in Atlantic City, October 1953. Leaders of the National Council were also seeking appointments and the women went through the protocol of asking the Council to include them or give them permission to seek their own appointment. Again no answer. Time was running out, so Mossie Wyker telephoned her friend, Bertha Adkins, the vice chairman of the Republican Committee, to ask if she could clear the way. She did. The appointment was arranged for Mrs. Wyker, Mrs. Abbie Jackson, Mrs. James Dolbey, Mrs. Leslie Swain and Mrs. MacLeod as the delegation to see the President.

As they gathered in Washington on the evening before, Mrs. MacLeod found Mrs. Jackson sitting in the lobby of the Dodge Hotel unable to claim her registration. Mrs. MacLeod went into action. The desk clerk could care less that they were there to see the President of the United States. Negroes could not stay at the Dodge Hotel. She telephoned another hotel to ask for two twin bedrooms. Late that night they claimed reservations without trouble. Some issues are only settled by action that sets its own precedent.

Their appointment with the President was for ten minutes, and the secretary indicated that he was running late on his schedule. Mrs. Wyker later recalled the experience as follows:

> Almost the first thing I did was to put that red, white and blue pamphlet in his hand and to tell him how we felt about what was happening to our country. We had published that Declaration of Loyalty and were going to get it across the country no matter what it cost us.

> The President was visibly moved that a group of private citizens had faced the issue and could see what was happening to the fiber of the country. He asked us questions about who we were, what we were doing. He spoke of pressures under which he was working and was greatly encouraged to find a group from the private sector with such understanding. Three times his secretary came to touch his arm and remind him that other

appointments had been scheduled and he would say, "Just a moment."

For almost half an hour they were with the President of the United States.

As they left, Mrs. Wyker said, "We do hope for an affirmative answer to our invitation that you speak to our Assembly."

"I'll think it over," he replied.

The secretary said later, "I think you can count on the President being there. I have never seen him so interested!"

1953 ASSEMBLY ATLANTIC CITY With a fanfare of trumpets, the sixth Assembly of United Church Women opened in the big Convention Hall in Atlantic City on Monday evening, October 5, 1953. *The Church Woman* later wrote that 'tons and tons' of women were present. All 140 pounds of me was among the 3500 delegates. Bishop William C. Martin, the president of the NCCC and Mrs. James Wyker, president of UCW opened the meetings by challenging the Assembly with messages on Christian Mission and Unity.

The President of the United States was to give greetings on the next morning at about 11 o'clock. Security required that all must be in the auditorium by 9 o'clock. The capacity of the Convention Hall was reached as many women came to the event from surrounding states.

By 8:30 thousands of women were eagerly climbing the long ramp that led to the auditorium floor. I was among them and slowed down my pace slightly not to pass an older woman who was pressing forward at her own pace. She looked at me anxiously and inquired, "Are *all* these people going to the rest room?" I smiled and shook my head. "The President is coming." It became a parable for me. There are some in every crowd who miss the big moment eagerly pursuing a personal goal.

But once in the auditorium, every woman was compelled to think of greater things. Walter Van Kirk had a captive audience as he spoke just ahead of President Eisenhower on "Christian Struggle for World Order." Over and over again the audience broke into applause as he called for honor to be restored in the nation. "The extent to which the United States has become a vast whispering gallery of charges and counter charges is almost unbelievable," he said. He went on:

> Only through living our democratic faith can we create the free society that such faith envisages. Only as such a free society is achieved can we expect other peoples to be convinced of the validity of democracy.

President Eisenhower picked up an additional theme of the "wasteful and devastating contest in producing weapons" which can only lead to "sudden and mass destruction." The other alternative—a just and durable peace—will come "only through courage, knowledge, patience, leadership . . ." He became more specific:

> We must respond to the legitimate aspirations and hopes of people.

> We must arrange trade systems that will provide each with the necessaries of life and opportunity for self-advancement.

> We must seek to resolve age-old prejudices, ambitions, and hatreds. These still scar great parts of the whole world.

> We must provide machinery and techniques to encourage peaceful communication and mutual confidence which alone can lift the burden of arms from us.

Others at the Assembly reinforced the note of freedom. Buell Gallagher, president of City College, New York, spoke of the plowing under of faith in leaders, and institutions, and other citizens which eventually would undermine both the Church and the schools. Pauline Fredrick, NBC radio commentator, pointed out that it was the "unofficial censors in this country who were trying to control the thinking, and consequently the speaking of Americans."

And Dr. Ralph W. Sockman, the national radio preacher, said "We can be fooled by our fears as well as our faith. The peril of our present national mood is that we shall believe too little rather than too much."

It was not only the speaking from the platform, but the

voices from the floor which made up the substance of the Atlantic City meeting. I will never forget the long lines which stood waiting their turn for the floor mikes as Mrs. J. Birdsall Calkins presented the resolutions from the business committee. In the most spirited session of the Assembly, the delegates expressed concern that the United States "opposed at the time the adoption of Covenants of the United Nations Commission on Human Rights; . . . called for the universal reduction of armaments . . . urged the strengthening of Point IV and the technical assistance program of the UN; . . . pressed Congress to authorize and promptly appropriate the U.S. share of the 1954 budget of UNICEF; . . . expressed our gratification that the refugee act of 1953 granting special non-quota visas to 214,000 uprooted persons and called upon church women to "assume their neighborly responsibility to these newcomers."

The Assembly said other things to its own constituency . . . urging every local council to have a training program looking toward full integration . . . pointing out that should the Supreme Court decision be affirmative, Christian women should find ways to meet the impact of the desegregation of public schools in their communities . . . wholeheartedly accept the disciplines contained in A Christian Declaration of Loyalty; and taking every opportunity to "emphasize positive social and moral concepts in press, radio, and television."

Myrta Ross, UCW's public relations director, had arranged a national radio broadcast in front of a live audience where Mary Margaret McBride, national radio personality, interviewed Assembly personalities. The frequent applause let the women back home know and share in the enthusiastic support of the message of this Assembly.

In the long run, the strength of a united movement of Christian women is reflected in the integrity of each individual woman who recognizes God's power at work within her and struggles for freedom and truth in her own place. So it was a benediction for us on the final evening to hear Rosa Page Welch witness through song and word of her recent experience with Christian youth in Asia and Africa. We are all of one loaf! After three overwhelming days we were ready for God's grace note as we sang in deep commitment: "Let us break bread together on our knees."

MINISTRY OF RECONCILIATION   Long after Senator McCarthy and the Committee on UnAmerican Activities were thoroughly discredited, the scars of this experience remained, particularly in the National Council, whose leadership had been the target of the unfair defamation of character. Risking loss in their own ranks, United Church Women generally could be counted upon to be loyal when the ecumenical movement of which they were a part was being attacked.

Mrs. Emlen Stokes, a courageous peaceloving member of the Society of Friends, agreed to underwrite a three-year ministry of reconciliation among church members themselves. The emotional stress pervading the churches could never be relieved by a written pamphlet of defense. So UCW and the NCCC were able to ask Mrs. Wyker to carry on a person-to-person ministry particularly through gatherings in small churches through the South. Mossie Wyker had a particular gift of absorbing the hurts and criticisms in her own being and was able to offer a touch of divine healing that the times required.

FOOTNOTES TO CHAPTER 3

1. Quoted from *The American Churches in the Ecumenical Movement* by Samuel McCrea Cavert, Association Press, 1968, p. 211.

2. Member Communions of NCC in 1950: African Methodist Episcopal Church, African Methodist Episcopal Zion Church, American Baptist Convention, Augustana Lutheran Church, Church of the Brethren, Colored Methodist Episcopal Church, Congregational Christian Churches, Disciples of Christ, Danish Evangelical Lutheran Church, Evangelical and Reformed Church, Evangelical United Brethren Church, Evangelical Unity of Czech Moravian Brethren in N.A., Friends - Five Years Meeting, Friends of Philadelphia and Vicinity, Methodist Church, Moravian Church (Northern and Southern Provinces), National Baptist Convention of America, National Baptist Convention, U.S.A., Inc., Presbyterian Church in the U.S., Presbyterian Church in the U.S.A., Protestant Episcopal Church, Reformed Church in America, Roumanian Orthodox Episcopate of America, Russian Orthodox Church in America, Seventh Day Baptists, General Conference, Syrian Antiochian Orthodox Church, Ukranian Orthodox Church in America, United Lutheran Church in America, United Presbyterian Church of N.A., The Federal Council of the Churches of Christ in America, Foreign Missions Conference of North America, Home Missions Council of North America, The International Council of Religious Education, Missionary Education Movement of the United States and Canada, National Protestant Council on Higher Education, The United Council of Church Women, United Stewardship Council of the Churches of Christ in the United States and Canada.

**General Department of
United Church Women
1950-1966**

chapter 4

A friend-filled circle

A movement takes on the nature of a personality. To describe United Church Women 'at her best' one would say she had a clear vision, fresh thoughts of her own and reflective responses to those of others, a capacity for a tender touch of friends, and the world in her heart.

Unless preoccupied by its internal housekeeping, a movement, like a person, normally gains real friends when warmly received, one at a time, into the family circle. Of course some are introduced by a member of the 'movement family' after meeting them somewhere else—at college, or an international conference, or the Commission on the Status of Women of the United Nations. Actually some are friends even before we meet them. Some common experience, like the World Day of Prayer, or a neighborly act after a destructive hurricane, or an exchange of letters expressing sympathy or confidence, binds us more truly together in friendship than many a casual touch.

It is for this reason that I always admired Miriam Evans, who was employed as the first staff person for Christian World Missions in 1950. It might have been her duty to stimulate mission study or handle last minute appeals for World Day of Prayer materials or receive overseas guests in her office, but you never would have guessed it! She had a manner of keeping the home fires burning so that all who surrounded her felt its friendly glow.

In this chapter I hope to describe some of the ways UCW widened the circumference of its circle of friends and thus enriched its own life and work.

INTERNATIONAL   Since all of the readers of this volume have
FELLOWSHIP - 1955   lived in the jet age when "breakfast in
                Kansas City and dinner in Paris" is as
commonplace among tourists as comments on the weather, it may be hard to understand the history-making significance of an international Fellowship Team which encircled the earth in 1955.

Leaving Los Angeles on February 18, Felicia Sunderlal (the Secretary of Women of the Church of North India), Mossie Wyker and Helen Baker celebrated the World Day of Prayer in 1955 in the Fiji Islands. Later joined by Josefina Phodaca (a Philipino lawyer and president of Protestant Church Women of Manila), the Fellowship Team was received warmly by Christian women in Australia, Indonesia, India, Pakistan, Kenya, Uganda, Egypt, Jordan, Lebanon, Germany and finally welcomed home by United Church Women in the U.S.A.

Helen Baker who accompanied the team as its manager was the chief interpreter to American women through the pages of *The Church Woman*.[1] The purpose was not to visit 'our work', not to see interesting sights, not to address mass meetings with messages from other parts of the world, but rather to find some living encounters with our sisters-in-Christ through conversations as they studied together the Letter to the Ephesians. Thanks to the written record of Helen Baker, we can share some of these experiences:

> *Dateline:* Suva, Fiji Islands on World Day of Prayer 1955
> It is nearing midnight in the Fiji Islands. Four times
> today the Christian women of Suva along with your
> Fellowship Team have been summoned by the
> Mighty One, God the Lord, to "abide in prayer" with
> Christians everywhere from the rising of the sun to its

setting, on this World Day of Prayer.

I heard the summons as I wakened even before "the rising of the sun" this morning. At first the darkness and the soft Fijian breezes in the palms deceived me, for I was certain it was raining. But as I threw open the wide doors to the hotel balcony, there beyond the palms and the clouds and the mountains were the first fair glimmerings of the new day—the day for which Christian women around the world were waiting; the day God himself must cherish, for he blesses it so faithfully year after year, in country after country, in heart after heart.

The first service came early, at six-thirty in the lovely little Indian chapel set back and separated from the street by such greenness as only tropical sun and rains can create. We arrived just as Indian school girls were marching in, all of them dressed in lavender-colored uniforms, with white scarves thrown gracefully over their heads, after the manner of saris. Soon women and girls filled the church, mostly from Indian homes. We stood for the first hymn:

> Jesus, stand among us
> In Thy risen power;
> Let this time of worship
> Be a hallowed hour . . .

No need here to search for the evidence of the working of His power; the evidences were pouring in upon the three of us so fast and so surely that, like the women at the tomb, we wanted to run back to you all at home to share the certainties.

Three other services followed that day, in different places on Suva. The welcome and warmth of the Fijian women with their multi-racial back-ground never ceased. Can you imagine the full hearts of the Fellowship Team as the day ended? Like a preview of a divine love story, the thoughts of the journeying sun brought images of women in their towns and all around the world answering the summons to pray on this day. Overwhelmed with their own experience, three women who had traveled far touched the hand of a woman from the Pacific Islands as they sang the closing prayer:

> The day Thou gavest, Lord, is ended:
> the darkness falls at Thy behest.
> To Thee our morning hymns ascended,
> Thy praise shall hallow now our rest.

Dateline: Surabaya, March 14th

And now it's our fourth and last day in Surabaya, East Java—a two-hour flight from Djakarta over irresistibly lovely islands. From the moment we stepped off the plane we have felt a warmth, a friendliness beyond words to describe. We keep asking each other, "What if we had missed Surabaya?"

Mrs. Wyker will travel far to find a more eager congregation than the one thousand strong which listened to her in the city's oldest and largest church. Benches in front cared for some of the late arrivals, among them a group of Indonesian soldiers (the navy held down the first row in the balcony); the choir stalls were jammed; the two entrances looked like a New York subway during rush hour. The organ was good; the singing of the hymns hearty. The Hallelujahs sung by the congregation a cappella as the pastor finished reading the Apostles' Creed were almost startling in their volume and intensity.

Dateline: Delhi, March 23

Mrs. Wyker was superb in every interview. Usually, Mrs. Wyker began by quoting the remark of the Governor of Bengal that women in India in the last ten years had risen faster than the women of any other country. Every woman we saw promptly and modestly denied this, saying it was true that women at the top had advanced spectacularly but agreeing with Mrs. Indira Gandhi, Prime Minister

Nehru's daughter, who regretted that the large majority of Indian women had not gone far. Village women must learn to accept responsibility, she said. Mrs. Wyker asked Raj Kumari Armit Kaur, minister of health, only woman minister, and a Christian, how we could best interpret India to America, her answer was as "going through the pain of travail."

Dateline: Uganda—Palm Sunday 1955

The reverence with which the African choir led us this morning in "Come to Dark Gethsemane" and "When I Survey the Wondrous Cross" could not have been surpassed in any Palm Sunday service anywhere. How the Suva and Kampala choirs . . . Every concern is overshadowed by *the* concern— the return of the Kabaka, king of the Kingdom of Buganda, a province of Uganda. Deported fifteen months ago by the British government, he is still in London while his million subjects are burning with humiliation and resentment and insistence on his return.

The Prime Minister of Buganda arranged an interview for us with the Kabaka's wife, Queen Damali. The Kabaka's absence was never mentioned in that interview but surely it was uppermost in all our minds. The Queen was gracious, and expressed sympathy with the purpose of the Team. She knew about United Church Women because our own Mrs. Emory Ross had asked her to send a word of greeting to the 1953 Atlantic City Assembly . . .

Asked by Mrs. Wyker what message she would like to send to American church women, the Queen replied, "We need your prayers in these troubled times." Then she remarked that she had read in *The Church Woman* about Sarah Chakko's death. This gave Felicia Sunderlal opportunity to talk about her former teacher. That particular conversation ended with the Queen remarking, "Miss Chakko had character."

Some of our outstanding impressions of Uganda? The overflowing hospitality which opened the doors of four African homes to lodge the Team members for their four-day stop. In no other way could we have come to appreciate the potentialities of the country or the warmheartedness of some of its Christians.

The consultation was as widely representative of the community as possible. The opening worship service was led by an Indian woman, with an African woman as translator. That afternoon the reporter for a buzz group on the "dividing walls of hostility" commented, "This morning for the first time in my life, I heard an Indian woman leading worship. I always think of them as traders on the road or in business. I did not know there was an Indian Christian woman in Kampala."

Dateline: Cairo

As we drove to our nine o'clock consultation, one of the first sights to intrigue us was the statue at the head of the main street "The Awakening of Egypt." With the Sphinx at her feet, a tall woman was throwing back her veil. Whoever the artist was, he was a man of perception; if only the ancient churches of Egypt had been strong enough to resist the culture that brought those veils so many centuries ago.

Dateline: Jericho

We had driven down to the refugee camps outside of Jericho where some 35,000 people are housed. No need here to describe refugee camps to United Church Women. The Arab camps, through our own World Community Day and through Church World Service publicity, are well known. We want here rather to record our amazement at what the YMCA and the YWCA are accomplishing in the schools for children, in the trade shops for adults, and in the general upkeep of the camp, and our dismay that there is evidently no more hope in 1955 than in 1948 that the families will ever know a permanent home . . We felt the same dismay in the consultation.

Moved by the morning's experience, Mrs. Wyker asked the women who, by the way, had studied Ephesians among themselves before our arrival, to talk about themselves. Each woman except one began her story with the words, "I am a refugee." Then, sometimes bitter, sometimes only weary, she would tell a story of heartache, deprivation, suffering, longing. These women are not among the 875,000 refugees living in camps and registered with UNRRA for pitiably small rations of food and clothing; they are among the 200,000 non-registered refugees, a goodly number of whom are Christians. Their husbands have found work, not perhaps equal to their abilities or to their vocations before partition. Their families have homes, though seldom equal to their previous ones . . .

Dateline: Jerusalem—Easter 1955

Early Easter Sunday, we joined the group of people worshipping at the Garden Tomb. It was possible in the setting of the beautiful garden to use our imagination and relive the story as if it were really happening, and somehow it seemed as if we might be women to whom our Lord was again saying, "Go quickly and tell."

Go tell? Tell the tragic things we have seen and experienced over and beyond what we have hurriedly reported or written home? The deep hurts of humanity, of people struggling and longing for freedom, tired, defeated, and war worn, of wandering refugees, tensions between nations and races. How can we ever tell it as it should be told?

Dateline: Germany

On the plane the stewardess has just handed me today's copy of *The Stars and Stripes.* It reports the opening of the Bandung Conference and the speech of President Soekarno of Indonesia. "We are living in a world of fear," he said. "The life of man is corroded and made bitter by fear. Fear of the future, fear of the hydrogen bomb, fear of ideologies. Perhaps this fear is a greater danger than the danger itself because it is fear which drives men to act foolishly, to act thoughtlessly, to act dangerously."

The therapeutic kindnesses began in Frankfurt, where four women from West Germany met the plane. Dr. Antonie Nopitch, whom so many American church women remember from her attendance at the 1948 Milwaukee Assembly, had come all the way from Nuremberg just to greet us as we passed through Frankfurt. With her were Miss Anni Rudolf, executive secretary, Evangelische Frauenarbeiten in Deutschland, Mrs. Olga Sander, president of Evangelische women's work in Frankfurt. Over the teacups, we shared the kinship that marked all our hours in Germany.

Dateline: Lebanon, April 18

We have not as yet written about the messages carried from one country to another and delivered in each consultation. When we left the United States, the Team took with them messages of goodwill to women around the world from the presidents of most of the national denominational women's organizations which help comprise the General Department of United Church Women. The women in each country in which we stopped added a letter of their own.

The Planning Committee sent with the Fellowship Team 500 wooden yokes, carved by a woman in Texas, Sarah Culbertson, to be used as gifts in the various countries. At the closing service of a day together, Mrs. Wyker would ask the group to form a circle and join hands. Then she would explain that the women of the United States wanted to send some token of affection which would also become a

symbol of what could happen around the world—
"the yoking of Christian women in prayer." The
Team members would pass out the little yokes, the
women would pin them on, and then Mrs. Wyker
would close with a prayer. Invariably, this became
the high experience of the day for both the Team
and the women of the particular country."

1955 ASSEMBLY
CLEVELAND, OHIO
The cumulative effect of this global
encounter permeated the Seventh
National Assembly. The theme was "The
Working of His Power in Us and Through Us." The Assembly
opened with Mrs. Wyker's account of the "Glory of the Church"
as she had sensed it anew during conversations with women
overseas. The Epistle of Ephesians had been the base of those
discussions and was used in the Biblical studies at the
Assembly under the leadership of Dr. Rachel Henderlite of
Richmond, Virginia.

The Fellowship Team had invited women from each of
the countries whose hospitality had been extended to them. In
addition, the presidents of the United Christian Women's
Colleges of Asia and many other overseas guests shared in the
program which gave some reality to the kind of world in which
God was at work.

There was no question that it was a revolutionary world.
Dramatic worship services especially written for the Assembly
by Margaret Applegarth gave substance to the sub-themes of
"The Church Faces the Revolutionary World" and "The
Church's Responsibility and Opportunities in the Revolutionary World." Speakers interpreted the giant upheaval that was
faced by the peoples of the world. Some of the memorable
quotes were:

Eleanor Roosevelt:
Peace can come only with confidence and knowledge
and the church women of the world can support inter-
change of knowledge among all peoples, as one of the
first steps toward that confidence.

Chester Bowles (U.S. Ambassador to India):

We cannot move from atomic stalemate to even the beginnings of peace, unless we reach an understanding with the masses of mankind. Man does not live by bread alone. He desires justice. He desires independence. He desires brotherhood.

M.A. Thomas (of the Mar Thoma Church of South India):

God is working out his purposes in and through the revolution. So our proper response is to understand what his purposes are . . . and that may mean something quite different from seeking to stop the revolution.

James Robinson (well known Negro pastor and lecturer in university and college campuses both in the U.S. and abroad):

There is no more profound Christian conviction than this—that if the truth of God, as revealed in Christ, should make a man free, he will indeed be free. The ultimate nature of this truth is that we can become free enough from the tyranny, oppression, and the limitations of this world to become children of God. This is the foundation of that mutual security, interdependency, respect and love—which make up the common denominator to the peace of the world.

Using material coming from the small discussion groups on the implication of the theme in the life of this nation, the women of the Assembly responded through their Message Committee:

We are filled with a sense of urgency because we know that today's revolution is world wide and explosive, and our human responsibility for facing its issues must be met not in centuries, but within a few short years.

Specifically they recognized areas of concern and action

relating to human rights as interwoven with foreign policy. They took official actions to protest when civil liberties are violated; encouraged disarmament; opposed universal military training; urged peaceful use of atomic energy; assisted in constructive process of change as Indians faced new adjustments in American communities; supported community agencies combatting juvenile delinquency.

It was appropriate that the climactic experience be around the deeper meaning of the life and death of Jesus Christ in a moving communion service. The Rev. Mrs. Mossie Wyker and the Rev. Eugene Carson Blake officiated as the bread and wine was offered through the hands of women elders.

PROTESTANT WOMEN OF THE CHAPEL As one of the NATO nations, the United States had thousands of men and women living in Europe and Asia helping to secure the peace and to interpret and build understanding. Never before had so vast a group of our people moved from one country to another by invitation of the governments of those countries. So in the 50's UCW began an important relationship with Army, Navy and Air Force wives and families living overseas.

In 1953 a group of women in Goeppeningen, Germany, organized *Protestant Women of the Chapel,* a companion to the *Protestant Men of the Chapel,* under the U.S. Chaplaincy. The movement spread to many military bases. There united efforts were made to meet special needs with similar groupings of Catholic and Jewish women. The program for PWOC was planned by a board in conference with the chaplain of the area and it was designed to meet the varied needs of those with different church backgrounds. It encouraged friendly relations with the people of the host country.

By the mid-fifties some UCW women in these overseas communities suggested to their chaplains that the UCW would be a good source of program help. For many years, UCW was asked to send a woman to participate in the fall rallies of the

PWOC in Europe and North Africa. Up until 1972, UCW coordinated the planning and production of the annual program guide which was used world wide under the guidance of the chaplains. This provided a helpful opportunity for association with representatives of denominations not working in the National Council of Churches. It also eventuated in the inclusion of the three UCCW celebrations in their program. These ties made it easier for women coming home to fit into the on-going program in their home communities or, being familiar with it here at home, to fit into the program they found in the U.S. military communities overseas.

GLOBAL NEIGHBORS   When the Reverend Mrs. Tamaki Uemura came to this country in 1946, there was a flurry about her officiating at a communion service at a Presbyterian National meeting since at that time women were not ordained in that church. Over the breakfast table in my apartment I tried to explain to her about men in the Presbyterian Church. She rolled her eyes upward and said, "Oh, I think I will go around creating more commotion! God give me wisdom."

I think this must have been Esther Hymer's prayer in the 60's. Her innovative approach to international involvement always created a God-given commotion.

GETTING ACQUAINTED   Following a conference in Europe, Esther Hymer flew to Africa on a three week visit to get acquainted with her Nigerian neighbors. She arrived in Lagos to find the hotel in which she had reservations had burned down. Settling into another hotel, she called an African woman whom she had known. A welcome party was arranged. Everybody wanted to know what she was there to do. "Nothing. I'm unofficial," was Mrs. Hymer's response. "I just want to listen to you by way of getting acquainted with Nigerian life." The next day thirty-five African women took over the hotel lobby just to talk about their concerns to some Westerner who wanted to listen.

Later she journeyed by car to Ibadan and went through

the same process. She returned to find imaginative women of diverse backgrounds already organizing themselves. She went to a meeting where a constitution was presented to the group. The African woman presiding said: "We have a constitution. I am going to be president. Now what do we do?" Eyes looked at Esther. She responded: "Whatever needs to be done. You decide." They looked again with wonder. "You mean *we* decide for ourselves?" After much talk, the priority which seemed to emerge was the need for nutrition education designed for women in village areas. How could this be done?

A plan was developed over the course of the next weeks. Five women should be sent to a church training school in the Netherlands where nutrition education appropriate to rural Nigeria could be obtained.

Hearing about the plan for nutrition education of their sisters in Nigeria, United Church Women offered to share the training costs for the five leaders and their initial program in the villages. In addition, American women assembled kits of basic materials according to Nigerian specifications and shipped enough so that each village woman would have one as she began her in-service training.

Following this rewarding experience in cooperation, it was the general practice to seek requests from the women of the country being studied and develop projects according to the specifications sent by them.[2]

NATION BUILDING   The struggles of the people of Indonesia for nationhood were marked by the emergence of women in positions of leadership. In the fast growing churches of what had become the largest Moslem nation of the world women had been ordained and held major responsibilities in Church structures and programs. Sensing the painful struggle against overwhelming odds in the new nation, Esther Hymer made inquiries to find out how American church women might help.

One of the guests at the National Assembly in Denver in 1958 was Mrs. Leimena, wife of Dr. Leimena, vice president of the Republic of Indonesia. She answered the question in general terms but urged Mrs. Hymer to get in touch with Tina Franz, a woman executive of the Indonesian NCCC, to work on some concrete proposal with Ernie Fogg, an American working with the Indonesian Christian Councils' complex relationships to English speaking churches and agencies.

They responded by introducing Dr. F. Kruyt, Director of Mardi Santosa maternity center in Surabaya. Dr. Kruyt, a Dutch woman born in Indonesia, had chosen Indonesian citizenship in order to carry on her life long mission to serve the women as a medical doctor. She was so well accepted as a citizen that she was elected to represent her region in the first constitutional Assembly held after independence.

Mardi Santosa under her leadership had become a center not only for pre-natal and maternity care but for family planning, child care and other services to women. Her dream was a facility where young women could live and be trained as visiting nurses. It was agreed that World Community Day offerings in 1959-60 would provide equipment and building supplies for expansion of the center and its facilities for training young women to bring health and counseling services to women in remote villages.

Working closely, Mrs. Hymer and Mr. Fogg were able to expedite the process by transferring funds from a New York bank to purchase steel in Hong Kong in time for it to be delivered in Surabaya without the usual inflation from skyrocketing exchange rates and the delays of transportation.

In 1960 every World Community Day packet had a study book and discussion guide written by Esther Hymer. The book was entitled *Channels for Peace* and focused on what was going on in Indonesia, as well as the aftermath of the struggles for independence and nationhood among other poverty stricken countries of Southeast Asia. The guide proposed a project that would enable American women to do something to show understanding for the hard working women of Asia. The project, called "Pieces for Peace", consisted of individual packages containing a new piece of cloth and a sewing bag with thread, scissors and sewing supplies. Literally thousands of these packages were brought to World Community Day observances that year as part of the offering. (The money and gifts doubled that year). Church World Service with its excellent delivery systems shipped the supplies to Indonesia, where for the first time in many years thousands of women made bright new clothes for themselves!

As usual, concern did not end with the year's special programs. Some time later Esther Hymer discovered that one of the field men for UNICEF was planning a trip to Djakarta to talk with government officials. "Would you mind running over to Surabaya to see how Dr. Kruyt is doing?" she asked in her most winsome manner.

The man looked a bit appalled but answered his friend, "Oh sure, its only 800 miles out of my way!"

It was worth the trip for all concerned. He not only was impressed with the competence and compassion of Dr. Kruyt but also by her capacity to make her services available and acceptable to all Indonesian people. He agreed to add a children's wing to the Center and CWS paid for furnishing it.

UN SEMINARS
1958-1960
Esther Hymer used resources from the United Nations as well as the Churches in writing preparatory study books. She would say, "The United Nations is here as a channel for us to use, but it is only one of many ways. We must concentrate on understanding the issues."

The women were eager to see the UN headquarters and therefore Esther arranged a series of seminars. State councils organized bus loads of participants for these UN seminars. During the period 1958-1960 nearly 1,500 women came to New York each year. This educational experience was reflected in the active interpretation of the United Nations in their home communities. It was exciting for women to recognize the possibilities UNICEF offered for the children of the world, or the Commission on the Status of Women to women, or UNRRA for international cooperation in development.

All of these activities were carried on from the national office at the Interchurch Center. When the Church Center at the United Nations was opened at the UN in 1963, United

Church Women was one of the first tenants. Upon her retirement that same year, Esther Hymer continued her work as a fulltime volunteer, developing friendships for the movement with many women delegates, the international civil servants of the UN agencies and the staff of many international organizations in the vicinity. Women in the metropolitan New York area always looked forward to the luncheon which Esther Hymer arranged for the women delegates to the United National Assembly.

EIGHTH ASSEMBLY   "Six hundred intrepid males ventured into
DENVER—1958   previously untrod petticoat territory
today. They converged upon Denver to attend the Eighth National Assembly of the United Church Women." This was newspaper jargon for recording the fact that husbands were invited to attend a national assembly of United Church Women. They were more than invited; they were encouraged to come by the bait of free registration. All sessions, including the work groups, were open to men; the fact that they had no vote did not keep them from sharing the business discussions!

The presence of men was one distinction of the Denver Assembly. The other was the outstanding group of international personages who appeared on the platform and assumed other leadership roles. One might have guessed that Mrs. W.W. Brooks (Gladys) of Minneapolis was chairman! Dr. Christian Baeta, of Accra, Ghana gave three Biblical interpretations of Christian Freedom which was the underlying theme. Dr. Leslie Cooke related the theme to the ever continuing and deeply humble work of reconciliation among peoples living under hostile governments.

A seminar on civic responsibility and the role of the Church was held for a week before the Assembly for a group of women leaders from 17 countries. This was possible through a grant from Lilly Foundation, Inc. and the planning of Esther Hymer who had come to the UCW staff some 18 months previously.

Most of the invited leaders were involved in social welfare or government roles: Rajkumari Amrit Kaur, chief of the Ministry of Health of India; Iris King, a mayor of Kingston; and Josefa Martinez of the Philippines, a UN technical advisor to Guatemala. In addition there were women community and educational leaders from Burma, Indonesia, Colombia and other countries where nation building was in process following the withdrawal of colonial powers.

At the Assembly itself Anna Lord Strauss, a member of the U.S. delegation to the UN, led a symposium where the role of women in today's world was discussed by women leaders from four major areas of the world.

On two mornings of the Assembly, participants divided into twelve workshops to consider simultaneously those concerns which should find their way into resolutions for the approval of the Assembly as a whole. Prior to the Assembly the topics had been discussed in local councils and a team of experts was added to each workshop to sharpen ideas into workable proposals. Mrs. Fred Patterson of Atlanta headed up the finding committee and introduced the resolutions debated at the plenary sessions.

In speaking to the domestic situation, the Assembly urged 1) the President of the United States to call a White House conference on integration as soon as possible, 2) the facilities of the churches be used for more inclusive fellowship, 3) the elimination of discrimination in housing, public schools, health and recreation facilities, transportation, and public accommodations, 4) more effective enforcement of civil rights legislation by the executive branch of the government, 5) increased financial support for public education and study of issues in proposed legislation regarding conditions of employment.

However, this Assembly will be longest remembered because of the South Pacific night. The curtains opened with an enlarged map of the Pacific Islands centered somewhere on an expanse of ocean. (Although the islands look close together in the midst of so much water, in reality the people who live on them are weeks away from each other by ordinary means of transportation). Recorded music typical of the islands was played. A young woman from the region studying in the United States made a presentation to the national president, Cynthia Wedel. Two members of the South Pacific Commission made presentations about the islands, pointing out that women lag behind in social development and that many of the health hazards were caused by the lack of prenatal and postnatal care of children.[3]

A plan was proposed that Marjorie E. Stewart, a British community development specialist, be sent for a short term to encourage the women of the South Pacific to undertake training programs for social and economic development. This endeavor had been endorsed by the Commission. United Church Women would be making this possible through their World Community Day offerings.

What a breathtaking experience the evening was for all 2,000 in the audience. It was like discovering an area of the world that had been overlooked—except perhaps that the dawn of the World Day of Prayer was somewhere nearby. Here was a new kind of interterritorial cooperation in government—a commission representing six governments. And a new kind of cooperation in mission. In this instance it was an intergovernmental commission concerned with progress in the Pacific seeking cooperation with a church women's organization in the United States.

Admittedly there was mild consternation among those of us connected with traditional mission agencies. How did this get started? Who cleared it? Why didn't we think of it? Being a working minority in most mission boards, could we have done it anyway?

WOMEN'S INTEREST IN SOUTH PACIFIC Such questions eventually had their answers. It started in a meeting of the Pacific Commission in 1953 held in Noumea in which a paper on the role of women's organizations had been read by a woman in the Papuan delegation. Its purpose to seek assistance for women's work was stated in a picturesque symbol of those whose livelihood was related to the sea:

> It is no use having a new strong hull fastened to an old, badly-lashed outrigger; for then, when the big waves come, the outrigger will break, the hull will be swamped,

and the people on the canoe will drown. It is the same with a village: the men are the hull, we women are the outrigger. If, while the men learn to do and to understand new things, we remain ignorant and backward, then we may cause the whole village—even our whole people—to be ruined. But if we work and train ourselves, then we shall be like a strong outrigger, and our village, like the well-built canoe, will be safe even in rough seas.

The Commission, stirred by this appeal and discussion, made a grant in funds for the purpose of exchanging information on women's activities among the islands. But this effort was not very satisfactory, and no wonder. The area covered was eight million square miles! So the next time the Commission met, there were requests from the delegates of territorial administrations for women's development with appropriate training programs. The problem of financing was their first obstacle.

Upon his return to Washington, one of the Commission members representing the United States telephoned Cynthia Wedel, then the president of United Church Women, to see if her organization could be interested. Indeed the executive committee after some consideration proposed that a grant be made from the World Community Day offerings to provide an officer for a period of two years. The Commission accepted this offer and made additional financial provision to take care of related matters, including securing help from the UN Food and Agricultural Organization (FAO) and the UN Educational, Scientific and Cultural Organization (UNESCO).

Esther Hymer, UCW director of Christian World Relations, worked with the Commission to find the right staff person—someone with religious motivation, as well as the suitable education and experience. A highly qualified person was found in Miss Marjorie E.T. Stewart of London. Mrs. James Birdsall Calkins, chairman of World Community Day, was traveling in the South Pacific at the time and cabled her warm endorsement.

Other expert assistance was also forthcoming, notably Miss Freda Gwilliam, OBE, JP, Women's Educational Advisor in the United Kingdom Colonial Office. With experience on every continent in development programs, Miss Gwilliam advocated training for women as homemakers, as contributors to community life, and as economically independent personalities. Needless to say most of these ideas meant a reorientation of thinking for both men and women in the South Pacific areas.

The heart of the project is conserved in letters exchanged between Esther Hymer and Marjorie Stewart during those two years. It is exciting to review the three-inch pile of carbons through which are sprinkled all over their pages fascinating names of islands—Aitutaki, Rabaul, New Caledonia, New Guinea, Samoa, Fiji, Tonga. Part of the reports were packed with information which was shared through *The Church Woman*. Under different dates here are some descriptive sentences from Miss Stewart's long letters:

Aitutaki, a tropical island five miles long and one and a half broad, is set in a lagoon sheltered by a coral reef some miles from shore. There are shadowy country roads but, contrary to expectation, practically no sea bathing . . . A population of 2,500 live in seven villages and grow citrus, tomatoes and copra for export, but shipping is irregular . . . There is no market whatsoever and the procuring of food is a hit or miss affair . . . oranges and tomatoes flood our house.

There is plenty of fish to be caught and the ground can grow vegetables of all sorts but the people have lapsed back to cassava. Tinned fish supplants the fresh delicacy of the surrounding seas. American occupation during the war introduced a tin economy. The one school just opposite our house with over 600 children up to grade 9 is well run and happy, but at 16 the boys and girls leave and enter a void, a dangerous one in its idleness leading to delinquency and child-begetting . . .

The need on the women's side is for an imaginative and capable Home Economist who can hold regular leaders' courses in sewing, dressmaking and cooking, and who can collaborate with the nurse in child care.

The people of the island, Maoris with some European intermixture, are cheerful, friendly, generous and always ready for songs, dances, games and a feast. We laugh until we cry over some of the games. . .

I have been on a tour in two of the Philippine Islands where I was shown some of their community development; I went also to Sydney for consultation with the South Pacific Commission Literature Bureau, and over to the French territory of New Caledonia . . .

In humid Papua and New Guinea consulting with their Department of Native Affairs and planning short leadership courses for the staff and voluntary leaders for women's work in that vast territory. By local plane to the British Solomon Islands . . .

In Fiji I had a wonderful six days meeting with representatives of twenty-two women's organizations, traveling to three quite separate areas, helping to shape policy for some kind of coordinating council for women's work . . .

Every time I enter a new area of the world, I feel as if I were starting all over again—knowing nothing, with everything to learn. Then to my relief some little store of previous experience reveals itself as useful and I fall back on what has been given to me in the past . . . should one ever be a moss covered stone instead of rolling freely around the globe?

The purpose of all Marjorie Stewart's travel and work was to design a women's program and establish a network for communication and education. Transportation was difficult so it was not unusual to have to remain for weeks on a tiny island after the particular conference or institute was over. "My clothes are weary of being packed," she wrote, but she never tired of pursuing programs which met the needs of the women of these islands.

Esther Hymer's letters to Marjorie Stewart were equally moving and informative—full of resources and of news about what United Church Women were doing in other fields. Obviously an affectionate relationship had grown up—both women responsive to the moments of discouragement that comes to every pioneer or their backers.

To culminate the three year program, a five week seminar was held for the leaders on the islands where programs had begun. This was the first opportunity ever afforded to the women of this vast area to have their representatives meet together to discuss matters of special importance and interest to women. Miss Stewart must have been gratified by the enthusiasm of the participants for assuming responsibility for the progress of women in their own areas. Later when she reported personally to UCW in the United States, Mrs. George Martin and her Committee on Christian World Relations must also have had deep satisfaction, for they had shared in the whole venture. Not often is a dream realized by those who envisioned it.

It was not to be a dream that disappeared with the passing of the years as I was to realize fourteen years later after I had become one of the staff of Church Women United. In planning for the Assembly in Memphis I was anxious to get a world famous woman, a Dr. Mata'afa Fetavi, the Vice Chancellor of the University of the South Pacific located on Fiji and the president of the Pacific Council of Churches, and I was looking for someone who would be our advocate. Dr. Fetavi was at that time being sought by many world committees and was speaking to many conferences.

While I was pondering on how I could be persuasive in an invitation, the receptionist called to announce someone whose name she could not understand. It could have been any one of several hundred overseas Christian women who called in our office while visiting the United States. After I had greeted her, she apologized for taking my time and quietly stated the purposes of the call. She was the translator of the World Day of Prayer service each year for her area in the Pacific and wondered how their local committees could have more direct contact with the International Committee for the World Day of Prayer.

Then she went on to say that the most significant program for women ever developed in the South Pacific had been a result of the interest and investment of United Church Women and she wished us to know of the gratitude of the Pacific Council of Churches as well as her own gratitude for the benefits she received from attending the Summer at the U.N. Like an internal combustion there exploded a sudden recognition. So this was Dr. Mata'afa!

SUMMER AT THE UNITED NATIONS In 1964 United Church Women celebrated the 20th anniversary of World Community Day with a training program for peace education. It was a noteworthy climax to the term of service of Mabel Martin, the chairperson of Christian World Relations. It also paid tribute to the vision and vigor of Esther Hymer who had retired the year before from her staff position, but as a volunteer returned to handle this special project.

Four training periods, each ten days in length were held at the Church Center for the United Nations in New York during May, June, August and September. Participating in this summer effort in 1964 were a total of 193 women, 145 from the U.S. and 48 from 30 overseas countries.

The program was developed from felt needs expressed by the participants: the need of factual information on the work of the UN and its Commissions, program planning to help in initiating programs in the local community, and a closer study of Christian responsibility in dealing with current international problems.

Homework was expected. Each participant received four Bible studies prepared by Dr. J. Carter Swaim called "God in the Midst of Change," a brochure on basic facts on the United Nations, together with additional pamphlets with an assignment sheet.

Once again it was a tribute to the reputation of United Church Women that even in the summer seasons the seminars could claim from international circles leadership of superior calibre: 31 members from the Secretariat of the United Nations; five members of UN delegations; a dozen from international organizations such as the World Council of Churches, Foreign Policy Association, United Nations Association; 10 from national denominational staffs related to international affairs.

UCW's invited guests, nominated by the National Christian Councils abroad, provided leadership from their experience in responsible positions in their own countries. Some of them led the worship services held each day in the Tillman Chapel at the Church Center for the United Nations.

A special group of international persons came for the session in late summer and were able to stay on for the Assembly being held that fall in Kansas City. Taking advantage of their presence, a consultation was held under the auspices of the Christian World Missions Committee. It focused on the nature and future of the worship materials for the World Day of Prayer.

So we come around full circle. American women may have expected a mere 'thank you' from overseas women but now they were the grateful recipients of the intellectual and spiritual insights of women from every part of the world. The most important part of all conferences is the person-to-person relationships, most of which are unplanned and often continue.[4] Twenty years after that summer a letter from a friend on Cape Cod remarked that her greatest gift from Summer at the United Nations was the steady friendship through the years of an Egyptian woman who had helped her family understand the multifaceted nature of the Middle East turmoil. Just because common convictions endure a friend filled circle offers hope even for a faraway peace.

1965
PEACE
MISSION   In 1965 the officers of the East Asia Church Conference invited six prominent American churchmen and the president of United Church Women to meet with the EACC executive committee in Bangkok, to consider the issues which Christians faced because of the continuing war in Vietnam. Enroute, it was arranged for Mrs. Sinclair to meet informally with groups of church women in Lebanaon, Thailand, Hong Kong, Japan, and the Philippines. Her coming was the occasion of bringing together women from various denominations in order for her to share the deep concern of Christian women in America for the comming of a just peace.

She stopped in Saigon to consult with Catholic and other women. She saw first hand the conditions in refugee camps; she noted the international service of women doctors, nurses, technicians working with the full cooperation of volunteer Vietnamese women. United Church Women was able to offer encouragement to a group called "Women of Good Will" who were providing a fresh start for many young women who had been orphaned by the war and, in destitution, were turning to prostitution for a livelihood.

On the train coming from Kobe to Tokyo, Mrs. Sinclair sat next to a Japanese shipbuilder who became interested in the reason for her journey. She explained that American Christians wished to come alongside Asian Christians in loving concern for the victims of war. Having previously observed the strong community feeling among the Christian minority in his own country, he asked: "Tell me why this Christianity seems to bring to you and others such joy and meaning to life." Edna Sinclair could be counted on to meet this challenge with a satisfying response!

75TH ANNIVERSARY OF WORLD DAY OF PRAYER On the first Friday of Lent in 1961, women gathered for the seventy-fifth time to pray for the world mission of the church. The changes year by year may not have been noticeable, but in the perspective of the years . . . what wonders!

Mrs. Paul Moser chaired the committee which planned the celebration of the 75th Anniversary. Appropriately enough, Sue Weddell was asked to write the workshop service "Forward Through the Ages." Miss Weddell had carried the correspondence with overseas committees and translators since 1941. Although the offering goal of $750,000 was not reached, the attendance and the offering were higher than any other time in history.

Joining in this celebration were women in 145 countries. Much of the growth and interest that this represented was due to the service given by Sue Weddell until her retirement from the Foreign Missions Conference (and to her successors Hazel Anderson and Irene Jones in the NCCC). Since the worldwide observance of World Day of Prayer had become its most meaningful attribute, the special feature of 1961 was to be a series of Prayer Fellowships, one on each continent to which

Christian women from neighboring countries would be invited.[4] In addition 32 Prayer Fellowships were held in the United States and Canada.[5] To each was sent an interracial and international team as a token representative of the world fellowship.

In all, over 2,000 women from 80 countries, speaking scores of languages, traveling in all kinds of weather—from wintry blizzards to tropical heat—took part in the effort to look together at their world and to pray together for their work. As Myrta Ross, the staff coordinator, looked at the file containing voluminous reports from all 37 Prayer Fellowships and which were filled with the concerns for which they sought the prayers of women throughout the world, she exclaimed, "What wonders God has performed!"

From these files I could dip into the descriptive story of each of the Prayer Fellowships. Each developed a different pattern, but all carried the common ingredients of Bible study, prayer, and sharing of concerns. Space compels me to choose only one of the Prayer Fellowships to describe, and so let me use the European Prayer Fellowship.

Dr. Marga Buhrig, who made all the arrangements in Switzerland, welcomed thirty women from fourteen European countries. In addition there were four members of the international team: Mrs. David Jones, Greensboro, North Carolina; Mme. D. Kuoh of the Cameron, whose husband was Ambassador to France; Mrs. Nassema Makdisi of Beirut, Lebanon; and Mrs. Paul Moser of New York. From Mrs. Moser's report come the following descriptive paragraphs:

> The gathering was significant also because it represented the Church in many kinds of areas. Some came from places surrounded by generally Christian influence; some from opposite situations. Most came from well established churches; a few represented churches which are tiny minorities of the population; a few came from areas where churches even try to oppress each other. No matter the conditions from which she came, each testified that it is always possible to pray, to witness to Jesus Christ, and to render service. Each said too, that the World Day of Prayer was the best tool for

expressing the openness of the family of God in the earth.

This was a praying group. Each day began with prayer and worship in a small church near Boldernhaus. Bible study and discussion on the incident of the woman at the well in St. John's Gospel proved so fascinating that there was difficulty each day getting the three different groups, divided according to language—French, German, and English—to end. Any self-consciousness disappeared as each prayed in her own language. During the Bible study each person expressed her ideas and insights in quite a full, free way. The women subordinated their denominational interests and gave no impression of being women from 30 different local churches of 18 different denominations. They kept their thinking and praying in touch with the whole world.

It was a working group. They gave close attention for hours at a time to the concerns of women in family and community life, especially to the social changes common to all in this period of history.

She continued to describe their experiences on the World Day of Prayer in 1961:

The sun was bright and warm enough to bring into bloom clumps of spring flowers.

The Prayer Fellowship group met for early worship at Boldernhaus instead of the small church as on other mornings. There was quiet excitement among the women. This was *the* Day; the day when countless Christian women in every continent and island were joining in a great chain of prayer. Mrs. Makdisi led the group using as her theme, "I am with you . . ." We spoke together of how others would be worshipping—some out of doors, others in schools, hospitals, places of business, some in mud huts or great churches—but all uniting in prayer to the same eternal Father.

At 7:30 in the evening, the great stone church seemed very cold and barren to me, as I entered it, alone, for the World Day of Prayer service at 8:30. I wondered if the warmth and oneness associated with the Day could be caught in this vast cathedral. Then the women began streaming in. Over a thousand came. Always I shall see and hear them coming, their vitality and purpose apparent in their fast quiet walk. Their shoes, some fashionable, with tiny high heels, but most of them good walking shoes, tapped out a steady rhythm on the bare resonant stone floor.

The music of the great organ struck our ears and swept into our souls as well as up into the vaulted arches, shaping thoughts of kinship not fully understood, yet not to be put aside.

The silence of prayer which followed it seemed fragile, yet I knew that here was a power welding criss-crossed lines into unity and lighting a flame no divisions could efface. Twelve young girls sat on a low platform behind the unusually large baptismal font. At the close of the service, they gathered the offering of over 2,000 Swiss francs in velvet pouches with long carved wooden handles and placed them, after the dedicatory prayer, in a semicircle, handles out, around the font.

Then Inez Moser concluded her report with the testimony:

I wish I could render more articulate the powerful emotions of joy,
Of kindled will,
The spell and balm of prayer that quiets the heart
And makes it stronger,
Making me feel on the edge of a miracle,
The forward thrust of the knowledge of each other's intercessions;
With a sense of the little of any worth given and the Much received,
I give this report with a renewed
Pledge of quest to find the gift of oneness in Christ
So little understood.

From such experiences held in 36 other places came the list of prayer concerns which were used in the petitions of future services of the World Day of Prayer. Although the illustrations were varied from place to place, the listing revealed the mutual burdens everywhere: materialism; youth;

education; migrant laborers; race relations; peace; women's development.

The common denominator underlying these worldwide experiences no doubt formed the basis of the next triennial Assembly which launched the emphasis "The Church Ecumenical—Its Oneness, Its Mission, Its Ministries . . ." We who are alive at this time are part of the wonder!

1961 ASSEMBLY   The ninth National Assembly of United
MIAMI BEACH   Church Women marked the close of the
                     observance of the 75th anniversary of World
Day of Prayer. Stimulated by a message from Mrs. Harper Sibley on the "Ecumenical Mind" the 1400 delegates discussed at luncheons the Ecumenical Church and concerns coming out of the Prayer Fellowship. Mrs. Sibley characterized the ecumenical mind not as the experience of the traveler but as the evergrowing awareness of each woman:

> This divine mind is ecumenical in its outreach. Christ's invitation was "Come unto me, *all* . . ." This is our mission. We cannot all go to far places, but a little piece of us can go to every corner of this great round world.

The Honorable Secretary of State, Dean Rusk accepted the invitation to speak to the Assembly because he believed in the tremendous potential for peace within the church. He pointed out that foreign policy was not made up of remote abstractions, states, sovereignty nor protocol.

> In this climactic period of history, foreign policy involves every citizen, lays its hand upon every home, and embraces our personal aspirations for the kind of world in which we hope our children can live. We in the Department of State are deeply interested in what United Church Women think about major issues of foreign policy. We follow your reports, appreciate your support when you feel you can give it, and pause to reflect if policy fails to commend itself to you.

Graphic meaning was added to each session of the Assembly with significant backdrops created by the artistic Claire Randall. Growing out of the personal spiritual anxiety of a young man caught in the tangle, it represented the confusion and lostness of our day. The background painting on that Christian Social Relations evening impressed the Assistant Secretary of Labor so much that she asked if it might be hung in the Department of Labor in Washington.

Esther Peterson spoke brilliantly that evening of the women in the labor market, perhaps inspired by the backdrop but more likely by the moving experience of dedication of the "women at the living level." (One of the overseas guests had used this phrase because she felt that "grassroots were envisioned in darkness far away from the source of nourishment.")

No doubt this Assembly will be remembered not so much for what was said from the platform but what each woman said to herself when Carrie Meares presented the opportunity to sign a card on which was written "A Declaration of Intent."

On the opening night of the Assembly there had been a processional of overseas guests to the Assembly, presidents of the denominational women's organizations, and presidents of the state councils of UCW, each of whom presented the printed program of its observance of the 75th Anniversary of the World Day of Prayer to be bound into a book. Helen Baker, moved by what this represented in common prayer for one another, asked herself some searching questions:

> *What was to be our next united act?*
> *To what mission was God calling us through that praying?*
> *What common testimony must we be making together?*
> *What common service rendering?*

Returning to the Roney Plaza where she was staying, she jotted down these questions on the hotel stationery (from which I copied them years later).

She had been asked to present *Assignment Race* the next night so she posed the same questions to the Assembly. She then described how the idea had grown. Word had come from one of the Communions (the Methodists) of their commitment to concerted action to achieve in their churches full participation for all persons without distinction of race. It was an invitation to all church women working within their churches and together in the community. Would it be possible to make this a great common commitment, a great common action, a great shared testimony?

Helen Baker went on to say:

> Here was a suggestion not alien to our common dreams. In words spread before the public year after year we had asserted our creed on the dignity of every person under the fatherhood of God. We had tried to demonstrate incarnate those words even though God, alone, knows how far we are from our goals. Your leaders knew, too, that across this country were hundreds of women suffering from the shame of our failures in the churches and in our communities, eager to take some new strong stand for justice for all, eager to move our churches out of the disharmony of the sounding brass clanging cymbal into the symphony of words ringing true.

She told how the idea was affirmed through many committee meetings, through commitment of all denominational officials, through the Board of Managers, through the coming of the check of $66,000 from the Field Foundation, through the availability of Carrie Meares for leadership.

The best was yet to come. Would the individual woman make a commitment . . . an assignment to herself of something real she would attempt in the place where she lived? In her hands was the card ready to indicate her *Declaration of Intent!*

FOOTNOTES TO CHAPTER 4

1. The complete record of Helen Baker's account of the visit can be found in the April, May & June issue of *The Church Woman.*

2. Through the years that followed a series of exchanges between church women in Nigeria and CWU in the USA were of mutual encouragement and illustrative of the kind of ongoing relationships among many peer groups during this period.

In 1964, Lady Ibiam, the wife of the first black African governor of the Eastern regions, was in the United States and attended one of the training sessions at the *Summer at the United Nations.* Impressed with the possibility of Christian women working unitedly together in her own country, she called together a group of women in Enugi, the Eastern provincial capital. By coincidence, I had made the 4-hour flight from Lagos that very day and was a guest in the government house. I took part in the dedication service for the first set of officers and later went with Mrs. Ibiam to see the site of a two-room African house which was to become a training center for women in the surrounding villages.

Rosa Page Welch was working as a volunteer in a girl's school in the Northern provinces at that time and she flew in for a visit with this enterprising unit in Enugu before returning to the USA.

In 1966, the Causeway team was received by church women in Lagos and in Enugu. Nigeria is such a big country that the two groups operated independently. Emily Gibbes, a member of the Causeway team, saw possibilities in using the Women's Center to develop commercial training. The next year CWU in Pennsylvania raised money for typewriters to begin the course.

In 1967, Phoebe Okehi of Lagos was invited to join the Causeway team to the USA and planned to report back to both units about the International Consultation in Anderson. However while she was here, the Eastern Region expressed its protest to certain actions of the central government by declaring its independence as the new state of Biafra. A bloody war followed in which thousands of people were killed and many villages in the east were laid waste by bombing and famine. During this time it was necessary for the church women to use a third party outside the country for communication. After the war, women returned to the devastated Enugu and cleared the rubble of their former center by hand. CWU in the USA offered $25,000 to build a new building for the Women's Ecumenical Center—more needed than ever.

In May 1974, our national office received a telegram notification of the death of Mrs. Ibiam signed by Phoebe Okehi, who flew to Eastern Nigerian region to join her sisters in CWU and lay the wreath on behalf of the Lagos unit. CWU in that area acted as an extended family helping with reception of thousands of mourners who came during the eleven days in which the body of Lady Ibiam lay in state. Those paying respects included the Archbishop of the Roman Catholic Church, and the heads of the Anglican and Protestant Churches as well as Africans from hundreds of the neighboring villages.

Each day from dawn to dusk a chorus accompanied by the police band led an interdenominational service.

"I have never seen or heard of a man or woman so well honored even by the heads of States," wrote Phoebe Okehi from the nation's capital city. "She was a good and true Christian, a humanitarian, an upright woman, a loved woman. Our women have asked that the Center be now named after its founder: the *Lady Ibiam Ecumenical Centre, Enugu.*"

3. The Commission represents the six administering governments of the various islands: Australia, France, the Netherlands, New Zealand, the United Kingdom and the United States.

4. Members of the Overseas Teams:

Africa—Kitwe, N. Rhodesia: Miss Norma Alampay, Philippines; Miss Dina Rizzi, Brazil; Mrs. Jesse Jai McNeil and Mrs. W.K. Evans, United States; Miss Ruth Lawrence, organizing secretary.

East Asia—Hong Kong: Mrs. Stanley I. Stuber and Mrs. W. Verne Buchanan, United States; Miss Wong Yuk Mui, Hong Kong; Miss Mavo Raymonde Ramamonjy Ratrimo, Madagascar; Miss Hazel Shank, organizing secretary (did not accompany team).

Europe—Zurich, Switzerland: Mrs. Paul Moser and Mrs. David Jones, United States; Miss Margaret Shannon, organizing secretary (did not accompany team).

Southern Asia—Madras, India: Miss Jocelyn Chitombo, Southern Rhodesia; Mrs. Stuart Sinclair, United States; Mrs. James Kinnear, organizing secretary (did not accompany team).

Latin America—Lima, Peru: Mrs. William Sale Terrell, Miss Margaret Lawrence, United States; Miss Hana Kawai, Japan; Miss Margaret Lawrence, organizing secretary (did not accompany team).

5. Regional Prayer Fellowships were held in 32 cities:

Little Rock, Ark.	West Palm Beach, Fla.	Albuquerque, N.M.
Nashville, Tenn.	Atlanta, Ga.	Dallas-Fort Worth, Tx.
St. Louis, Missouri	Charlotte, N.C.	New Orleans, La.
Montreal, Canada	Wilmington, Del.	Pittsburgh, Pa.
Boston, Mass.	Washington, D.C.	Columbus, Ohio
New Haven, Conn.	Richmond, Va.	Rochester, N.Y.
Detroit, Mich.	Winnipeg, Canada	Los Angeles, Cal.
Chicago, Ill.	Minneapolis, Minn.	Phoenix, Ariz.
Louisville, Ky.	Omaha, Neb.	Salt Lake City, Utah
Denver, Colo.	Portland, Ore.	Anchorage, Alaska
Seattle, Wash.	Vancouver, Canada	

**General Department of
United Church Women
1950-1966**

chapter 5

Human rights for all

Because of the current emphasis on human rights, both in the church and in the world community, we *reaffirm the historic stand* of United Church Women on the inclusiveness of our Christian fellowship across denominational and racial lines, and we *determine to take next steps* toward the fulfillment of our Christian purpose. This constitutes a joint responsibility on the part of all racial groups. We begin where we are and go forward from here.

From the Preamble of a Resolution of the executive committee of the General Department of United Church Women, Omaha, Nebraska, October 7, 1952.

Along with all other Americans, church women were facing a decade of learning through action. Two phrases in the Omaha resolution on racial justice reflected an important transition. How does one get from reaffirming a "historic stand" to taking "next steps?"

The long resolution went ahead with specific proposals, appropriately enough beginning with their own organizations: appraisal of meeting places and program participants; examination of delegations and officers; changes of attitudes; interpretation of human rights to the churches. Easy enough said, but not so easy to act in such a way that a large number of another race felt at home in the situation.

Then an action by the Supreme Court demanded a response from thinking people of all races. In an appeal case entitled Brown vs. Topeka Board of Education, the Supreme Court ruled that racial segregation in public schools was unconstitutional. This immediately challenged the legality of most school systems in the South as well as de facto segregation, due to the housing patterns, of many schools in northern cities. There followed a whole rash of incidents through which the racial struggle in the fifties found expression.

Simultaneously there were spontaneous and scattered efforts by persons of goodwill some of which advanced the goals more than others. Yet there was a tolerant acceptance in the beginning of any contribution as long as the intent was to work side by side or to use one's clout in circles closed to other races. As the decade advanced, a new kinship grew among those "in the freedom movement." Black and white buttons of equality were worn with a real cause by Negroes as well as by white persons who found satisfaction in being openly counted.[1]

Like most white women, I was too sheltered to sense the depth of feeling that had penetrated the Negro community for generations and that had eventually forced this social revolution. Yet there were learnings for us all, some of which are reflected in the human elements in the episodes that follow. I am deliberately selecting quotations from those who found racial action a religious experience. One must not assume that all Christian women were at one in this issue. The dramatic events revealed hidden facts of which no one was aware: families split, congregations polarized, individuals were ambivalent on personal involvement. In some cases women acted as individuals joining in various civil rights activities as they could; in other cases United Church Women formed the channel by which women could confer and act together.

CONSULTATION FOR SOUTHERN LEADERS   Women leaders of 15 southern states met in an historic conference in Atlanta, Georgia, June 21-22, 1954. Their purpose was to study the specific problems facing the desegregation in public schools. Presiding were Mrs. Leon Ellis and Esther Stamatz, chairman and director of the department of Christian Social Relations.

New courage is found in the knowledge that one is not alone. Those who carried responsibility in these crucial days found power flowing from companionship. Together they . . .

expressed grave concern over the fact that attitudes and prejudices are now being instilled in white children at home and in public schools; . . .

recognized the fact that few ministers had spoken openly and decisively in favor of the Supreme Court decisions; . . .

decided to repel every suggestion that the churches should be used to continue segregation by creating private Protestant parochial schools; . . .

realized the plight of the Negro teachers who might not be employed in biracial schools and whose unemployment could cause much hardship; . . .

pinpointed the problems inherent in population ratios and school facilities.

Finally the women prepared a statement which affirmed the Supreme Court decision as translating into reality Christian and democratic ideals. The women felt that working together was of great importance in changing public opinion and in negotiating a peaceful adjustment.

ATLANTA MAKES The stamina of United Church Women is
HISTORIC STAND tested when its historic stands are
reaffirmed in the light of place and time.
Church women in the South knew that race was a world
problem, but they also knew that their particular responsibility was the place where they lived. A year after the Supreme
Court ruled on desegregation, the State Board of Education in
Georgia "revoked forever the teacher's license of any member
of the NAACP or anyone in sympathy with that organization."
Seeing this as a threat to all freedoms, a group representing
the local council of UCW began to work on a carefully worded
statement reflecting this point of view. The statement was published on the front page of *The Atlanta Constitution,* and there
soon followed on its pages statements from other
organizations. On August 15, 1955, the *Atlanta Journal* carried
a headline BOARD BACKS DOWN ON TEACHER FIRING!

The months of preparation for the actual achievement of
an integrated school system were ones of sobering realities.
Mrs. Fred Patterson (Ida Milner Patterson), whose leadership
always blended genuine wisdom, great courage and good
cheer, reported for Atlanta in *The Church Woman,* December,
1961:

> When all the preparations for desegregation in our
> schools were being discussed I could not help but think
> we could not have made more preparation for the
> Russian army with tanks . . .
>
> As I watched WSB-TV that Wednesday morning tears
> welled up into my eyes. Many others shared this
> emotion. Why? I suppose it was relief that our 'blood,
> sweat, and tears' had borne fruit. It was the climax of at
> least a year's active preparation for and many years of
> grappling with the problem, with almost no discernible
> progress.
>
> My mind flashed back to June 1954 when Margaret
> MacDougall, as spokesman for UCW of Atlanta, the
> executive committee of the state League of Women
> Voters, and the executive committee of the state PTA,
> upset a Georgia Education Commission hearing by
> suggesting that Georgia comply with the United States

Supreme Court decision by appointing a biracial committee in every town to work out the details. We were roundly insulted that day . . .

In January the Legislature met, full of sound and fury. Many of our political leaders were 'experimenting with ignorance' according to one judge, as they passed law after law to circumvent the decision.

Out of the threat of closing our schools rather than compliance with this "iniquitous law" came HOPE— Help Our Public Education. HOPE rendered the state invaluable service, organizing chapters all over the state arguing neither for segregation nor integration but for open schools.

Out of HOPE came OASIS—Organization to Assist Schools in September. Parents were contacted by telephone, by letter; teachers and children and parents met frequently with the Atlanta school superintendent. Churches held discussion groups the last four Sundays in August; a week-end of prayer was observed just before school opened . . .

Tears, yes, not only in my eyes but in the eyes of many who watched Atlanta schools desegregated that morning—liberals (so-called), desegregationists, segregationists, integrationists—all were moved as they watched a city change 'its way of life' with dignity and restraint.

WORKSHOPS ON CONTROVERSY There are times when the whole society has dyspepsia—everybody seems upset with other people and with themselves. UCW did not pretend to be a "cure-all" but they did what they could to help their own community leadership to focus on *What* and *Who* needed to be appreciated and *Who* and *What* needed to change.

Using a small grant from the Fund for the Republic, a plan was set up for a community workshop. Resources such as short movies, role playing case studies, group analysis were provided. Interracial teams were trained to work with local sponsoring committees.

Each workshop would proceed somewhat as follows. The Leadership team would act as a panel for discussing the general content on some such subject as "What constitutes freedom today?" followed by a panel of local citizens describing "our town." Then the workshop participants would ask each other: where do these attitudes stem from? Who are the respected citizens in this town and why? Who really is the power in the schools, the labor market? the churches? the welfare system? the real estate? On another day they pursued questions of changing unethical attitudes, lack of communication among people of different racial or economic or age groupings, how to deal with a closed mind; a vicious tongue . . . The last session was spent in discovering what they had learned and to plan for the next steps. Before the workshop ended, it was important to discover where they were going in the community.

There was improved climate within the community. Essential to the success of any law is the willingness of the citizens to let it happen. How important it is to surround with a friendly atmosphere the first ventures of Negroes in a formerly "closed" area of work. Mrs. John C. Norman of Charleston, West Virginia, who had been active in the development of the Workshop, was one of the first Negro teachers to be welcomed into the integrated high school in Charleston. She found it such a happy experience that Myrta Ross arranged for her to have an interview with the well known radio personality, Mary Margaret McBride, over national radio network. This illustrates how a national office can often enhance the witness of local UCW effort to influence a wider constituency.

The interracial teams not only found much in common by working together but the workshop participants also learned not to stereotype by race the strengths or weaknesses of their leaders. Rosa Page Welch, a national vice president and general leader in this field, took assignments on a number of the teams in West Virginia, Texas and Mississippi. At that time she normally expected to be in Negro homes on these itinerations, but several times she was surprised to find she had been invited to be a guest of a white family. She told me some 15 years later: "I found myself feeling fear for that white family living in an all white neighborhood. I really was more concerned about them than myself.

UCW established the fact of their strength in a local base by satisfactorily completing the workshops and the follow up evaluation. This put them in good stead to apply and receive the large grant from the Field Foundation which enabled the priority program of Assignment Race *during the 60's.*

ASSIGNMENT: RACE On opposite pages of *The Church Woman* (April, 1963) are portraits of two women. They could have been sisters except for the fact that they were members of different races. They were indeed sisters-in-Spirit. Each held her head high with confidence; their steady eyes and almost identical smiles reflected an inner beauty deep within each woman. Under the title ASSIGNMENT: PERSONAL, each had written an article to answer the question: "What, as an individual, is my assignment?"

Both were on the national advisory committee of UCW project *Assignment Race.* The Negro woman, Juanita Saddler, Texas born, graduate of Fish University and later its dean of women, had many years of administrative experience in the local and national YWCA. She lived in New York City where she was a deacon in Riverside Church.

The picture on the opposite page was that of Mrs. Kyle Haselden (Elizabeth). In Minneapolis she had served on the Mayor's Commission on Human Relations, and in Rochester, New York and Charleston, West Virginia, she served as chairman, Women's Human Relations Councils. She was chairman of Christian Social Relations in her local council, UCW of Evanston, Illinois.

Assignment Race had been launched at the national Assembly in Miami, Florida in 1961. Each woman was asked to write down her personal intent in carrying out the national goals for justice in a multi-racial society on the printed commitment cards. These personal assignment cards were then sent out to thousands of other church women with the request that they be returned to the national office. Later the national advisory committee utilized the commitments which had been written to mold the format of its program.

The Church Woman, as part of its continuing service in the program priority, requested various women to reflect on their experience after signing the statement.

In that issue Elizabeth Haselden wrote of her strange sense of fulfillment as she signed her card, seeing her assignment as an opportunity to close ranks with other Christian women whose names she could not know but who would be working in this common endeavor. She wrote:

> . . . Memories engulfed me, and I thought of the various activities in which I have engaged in the years past. I felt again the strictures of inadequacy, the frustrations, the spiritual weariness on the part of both Negro and white women.

> . . . Surely this little piece of paper before me would bring to light many women who held convictions hitherto unexpressed.

> . . . There was no agreement on techniques, no course of action, no particular procedure; but concern and acknowledgement of Christian obligation became the framework of future devotion and service . . .

> With real emotion I mailed the paper. I thought hopefully of thousands of others mailing it, timidly or eagerly, and waiting for results. Here indeed was a quickening of the Holy Spirit among us, leading, guiding, urging us along the path toward wholeness and obedience.

Juanita J. Saddler wrote of her Assignment in terms of provocative questions which had risen in her reflection as a Negro leader of long experience.

> Do I suffer from such blindness that I do not see that the greatest evil in our society is poverty?

> Do I have a conviction of relationship? Do I believe that we are related, belong to each other, belong to God?

> Have I a right to accept *separatism* either because of poverty or color when a substantially satisfactory existence depends on my efforts to achieve wholeness?

> Isn't token representation on staffs, boards, commit-

tees, being integrated separately?

I can't answer my questions once and for all. I keep trying to measure my internal growth and progress, lest I become one of those gentle or not-so-gentle persons of prejudice who use color, poverty, crimes of the poor, neighborhood deterioration, civic apathy, moral irresponsibility as justification for their fears, annoyances, and hate. All this is worth struggling against not only because of what it may do to the other person, but because of the growth in wholeness that comes to anyone with the courage to face such questions.

The planning for this timely endeavor was initiated in the national Committee on Christian Social Relations, which was chaired by Mrs. J. Russell Henderson of Little Rock, Arkansas and staffed by Eleanor French (both persons of great vision and a lot of common sense.) The grant from the Field Foundation "for the purpose of mobilizing and training women to work toward improved race relations" included the funding of a director for a three year period. UCW was fortunate that Carrie E. Meares was available. She had worked professionally with the YWCA for 21 years including a couple of years in South Africa.

There was real satisfaction when Mrs. Leo Marsh (Bessie) of Montclair, New Jersey accepted the chairmanship of *Assignment Race.* Active in the local and national UCW since she was a young woman, she had wide experience in community relations both in Ohio and New Jersey where she was currently serving a five year term on the school board in Montclair. As chairman she interpreted the program to other national boards with similar goals and worked out cooperative efforts. Yet she participated fully in the field program of *Assignment Race* seeking local response and "troubleshooting" in case of friction.

Each local council appointed a chairman for *Assignment Race.* This person not only assisted women in wanting to work on this issue to find each other, but also was able to keep a steady report going into the national office. Carrie Meares somehow knew exactly how to stimulate and respond to the particular situation. She was sensitive to the fact that what happened to the individual woman in a changed attitude was of supreme importance even though it could not be wrapped up as a statistic in any final report. A widespread program of leadership training of peers was carried out through the same process of interracial teams which had proved valuable in a more limited scope in the Workshops on Controversy. Members of the national board were trained and still have vivid memories of going out two by two following their meeting in San Antonio to other cities to "spread the word."

In reminiscing on this period ten years later in my living room, Bessie Marsh talked about her philosophy of program. She has said, "A project of this dimension depends on the soundness of its purpose and its ability to command consistent involvement. *Assignment Race* had those qualities, and thus was able to be the ground work on which other programs could develop within the Church Women United." She then spoke of her warm affection for the women leaders who had been so loyal throughout this whole effort, among them Juanita Saddler, Ann Bennett, Anna Arnold Hedgeman, Thelma Stevens, Margaret Kuhn, Emily Gibbes, Ernestine Henderson, Mrs. Shaw, Mrs. Mary Ross, Phyllis Bedford and other leaders of the Nego denominations. Louise Wallace, the national president, was right at their side throughout the whole endeavor, not only giving herself unstintingly to a heavy field schedule, but writing constantly to remind the women of the churches that *Assignment Race* was their effort, not something they could watch or receive as a report from the national office.

I wondered if anyone ever could realize the personal toll which just the travel takes from volunteer leadership. In one instance Bessie Marsh was teamed with Louise Wallace for work in the New England area. Their plane was grounded in New York for two hours in fog, then got as far as Boston only to circle for two more hours not being able to land. Finally they got down in Providence, took a bus and arrived at their meeting only eight hours after the meeting was scheduled to begin. Later in the same trip, they found that intense cold weather in Maine together with their weariness was bringing serious head colds. The local chairman took them in hand, wrapped them in huge flannel nightgowns and caps, and tucked them between featherbeds. They recovered for the meeting the next day only to find that the participants didn't think there were enough Negroes in their area to make race a problem.

They were full of their own problems: a possessive local treasurer who dictated all the decisions on the use of their money. "Louise was flexible and took that problem on," recalled Bessie Marsh. "That's what national presidents are for!"

Louise Wallace moved with strong convictions and a quiet humor among the women of the churches during a period of acute national problems. Her leadership was also felt in cooperative efforts with the NCCC after she was appointed to the Commission on Religion and Race by President Irwin Miller. "How she found time to participate so wholeheartedly is a matter of no small wonder," once commented Robert Spike, the director of the program. He went on: "We value her sensitivity to the issues of racial justice, her deep commitment in all the aspects of the program and her intelligent guidance in basic policy matters. We cannot get along without her."

In 1963 regional meetings were held in each section of the country and were attended by hundreds of women. Bringing together women from a region under the aegis of *Assignment Race* had a tremendous impact. They shared both frustrating and fruitful experiences. Both Negro and white women became aware that the greatest assistance to an individual's effort is the simple association with others making the same effort. Personal involvement in community interracial struggles inevitably brought insight to the wider struggle going on in the nation and the world. There was a new understanding of vulnerability among peers of both races which brought about mutual trust in the issues which confounded us all. In some instances the only results had been an awakening to the fact that there was a problem affecting human beings in the community. However just waking up often leaves people disgruntled and therefore there was follow-up work to do.

In other instances real changes were made in community institutions for Phase II of *Assignment Race* which stressed the impact on the community. Intentions were determined by local Boards, which meant that substantive discussion had to take place.

Survey questions which measured progress or analysis also had to be answered as a group, thus offering less temptation for an ambitious individual to report what she wished might have happened. Church women were able at that time to get at the cause of many elements of discrimination: open housing, training for jobs, fair employment, use of the ballot box for general reform.

A supplemental grant by Field Foundation made it possible to engage Rhetta M. Arter and Corinne Morrow of the Research and Action Associates, a professional firm, for a social action survey. Their extensive report accumulated and classified the findings of hundreds of communities. From their study they made certain recommendations as they presented their report and evaluation to the executive committee of the General Department of United Church Women in the spring of 1966.

One of the recommendations was that UCW study the basis of membership and the general plan of representatives coming from women's organizations in local churches for various meetings and projects. It was felt that the nature of UCW militated against persons of darker skin finding an easy access on their own into the larger fellowship. The new bylaws proposed that United Church Women become an autonomous movement and meet this objection by defining the nature of United Church Women as a channel through which any individual Christian woman could work with others to carry out its purpose. Thus the employed women of any race could take the initiative necessary to share in our life and work.

In the long run the value of Assignment Race *may well have been not so much what UCW contributed to human rights in many specific places throughout the country, as what* Assignment Race *caused to happen in the constituency of UCW itself.*

The Christian Social Relations Committee locally related directly to the national committee thus strengthening a sense of national identity and effort. Often these local committees were a rallying point for local study and action. These local groups grew into intense fellowships, the effect of which is still felt in many communities. They became a "sanctuary" for many concerned individuals in that they gave an opportunity for understanding and action not found elsewhere in their churches. These study and action groups brought local UCW units into the many civil rights coalitions which sprang up in most communities and laid the groundwork for cooperation with the larger metropolitan efforts which came about in the more violent "crises in cities" that occurred in the next decade. As official studies brought out the actual nature of the separated societies in the United States calling for adjustments in schools, churches, housing, and employment practices, the experience of United Church Women during the previous six years made them better able to cope with the social upheaval which was to mark the coming years.

In the following two sections there are described the human and religious elements in the movements of Civil Disobedience and the Freedom Marches. In each of these events there were many persons whose motivation and backing came from their church. The upheaval which resulted because some were more active than others cannot be measured; nor can the participation of any individual be valued separately from the result as a whole.

Many of us interpreted the social struggle of the 60's as birthpangs of hope for our nation. Hope for the inalienable rights of many black citizens; hope for a truly multi-racial society for the benefit of us all; hope for spiritual renewal among Christians and Jews together in the crucible where our claims for a God of justice were being tested.

A professor of bio-chemistry, whose native home was India, sat looking at the television in my New York apartment. As he saw the Blacks linked arm in arm, singing hymns on the steps of a white church disbanded to be met by hostile crowds with sticks and stones, he remarked that the Church must be very successful in this country. When his hostess protested mildly that in many ways church people reflected too nearly the culture which surrounded them, he replied simply enough: "Just because some churches appear dead is no reason why you shouldn't recognize the Holy Spirit alive and at work among God's people."

CIVIL DISOBEDIENCE As the timetable of results brought increasing disappointment, there was a growing number of persons who came in "from outside" to stand with the oppressed who stood or knelt in protest in front of churches and public buildings. This only aroused the ire of those whose duty was to preserve the status quo. Wherever this could be interpreted as a violation of local laws, people were arrested. As had been true for centuries, some creative writing emerged. Martin Luther King, Jr.'s "Letter from a Birmingham Jail" was written on toilet paper from behind the cell bars and smuggled out to his associates.

On the question of civil disobedience, sharp differences of opinion were expressed in local congregations. Some of the breaches within families or churches were not likely to be healed quickly. Generally speaking the national church bodies were supportive of those who witnessed to their convictions and were able to offer legal defense funds and other ministries. The experience of these "offenders" is reminiscent of similar periods in every century of Christian history and is significant in interpreting the Christian faith. Let me offer several stories as they were told to me:

Orangeburg, South Carolina, a community of 12,000 with two Negro colleges, witnessed something it had never seen before during this period. In the early student demonstrations in 1961, 1,600 young people and children were arrested in three weeks and were handled in a rather inhumane way. In a similar protest nearly two years later a group of citizens composed of school teachers, meat packers, union leaders and the seven ministers in the city joined in another demonstration. Since it was the weekend ahead of Worldwide Communion Sunday, the ministers carried with them their individual communion sets used for hospital calls. A student pastor records his thoughts:

On Saturday preceding the world-wide communion, we had a fullscale service in the same stockade into which hundreds of young college students had been herded two years previously—when they stood in 19 degree weather, drenched by fire hoses and tear gas, and with icicles hanging from their hair. The shivering youngsters had stood for hours awaiting bail bond, but even then their cry was: 'WE WANT TO BE FREE.' A blind girl, an honor student in that march, never knew what struck her; she thought it was water, but she did not turn back. This was Christ in action as seen by the blind.

Maybe it is true that all of us felt free for the first time. These ministers feel now that they did what Christ wanted them to do—to witness for him in season and out of season—in Orangeburg, in church or jail, to commune with Him and His people in spirit and in truth.

It is our belief that this experience was really the new blood in the hearts of many, including the power structure of a hardcore town in South Carolina. This might well be our means of saying to the world, "LET US BREAK BREAD TOGETHER."

In the communion service the next day, it was necessary to substitute the elements with prison fare, but the spirit was genuine. The jailor was offered communion by a Negro pastor. What better way to celebrate Worldwide Communion!

A white university professor goes South to face the charges brought against him while participating with a demonstration on civil rights. He ends up in jail. He writes of his new experience with the "people of God."

Ecumenism is a word you begin to appreciate in a new way when you are behind bars. For you discover very soon that although the law can keep you in jail, the law can't keep the Church out of jail. You realize that you are not alone. You do not have a heightened mystical sense of the presence of God, but you do have a heightened tangible sense of the presence of the communion of saints. The telegrams of support begin to come: from a Catholic layman in California; from a white southern Presbyterian couple in Arkansas; from a group of priests, nuns, lay people and Protestant ministers on joint retreat; from a Catholic seminary professor; from members of the rabbis' congregations; from your own denominational officials; and, most humbling of all, from Martin Luther King, Jr.—humbling because he has been in jail dozens of times more than you have, and how many telegrams did you think to send to him?

It's not just the telegrams. It's the fact that almost all the telegrams remind you that the senders are praying for you and have groups of people praying for you. And you realize as you sit in jail that Protestants in Hot Springs, Catholics in Menlo Park, Jews in Springfield, Negroes in Newark, "Wasps" in New York City, and many others you know not of are upholding and supporting all of you by a great web of love and concern and intercession.

In a hotel in Atlanta, a young white girl told her story simply. She had come out of jail that afternoon and had a number of times suffered beatings on the part of those who just didn't like the protest that was being made. But she smiled. She used to live in Philadelphia where her folks were church members, she said. She had been in jail there, too, several times for not too good a reason.

Then when the racial struggle began, she went South and offered her services. The Negro captain in that area, a wonderful Christian girl, explained to her why faith in Christ made it possible to keep on loving people. When she was in jail, she had "time"—that's the main thing you have in jail—and she read the Bible and learned to pray. Then she added, "And now I believe I am Christ's disciple, and that I can do almost everything all Christians do—well, except going to some churches with my Negro friends."

A bomb explodes in a Negro church in Birmingham and four little girls are dead. Four families in grief and sorrow. All across America countless mothers ponder this thing in their hearts; countless fathers wonder how it could happen in this land of the free; countless little girls go to Sunday School and sing "Jesus loves me, this I know . . ."

The following Sunday in the Church of the Master located in Harlem in New York City, the members arrived with white arm bands of mourning as a sign of identity with their sister congregation in Alabama. Imagine our surprise to find special visitors in the congregation—the mother and father of one of the little girls. The pastor asked the father if he wished to make a statement. He said:

> We are deeply hurt over the loss of our daughter, as other parents are deeply hurt over the loss of their daughters. But I don't think my turning to violence and forgetting love will help anything. We must keep love in our plans; otherwise we will be doing just what will help our enemies most.

> The blame for this tragedy is broad. It cannot be pinned down to any one person. The every-day person shuts his eyes to things and says, 'It doesn't concern me.' And then suddenly something dastardly happens and we all feel guilty; we should have spoken out. You don't have to go to a certain place to speak. You can let your neighbor know how you feel about this thing. Be brotherly where you are, resort to love, and work for the betterment of mankind. Now that Christ and the Church have carried us so far, we must not give them up.

FREEDOM MARCHES The cradle of injustice began to rock slowly in Montgomery, Alabama when Rosa Parks got on a bus, paid her fare, but refused to sit in the assigned back seat. She was arrested. Her pastor, the Rev. Martin Luther King took up the cause.

The bus strike was on. The labor force was stalemated. The nation was alert that the social system must change as 50,000 Negroes substituted their tired feet for their tired spirits in a protest against indignities in the simple necessity of a bus ride. They began their long walk for freedom. For more than a year they walked in dignity rather than ride in humiliation— walked to their jobs—walked home—walked to school— walked to the shops—and walked home again. One old grandmother, obviously worn out by her walking, was asked, "Why don't you give up and ride?" She replied, "No. I'm not walking for myself. I'm walking for my grandson. I want him to be able to get in a bus, pay his money, and take a seat."

Walking became one of the great democratizing symbols of the freedom movement. Almost anybody black or white, young or old, rich or poor, unknown or famous had two feet one of which, put in front of another and pointed in the right direction, could respond to the rhythm of persons close by. Thus in thousands of places, as one company we sang the marching song, "Deep in my heart, I do believe, we will overcome someday."

There were many small groups who walked in front of segregated churches and lunch counters with increasing effectiveness as TV and news coverage spread their influence. The great marches took a mobilizing skill effectively exhibited by the Rev. Andrew Young and other members of the staff of the Southern Christian Leadership Conference.

During these years students, women, churches, professors, laborers all worked on their own constituency, but in the March they were together as a force for freedom. Let us recall several of the major ones.

Washington, 1963

The convergence of a half million people on the city of Washington on August 28, 1963 was a happy foretaste of a "great camp meeting in the Promised Land" . . . "Oh walk together, children; don't get weary . . ."

From every part of the nation came hundreds of chartered buses, planes, vans, and private cars which pressed into the capital city. Fortunately the preparatory work had been superb. The Washington Committee working with the police and civic authorities had set aside acres of parking spaces near the Lincoln Monument and provided health facilities and clear directions of all the cooperating community delegations. One can hardly fathom all the energy and organizing skill that was behind this gathering of a hundred thousand persons, the promotion, renting of buses, the direction for the drivers and the heads of the delegation, the publicity in the newspapers, the mountains of sandwiches, the jobs and families that needed to be planned for.

Someone ought to write an eulogy to Anna Hedgeman who handled the church promotion on behalf of the National Council of Churches. She calmly outlined the Plan for the Day and the part the churches were to have in the delegation visiting the President afterwards at a breakfast meeting for church leaders from all over the country. No one could have guessed the details which had already gone through her hands. Among those leaders was Louise Wallace, the national president of UCW who recognized that her personal involvement in this issue among the rank and file of church women was probably greater than any other.

Although the doors and windows along the path of the March in Washington seemed tightly closed in the apprehension that "something might happen", the spirit of the marchers was as open and friendly as a giant Sunday School picnic. We saw people we had not seen for years; we visited with strangers as if they were old friends; we were exhilarated to be among a multitude ready to go over the hill for victory. The celebrities on the platform were those who were giving priority to the civil rights legislation and came from many walks of life.

The program of music and prayers and greetings climaxed with the famous oration of the Rev. Martin Luther King, Jr., the 33 year old leader of the Southern Christian Leadership Conference. The crowd roared its approval after each of his famous lines.

Even though we face the difficulties of today and tomorrow, I still have a dream . . .

I have a dream that one day on the red hills of Georgia the sons of former slaves and the sons of former slaveowners will be able to sit down together at the table of brotherhood.

I have a dream that my four little children will one day live in a nation where they will not be judged by the color of their skin but by the content of their character.

I have a dream that one day every valley shall be exalted, every hill and mountain shall be made low, the rough places will be made plain, and the crooked places will be made straight, and the glory of the Lord shall be revealed and all flesh shall see it together.

Selma, 1965

Tuesday, March 16th, began rather quietly in the sealed-off compound in Selma, Alabama. Lines formed beside the church as people waited to be fed from the tiny kitchen where women took turns in preparing and serving the food. Small groups gathered on the grassy plots to discuss the next steps in preparing for the well advertised March from Selma to Montgomery. Occasionally a freedom song or spiritual could be heard from one of the neighborhood gatherings which welcomed hundreds of newcomers from all over the country who had come to join in the demonstration. Suddenly sirens broke in on the temporary calm and there was a rush of people to the area in front of the AME church. Medical nuns were getting into ambulances en route to Montgomery where acts of police brutality had been reported inflicted upon a group of students in a SNCC demonstration. Within half an hour everyone had taken a position, standing or sitting, on the church steps or on the sidewalk. The police encircled the crowd and filled the street with their cars and reserves. Across the street an angry looking posse waited to see what would happen.

What did take place was not unusual since it had been happening in Selma every day. For hours on end the air was filled with the songs of the freedom movement, with prayers, testimonies, speeches, and sermons. An account of one event of that long evening comes from the notes of Bruce Rigdon, who with other seminarians, had flown in from Chicago:

> The demonstrators who had come from all over the country numbered in the hundreds. Those in the back were "eyeball to eyeball" with the state police line. Some newcomers to the discipline and spirit of the Selma demonstrations had begun to jeer at Sheriff Jim Clark, standing by his car in the middle of the street. Unlike many of the police surrounding us who appeared relaxed and even smiled occasionally at the lyrics of our songs and the humor of the speakers, Clark wore a stern expression, and several times interrupted proceedings with his electric bullhorn to take issue with what was said. Before this situation could develop further, one of the leaders of the SCLC leaped to the microphone on the steps and began to speak:
>
> > Those of you in the back who are taunting Sheriff Clark, listen to me. Sheriff Clark is not the enemy—we

are not fighting against him, but for him . . . Like most of us he has grown up under a system that has made him a cripple. It has twisted and perverted his life and ours with lies, suspicion, hatred, and fear . . . We are fighting to destroy the system that has crippled him and us. We are fighting to make it possible for all of the Sheriff Clarks and Jim Crows to begin to live as human beings, with dignity and compassion.

I believe that nothing new and creative comes in human society except through suffering and crucifixion . . . We have a choice to make: we can allow this history of suffering to become a cup of bitterness, or we can so try to live that this suffering may become a source of creative change and new life for the whole nation.

As for me, I have a sense that something amazing has been taking place among us during these last years. There is a new stirring, a new moving of the Kingdom of God in our lives. It is powerful, it cannot be ignored or stopped. It calls all of us to respond to what God is doing in the history of the nation.

All along the way were persons of both races doing the tough preparatory work. Once they crossed the bridge at Selma over the opposition of the local police they were into the March which was scheduled to take four days, their final destination being the steps of the Alabama State Capitol. Their object was to accumulate pressure for state civil rights legislation.

Some depended on the tenant homes of rural farmers to find beds, water supply and other needs in case of emergency. Hundreds of temporary latrines were erected, and facilities for food and health care were provided.

During one of the Selma days, the annual meeting of the Committee of 100 United Church Women was being held in Washington, D.C. and Lady Bird Johnson had been invited to their luncheon. Uppermost in most of their minds was the possible significance of the Selma March. It was the general feeling that the UCW president, Edna Sinclair, should fly down to join the last day of the March to sustain the strong position of UCW and to undergird Coretta Scott King, who was serving her first term on the national Board. Mrs. Sinclair asked the opinion of Abbie Clement Jackson, a member of the Committee, who immediately said, "I've been thinking of doing the same thing. I'll join you." So they flew to Montgomery. They found many friends who had come from across the country as well as leaders of UCW in Alabama. Beside them walked Dr. Rachel Henderlite, in spite of the hazard to her health, just because she needed to live out her Christian conviction. There were noisy helicopters overhead, and armed police were everywhere. Yet as they walked through the streets of Montgomery, turning down the street past the church of which Dr. King was pastor, and walked to the steps of the State House, there was among them quiet certainty that their cause was righteous. Along the curb many watched for their friends or family who weren't quite able to join in the open demonstration. Mrs. Sinclair recognized many of her friends who waved her onward. Later it was a great satisfaction to know that on the next World Day of Prayer for the first time Negro and white women joined in wonder and joy together at lunch. As Dr. King spoke to the huge crowd in front of the capitol, he began quietly and rose to the inspirational quality which he gave the movement.

On the way home in the plane, the tired participants talked of the meaning of the experience. Next to Edna Sinclair was a young Catholic priest who said something like this: "I now know why the incarnation of God in a human being was so important. Its meaning came through to me as I witnessed today in young Negro leaders the very presence of God singing 'His truth will make us free . . . deep in my heart I do believe.'"

Memphis, 1968

On November 22, 1963 Coretta and Martin King were at home together and like millions of others witnessed the assassination of President Kennedy on their TV. Touching his wife's hand Martin remarked: "If the President of the United States can't be protected from this sort of thing, you know that there is no way to protect me." They both had recognized his vulnerability, the price of leadership of a freedom movement.

In October, 1967 the national Board of Managers, on which Coretta King was serving her second term, met in

Atlanta. She invited the executive committee to her home for supper one night. As we talked together, she shared many of her personal reactions to what was happening; how it felt to have her husband arrested on the pretext of a traffic violation, their home bombed, threats and abuse over the phone, their longing that their children could have a picnic in the public park on Stone Mountain.

The priority of the civil rights movement by this time had moved from voting registration to a struggle to overcome discrimination in the economic field. Dr. King, who had mounted a campaign that summer in Chicago, was planning a "Poor People's March" to the national capital. Meanwhile he flew to Memphis to show sympathy with a strike among poorly paid garbage workers. It was there on April 5, 1968 that the bullet was fired which took his life.

Nina Boswell and I were working late in the office that night. A friend who had heard the news over TV thoughtfully called and before we could adjust to the shock, a call came from Abigail McCarthy in Washington. She was going South the next morning and would stop on behalf of Church Women United to see Coretta King. I telephoned Mary Hoyt (president of CWU in Georgia) and Dot Dolbey (the national president of CWU) about procedures. The Memphis March at which Dr. King had planned to speak was scheduled for the following Monday and therefore it was not expected that the plans for the funeral would be announced for several days. Mrs. Dolbey named the official delegation for Church Women United for the funeral, and agreed to fly to Memphis with Helen Turnbull to participate in the Memphis demonstration.

Church Women United in Memphis had been in action as advocates of the workers since the beginning of the strike. The president of the local unit, Helen Hardesty, was able to make arrangements for reserved places on the platform for the national president. Coretta King flew to Memphis to share in the rally. Her courageous statement was gratefully received by the crowd which numbered in the thousands. The Mayor had previously announced that the City would accede to the demands of the strikers. Having to leave early to meet a plane schedule, Dot Dolbey passed a note to Coretta King saying,

"We're with you all the way."

A few days later the funeral was held in Atlanta with thousands of persons pouring in from all over the nation: persons in public office, celebrities from the entertainment world, officers from the churches and educational institutions; most important were the common people, Negro and white, old and young, who had worked and walked under his leadership for nearly a decade tempering the nation's conscience.

I shared a hotel room with Claire Harvey, a member of our Board, who had come in from Jackson to do the ground work for the group representing Church Women United. Before five o'clock I heard her up and when I asked about it she replied, "My heart is troubled. I must get among the people. I am going to the Church!" "I'll go with you," I said, wondering who would be at the church at that time of the morning. But they were there—hundreds of them who had come in by the bus load. There was an amazing spirit of oneness—as if they all knew each other personally. Many of them did, for one could hear them recalling various church meetings or civil rights events as they greeted each other; but mostly the oneness was a result of a common experience as a race and therefore they could comfort and cheer each other. It helped me understand later the importance of the movement for black identity.

After this high day of national tribute, there could not help but be a despondent hangover as the multitude dispersed to go home. What next? Without a great leader would the struggle for human freedom go on? Did we really believe that "deep in our hearts we would overcome someday"?

EVEN MISSISSIPPI   I have a dream that one day *even the state of Mississippi,* a state swelling with the people's injustice, sweltering with the heat of oppression, will be transformed into an oasis of freedom and justice . . .

-from the oration of Martin Luther King, Jr.
at the Lincoln Memorial, Washington, D.C.

Mississippi was a particular challenge for all those who cared about achieving human justice or relieving human misery. A century had passed since the Emancipation Proclamation, yet many poor Negro farm workers remained subservient in spirit and mentality—and many white people had not grown past the mentality or spirit of the slaveowner. Mastery through economic oppression and intimidation by brute force was common enough.

When the leaders of the national civil rights movement decided to concentrate on Mississippi in 1964-65, they had in mind at least two objectives. 1) the need to reinforce a remarkable group of persons already at work in their native state; and 2) the need to focus the light of public opinion on law enforcement officials in Mississippi. Hundreds of students, church leaders, and freedom riders came into the state to challenge the segregated public facilities, to become a presence in the courts, to assist in voter registration, as well as job skills, literacy or health efforts, to join in the state-wide marches of protest, and to observe first hand the rough treatment of the powerless poor.

In the midst of these general activities, United Church Women in Mississippi were at work doing what was possible under the circumstances. Let me list a few illustrations of the varied ways in which women became advocates:

Just because it was not a simple matter to keep the Mississippi UCW alive during this particular period of crisis, the national president, Edna Sinclair, and I flew to Mississippi in the late summer of 1966 to confer with responsible leaders. The state president, Ann Hewett, welcomed us at a dinner in a downtown motel where there was almost an equal number of Negro and white women.

We drove up to Greenville where Mrs. Jesse Brent (Ruth) had in her home for lunch about 30 leaders of both races to discuss the problems besetting the Delta ministry. I remember having a distinct feeling of what a "saving remnant" could mean. By remaining loyal to the national inter-racial policy, United Church Women in Mississippi was itself a witness of an open visible fellowship in a society which was

One evening Clarie Collins Harvey, a member of the National Committee of 100, came by in her car to take us over to her place of business—the Collins Funeral Home—which was just settling in to beautiful new quarters. Everything spoke of a sensitive ministry to the bereaved, such as the beautiful chapel in which Christian art was tastefully placed, the quiet place of privacy with a few devotional books at hand for family or friends of the deceased. She pointed with pride to family heirlooms—a photo of her grandfather who had been born a slave and was later emancipated; the tiny trunk in which her father had packed all his earthly belongings and carried them to Rusk College to get his education. She showed us the office of her mother, the first Negro librarian in Mississippi, who since her husband's death, had managed the Collins Funeral Home where now Clarie was actively associated. We went into the office which Clarie used and again felt the good taste of this remarkable business woman.

The conversation came around to the development of a movement called *Womanpower Unlimited,* which Clarie had organized. It was made up of women willing to undertake some risks in order to be of service in the crisis of their native state. One of their concerns was for the victims of selective and over-zealous law enforcement whose suffering was particularly acute during periods of high racial tension. Clarie Harvey took a personal interest in the young idealists who came to Mississippi from other sections of the country and often found themselves involved with local authorities on some trumped up charge. Families of these young people were grateful to have responsible Mississippi citizens willing to offer a helping hand.

It is an overwhelming experience to meet *Clarie Harvey* on this platform. Although we have never met, she played an important part in rescuing me from an incredibly painful experience. In the summer of 1962, I boarded a Greyhound bus in Nashville headed for Jackson, Mississippi.

As I had anticipated, there were dual facilities in the terminal in Jackson—one marked for "White People Only" and the other for "Colored." Wishing to test the interstate law, I went into the waiting room marked "Colored" and sat down at a counter to order a cup of coffee. Several other white people whom I don't know came in about the same time. Immediately the police entered and ordered us to move on. I said I was waiting for a cup of coffee before returning to the bus. Again, the order "All of you—move!" In a few minutes the police closed in on us and evidently on some black persons who were in the waiting room for whites. I was arrested for disobeying the orders of a policeman.

After five minutes in the courthouse, a judge fined me $250 and set bail at $500 which money I did not have. We were put into the city jail, of course, separated by race, and remained there for a few days. Then without explanation an armed guard took me to the county jail which was even more crowded. Once again, after a few days I was moved and taken a distance from Jackson to the Mississippi State Penitentiary. There I went through a grueling experience—a rough body examination by the jailers, meager food and water, and was placed in maximum security. Prison conditions were especially filthy so packets of sanitary supplies, and a bar of soap were received gratefully from a group called *Womenpower Unlimited.* I obtained a black lawyer who posted my check for bond;

It was a strange feeling to be released and walk out all alone. A black man approached me and asked if I were Shirley Smith. He represented *Womanpower Unlimited* and took me to a nearby Negro church. There were women waiting for me with clean clothes and a place to wash and warm food. I was taken then to a beauty shop where a black operator washed my hair—a blessing beyond description. Any one of these persons could have gotten into trouble, but in the wonderful communication system which is theirs I was cared for until I boarded the plane for home.

So you see why I want to thank Clarie Harvey and *Womanpower Unlimited* on my own behalf and on behalf of other young people who needed some Mississippi citizen to take the risk of kindness for an outsider.

PRAYER AND PERFORMANCE With a reputation throughout the South as a sensititive leader of spiritual life retreats, Mrs. W. Schutt (Jane), president of United Church

Women in Mississippi, was a natural choice to lead the regional prayer fellowship in New Orleans during the 75th Anniversary Celebration of the *World Day of Prayer.* The experience of Negro and white women praying together about concerns which they had selected was deeply meaningful. Why should it not be true of Jackson? She returned determined to find a way to make possible an interracial fellowship of prayer. She found that even a small interracial group could not meet in her own church, an all white Episcopal Church in the city. However the Pearl Street Baptist Church, one of the Negro Churches, did open its doors for their weekly meetings. Each week each woman shared the problems which troubled her and together they sought God's presence and guidance.

Prayer begins as well as ends with "Amen." So be it! Jane Schutt and her friends were soon to find God's presence in the midst of the daily action in the streets and neighborhoods of Jackson as well as in the church. Glimpse some of them: Frequently Jane was on the phone as long distance calls came from her sisters in UCW in other states: "My son is on his way to join the marches round the state . . . My daughter wants to spend the summer helping register voters . . I gave your name . . . Won't you keep your eyes open for them?"

Her backyard and the garage were stacked high with gear and extra suitcases. Her counsel over a cup of coffee helped these eager strangers to be where the action was and to know how to handle themselves. At another time she organized a soup kitchen on a street corner in Jackson, ready to welcome the tired and hungry participants from the five day march around the state.

On one day, she could be found reading a letter from a rabbi writing from Florida. He had finished his work with demonstrators there and would like to put effort into Mississippi. He needed free room for the summer and some guidance as to activities. Jane was able to relate the request to an unexpected ally who had telephoned the day before to say, "I'm free, white and 81. How do I get in on your fun?" Jane called this wealthy woman from one of the old families to ask if she knew someone who would give the rabbi a room. The woman agreed to take him herself! She then used her social clout to get appointments with some of the leading businessmen of the city. She persuaded her guest to undertake a listening ministry all summer so that the upset upper class could vent some of their feelings. Each evening they talked of his experiences of the day. "It was like living with John the Baptist," she later remarked to her UCW friends.

Or you might glimpse Jane Schutt getting ready to lead an interracial workshop in Montreat or in Alabama, or counseling with a State or National Committee of United Church Women who wanted to open up some special service for the poor of Mississippi, or praying with her fellowship of women over an opportunity to serve on the U.S. Commission on Civil Rights in Washington (which they decided to reject because it would lessen her influence in Mississippi where she was needed).

Yes, go with Jane Schutt as she looks out of the window of her home one night to find a cross burning in her front yard. The traditional Ku Klux Klan warning, meant to strike fear, sputtered and burned itself out in futility.

One can start and end most days with prayer but there is lots of living in between.

WEDNESDAYS IN MISSISSIPPI The genius of women working for social change is not only "what they do" but also "whom they know." Being able to call on women with influence multiplies the chances of actual achievement. Every woman linked through one project, begins to be the center of ever widening circles of other action. Many more angles on what is really possible in the areas of social tension are generated from these living centers of activities than could possibly come from a structured long range plan where conformity is an element of success.

In 1964 and 1965 *Wednesdays in Mississippi* was organized upon the initiative of the National Council of Negro Women with the cooperation of other organized women's groups, including UCW. The plan called for groups of women from northern cities to go to Mississippi each week of the summer to try to build a bridge of communication with their southern counterparts.

Interracial groups of women went to Mississippi each week in 1964-65. The team members were recruited to respond to expressed needs of a coalition of women in Jackson, the key persons of which were from UCW, the only integrated group of women existing in that city at the time.

There were requests, such as from a Catholic Mission struggling in a poverty area, to provide a specialist for the Head Start project, and to offer resources to librarians and social workers. Their real intent was directed toward ease and understanding of communication among women of all races. Response came from Boston, Columbus, Detroit, Minneapolis, Chicago, St. Paul, New Jersey, New York, Philadelphia and the Washington-Virginia-Maryland area. Each visit took approximately three days plus travel time and was financed by the team members. Recognition was given to the importance of Human Relations Committees functioning in many parts of the state. But the simple framework of common working goals, common concerns of women, of sharing of literary and musical pleasures, creates a mutuality of interest which cannot be found by the sole contact of races when they sit next to each other at formal meetings. Every effort was made to avoid publicity either while in Mississippi or upon the return home. Each wrote a report upon returning home. The following observations offer typical insights:

> There was a sense of *relief* on the part of most people I met, a feeling that a change of climate and mood had taken place. 'We can breathe again,' said several. 'We can talk to each other again. And we have found that there are other people who agree with us.'
>
> •••
>
> I found real grounds for hope that the best qualities of the southerner would prevail and that the new relationships will be enriched by the finest aspects of the traditional relationships between the races in the south.
>
> •••
>
> The tremendous response to the challenge of *'Headstart'* seemed to indicate an eagerness to bridge

the gap of inequities in culture and education on the part of the Negro and a recognition of the importance of this in the resolution of civil rights issues. The tragedy here, it seemed to me, lay in the fact that no official body of the city government or the schools would assist in this crucial effort and that the heavy load of responsibility for the large program was carried by too few individuals.

• • •

The 'power structures' of the city seemed still unmoved, even though members of the Committee on Mississippians for Public Education whom I met seemed rather confident that the Superintendent and school board would act responsibly with the desegregation of the schools in the fall.

• • •

The small committee trying to recruit girls for the job corps faced almost insurmountable problems and no cooperative women's job corps from the city. The committee showed wonderful spirit and dedication but great frustration.

• • •

Even though I have indicated signs of hopeful change, I was also quite aware of the spirit of fear and uncertainty which still exists. This was also made clear through conversations with several people. The John Birch state of mind, the religious extremes, hatred of the National Council of Churches, and general suspicions certainly blanket the area.

• • •

CONTINUING QUESTIONS By 1965 most Americans were aware that they were in the midst of a social revolution testing whether white and black peoples together could achieve equal opportunity in this country. Although they had experienced only one phase of a continuing struggle, the first decade provided a natural occasion for consolidation and evaluation. Both black and white writers were raising two queries: What have we achieved since 1954? What can we expect in the next decade? Listed among achievements were: 1) greatly increased awareness of the racial problem; 2) an awakening of the American conscience to the moral and human implications of discrimination; 3) a disclaimer that the black in the South was "content" where he was; 4) the Supreme Court ruling that any discrimination practice due to race was illegal; 5) Congress after many years of silence on the subject passed two civil rights acts, thus bringing pressure on the Justice Department for their enforcement; 6) peaceful protest in the South had caught the imagination of other sections of the country; 7) public facilities, lunch counters, hotels, and transportation were open; 8) individual blacks were seen for the first time in formerly all-white stores, both as clerks and customers, in school systems, both as students and teachers as well as on controlling boards in civic organizations.

But in a democracy, the political system can go only part way. Much awaited the general change of heart and practice among the people themselves. In every revolutionary process the amount of individual hate, frustration, irrationality, and prejudice which spills over into the general life of the community is not easy to mop up.

As these conditions were complicated by other facets of social unrest in the United States, the next decade would be more chaotic and confused as the racial struggle reached national proportions. Would the growing realization of two separated societies hamper or excuse participation in the cause of human rights? Would new black leaders be able to control the struggle within a framework acceptable to enlightened white opinion? Would the continuing frustration result in anarchy—rejecting the whole system? What handles would then be unwittingly offered to white reactionary persons still holding much economic or political power? These were questions raised in 1964 and 1965. They were questions which were waiting for answers during the next decade.

PEOPLE, POVERTY   Beginning in 1965, a three year emphasis
AND PLENTY   around the theme "People, Poverty, and
                       Plenty" was launched and featured in the
next three May Fellowship Days. It was said that the UCW study guide "One Fifth of a Nation" came off the press one day ahead of President Johnson's announcement of his war on poverty! Eleanor French, the staff director of Christian Social Relations, focused her attention on aiding volunteer women

to be both competent and compassionate. A thorough educational process was sustained over the triennium period. For some it seemed repetitive. (We've decided to give up poverty for Lent," a leader in a small community in the middle west once told me.) For others there was opportunity for growing awareness of the complexity of sharing with the "have nots" in a country of great plenty.

Following the announcement of the "war on poverty", there was a rash of meetings of business and civic and religious organizations seeking to form coalitions of various kinds to alleviate some phase of the problem. UCW decided to work with a number of national women's organizations on the problems of women who were disadvantaged by poverty. The Committee on Household Employment was organized to concentrate on protecting the rights of women in domestic service, and eventually incorporated and financed its own program.

WICS   One particularly congenial coalition which had worked together through the Civil Rights Movement formed the Women's Inter-organizational Committee, composed of the Young Women's Christian Association, the United Church Women, the National Council of Negro Women, the National Council of Jewish Women and the National Council of Catholic Women.

It was to this coalition of women's organizations that the President's Task Force on the War on Poverty turned when Congress, pressed by Edith Green, authorized the inclusion of women in the Job Corps. Girls needed a helping hand to break out of the poverty cycle. These organizations were asked to provide volunteers to recruit and screen young women for the Job Corps. Although the YWCA was already committed to administering another government program in the training field, the members of the other four groups incorporated as Women in Community Service in December 1964 and undertook the job. They were joined in 1969 by the National Auxiliary of the American GI Forum (a Spanish speaking association of women).

At that time there were questions about churches

receiving money directly from government sources, even for community services. As a separate entity, WICS could apply for government funding. However, Mrs. Stuart Sinclair, who had been elected president of the UCW a few months before, was able to clear the matter with the General Board of the NCCC. To stabilize the operation it was hoped there would be additional funding from foundations, and from the parent organizations themselves.

WICS was built on the solid foundation of responsible women nominated to its Board and Corporation by the parent organizations, and by the personal involvement of strong leaders like Dorothy Height (NCNW); Jo Weiner and Hannah Stein (NCJW); Margaret Mealey and Rosemary Kilch (NCCW); Edna Sinclair and Eleanor French of UCW. Major credit for coping with complexities of government administrators and the ramification of a national volunteer set-up goes to the able executive director, Mary Halleran. In addition to a small staff in the Washington office and area coordinators, each parent organization was allowed a liaison person within the WICS budget. UCW was ably served by Louise Pheutze, Helen Turnbull and Dorothe Dow through the first decade. UCW offered the services of its public relations director, Maza Tilghman, who chaired the WICS committee on interpretation and managed press and TV relations.

The first WICS office was one corner of a desk at the National Council of Catholic Women in Washington, D.C. By January 1965, it had grown to two rented rooms. By July of the same year, it had expanded over an entire floor of an empty government building. By the time the holes in the floor were filled with plaster, the fly-specked walls hidden under a coat of paint, and borrowed card tables and wooden boxes replaced by desks and chairs, the government decided to raze the building! One more move did it!

The anxiety rhythms of WICS seemed to surround the periodic negotiation of the contract with the Office of Economic Opportunity. The agreement covering a specific length of time, as well as the particular circumstance of the Government's budget process, called for the commitment of WICS to recruit a specific number of girls for the Job Corps for which WICS received a sum of money covering a detailed overhead budget.

Then began the pressure, training, and reporting that were required to realize their numerical goal. Surely the WICS office must have been one of the liveliest offices in the country. For instance in 1970 WICS agreed to provide 4,000 enrollees for the Job Corps. By adding 30% more girls for "no show" applicants, a total goal of 5,700 girls had to be recruited.

The early response from volunteers was enthusiastic. From a baker's dozen at the beginning of 1965, WICS volunteers numbered nearly 10,000 by the end of 1966. More than 20,000 women had contributed many hours by the spring of 1969. The six screening centers established in 1965 had proliferated to 290. In addition, WICS had contacts in 300 more cities.

No sooner had the enthusiastic mobilization of volunteers reached its height than a moratorium was called on the whole program. It was to occur twice more in the years ahead. This, together with the variation and uncertainties of the contracts, inevitably resulted in loss of morale and numbers among the volunteers and disillusionment and disappointment among their young recruits. It was unfortunate that a program which was intended to provide greater security for the individual girl should in itself be so insecure. Women engaged in this community service demonstrated the important value of volunteers who continue their commitment in the place where they live, whereas an employed worker has no choice when regional and national offices are closed.

WICS volunteers were an "anchor to windward" for many girls beset by doubt and uncertainty. WICS volunteers brought strength and stability when the program was being considered each year by Congressional committees (as when the hopes of many were dashed by the closing of 59 Job Corps Centers in 1968 and 1969).

These volunteers organized literacy classes, taught homemaking and child care, and tutored girls in basic school subjects. They introduced young women to the world of work and helped them find suitable low cost housing. They placed many on jobs and provided advice, encouragement and friendship during periods of anxiety, financial stress, or personal misfortunes. Working together across racial, religious and cultural lines, artificial barriers were eliminated.

WICS volunteers gave over 7.35 million hours of work without compensation to help young women from the seriously blighted economic sectors of the country. They recruited and screened more than 51,000 acceptable applicants for the Job Corps, and interviewed, referred to other programs, or provided needed assistance for 230,000 others.

The closing paragraph from a 1969 WICS Bulletin reminds us that it has always taken faith to fill the circle of the possible in what is, humanly speaking, an impossible situation:

Whatever lies in the future, WICS must not forget its past. It was born of a wedding of civil rights and human rights. Today WICS has a contract and a commitment— a contract to help alleviate poverty by assisting young women to break away from the treadmill of deprivation to which they have been chained; an unwritten commitment to help excise prejudice by working across racial, religious, and cultural lines. There is a terminal date on the contract. The commitment is open ended.

1964 ASSEMBLY The racial upheaval of the 60's affected every **KANSAS CITY** household, every local church, every community, every business establishment and every section of the country. If the Church were to have any impact on this social revolution, it could not be shoved off on a mission board or the pastors of local churches. This was everybody's business. Whether or not they had accepted the call, the 1,400 women who came to the Tenth National Assembly in Kansas City knew full well the intention of the theme "Laity in Mission."

A panorama—using drama, painting, music, and dance—depicted the loneliness of the individual person and the estrangement of the neighbor: the inhuman automation, the aloneness of the divorcee, the emptiness of the marriage, the frustration of the man who must spend his life "goose-stepping," the hatreds and indignities that prejudice spawns in any society, fear of the atom bomb. The panorama demanded that all of these must be accepted as part of the "world" to which our faith and our lives should make some purposeful response.

"If the modern lay woman wants prophetic direction for her life," said the Biblical interpreter, Father Paul Verghese, "she can find it in ancient words." Outlining the parable of the Pearl of Great Price (Matthew 13), he asserted; "The ministry to which we are called requires the whole of our being, the whole of our time, everything we have . . . It is a ministry which will make us tired and torn. It is a ministry which will make us despised and rejected . . . "

Challenges were made through panels on laity—Edith Lerrigo, Arnold B. Come, Alden D. Kelly, Franklin Littell, Margaret Frakes, Frederick K. Wentz. Consciences were stabbed awake by Ambassador Chief Adebo, David Stowe, Kenneth Maxwell, Honorable Constance Baker Motley, Dr. Daisuke, Cameron Hall, Wayne Hartmire, Daisuke Kitagawa, Madeline Barot.

The issues would have been dismissed like the body rejects foreign objects had it not been for luncheon meetings where the same group of fifty women ate together for three successive days and talked about the questions which haunted them: Are people really beneath us because they are undereducated, poorly clothed, without a job? Will we accept all people as having inherent worth and real potential?

The Message from the Tenth National Assembly was presented by Abbie Clement Jackson, the chairman of the Message Committee. Rather than calling on the government, the emphasis was on making the laity of the churches conscious of their unfinished business. The subject matter was reminiscent of the ever growing spiral and included some suggestions which were within the circle of the possible:

> *On Christian Unity:* We would join the thousands of Christians around the world, Roman Catholic and Orthodox and Protestant, who daily and especially during the Week of Prayer for Christian Unity, pray that "they all may be one." And on our own World Day of Prayer may our prayer for unity in mission be answered

in part by our willingness in each place to "act and speak together as occasion requires for the tasks to which God calls his people."

On Race: During the past triennium, through *Assignment Race,* we have worked for full participation of all people, without distinction of race, in the local church, the community, the denomination, and the councils of church women. We believe we have moved forward, but to lessen this emphasis now would be unthinkable.

On Poverty: Today the causes of poverty lie primarily not with the individual, but with society. Today compassion must be joined to social imagination and social responsibility.

The love of our Lord demands that we stand with people who are poor, recognizing our oneness with them before God—our oneness in need and in grace.

On Peace and Justice: There is no short cut to peace or to security. Our nation must persevere with other nations in the search for reliable arrangements to eliminate weapons of death and reduce the burdens of armament. Nuclear weapons of war have become an intolerable threat to human survival. Their elimination will be possible only when the nations have created international institutions capable of keeping peace.

The planning committee had envisioned a commitment service which would sum up the message of the Assembly so that each woman could take its picture in "the Kodak of her heart" and take it home with her. At least that is the impression which Louise Wallace left with me when she asked me to write the closing service. The committee had already chosen the persons who would participate, namely, Coretta Scott King, Father Paul Verghese, and the incoming president, Edna Sinclair. It was like finding a frame for three genuine originals who, without further embellishment, would have been enough.

During the summer I spent a few days in Rome with some officials of our Church who were there on official business. One afternoon we had tea at the home of the

American Ambassador who was living in an old Italian villa. As our hostess walked around the garden with me, she pointed out the entrance to the catacomb connected with the house. Later we visited the catacombs designated as "belonging to the House of Priscilla." It dawned on me that catacombs had frequently been connected with homes like neighborhood tornado cellars in our country.

Yes, that's what Coretta King was making of her home—a place where her husband could come for comfort and blessing before returning to the struggle which later claimed him as a martyr. Every Christian woman should have a Catacomb of the Home.

In fact, every one could create a Catacomb of the Heart—on the walls of which would be depicted the sign of service, the basin and the towel, and the symbol of faith the outline of a fish, the word which in Greek is an acrostic for Jesus Savior Lord. Into the Catacomb of the Heart, each woman would welcome the hurt, the angry, the humiliated peoples of this earth; through her prayer and loving kindness, they would be comforted and blessed.

**General Department of
United Church Women
1950-1966**

chapter 6

On the way to CWU

United Church Women began as an autonomous movement and established many practices of independent action that were never abandoned during its fourteen years as a General Department of the NCCC. During this period a vigorous training program for state leaders was carried on, resulting in effective educational background in the program departments: Christian World Missions, Christian Social Relations and Christian World Relations; and the three national observances of World Day of Prayer, May Fellowship Day, and World Community Day.

In the period when the National Council of Churches faced unprecedented and frequently unfair criticism, UCW was also valuable in public relations and interpretation. A Committee of 100 outstanding women was developed for this purpose under the chairmanship of Mrs. James Dolbey and later Mrs. Dallas Sherman. One of its members, Mrs. Emlen Stokes provided funds for staff so that the Committee of 100 had the able services of Mossie Wyker for four years. The need which called for this special effort of interpretation seemed to subside so that in 1967 the committee formally dissolved.

In 1963 the Committee on Restructure of the NCCC proposed a plan for greater program coordination. There was created a new Division of Christian Unity composed of a Department of Faith and Order, the Departments of United Church Women and United Church Men, as well as Departments carrying relationships to Youth Work in the denominations and relationships to State Councils of Churches.

On the chart this looked like a loss of status for the women, inasmuch as the General Department of UCW previously had direct access to all program divisions and its director was on the cabinet of General Administration. This seeming loss was offset by the fact that Cynthia Wedel was elected as Associate General Secretary for the Division of Christian Unity. Her leadership assured UCW of an understanding colleague and an advocate in the higher echelons of the NCCC.

The Division of Christian Unity included those departments which dealt with various aspects of the participation of laity in the Churches and gave us all access to the theological studies in the Department of Faith and Order. The dynamics of our separate departments were so different that our operations were largely self-contained and we were free to confer with any other department in the NCCC on matters of mutual concern. The Division was destined to be shortlived, however, since from the beginning, it had a tough financial problem. There were no clear lines of support from denominational sources such as those enjoyed by Divisions of Mission and Christian Education. Only the Department of United Church Women was completely self supporting and able to contribute its full share to the overhead cost of the Division.

SPECIAL STUDY COMMITTEE—UCW The times called for self study of the program of United Church Women to see what thrusts would commend themselves as possible next steps. Toward that end the national president, Edna Sinclair, appointed a board-staff committee to set some directions for the future. The committee was chaired by Mrs. Percy Rex (Ruth) of Delaware. Her experience, plus her great belief in women of the churches, added much to any evaluation process. Although Dorothy MacLeod was doing the staff work for the committee, I was invited, as her proposed successor, to attend one of their committee meetings in the fall of 1965.

At that meeting, the ten women present were analyzing themselves in relation to the recent reorganization of the NCCC. With the growing centrality of the denominations in the NCCC, UCW was increasingly envisioned as fulfilling the same supportive role in the NCCC as women's auxiliaries had fulfilled in their respective churches.

As I listened to their comments during the preparation of their paper, clues as to their mood at the time emerged. Perhaps they were over sensitized to being part of the laity. Sometimes this meant withholding some of their opinions, rights, and power as women in order to appear cooperative with the plans of others. Too much time was absorbed in cooperating with the departments of the NCCC in the traditional categories of social action. There seemed to be a longing for women to initiate programs and define tasks both on local and national levels—particularly in some of the new areas of inquiry such as human sexuality.

It seemed too, that United Church Women was not as homogeneous theologically as once assumed.[1] There was a felt need for Biblically based workshops which could assist women in thinking through the content and expression of their faith. Their present program departments were content-centered and overlapped when it came to practical application in short term projects.

As I was to observe many times later about national committees of UCW, this group of women from different parts of the country worked with real integrity of purpose. Each spoke openly about the situation as she saw it; together they took the risk of facing reality, yet were not defeated when there was no immediate solution. They listened courteously to each other, even though some proposals seemed a little far fetched. They came together on points of agreement which made possible a recommendation for the next step. Their conclusions always looked past the present, which allowed for the time lag necessary before they could be considered by local and state units.

During the next months we took every opportunity to

brainstorm about the nature of the movement. Conversations, retreats, committee meetings, all ended in expressing the lively hopes among the constituency.

Realizing that some of the intangible ideas must be widely felt before any organized specifics were determined, we particularly welcomed the 150 state program chairmen who came to New York for the annual training period. In discussion, the question was often posed: "What would we like to see happen in the local councils of UCW?" Here are some of the concerns often expressed:

- We want to be a national movement. We don't want to be thought of as little local women, with some people who are not "us" determining what happens.
- We look and act like a homogeneous group of white Protestants. How do we get participation from persons of other races?
- How can we get the skill and service of employed women?
- How do we involve young women without their wrecking the program we already have?
- What are we supposed to do about Catholic women some of whom want to "join"?
- What will happen if the present trend continues, when "our" women move from the central city to suburban communities?
- What shall we do about the morality problem and sex education among youth?
- Are we really facing the fact that we are not prepared to interpret our faith as Christians in an age increasingly controlled by technology?
- After thirty years of peace education, why have we been so ineffective?

There was a strangely similar aftermath to all these exploratory meetings. The ideas generated were so affirmatively acceptable that many believed them to be the stirrings of the Holy Spirit. This may have resulted in an overdose of 'spiritual security' which was corrected during the succeeding months by our pragmatic sisters. It ought to be, but how?

At a luncheon arranged for me to talk with a dozen

members of the YWCA national staff, I shared some of our new directions. At the conclusion, Edith Lerrigo, the General Secretary, commented: "Aren't we glad we knew her when she thought it was possible?"

INTERPRETIVE LUNCHEONS Filling the circle of the possible on every occasion was what was called for. Generally speaking United Church Women had been regarded as a pan-Protestant movement, but after Vatican II, we realized that there was another possibility. In the fall of 1965, the Board of Managers met in New York City. The Board's Committee on Public Relations, chaired by Mrs. John Norman of West Virginia, together with the staff director, Maza Tilghman, planned a luncheon program at the Statler Hilton Hotel to which 500 women from the vicinity, including Roman Catholics, were in attendance. Besides the apparent fellowship around the tables, the program consisted of the observations of the Vatican Council as described by a Protestant and a Roman Catholic. One of the speakers was the only American woman named as an official observer, Sister Mary Luke Tobin, the president of the Leadership Conference of Women Religious. The other was Mildred McAfee Horton, formerly president of Wellesley College, who had accompanied her husband, Dr. Douglas Horton, one of the Protestant observers. Both women spoke with sparkling simplicity making the most of the human aspects of this famous Council of Bishops.

So successful was this first public relations event that a second popular luncheon was projected for later in 1966 to interpret UCW through one of its major programs—citizen participation in the "war on poverty." We hoped to use the occasion to honor Representative Edith Green who had earlier pressed for the inclusion of women in the Job Corps Training Program. A major press conference was scheduled prior to the meeting. The challenge was to round out the program so that there could be demonstrated an interweaving of our program and the diversity of our constituency. Thus our public relations would authentically reflect our purpose and nature.

Largely through the enthusiastic work of Elsie Jones and

the support of state presidents in the northeast, we reached the goal of having a thousand women present at the Americana Hotel in New York on February 28, 1966. The seating plan called for at least one employed women, one young woman, women from at least two racial backgrounds, and an international woman to be at each of 100 tables. The verse speaking choir from the Women's Job Corps Center in Charleston, West Virginia, gave two selections under Ruth Norman's direction. United Church Women in Tenafly, New Jersey, had arranged hospitality in private homes and planned for a sightseeing trip of the United Nations Building and some other major sights in New York. The presidents of each of the four organizations cooperating to form WICS were at the head table and four young women presented each of them with a radio made by the girls at the Job Corps Center in West Virginia. A professional woman whose hobby was leather work made a portfolio in which was inserted the citation to the Honorable Edith Green. When Dr. Eppie Castro, on behalf of the Asian Church Women's Conference, presented a gift from the Fellowship of the Least Coin to Dr. David Hunter of the NCCC for its program of Christian ministry among farm workers, Dorothy Height, president of the NCNW, mumbled to her neighbor at the head table, "What-do-you-know-about-that?"

Mossie Wyker welcomed to the platform several four year old girls of different racial backgrounds as a salute to the future. Sargent Shriver accented the forward thrust of the government program to alleviate poverty and departed from his manuscript to answer questions which were coming from involved groups such as ours. I closed with a statement of why Christ's women would always be among the poor—listening to and learning from one another.

Martha Kiely flew down from Buffalo to be the "cocked ear" from outside the area as she moved among the 100 tables. She had been invited to be a guest editor of the June issue of *The Church Woman.*

The event had been a success. We had mobilized hundreds of women of diverse backgrounds from our own constituency in three weeks! By demonstrating that each part of program was essential to all others, and our national poverty problem as part of a worldwide one, then both giving and receiving was called for on the part of all involved. We had borne witness to our faith in action before representatives of the press and national government and given new heart to those of our number who were recruiting for the Job Corps through WICS.

We demonstrated how all phases of our program were essential to the one which we were emphasizing. We had shown that American poverty was part of a world problem and demonstrated that there is both giving and receiving on the part of all involved. We had borne witness to our faith in action before representatives of the press and national government and given new heart to those of our number who were recruiting for the Job Corps through WICS.

There is a postscript in a national office after any exhausting and exciting event. A Board member enters to exclaim exuberantly: "SEE, I told you we could do it!" She does not notice the stacks of undone regular work or the prone bodies of the worndown staff! Just because ongoing work for thirty years has established channels, a SPECIAL EVENT can be pulled off in three weeks. A movement is energized by the alternating currents of drama and drudgery.

EXECUTIVE COMMITTEE
MARCH 1966
Inasmuch as the executive committee meeting was coming up within a few weeks, there was plenty of staff work to be done. There is always a solemn feeling about these official meetings. No matter how careful the staff preparation, or competent the committee work, only the elected Board can make the final decisions on behalf of the whole movement. This executive committee was making plans for the Board of Managers meeting to be held October 10-14 in Omaha and the Ecumenical Assembly was called for the following August. Each of these official bodies must act responsibly on certain matters in order that the other, in turn, can act responsibly!

At this meeting the report and evaluation of the *Assignment Race* was presented by the team of social research. A program of *Christian Causeway to Africa* was approved for the summer, a sabbatical for Helen Turnbull to study Orthodox Churches was approved.

Of special interest was the report of a Committee charged to replace the bylaws of the General Department of United Church Women with a set of standing rules in line with other departments in the new Division of Christian Unity of the NCCC.

A set of standing rules was a simple affair for other departments which were governed by small departmental committees of national denominational representatives. UCW with its vast constituency of over 2000 local and state councils of Church Women as well as 23,000 local committees of the World Day of Prayer could hardly be captured in the same framework. Besides it was clear that if we were to emphasize the 'movement' aspect of UCW, local and state units must have a recognizable national identity.

After a number of conferences with the officers of the NCCC, the special committee proposed that two documents were necessary: (1) a set of by-laws describing the nature and function of a national movement, and the responsibilities of a Board of Managers; (2) a separate set of Standing Rules that defined the duties and relationship of a Departmental Committee on Women's Relations within the NCCC. The first would effectively free the constituency to control its own national movement. The second would be submitted to the appropriate committee of the NCCC for approval.

Since the Departmental Committee members would generally be the same as the executive committee of UCW, there would be no conflict of interest. This smaller, more accountable body followed the general organization of the rest of the other departments of the Council. The development of these two documents was referred back to the Committee, which was charged to bring the bylaws to the Board of Managers in October.

The treasurer made a report of income and expenditures for 1965 which, as usual, had a slight balance.[2] She gave an appropriate tribute to the shrewd skill and continual optimism of Dorothy Nossett, Associate Executive Director for Administration.

Mrs. Leroy Walcott (Elnora), the forward looking chairman of the Finance Committee, presented the budget for 1967. The Finance Committee was concerned that some new approach should be made to obtain more income so that UCW would be free to move among a greater variety of women, opening new program areas to involve them.

The executive committee gave its full attention to the financial report. They recognized that it would be necessary to have a greater annual income for the movement to grow. On the other hand more program was needed according to some to stimulate gifts inasmuch as the funds from the Ecumenical Register had been exhausted in 1958. It was a sort of which-comes-first-the-chicken-or-the-egg affair. Being women with experience in such matters they approved a balanced budget based on realizable income. Hope must come to terms with expectation in the day by day operations. Both must be kept alive for a better tomorrow. And tomorrow would begin for UCW only when it dawned on the women themselves.

BOARD OF MANAGERS MEET OCTOBER 1966 Ahead of the business session the Board of Managers sponsored an open luncheon on October 10, 1966 for church women in the surrounding region. Invitations were issued with the hope that each carload would reflect a diversity of age, race and experience. Over 300 women responded from Iowa, northern Kansas, Missouri and, of course, Nebraska—so that the members of the National Board scattered among them could get a feel of the midwest constituency.[3]

Three women whose pioneer courage had inspired earlier boards, challenged all present to undertake continuing responsibility. Mrs. M. E. Tilley (Dorothy) of Atlanta, Georgia, who for fifty years had been a leading activist for human rights in the South and an advocate for children in trouble, reminisced with humor about past struggles and expressed firmly her convictions on issues of the present day. Then Mrs. Harper Sibley, a beloved leader through the years, and president from 1944-1950, placed the responsibility of the new era for this ecumenical movement directly on the shoulders of the women sitting there. "Unless you have the faith to cope with change, get out of this movement," she said, and then she continued with a warning that changes are of different kinds, quoting lines from two old hymns: "It could be 'change and decay all round I see' or it could be 'change from glory into glory'. That depends on what you see and what you do."

Margaret Applegarth had written the dedication service especially for the occasion. It was built on the children's finger play "Here's the church and here's the steeple; open the door and there are the people." Three hundred "open churches" were formed on the tables as we visualized the Church that was humanly speaking in our hands.

DIRECTION 1966   Change became a lively reality through the actions of the Board during the next three days. The statement on Roman Catholics was adopted as Board policy. It was voted to cooperate with other women's organizations in an exploration of the Federal School Lunch program. Ida Patterson, the chairman of a Special Committee on Sex Morality, presented their findings and some analysis of the problem.

In a once-in-a-lifetime hearing, I was given a generous amount of time to present what, in my judgement, were major assumptions which must be taken into account by church women planning together in the next decade.

An open invitation to examine where we are and where we go from here" is sensed in the following excerpts:

Concerning our times:

The 20th century marks a great transition in the history of mankind—drastic changes in family, in government, in education, in ideologies, in religious practices . . .

Technology and science have become an organized social factor . . .

25% of the human beings that ever lived are alive now and their problems are intermeshed across all continents.

The evaluation of our program must be undertaken out of our understanding of God's intention for this period of history.

Concerning the ecumenical movement:

A crisis in many ecumenical organizations has come about due to their preoccupation with operational structures—which often limit participation to officials and those appointed by them. Only as the whole membership of the church shares in ecumenism will there be an upsurge in Christian unity . . .

The program and channels of UCW are ecumenical instruments of the women of the churches as they carry out together their commitments as Christians in the life of the world.

Our age is characterized by the millions of Americans who are living for sustained lengths of time overseas, in business, graduate study, military service, as political refugees, as youth adventurers, as peace-time volunteers. The ecumenical movement can be of real service during a time of international living. A breakthrough to the hearing of the gospel may be found in many areas where the traditional structure remains paralyzed.

Concerning women:

Let us consciously lift up the natural gifts of women—those which are a result of traditional environment, those uniquely possessed by an individual and those God given charismatic gifts which relate one person to another . . .

Increasingly the number of employed women or women who have complex family obligations must be enlisted for a different kind of short term service to the church . . .

Women, who had a traditional role both in maintaining and developing a civilized society, now find themselves with a new question: What does the 20th century transition mean to neighborhoods, schools, families and churches—places where women could readily begin to play a creative part?

How can we assist the individual woman to discover wholeness if she is handicapped by circumstances: the 'woman alone'—single women, divorced women, and widows; the unwed mothers, the breadwinners for families, the older woman, the modern young woman who has sold her freedom too cheaply?

Concerning dimensions of new growth:

We cannot afford to allow our Christian faith in the USA to be expressed in isolation. Let us learn from those in other cultures in developing nations, or those working in different social and political contexts.

We must re-train women for responsible action. Our job is not limited by observing or commenting about the issues of our time. Ours is a task of finding out what lay women will do in the technological revolution. What values will accent our contribution.

We have scarcely begun to understand the devotional practices or the theological meaning of traditions other than our own . . .

We must set up pilot efforts of disciplined Biblical study and move in obedience as instruments of God's grace and mercy in our world.

During any transitional period there is bound to be tension. Many will disagree as to what to do, how we do it, and most critical of all, why we are doing it. We must use these tensions creatively to further establish meaningful goals to which a greater number can subscribe.

We must engage in genuine prayer, prayer that requires forgiving one another before we begin, and, belief in a living God as we continue.

Although these statements might have sounded a bit expansive at the time, during the next nine years the national movement stimulated concrete programs in all of these areas. Not enough. No significant change. Yet, who can tell?

Ruth Rex presented the report of the Committee on new bylaws with the confidence and simplicity of offering a new recipe to a near neighbor.

"We are one national movement," Mrs. Rex said, as she

introduced her report. "There are certain things that are done for the good of all concerned nationally. Other functions can best be done by state units, and much action will only happen if it takes place in particular communities. Every church woman is a part of the movement in all three spheres. These bylaws concern the nature, functions, responsibilities, and organization of the national movement . . . " She led them through each section, pointing out the different aspects which were necessary to assure a flexible movement.

A movement must have a purpose which calls women to form their own concrete objectives and to move together in action. The proposed purpose was:

> . . . to encourage church women to come together in a visible fellowship to witness to their faith in Jesus Christ, and, enabled by the Holy Spirit, to go out together into every neighborhood and nation as instruments of reconciling love.

And who composes the movement? From the article on the nature of the movement we read:

> . . . a national movement, through which Protestant, Orthodox and Roman Catholic women may express the ecumenical dimensions of their faith and work. Units in state and local communities are organized around their own bylaws, it being understood that such bylaws may not conflict with those of the national movement.

> . . . is open to all who are members of churches who confess Jesus Christ as Lord and Savior, and who desire to manifest their unity through fellowship, study, and cooperative action . . .

In determining that the movement should be composed of individual church women rather than organizations, the Board was meeting a number of issues:

> . . . the many women who were not members of church societies.

> . . . the finding of the Survey on Assignment Race, calling for more flexibility in membership in order to

include individuals from racial minorities on their own initiative.

. . . the recognition that Roman Catholic women had a variety of organizations for Christian services.

The power to elect the Board of Managers, and the officers, and the nominating committee of the national movement was given to the Ecumenical Assembly which should, normally, be held every three years.

After answering questions on the various charges, the articles of the bylaws were voted ad seratim. Not wishing to start with a debate on semantics, Mrs. Rex omitted until the end the first recommendation which had to do with the name. In the draft, the Board was to choose a name—either United Church Women or Church Women United. Since the chairman needed to make a definite motion, Mrs. Rex put forward a new name, "I move that the name shall be Church Women United." Almost instantly it was seconded and all discussion was over in a few minutes. The vote on Article I was nearly unanimous.

"When does it begin?" shouted a woman from the floor. Mrs. Sinclair, Mrs. Rex and I all looked at each other. The president asked me to make a ruling. I said, rather tentatively, "This Board voted bylaws including a name. We are already Church Women United!"

The name was appropriate for a flexible movement: Church Women United in Oregon; Church Women United for peace; Church Women United in prayer; Church Women United on our way together!

The national movement was once more autonomous. In the same bylaws, however, the administration was assigned to the Departmental Committee on Women's Relations of the Division of Christian Unity of the NCCC.

ON OUR OWN   So we settled into a comfortable ambi-
dextrous arrangement. With one hand (the
right one, of course) we offered services to
Church Women United and with the other cooperated through the Division of Christian Unity with the NCCC. The fundamental difference was that the constituency of the NCCC was

made up of national denominations and the CWU was a movement open to individual Christian women. The tension between movement and structure is a healthy one as long as each performs its role in recognition of the other. The arrangement might have lasted a long time had it not been for the financial pressures with which both the NCCC and the CWU had to deal.

Early in 1968, Cynthia Wedel resigned as Associate General Secretary and returned with her husband to Washington. She was to be elected a few months later as the President of the NCCC. The officials of the NCCC, realizing they had been absorbing an annual operational deficit from reserve funds, decided to dissolve the Division of Christian Unity and two of its departments which required subsidies from the general funds.

The Department of Women's Relations was related to the NCCC bylaws only as a department in a division that was no longer in existence. This required another study. However before that could take place an unanticipated action in a meeting of the executive committee of CWU changed the course of events.

In September 1969 an enlarged meeting of the executive committee, including denominational leaders, was called to take a fresh look at what was happening to minority women in the midst of the 'crisis within the nation'. Most of the denominations had set up Commissions on Racial Justice with program funds, but these were largely in the hands of black male clergy. CWU's lack of available program money was a handicap to any creative planning and most of the denominational women had the same problem.

The presiding officer, Mrs. James Dolbey, was surprised when out of the blue a motion was made by one of the vice presidents, Mrs. Leo Marsh, to the effect that "the officers of CWU be instructed to confer in the light of what CWU is becoming with officers of the NCCC and report to the Board."

Although none of us, including the maker of the motion, understood the full implications of the action, there was a general feeling that something must be done to put CWU in a position in which we had more flexibility to use our own funds.

The allocated costs for general services in the NCCC, including public relations and personnel, were steadily increasing as were those of business management. CWU's income looked large to other departments but, unlike them, the greater proportion was designated to be given away. There always was a strain to keep our operating budget in hand.

What was clear about the motion was that the officers wished to deal with their peers, the lay officers of the NCCC, and not leave the matter to interstaff negotiation. In this matter they were acting as officers of the the Church Women United (rather than as members of a Departmental Committee) and they drew up a paper of administrative adjustments which would make CWU a more viable operation. When the meeting took place in February 1971, they were disappointed that except for the president, Cynthia Wedel, the others present were from the general secretariat of the NCCC.

Cynthia Wedel presided with fairness, opening with a sympathetic statement in which she pointed out that ever since the beginning the women had the problem of a different kind of operation. She recalled the endless meetings when she had been president of UCW trying to work out an understanding. Dorothy Dolbey read a statement of adjustments which would release money for stimulating relevant programs in crucial areas.

The heads of the two Mission Divisions spoke for accommodating to the request of CWU, for they saw that our participation had values beyond monetary concessions. Although our officers were prepared to compromise on any one of the statements, in the long run the business administration of the NCCC ruled that CWU would have to accept all the obligations and privileges of the NCCC or none of them.

The officers reported through the executive committee to the Board of Managers meeting in St. Louis in March 1970. Following the recommendation of its executive committee, the Board quietly but unanimously voted to handle its own administration and to adjust its bylaws accordingly.

SEPARATE OPERATIONS So in 1971, Church Women United began to mind its own business. In the months that followed agreements were reached on separate operations. CWU continued to rent the same offices and to enroll their employees in the NCCC pension plan.

An outside firm set up the bookkeeping system, appropriate records of the source of income, and the categories of annual expenditures. Dorothy Nosset was able to handle this new system with the staff which she already had. We employed Shireen Subramanya to handle our large printing contracts. By being able to accept competitive bids, the cost of our publications in 1971 was $30,000 less than the previous years. As a small operation we were able to dispense with some services. All in all, CWU was less encumbered going over the economic rapids of the next five years.

Although the immediate reasons for a separate operation were pragmatic in nature, there were deeper values which soon became apparent. Cooperation on special projects in mission, relief and social concern continued but the impact of two visible yet different constituencies was greater. Each organization had an identity and knew for whom they were speaking and what they could deliver. The fact that Church Women United was on its own, able to speak freely, offered a flexibility for sharing fully in the women's decade.

And perhaps more important than the financial relief was the fact that the administrative staff was now free to devote its full energies to the renewal efforts of church women themselves.

It was time to pull ourselves together and be on our way. Ahead were new dimensions in our continuing commitment. Women must be alert to each breakthrough for Christian witness in a fast changing world. We were on a journey toward wholeness in a fragmented world. As participants in the live documentary of a secular world, we must make our mark with signatures of faith.

FOOTNOTES TO CHAPTER 6

1. Early in the 1950's the National Association of Evangelicals began sponsoring a separate World Day of Prayer using the traditional date (first Friday in Lent) set by the National Committee of the World Day of Prayer in 1920. Since a second approach in the local community could be divisive or confusing, the national office of CWU approached the office of the NAE requesting conversations to resolve this problem, but received no answer.

For other reasons, the International Committee of the World Day of Prayer meeting in Sweden in 1968 changed the date to the first Friday in March and designated Church Women United as its only sponsor in the United States. The NAE also changed its advertised observance to the new day. Hence if competitive services in a local community seem to hurt the spiritual significance of women uniting in prayer, the local unit of CWU will need to handle the problems of reconciliation.

With deep appreciation of our heritage of 90 years in praying together across denominational lines for the mission and unity of Church, and in loyal commitment to Christian women in 160 overseas nations who join us on that day each year, Church Women United continues to value the World Day of Prayer as the highpoint in its experience.

2. In 1965 the sources of income for the General Department of United Church Women were as follows:

State Councils	$ 65,381
Denominations	30,787
Individuals & family foundations*	10,000
Fellowship Fund**	49,000
Offerings:	
World Day of Prayer	487,709
World Community Day	134,431

* included annual income from an irrevocable trust set up by Mabel and Venette Sites, of Fort Wayne, Indiana.
** Fellowship Fund came from an annual mail appeal to 42,000 small donors. It was established to replace the residue funds from the Ecumenical Register, which were exhausted in 1958. An evaluation indicated the cost of promotion and processing was out of proportion to amount of income. The Finance Committee substituted a Share-in Plan for small individual donors, and placed it into the hands of local finance committees.

3. The change which each generation brings in leadership roles, was suggested by the young women who introduced the speakers. Coretta Scott King introduced Mrs. Tilley, and Kayo Takeda Cho, a graduate student at Yale, introduced Mrs. Harper Sibley. Later Dr. Cho became one of the presidents of the World Council of Churches.

Section 3: Kar

ouches Rand

JUST BECAUSE

Jesus Christ is alive

and at work in the midst

of kaleidoscopic change

heart responds to heart and . . . . . . **HAND TOUCHES HAND**

A CATHEDRAL
to the glory of
Jesus Christ our Lord
is being built each moment
    as
Hand touches hand

We **long for . . . listen to . . . lift up**
and **love one** another
    so that
All in each place
May **offer others gifts God has given us:**
Integrity in relationships
Joy and Peace in faithfulness
Strength to do **more than we ask or imagine**
through
    The Church

Who has not awakened in the night with the clanging of an inner alarm? Some major decision has been made; one's future is determined, yet there is not the foggiest clue to the next step.

One dark night in December 1965, I had such an experience. Formalities had been finished with my new employer (Church Women United); farewells had been said to my former colleagues; what would there be in the path ahead?

I became acutely aware of the framed print on my bedroom wall faintly illumined by the ground lights outside the apartment. It was a photograph copy of Rodin's sculptured piece entitled, "The Cathedral". Two slender hands, seemingly feminine, emerge from the common base of humanity, arch gracefully each in its own sphere, and gently touch each other. They are intertwined yet free; as the fingers touch, they form a "Cathedral spire," lifting its praise to God.

What would be the shape of a "spiritual" Cathedral built by the hands of women touching each other in very human ways? What would be the nature of the theology which was spoken to and by women as heart responds to heart? Would our testimony be from a pulpit high above our listeners, or like the Eastern Orthodox, would the chief symbol of the Cathedral be the floor where all stood on the same level before God? Who would form the "priesthood of all believers"—listening, learning, loving and walking humbly before their God?

Would the symbol of leadership be the gavel—or the courteous word and cocked ear? Would the congregation be a great diversity of people who belonged to each other just because of what God had done for each of them?

Like the Hussites in Bohemia a thousand years before the Protestant Reformation, would the Cathedral be built in the market place—enclosing the well so that the poor might get their water as they received inspiration from the scripture on the walls or heard its proclamation from the pulpit? Surely the Word and the Well belonged as a symbol of God's grace, and every day should be the "Lord's Day" to offer thanksgiving in worship and in service.

All of these were ponderings of my heart in the middle of

that night. I turned on the light, sat up in bed and wrote these lines:

A CATHEDRAL
to the glory of
Jesus Christ our Lord
is being built each moment
　　　as
Hand touches hand
In very human ways
　　　and as
Heart responds to heart
We long for . . . listen to . . . lift up
and love one another
　　　so that
All in each place
May offer others gifts God has given us:
Integrity in relationships
Joy and peace in faithfulness
Strength to do more than we ask or imagine
through
　　　The Church

We now had a poetic image to dream into reality. The overall conception—a Cathedral—was only a graphic way of saying that the ultimate building of Christ's Church on earth did not begin with us nor would it end with us. We were among those artisans from all time and from many places who were adding earthly substance to its divine design.

The times were described by others as the most rapidly changing historic period of any since prehistoric man caused fire to come from flint. Even in 1966 we could see what this meant in human terms. The following message was sent to the president of every local unit along with an interpretation of Rodin's *Cathedral*

God has showered women with many gifts . . .
These gifts were given to us in order to give away.
In this complex world of specialists, where
the gulf between persons grows wider each year, let us
become a nation of neighbors.

Among lonely and bitter hearts, let us be hospitable members of the household of God, offering healing and reconciliation.

In the struggle of race and class, of nation against nation, let us so relate to all human beings all over the world that we may find new energy to bear one another's burdens and new excitement in responding to a Christian's highest calling.

chapter 7

**The movement itself—
longing, listening, lifting, loving**

Since the 1966 bylaws provided a framework within which we could work, we were ready to trust Church Women United to church women! The movement would grow as "hand touched hand"; it would have meaning as "heart responded to heart". By the inspiration of the spirit, women would be able to love, to listen to, to long for, and to lift up one another. Their voices would raise songs of thanksgiving in a Cathedral of God's own making. They would walk along the paths of many countries and down the streets of many cities sharing gifts they, too, had received—joy, peace, integrity, and strength for the living of these days.

The national office could not do this for them. At most, it could provide instruments which would give their individual notes a national rhythm. Eventually a simple pattern of organization for Church Women United in the community must be determined, but first we must find out what church women wanted to do together and what signposts would offer direction on our way.

An Ecumenical Assembly called for July 13-16, 1967, would provide some days for national agreement. So it was proposed that we have an *assembly line* on which every church woman could voluntarily work in appropriate time shifts toward the goals and program projects which could be done best by united action.

The *assembly line* began with *Explore Units* of four to eight women (self-starting and self-stopping at the end of their work). Each *Explore Unit* agreed to work on one assignment and report its conclusions on program proposals. A layout of suggestions for each of the following areas was available from the national office: Christian faith in the contemporary scene; living in a pluralistic society; problems of urbanization; women in today's world; potentials of new leisure; human values under present pressures; recognizing and releasing gifts in individuals; helps and hindrances to a peaceful world. Nearly 30,000 women shared in the *Explore Units.*

Meeting during the same period were five consultative groups of professional women with special experience in five subjects which needed an analysis of issues and resources. In all, about seventy-five professional women worked with us in these consultations without honoraria and in some cases taking leave of absence from their work. Each of the consultations proved to be a new dimension for the staff members assigned to it, not only to share in the thinking of the participants but also to share their enthusiasm in being of some service to the Church. As one whose training was in special education remarked, "You'd think my local parish would ask me for some help with the young people. . .but no, I've only been asked to bring a batch of cookies to a reception!"

Dr. Barbara Ward, who was part of the Consultation on Mobilization for Peace, was eager to bring about citizen pressure for 1% of national income for social and economic development. She thought it important that every woman know enough economics to be able to talk with the local banker and editor. Before the end of the meeting, she offered to write a primer for us. It turned out to be a book, *The Lopsided World.* It was a little above the primary level but then so are church women! Not only did these professional women contribute to the quality of our program development, but they also gave us new confidence in our own constituency, sometimes being more impressed with our potential than we were ourselves.

NEW DIMENSIONS As the time of the Assembly approached, the new president created a Commission on New Dimensions from those women who were in nomination to become national officers plus one person from each of the national Listening Teams. Their task was to review the work of the *assembly line* and to classify program suggestions under several categories for the selection and use of CWU in local communities.

In addition, the Commission outlined proposals for new program ventures to be undertaken by the national movement when financial resources were available. The Commission worked for two days in May formulating their report. When they had finished their outline, one of the incoming officers queried, "Just what's new about these new dimensions?"

It was a natural question for in general terms they spoke of familiar human ills. Yet those who wrestle with the record of many conversations always feel the result has a new quality. The Commission carefully safeguarded its report with this introduction:

To YOU—a personal word—

In the past few months you have heard 'New Dimensions' many times, and so you have come to this Assembly with a sense of eager anticipation—perhaps longing for something new.

Yet, strangely, this report is not new—for it has come out of *your* experience and *your* concerns as you have shared them in the many explore units and listening teams. In fact, many of the sentences are yours—without quotes!

The new is *You* . . . . .
in responsible discipline, encounter and action!

Most of the Commission was present for the Assembly, and various members presented selected parts of their long report which was in the hands of those present. In unison, however, the Commission read aloud this section:

We are new human beings through Christ. We listen with new ears and are led to find in our midst: ↳

. . . a *new awareness of who we are* and what we must do as church women

. . . a new way of *looking* at all our *activities in the light of today's world*

. . . a new *choice* of plans *for action* so that those in each community may discern their most pressing needs

. . . a new *diversity in the company* with whom we will be doing our work

. . . a new *emphasis on wholeness* as persons; as a fellowship of Christians; as citizens of an inter-related world

. . . a new excitement when the *gifts of many different* kinds of *women* are discovered

. . . a new *challenge for women* to qualify themselves for significant tasks in helping form human values and human relations in a technological age

. . . a new *spirit* as Orthodox, Roman Catholic, and Protestant women walk together *the ecumenical way*

NATIONAL GOALS The selection of goals is an interesting process when a group of twenty women handling reams of papers identify the aspirations which women have expressed. You can be sure that much is determined by the 'sieve' with which each strains the many words to extract her own formula! It was my custom to bring to any meeting an empty hand and I left with no more than five propositions—one for each finger! This meeting was no exception. There emerged five goals beginning with the pointer finger and concluding with a goal on the thumb which could touch each of the other goals encircling each into a whole. Each goal starts with an action verb:

Venture in new forms of Christian witness

Accept responsibility for justice and peace

Seek creative and healing encounters in the midst of the human community.

Release the full potential in every person

Develop maturity in faith and discipline in commitment.

VISIBLE FELLOWSHIP The purpose of Church Women United is to encourage church women to come together in a visible fellowship to witness to their faith in Jesus Christ and, enabled by the Holy Spirit, to go out together into every neighborhood and nation as instruments of reconciling love.

Therefore the New Dimensions report opened with a section on the visible fellowship:

When church women come together in a visible fellowship, we celebrate the presence of the living Lord, the Revealer of God's reconciling intention. We also find together new direction as to the ways God will use us to carry out His purpose.

Thus the three national observances, World Day of Prayer, May Fellowship Day and World Community Day, were continuing commitments and came to be known as celebrations.

The Consultative Group on Spiritual Renewal, of which Dr. Beverly Wilding Harrison of Union Theological Seminary was the coordinator, recommended that Church Women United should develop a pattern that encouraged small groups of women to come together regularly over a period of eight to twelve weeks in spiritual support of one another.

It was more than a coincidence that about this time a letter came from Charlotte Browne-Mayers, an executive in the Standard Oil Company of New Jersey, with this encouraging word:

One of the things that has stimulated me most in recent times is the vision, which I think you have, of the United Church Women as a movement influencing the quality of life in our society. The whole world seems in revolution and, as we know, there is revolution in our environment, our neighbors, and our family life.

The quality—pervasive, charismatic, and catalytic—of the "revolutionary ranks" is perhaps the special task for Church Women United. A revolution is needed that carefully cultivates new life and better growth not just in patches of society but for all the grass roots.

I responded by inviting her to a luncheon conference to ask what concrete proposals would enable us to influence the quality of life. The suggestion coming from this business executive sounded new, even though it was one which had always been possible: renewal coming from small groups of Bible study and prayer. A movement of our nature should respond to the yearning for relationships with Christian women with diverse backgrounds. We spoke about finding a name which would serve as a trademark and came up with "The Well." Charlotte commented, "Water from a well is no longer a commonplace experience in urbanized America, but it is not beyond the imagination of most of us, and the need for clean water is universal."

The New Dimensions report took time to describe this proposal:

In the pressure of today's urbanized society, it is essential for us to find renewal in informal groups discovering a new style of study in scripture and relating our faith to everyday life.

We can see a business woman in the heart of a large city opening her apartment for a breakfast fellowship; an apartment dweller discovering her associates in the laundromat, and agreeing to meet several evenings together; an unused parlor in a large house in a small town being set aside as neutral ground.

This experience will be reminiscent of the Samaritan woman who went out of the city and found a Jew at the well. Each expressed a need the other could meet. Here honesty and depth in conversation found ready acceptance. Here Jesus pointed out that true worship was distinguished not by locality or tradition but by Spirit and Truth. Here a woman was able to know a new life through Jesus Christ, and gladly went back *into* the city to proclaim it. These experiences may become known to us as *Wells,* where openness and differences and spiritual renewal and patterns of obedience form a natural place to be together.

So invite another to 'Come and join us at the well.' Remember that part of God's work is to make friends out of strangers. Expect great things from honest persons who seek to share these experiences—even if they are not among the established women in the church.

Other programs were proposed where the claim of Christian kinship could become more visible: *Christian Causeways, Fellowship of the Least Coin; Dialogues of Discovery,* and a plan of *Hallowed Hospitality* where families included the stranger within their circle of love.

RESPONSIBLE   Since our purpose included going out
CHRISTIAN ACTION   together into every neighborhood and
                         nation as instruments of God's reconciling love, it was appropriate that the New Dimensions committee should outline inter-related programs under the general headings of Peace Building, Community Services, Metropolitan Ministries and Women's Rights. This section of the report was entitled "Responsible Christian Action."

Although the specifics of these programs varied from year to year and from community to community, the general framework did not change during the next ten years. Each subsequent Assembly reaffirmed the goals and outlined the specific intentions for the triennium.

The report on New Dimensions contained a third section calling for initiatives in the national office in the areas of "new vocation of women," theological training, sex values, specialized ministries among women living alone (single or divorced women), a wider program for the international community living in the United States and the American communities living overseas. However, such initiatives were dependent upon the vote of subsequent national boards and of available funds. Income did increase somewhat during the next nine years.[1] However, so did inflationary costs. Hence, except for those programs financed by foundations or Intercontinental Mission funds, the national program initiatives were limited.

PATTERNS OF CWU UNITS   All effective movements have appropriate organization although not all organizations move![2] Church Women United is organized according to separate bylaws in the local community or county, in state or other regional boundaries by an executive board, and on the national level by a Board of Managers. These three spheres of action do not form a hierarchy since each has distinctive functions and is free to initiate ways to carry out its own responsibilities. The term 'unit' was adopted to define a local or state or regional area operating under its own bylaws which must be in harmony with the national purpose. Thus one national movement is composed of many 'units'.

The recommended bylaws for a state unit made provision, then, for functions which neither the national or local units could appropriately do but which needed to be done for the sake of the whole movement, namely: 1) nurture of local units; 2) cooperation with state denominational programs; 3) financial support of CWU beyond the local unit; 4) advice as to state and national legislative issues; 5) resources and training for current programs; 6) provision for state assembly or regional institutes for leadership training; 7) communication through newsletters or regional media.

It was relatively simple to come to an agreement on patterns of state and national bylaws inasmuch as all the representatives of concern units were present at a meeting of the Board of Managers in October 1933. It was quite another challenge to discover a pattern of operation to recommend to local units of CWU—one which would express the purpose and nature of the national movement.

How could participation be enlarged to include all church women of every race and Christian tradition—whether or not they were active in church women's organizations? How could planning take into account new women in the community, new interests of younger women, new involvement of employed women? What new life style on the part of CWU was called for in order to give a greater variety of women a quick access to central decision making and personal involvement in special action projects?

A survey called "Looking Past the Present" sent to every local president brought answers from only about 300 women and their grievances were understandably more clear than their recommendations. In preparation for the 1967 Assembly, Mrs. Sinclair appointed a committee of local presidents representing different sizes of communities and different states.

The meeting was convened by Ada Black (Mrs. H.H.) who was then the president of the unit in Buffalo, NY. As each of the 7 women introduced herself by modestly describing the situation in her unit, an unpromising atmosphere settled on the gathered. What committee could presume to advise 2000 different units each in their own peculiar circumstance? Then Edna Sinclair, whose spirit always conquered gloom, described the possibilities of a national movement calling forth the gifts of Christ's women in the place where they lived. Ada Black quickly added her affirmative experience with some evening forums and open board meetings in Buffalo. Norma Docket, who had come from Iowa to represent the small rural unit, was positive in finding the way different patterns could be adapted to situations like hers. They were all agreed. Nobody should be expected to "go it on her own" in CWU.

All were agreed that planning groups around the essentials for survival and growth of local units would assure a more ecumenical approach as well as more satisfying results. The four areas needing constant working goals were: 1) CELEBRATIONS—the visible national fellowship of worship on the three traditional observances; 1) ENABLING SERVICES for maintenance of unit: stronger finance, discerning nominations, effective public relations; 3) GROWTH OR DEVELOPMENT of CWU to include a greater diversity of women and to enlarge relationships with other organizations with similar goals; 4) ACTION both in community service and in advocacy for justice as citizens. It was readily agreed that depending on available resources and local situations, the choice of projects and procedures should be decided by those involved in each place. Forums open to all church women further enlarged the circle of consultation.

The end result was a creative plan of operation which in itself was a true expression of the spirit of the national movement. No one would ever be lonely in leadership who accepted a place in this imaginative scheme. I remember walking out of the meeting as if buoyed up on the mythical cloud Nine and saying to the staff: "If there is a renewal among the grassroots it will be due not primarily to the Commission on New Dimensions but to the Committee on Local Structure. Hope is greater than history." I know some bulbs bloom early; some later!

On behalf of the committee, Mrs. Black presented the report to the 1967 Assembly. Her realistic approach to local units was clear in her introduction and her natural optimism in the recommendations was convincing. She began:

> In each place, church women work together in a way that is appropriate for the size and scope of the undertaking. Many local communities are only involved at present in the three national observances which can be deeper experiences if carried out in the spirit of our new goals. The purposes which we highlight in these observances will open doors for other services and thus a minimum organizational structure will unfold as needed. This report is not made as a mandate, but it is hoped that its general design is simple and flexible enough to be helpful for any local unit of Church Women United.
>
> The pattern we propose is in itself a part of our fellowship, for it is composed of a series of groups which plan and pray together. Such words as *listening teams, planning groups, task forces, executive committees, forums,* are only descriptions of groups of women gathered around a specific function.

At the Assembly opportunity to clarify the plan in small groups was given ample time and the report was unanimously received. Back home, it was not so simple to transmit the *why* and *how* of change. Some local units merely changed names of the old committees and thus complicated rather than simplified the structure. However, many found in the new style the excitement of finding colleagues and developing understandings which allowed for flexible movement. As hand touched hand in very human ways, the leadership learned the disciplines of longing, listening, lifting, and loving (not always in that order!).

ON-BOOK   Both the local pattern of organization and the program proposals of the new dimensions were described in a brochure called, "On Our Way Together." The *On-Book,* as it was called, had a colorful red and yellow cover and was loaded with cartoons to illustrate how human and how different were the women who were united through this movement. In one state university it was used in a sociology class as a pattern of community mobilization. In two years, 20,000 copies had become the property of those who cared enough to join women from other churches and be on the way together. In 1971 a revised *On-Book* was published to update the program.

FINANCIAL   The growth of CWU depended on a more
GROWTH PLANS   adequate financial base. Each state had
                   developed its own process of encouraging
contributions from local units. In 1970 the finance committee made an attempt to develop a more uniform system and to recommend that materials be prepared which would assist local women to understand the needs of the state and national program and to urge that they solicit local contributions from individuals through an annual appeal to SHARE IN the work of Church Women United. If a local unit grew in strength and participation, it would take a more responsible share of the state and national budgets. It envisioned that the executive committee in each local would look ahead and set its own goal. At the end of three years there were about 800 local units who were willing to project a goal in faith. This growth in responsible financing also helped the state and national movements to adjust more accurately their program to an expected income.

FUND FOR   In 1971 a Fund for the Future was officially
THE FUTURE launched with Dorothy Dolbey its first chairman.
                Its purpose was to seek major gifts from indivi-

duals and family foundations to meet anticipated opportunity or any annual dip in income. Special stationery with the purpose of this fund in the acrostic LOVE indicated that more money would mean CWU would have more

Long range planning
Operating funds
Ventures in Christian witness
Endowments to assure the future.

During the two years in which Hilda Dail was the development director, she carried out a successful training program for 50 women in the western states. She prepared kits of material for volunteers to use as they approached their peers for contributions. The Finance Committee placed in the Fund for the Future all money that could not be anticipated when the annual budget was projected: bequests from wills or trust funds, memorials or living tributes for outstanding service. The interest earned was added to the annual income. Thus the Love Gifts from individuals could add strength to CWU every year forever!

PRIORITY PLAN 1971   In 1971 an Ecumenical Assembly in Wichita, Kansas, voted the priority of the new triennium to be "the expansion and deepening of Church Women United as a national movement which finds expression in a local community." Basic to a dynamic movement is the comprehension of our faith as Christians and of ourselves as women.

One of the vice presidents, Margaret Sonnenday, assumed the responsibility of developing the priority program. A planbook was issued in which the goals of 1967 were reaffirmed and specific intentions relevant to their times were outlined under each. A practical check list was created to assist local units in determining their own profile and in defining those areas to which they must give attention if they were to grow in fellowship and in program.

The major program funds available in 1972 and 1973 were used in providing tools to increase the skills necessary for growth in the movement. The first was how to listen and how to respond. A teaching record was devised with professional advice. The record was adapted to the language and program of CWU by volunteers in California. An interesting future reference was that Martha Edens was among the 'volunteer critics'. Together with a manual, the recording was sent to every local unit. The Listen-Respond device also collected data from many women and was sent to the state "Listening Group." At its meeting in Phoenix in the spring of 1973, the Board of Managers received from state presidents a summary of the topics touched in response to this vehicle of communication.

In 1973 a series of workshops designed to increase competence in action skills was called *Response-Ability* (responding to a need with ability). After conference with state presidents, a coordinator was selected to develop each of 30 workshops. All coordinators came to Oklahoma City to assist in designing the workshops under the professional leadership of Nancy Geyer.

Using the current program, the design included several techniques which could be transferred to other subject matter in later years. For instance, the women learned how to interview and summarize findings by practicing on a 'teacher' and a 'pupil' in order to discover their awareness of education for global living in elementary schools. Around case studies there was purposeful discussion about health delivery services. In order to learn about the revenue sharing plan, the group used a simulation game which had a package of records with appropriate sound effects. Worship and get acquainted periods were analyzed after the event. In some cases, worship created by the participants themselves around the experience of the workshops was used in dedicating their learning.

Elizabeth Gripe, as staff director of cultivation, acted as trouble shooter. A member of the staff was assigned to assist each of the program coordinators. It was my privilege to share in five workshops, two of them for women in the far West, one for those in the Dakotas, and two for women in the middle West. After sharing in all the office turmoil in developing this kind of program, it was a great satisfaction to be among the women and see the great variety of leadership skills available in our midst. Clarie Harvey's advice was right, "When your heart is troubled, get out among the people."

ADMINISTRATIVE ADJUSTMENTS Fortunately the national staff was enthusiastic about the renewal of the movement and saw that there was no place for rigid departments which channeled materials to their counterparts. To establish the rhythm of the movement so that local, state and national officers carried initiatives in their own sphere, the staff became generalists and some changed roles with the emphases of the triennium. We saw CWU's primacy to be of women not subject matter—hence our staff assignments had to do with the role a woman was carrying in CWU at the time. Some women were carrying volunteer administrative roles as presidents and as treasurers. A staff member was asked to provide the necessary services for them. Some were volunteers in community services, others being citizen advocates; some were participants in an international community. So it was that our staff work provided the tools for church women to maintain relationships which would make women more effective.

The issues might vary from one year to another or from one community to another, but the skills and learning were easily adapted. Our staff also perceived the import of both local and global aspects of the problem. As citizens, women should be as interested in action to eliminate discrimination in a community swimming pool as in changing economic and governmental policies in South Africa.

When a woman heading a training program for midwifery in Nigeria arrived, it was a great satisfaction to me to introduce her to Alice Leppert and know that within 10 minutes she would have a handful of helpful material and addresses and an introduction by phone to the finest resources in the country for her to follow through her own research.

INTERCONTINENTAL MISSION Intercontinental Mission is the CWU program of greatest dimension: its roots have been productive from the very beginning of united work; its scope in concerns and geographical terms as well as its budget is larger than all other programs combined; it receives support from our whole constituency. By Intercontinental Mission we mean that part of our total Christian witness which is carried out through other recognized agencies or one of our peer groups of women in other countries. We are able to stretch our strength through those who are close to the places of great need, who speak languages we do not know and who have human resources and skills which are not available to us.

Along with other aspects of our administration previously carried by the NCCC, in 1967, CWU became responsible for the collection and distribution of its mission monies. As an auditing firm set up our books, it was proposed that all programs, regardless of size be in clear categories in one unified budget. This made it possible to check on accountability and to save considerably on overhead expense of bookkeeping and audits. We also were able to assure our grants to other ongoing programs without their being penalized in a year when a snowstorm might decrease the offering. It removed the tension when some programs administered by CWU staff were similar in nature to those which we were funding more generously through other agencies. It also gave all participants in our financial growth, individual donors, states and others, a sense that they were sharing in the total task for which CWU had come into being.[4]

Nevertheless, the stewardship of nearly six million dollars over the course of the decade merited the special attention of an Intercontinental Mission Committee whose members carefully scrutinized all aspects of requests and received evaluations from these program grants before making their annual recommendations to the larger Board of Managers. Having shared in the deliberations of this committee, I can testify how prayerfully its total inter-racial membership weighed even the smallest grant with compassion and competence.

Under the leadership of persons with the spirit of Bessie Marsh and Olive Tiller, both givers and receivers became stewards of God's loving kindness.

ECUMENICAL ASSEMBLIES
1967 - 1971 - 1974
When church women from all over the nation meet together to consider their commitment to be reconciling agents in the world, they are a visible fellowship. Like other parts of the movement, an Assembly is open to Protestant, Orthodox and Roman Catholic women who wish to identify with its purpose. Although they were members of churches, the participants were not delegates of them. Often the financial arrangements were shared by state and local units, yet the individual did not speak for the unit. The Assembly was another form of mobilization as "hand touches hand" to form a national movement.

We began to call the national meeting an Ecumenical Assembly sponsored by Church Women United in order to make clear that all Christian women were welcome to participate freely - including Roman Catholics and those whose church membership was in overseas churches. Since each Ecumenical Assembly highlighted the encounter of church women with their times, we will review all three of these Assemblies as a preface to other chapters which describe how our purpose was carried out by our program.

1967 ASSEMBLY
LAFAYETTE, INDIANA
There was an infectious spirit of expectancy that something new was about to happen among the 1750 women who gathered in Ecumenical Assembly at Purdue University in West Lafayette, Indiana, in July 1967. Yet the purpose in coming there was our affirmation of a continuing commitment of Church Women United. As a bus bound homeward pulled away from Purdue on July 16, one woman was heard saying, "I'm going home to wash dishes, but it's a new woman that's going to be washing them!"

Just as most of the women had shared in forming the program of New Dimensions, they were involved fully in every phase of the Assembly itself.

In the opening night play, "No Longer at Ease," some identified with a church woman who did not want to face "people with needs I don't understand, with problems I don't want to know about, and whom I can't help." Hers were the questions put to Sister Ida Gannon, President of Mundelin College, and Dr. Esther Swenson of Maryville College, as they carried on "dialogues with the Bible" each morning.

"New Dimensions for Modern Women" were explored with Dr. Mary Calderone and Violette Linbeck. Many were already living in the situation conditioned by "Our Urban World" interpreted Calvin S. Hamilton, the city planner from that great metropolitan area in southern California, and Benjamin Payton, President of Benedict College.

There was keen interest in the "rap" session among four teenagers discussing how it felt to be a part of a "New Generation in a World without Precedent." Malcolm Boyd listened to their discussion from a hospital bed in Washington and commented on their remarks over piped-in telephone facilities.

Then, as an experienced TV moderator, Esther Stracher, interviewed twelve women from every continent who sat at the peace table—the whole Assembly realized peace was not a quiet time, but a dynamic time when things happen, when justice must be established, when truth must be told by the media, when freedom is felt by the common people. If opposing forces to justice, truth and freedom were considered a 'wartime seige,' it explains the 'battle fatigue' which beset many God-fearing persons in the decade coming.

From the opening "Hallelujah Chorus," sung in the midst of film clips of our contemporary life, to the closing commitment service when seven women presented the program on New Dimensions, the Assembly radiated a sense of dedication, and demonstrated willingness to face realities. Inwardly many of us accepted as a continuing commitment, a life of discipline and prayer, led by a woman kneeling at the foot of a large wooden cross, Dorothy Dolbey, the newly elected president of Church Women United.

1971 ASSEMBLY
WICHITA, KANSAS
By 1970 almost all Americans were aware that they were in the midst of a technological revolution which was rapidly changing relationships among human beings. In everyday life the computer and the labor saving devices seemingly offering

freedom, yet at the same time enslaved us in new systems. The projections of a 'post-civilized' era by the year 2001 were both thrilling and threatening as we looked to the future.

The national Board of Managers issued the following Call to the Ecumenical Assembly:

> • *explore the implications of the extraordinary claim that God in Christ made a radical breakthrough into history; and*
>
> • *discover what this faith compels us to do in the midst of the radical breakthroughs in technology and social patterns.*

On the evening of April 22, 1971, in the Concert Hall of Century II in Wichita, Kansas, there gathered 2,100 church women from all fifty states and from fifty-two other countries. The president, Dorothy Dolbey, convened the Assembly with these words:

> Let us enter into these days—sometimes in periods of silence and sometimes in periods of much talking; sometimes in tension, sometimes in celebration.
>
> Let us see that God is working his purposes out and that we belong to each other because of what God has done for each of us.
>
> Let us rejoice in every breakthrough of God's power among us. Together let us claim victory and together give God the glory.

The Assembly opened with a celebration of God's breakthrough into history. The environment of shapes and color was made with unique wire sculptures by a creative team from Cincinnati. To the background music and the sound of a woman's voice reading from the Biblical stories of the Creation, the Covenant, the Passover and Exodus, the Incarnation, Crucifixion and Resurrection, and finally the Pentecost. Members of the American Baroque Theater interpreted the Scripture through dance designed by their leader and choreographer, Irmgard Altvater.

During the week small groups of women gathered to grapple with the theological insights of our purpose stimulated by a theological team of two women and two men whose discussions were brought into each room through the facilities of KPTS, an educational TV station. On one evening a multi-media presentation and a conversation among four persons of different scientific backgrounds who formed the "Think Tank" exposed the shape of the future.

But women also faced their task as loving human beings and responsible citizens in the midst of the fast-moving age. At an Agape breakfast, the words and music of Sister Teresita Weind spoke of the ways of mercy and justice in today's world. The requirements of taking seriously the need for social development among the peoples of every continent were presented. The Assembly accepted *Calls To Citizen Action*— to share in the shaping of new social structures; to open opportunities for women in transition; and to engage in peace building.

From a balcony outside the convention hall hung a huge banner for all to see with the words, BLESSED ARE THE PEACEMAKERS. As 2,000 women stood below in silent prayer, the voices of women called from the balcony, "Blessed are the peacemakers" in nine languages, including Vietnamese. Our national president read the statement of the Board of Managers calling for the cessation of the Indo-China War. At the conclusion, as we sang, "God grant your people peace," a butterfly flew across the full length of the banner. This happy surprise caused a ripple of excitement for the butterfly, an early symbol of the resurrection, was used by the Assembly to represent breakthrough of new life.

The implication that we might be living through periods of anarchy as the old patterns were left behind called for a serious look at the role of Christians in the next thirty years. Often a parallel was drawn to the wandering of the tribes of Israel in the wilderness on their way to their Promised Land.

In the book of Leviticus we learn of the naming of Aaron as priest and the ceremony which dedicated his ministry:

> Moses took the blood of a lamb and put it on the tip of Aaron's right ear, and on the tip of the thumb of his right hand and on the big toe of his right foot.

As the mime acted out this same ceremony in the conclusion of the worship service, we recognized that, far from running in escape, our calling was to be priests in every neighborhood. We must live in the midst of the people who are confused and grumbling with disillusionment. We must dedicate our ears to listen to what they are saying, our hands to the creative and courageous work that is ahead, and set our feet to walk in the direction of God's will for our time.

1974 ASSEMBLY   "A Journey toward Wholeness" was the
IN MEMPHIS   theme which called church women from
                      across the nation to the Memphis Assembly.
There were some who had been on this journey from the beginning of their lives; others were caught up with the more seasoned travelers as they responded to the interviews of the Committee of 74 who had conducted a significant test of the aspirations and fears of church women ahead of the meeting; others began the journey in small groups around the preparatory booklet, "One in Spirit," where they shared their yearnings for a fresh vision of what Jesus called 'living life to the full'.

Those who had held some state or local office were vaguely aware that the word 'whole' had been used in relation to program development since 1966—a word akin to holiness, to health; a word implying integrity, oneness, interrelatedness. But wherever each woman was on her journey toward wholeness, she knew she could not make the journey alone.

So in bright October, Christ's women from all directions of the compass gathered at the Cook Convention Hall in Memphis on the banks of the Mississippi to experience together four special days on their journey toward wholeness.

Extra Special Places were set up for people to find each other as they browsed over books or exhibits or shared creative skills. We discovered all kinds of hidden resources among ourselves as they talked together in the mini-communities.

There were a lot of "extra special" people at this Assembly. More than one third of the registered participants were from American minorities. Several hundred employed women arrived for the weekend. The international participants were all vocal, since social change in their own countries was so greatly involved in the Assembly theme.

"This is the most authentic audience I have ever seen," said a nationally known speaker to Dorothy Barnard, program coordinator. Those who spoke from the platform were genuine originals—every one of them speaking from deep personal experience and caring a great deal about those who "had ears to hear" them.

On the opening night, the Assembly turned first to worship God, where wholeness begins. A call to "Become Perfectly One" came to the Assembly from three members of the Women's Ecumenical Prayer Fellowship of Egypt who had prepared the 1975 World Day of Prayer service on that theme.

"Our Heritage—The Gathering and Scattering of Light," was the title of the subsequent portion of the program. Norma Levitt, immediate past president of the National Federation of Temple Sisterhoods, and Archbishop Iakovos, of the Greek Orthodox Church in North and South America, offered fresh interpretation of our heritage. In many ways our faith came from the story of many journeys—the diaspora of the Jewish and Christian peoples. The circumstances were often tragic—enforced exile as slaves or persecution in ghettos. Yet, in every migration the lantern of their faith was carried, scattering its rays and gathering them up in circles of light.

Norma Levitt had written a beautiful prose poem to share her experience of Judaism, the roots of which are conserved in Jewish holidays but the meaning of which is part of God's revelation to all His people. She spoke of our partnership with God in continuing creation, of the meaning of the Sabbath and the promise of the rainbow; of the revelation of One God and One Humanity; of the Passover and Sinai experiences as people were gathered into community; of the redemption of the world around the strong concept of justice, and of the affirmation of life and hope in the greatest of Jewish holidays, Yom Kippur, the Day of Atonement.

Archbishop Iakovos interpreted the distinctive heritage gained from the early Christian believers: the incarnation of God in the likeness of man—our Christmas celebration; the experience of the church as co-workers with God in the continuing processes of renewal; the resurrection power in discovering truth, freedom, and salvation; the community of mankind as the Spirit gathers together the people of God in unity.

As they finished, the lights began to stretch across the stage as a lyric voice sang these words from Ephesians:

One is the Body, one is the Spirit,
One is the hope to which we are called;
One is the Lord, one is the faith,
One is the God who lives and works in all.

The voice was that of Sister Jane Marie Richardson, who had come from her life as a contemporary recluse in a tiny hermitage in Loretto, Kentucky, to sing the Scriptures which beautified the service. She had made her own translations and set them to music.

The service climaxed with testimony to the presence of God in the trying circumstances of today's world. Christians now form a global diaspora. On every continent there is racial tension, great disparity between the rich and the poor, the repression of human dignity, and the personal crises of grave illness. As the Assembly listened to the voices from Brazil, Korea, South Africa, and the United States, they rejoiced that the light of life cannot be quenched by darkness. The voice of Sister Jane Marie caught up the refrain in each believer's heart: "Far beyond dream is the love of the Lord."

A kind of spiritual tourist's disease had previously attacked most of those who were making the journey together in Memphis. It was an inevitable result of jet-age living— overstimulation and overeating. This spiritual malaise had taken hold of each of us differently. If we were to get back on the main thoroughfare together, it would take some fairly bold guideposts.

Spiritual Signposts were the highlight of the Assembly. Mary Louise Rowand was persuasive and forceful as she outlined the Biblical perspectives for becoming a whole person.

On another morning, Dr. Isabel Wood Rogers, with a down-to-earth approach to a difficult-to-understand problem, developed from the prophets and the teachings of Jesus, God's design as we move toward a just global society. And

God's judgment was just as clear: "Whenever walls begin to be built on top of the natural lines among people, divine intervention is necessary to break down the walls."

The Assembly listened to the realities expressed in lives of women when the vacuums were created by the circumstances of extreme poverty (Irma Mazelis), and social ostracization as was true of the woman offender (Euphesenia Dean), as well as scarcity of faith, presented by a panel of participants. One evening was spent in considering the crucial needs of children, many of whom enter adulthood with crippled personalities.

As background for the day on which the Assembly considered the claims of the global family on Church Women United, a panel of women from poverty pockets in the United States and overseas emphasized that the path to food is the one most frequented by women. Saul Mendlovitz, president of the Institute for World Order, spoke of the necessity of economic welfare, social justice and ecological balance being available for all people if we want a peaceful global society.

"Dedication is deciding to do what must be done," was the repeated direction of Margaret Sonneday, responsible for stating the triennial goals. The Assembly was divided into 50 mini-communities each afternoon. On the first afternoon each mini-community concentrated on what could be done in the local community to assure a fuller life for the woman offender, the woman restricted by poverty, and the woman needing a more genuine religious experience.

On another afternoon, each mini-community concentrated on the ramifications of meeting the problem of hunger from the point of view of education, political action, communication, child advocacy, social involvement. Placards with *Grievances* and *Great Solutions* were made ready for the evening mass meeting when the next steps to a preferred world were to be agreed upon.

The Assembly moved into a new position, a hall was divided by colored paper "walls" separating the various points of view represented during the afternoon's mini-community discussions. A note in the program explained, "Together we make up the spectrum of a rainbow of hope, but each group is symbolically cut off from others, by seeing their world primarily through one color."

Barbara Marx Hubbard, founder and chairperson of the board of the Committee for the Future, Inc., was the skillful moderator of a panel of twelve who attempted to answer the questions: "What can we do now to achieve a preferred world?" and "How can women of the world, using a variety of means, arrive at this goal?" The assemblage sang, "If we only have love," and suddenly the "walls" came tumbling down! Confetti, and ticker tape made up of all the colors which once had been dividing walls were released over the hall in a rousing finale to celebrate the fact that contributions from all persons can meet the global expectations of our time.

Somewhat sad at having to say farewell to our Assembly friends, and somewhat glad to be going back to the day-to-day work at home, Church Women United came to their closing dedication at breakfast on Sunday morning.

"Come, let us have breakfast," was the invitation of the retiring president, Clarie Collins Harvey, as she reminded us of the post-resurrection experience of the disciples on the seashore as they brought in their fresh catch of fish. The women re-enacted the sharing of the loaves and fishes, as a living sacrament that their daily work would always have the fresh assurance that Christ is alive and at work in our midst.

The new president, Margaret Sonnenday, spoke of commitments in the days ahead, of the calling of a new kind of leadership which would start from any point and move out to include others, giving and receiving as might be required in order to get the task done. Such leadership, she said, would require a new sense of the wholeness of the movement—a new sense of values, of learning God's will through our failures as well as successes, of expressing confidence without arrogance, assuming responsibility without regimentation, of becoming accountable to the whole without claim of credit.

In a final ceremony of light, Margaret Sonnenday said to women, soon to scatter across the nation, "In the darkness each of us must claim for herself the burning light of faith. Remember, The *Lord* is your light and your salvation . . . *Your* spirit is the candle of the Lord.

"Look across this room," the new president urged the women. "Look across this room and you know what our individual lights together can do. Women in our home towns all around the world also reflect the candle of the Lord. Together there is enough light for our lifetime journey toward wholeness.

All the little candles winked and flickered. Hands came together across the tables, and the candles joined into one steady totality of light. Twenty-two hundred church women were going home, each with the light of the Lord in her heart, renewed and burning with new purpose.

Like a Cathedral, the maintenance of a movement requires continual repair as well as construction work. For on the foundation of solid inter-personal relations rises the superstructure which gives it visible shape—all the offerings, all the programs all the community services. It is on this foundation that all in each place find equal footing as they gather to worship.

It takes skill to be "people-movers." It takes time to appreciate and use diversity of religious and cultural tradition. It takes patience to iron out differences in points of view, knowing that the continuing fellowship is more important than unanimity in a current controversial issue. It takes faith to be an instrument of God's reconciling love in a decaying neighborhood.

One of the great things about being a national movement is that all of us can be in more than one place at once! We can thus stretch our strength and reinforce those who are temporarily handicapped. We all need each other at some time or other and find our inspiration coming from sources we never could have anticipated.

In later chapters will be described some of the efforts as a national movement to fulfill our goals through ecumenical development or growth (Chapter 8) and ecumenical relationships (Chapter 10) and ecumenical action (Chapter 11) during the period from 1966 through 1975 often known as the Women's Decade (Chapter 9) all of which gave us new hope to plan for our future (Chapter 12).

FOOTNOTES TO CHAPTER 7

1. In 1975, the sources of income to CWU were:

State Units	$87,787
Denominations	37,858
Individuals & family foundations *	58,784
Investment income **	32,916
Offerings:	
World Day of Prayer	495,673
World Community Day	137,604
Gift Certificates for material aid	334,846

* Includes income from Sites Trust.

** Interest available from several forms of money management including Fund for the Future. The Fund for the Future was set up by designated gifts from donors, plus money from wills and memorials. In 1975 it amounted to $108,566. Its annual interest is used for current program needs. The principal is available for unanticipated deficits or special opportunities.

2. From New Dimensions in a Continuing Commitment.

Definitions of movement terms:

Listening Teams—a liaison between the women of a local church and a local unit. A listening team is made up of several individual women who both listen and respond to other individual women. It allows for an exploration of an idea to be made informally among a wider group of women. The chairperson reports to the Forum or the Executive committee the general consensus of church women without commitment until the CWU unit has an opportunity to develop a plan which seems to respond to the needs of most churches. (This replaces the former utilization of Key women.)

Forum—a place and time for encounter, for evaluation, for sharing concerns and for proposing approaches to the problem. It is open to any church woman interested in the subject and should also include at least one member of the Listening Teams.

Planning Groups—the grouping of like programs for planning and mutual support.

Celebrations—World Day of Prayer, World Community Day and May Fellowship Day services of worship and related activities.

Ecumenical Development—the increased participation of church women from all races and Christian traditions, as well as opportunities for wider fellowship through Wells, the Fellowship of the Least Coin, and interreligious dialogues, and international visitors.

Ecumenical Action—projects for voluntary services and Citizen Action.

Enabling Services—which kept the movement going: Committees on Communication, Finance, and Nominations.

Executive Board—is the official policy and planning group defined in our by-laws. The chairperson of Planning Groups and Standing Committees are members.

3. It was envisioned that Planning Groups would consist of two or three persons which could be expanded as the occasion called for. Their objective was to develop work projects in three essential areas of growth:

Ecumenical Celebrations: three national observances where the whole movement looks at the whole Gospel in the whole world;

Ecumenical Development: growth in participation and understanding of all Christian traditions; involvement of Christian women of all races and all age groups; relationship with Jewish women and others with;

Ecumenical Action: opportunities to study, speak and act on conditions and issues in each community.

Finally there would be the important *Enabling Services,* which would ENABLE adequate financing, enable the movement to grow in depth and meaning through interpretaion to its own members, and enable its work and concerns to be understood by the public at large. So to this group fell the task of obtaining volunteers, carrying on effective public relations, presenting nominations, and raising sufficient funds to support the ongoing work and program.

4. Speaking on "Biblical Perspectives on the Wholeness of Persons", Mary Louise Rowand focused her message on the women assembled there who were hiding behind their 'reliable, responsible, religious' facades. She analyzed our situation in the midst of the women's decade:

"When human culture goes out of kilter, its not surprising that the concept of women tied to that culture goes out of kilter. From the beginnings, the essence of the womanly was encompassed in the word WAITING————

Woman *waited* while man preached; while men governed, while man decided to marry her, while she was bearing children. . . She *waited!* She was supposed to wait! WAIT was the Sampler she sewed her life to. WAIT until you can wear make-up, have a date, go steady, get married. WAIT until your man makes money, until your children finish college, until you have time to be a grandmother. . .the WAITING game!

"THEN came the 50's and the stirrings: you're as good as a man, THEN you're the same as a man.

**Church Women United
1966 through 1975**

All in each place had a particular challenge for Americans when it came to ecumenical development in the 60's.[1] Where else would there be so many Protestant denominations, let alone the many do-it-yourself religious fads? Roman Catholics were going through. a period of renewal in the wake of Vatican Council II. At long last an American expression of Eastern Orthodox faith was flowering from multi-ethnic European roots. American citizens coming from many racial and ethnic minorities were claiming their long delayed birthrights in a pluralistic society. And all these factors were coming together in the sprawling metropolis, where today's corruption collided with tomorrow's aspiration.

In 1966 Church Women United staked out its claim of a movement open to all of Christ's women in each place. We filed it officially in the bylaws. We knew it would not be easy to shape up into the kind of movement we claimed in our intentions. We did not know whether we had the perseverance and strength "to work the claim" long enough to realize a diversified yield. Considering the ecumenical climate the first 25 years of its life as a national movement, it is not surprising that United Church Women was largely composed of

Protestant women from churches which were congenial to cooperation. The original distinctions rising out of a particular historic situation in Europe or Great Britain were superceded by an American lifestyle. Many of these churches had similar worship patterns and their congregational life included a woman's society of some sort. Since differences were only a matter of degree, interdenominational programs were readily communicated.

But times were changing. It would have been tempting to offer the security of a homogeneous religious club, but Church Women United must respond to its God-given calling to be open to all in each place.

... including all Christian traditions.

WITH EASTERN
ORTHODOX CHRISTIANS
It is no wonder that the Orthodox refer to their constituents through the generations as "the faithful," for a dynamic tradition connects the Orthodox with the development of the Christian Church from its beginning.

During the early centuries, patriarchates with many geographic and ecclesiastical subdivisions came into being. Beginning in A.D. 325, a series of Ecumenical Councils were convened to develop the dogma of the Church based on Holy Scriptures and Holy Tradition (the encompassing experience of the Church). When certain Churches in Syria, Egypt, Ethiopia, and India disagreed with the Council of Chalcedon in 451, another major association of Orthodox Communions came into being.

After several centuries of deteriorating relationships between patriarchates in the East and the West, the Great Schism of 1054 resulted in the formation of the Roman Catholic Church. Five centuries later, the protests against Rome at the time of the Reformation further divided the church.

The Orthodox Churches became a prime factor in shaping cultural traditions of the nations of Eastern Europe. Encompassing so great a proportion of the population, the Churches in many cases became virtually state or national churches. As missionaries and tradespeople migrated to the Orient and to Alaska and to other parts of North and South America, they carried the names of their home churches— Greek Orthodox, Rumanian Orthodox, Russian Orthodox. The large migrations from Eastern Europe coming to the United States in the late 19th century brought their churches with them. Orthodoxy, which had been the heart of community life in their former homeland, also became a cohesive force in the new situation.

It must have been somewhat traumatic for persons who found identity within large "state churches," where culture and religion were interwoven, to find themselves one of many ethnic minorities in a country which separated church and state. Although each national Church is administratively autonomous, they are bound together by historic faith and maintain cordial relationships through the Ecumenical Patriarch in Istanbul. At least seventeen different Orthodox jurisdictions emerged in the United States from these ethnic origins. They maintained continental relations through the Standing Conference of Canonical Bishops. Prophetic voices are even expressing the hope that one day there will be one Orthodox Church in America contributing its gifts as an integral part of our national pluralistic life.

Although the door had been left ajar for many years, very few women of the Eastern Orthodox Churches had ventured into Church Women United. How could they be encouraged? Perhaps a clue was in their own culture. In the villages of Eastern Europe, gracious hospitality to the *stranger-guest* is the way of life in every family. Therefore, it is not surprising that a cordial approach on a one-to-one basis brought a warm response from Orthodox women.

In the course of getting acquainted with the interests of my staff colleagues in 1966, I found that Helen Turnbull had a deep appreciation for Orthodox Christians. While serving on the staff of the World Council of Churches in Geneva from 1956 to 1959, she felt a need for exposure to the spirit of Orthodoxy. Her friendly interpreter, Metropolitan James of Melita, later became Archbishop Iakovacs, primate of the Greek Orthodox Church in North and South America. He introduced her to Clara Nicholson of Boston, who was helpful in arranging for her to meet Orthodox friends in the New York area.

Our Personnel Committee readily agreed to Helen Turnbull's proposal that her sabbatical leave in the fall of 1966 be used in seeking a greater exposure to Orthodox Churches around the world. Over the course of five months, she shared in a wide range of activities in Japan, South India, the Middle East and Europe.

In evaluating the sabbatical assignment, Helen Turnbull noted the following lasting impressions:

1) the devotion, the beauty and the mystery of the worship in all Orthodox churches;

2) the tradition and history of the Orthodox Church about which we western Christians still know so little;

3) the faith and courage of many who had suffered greatly in all kinds of political, sociological and ecclesiastical upheavals; and
4) the responsible participation of the laity.

Eager to share her experiences, Helen Turnbull sought contact with the head of the women's organizations of each of the various Orthodox Churches in the New York area. Archbishop Iakovacs, recognizing the wisdom of gathering women of different ethnic backgrounds who shared a common American experience, arranged for a small group to get together. Out of this gathering grew the Orthodox Christian Women of America. Mrs. John Linakis was elected its first president. In the winter of 1972, this pan-Orthodox women's movement entertained Mother Alexandra, the former Princess Ileana of Roumania.

It was an enriching experience to include leaders from four of the Orthodox communions on our national Board. We were welcomed in special social occasions by Orthodox women in Pittsburgh and Detroit when the Board met in those places.

Of particular value to these relationships were three women who served on our executive committee, Yorka Linakis, an attorney and later judge of the family court, often counseled us in legal matters relating to our bylaws and acted as parliamentarian at Board meetings and national Assemblies. Vivian Hampers was a valuable liaison with the Philoctopas, the women's association of the Greek Orthodox Church, and like the others, was a reliable interpreter of the hierarchy and traditions of Orthodoxy. Clara Nicholson was elected a national officer in 1971 and later served for a term as the chairperson of the Personnel Committee. To perform these duties effectively Clara took time from her annual leave, demonstrating that concerned professional women can find time to render valuable ecumenical service.

The Church Woman undertook to interpret Orthodox Christians and their churches to the wider constituency of readers. The May 1973 issue was a masterpiece combining the tradition and dynamics of the Orthodox Churches both in Eastern Europe and Asia, as well as the Americas. At an annual meeting of the Philoctopas in New York, Archbishop Iakovacs commented how remarkable it was that a predominantly Protestant organization should put out a magazine interpreting the Orthodox when Orthodox Christians had not published similar information about Protestants.

We were learning that it is not the diversity of our church traditions but the freedom in unity which became the new experience in CWU. We do not need to understand everything about the art form or liturgy of others in order to experience something of their meaning. There is a certain attitude of humility which Orthodox liturgy inflicts on the Protestant, but it is better to deflate the ego than to debunk the inspiration it creates!

Perhaps this can be illustrated by sharing some of the insights into their tradition and worship which I gained by spending the Greek Orthodox Holy Week on Crete in 1972. The occasion for the gathering was a WCC Consultation on "Centers for Social Concerns and Related Christian Movements." We were the guests for ten days of the Orthodox in one of the new buildings of their Lay Academy in Gonia, Crete. Nearby was a monastery and church (built 1618-34) where we joined the people of the community in Good Friday and Easter worship services.

Father Ireneus, whose gentle authority pervaded the conference, began his interpretation of the Orthodox observance of Holy Week by saying, "My first anxiety is how not to make you tired with explanations."

One of his suggestions was that the women dress appropriately for the Good Friday Service. He was immediately challenged by a feminist from Holland, "Why women? Men can wear shorts or bathing suits too. The peasant women on Cyprus are wearing pantaloons on the road." He explained that the village people knew what was considered appropriate to wear to church. "You have been well publicized as Christians from all over the world. You will be making an ecumenical witness to a weary people!" Both had "over made" their points, but it reminded us all that culture and religious expression are related.

Something of the lifestuff of Christian continuity is felt from the Orthodox manner of embodying concepts in human form. Their churches are full of mosaics, oil paintings, frescoes, life size statues of Jesus showing his human sorrow, suffering, compassion and tenderness. Icons relate the saints to the believers of all time. Pursuant to the early tradition of the priesthood of all believers, laity share equally in the responsibility for the preservation of the Church and the propagation of the Christian faith. Even though their conservative tradition guards many sacramental functions as exclusively for "the faithful," the Orthodox folk have a way of welcoming the *stranger-guest* and accepting her into the family.

How well I remember their open cordial reception when I was in the Middle East in May 1972 for a visitation on behalf of the International Committee for the World Day of Prayer. Vivian Hampers had written ahead to friends in Istanbul hoping they could arrange for me to be received by the Ecumenical Patriarch Athenagorus I. Although his age and his health might have suggested more caution in receiving an undue number of visitors, he happily accommodated a friend from his beloved American family.[2]

In the two days I had been in Istanbul, I could feel the pressure that was on the small Christian community, and marveled at the courageous witness of those who maintained a Patriarchate beleaguered in a Moslem country. Katerin Halepli (who had been a participant in the Causeway 1967 in the United States) and I went to the beautiful Byzantine Church in the compound where His Holiness resided.

It was Pentecost Sunday and the liturgy became meaningful as Katy translated so that this stranger-guest could understand.

Afterwards in the courtyard, we greeted the venerable old Patriarch, with his broad shoulders towering above the crowd, his kindly smiling eyes lighting up a strong face, and his flowing white beard covering his chest. He indicated as we talked in the courtyard that we could talk alone as soon as he had given a message to a group of 30 theological students from Athens.

Sitting in the back row, I did not take my eyes from his

face as he earnestly talked to the students for a half hour. Whispering in my left ear, Katy indicated that he was speaking of his lifelong commitment to Church unity and world peace. After he finished, the students were served refreshments which seemed to consist of a glass of cold water in which there had been inserted a stick with some taffy at one end.

His Holiness was tired and we visited only briefly in English. He repeated his concern about the long duration of the Vietnam war and said he had cabled President Nixon within the week urging him to negotiate peace. I told him how Church Women United was seeking to be a channel for unity and peace and ask for his prayers. In offering me his benediction, he added the words: "You now are my god-daughter." He died a few months later. The memory of his face made strong by loving kindness remains an icon in my heart.

WITH ROMAN   The election of Pope John XXIII in 1958
CATHOLICS   heralded a new era for Roman Catholics to
                  share in the ecumenical movement. Pope John's great love for humanity and his pastoral concern for his colleagues were translated into an amazing set of social reforms for the poor, vast aid for developing countries, and an openness in relationships with Protestant and Orthodox Churches.

Those who felt that the election of the seventy-seven year old Patriarch of Venice was merely a holding action must have been astounded when on January 29, 1959, Pope John quietly announced his intention of calling an ecumenical council "to consider measures for the renewal of the Churches in the modern world, the promotion of diversity within the unity of the Church, and the reforms which had been promoted by the Ecumenical and Liturgical movements." This Second Vatican Council was convened in 1963 and produced sets of documents which became the source of renewal in Roman Catholic thinking and gave momentum to cooperation among Christians all over the world.

The immediate response from national church bodies in the United States brought about a series of official conversations on selected doctrinal subjects as agreed upon with the

Bishops Commission on Ecumenism. These efforts were valuable among a limited number of theologians and other leaders and no doubt kept official doors open for further steps in cooperation.

By its very nature, Church Women United was prepared to welcome the participation of Roman Catholics on a widespread community basis. The national, state and local units eagerly began planning so that women could share in this new ecumenical experience.

We were fortunate that the Jesuits had assigned Father David Bowman to the NCCC to assist its various departments to relate their programs to Roman Catholic thinking and action. Always attentive to the distinctive purpose and nature of CWU, Father Bowman had a genial way of facilitating through the maze of Roman Catholic structures whatever we wanted to do. Any conversation with him pinpointed the essence of a proposal and deftly made the peripheral problems disappear.

One day Father Bowman dropped into the office to introduce two friends of his from Washington. One was Sister Joan Bland, Vice President of Trinity College, the oldest Catholic College of liberal arts for women. The other was Mrs. Eugene McCarthy, a member of the Bishops Commission on Ecumenism.

Almost immediately we were involved in a conversation concerning the possibilities for women in the ecumenical climate following Vatican II. We agreed that we must be sensitive not to go through the forms of Christian unity where there was no meaning for those involved. We talked about the participation of Roman Catholic Women in Church Women United, about the enrichment of our faith through mutual exploration of the various traditions, about corporate action on issues of peace and justice which would offer inspiration for the days ahead.

I spoke of our satisfactory experience with the National Council of Catholic Women in the program of WICS and of the cordial way in which its executive committee had received me at the Villa Cortona in its January meeting. They pointed out the weakness of expressing the ecumenical dimensions only through organizational cooperation. It was more satisfying, they thought, for each woman to be identified as an individual where she could be fully herself. As often happens this unplanned visit of forty-five minutes grappled with more issues than many a two-day consultation on policy and inter-church relations!

These informal conversations were helpful during the next weeks as we prepared statements to answer questions coming from our local and state units, on whether it was "legal" for Catholics to hold office. Considering the historic period through which we were going it was felt wise for the Board of Managers to adopt an official statement on *Further Association with Roman Catholics* in October, 1966. The Statement reminded us that Christians of all traditions share as one their faith in Christ, that our common heritage included the early centuries of church history, and that genuine differences of polity and theology had separated us in the 16th century, some of which still require solid work to resolve. We were called to reason together about what is required of all disciples of Jesus Christ.

The Statement urged that we get acquainted with the devotional practices of both traditions, and that we reinforce each other in the pursuit of justice, peace and Christian unity. Since we were bound to discover commitment and competence among Roman Catholic leaders, we would want to recognize emerging leadership in normal and appropriate ways within our organizational structure.

As our way of working called for local and state boards to take the initiative in their own spheres, the national nominating committee adjusted immediately, and Roman Catholic Board members were elected at the 1967 assembly. From the beginning they accepted responsibility for the whole movement and did not speak or act from a sectarian point of view. Among those who served as officers were: Sister Mary Luke Tobin, Abigail McCarthy, and Nobuko Haworth, Sally Cuneen, Lily Badre, Sister Maureen O'Keefe, and Lillian O'Conner were appointed to special leadership roles.

In many local units Roman Catholic women were already participating. With this encouragement there were many World Day of Prayer services held in Catholic sanctuaries in 1967 with women leading the liturgy. Protestant and Roman Catholic women alike found real excitement in showing love for one another and thus honoring the Lord of the Church.

CONGRESS OF LAY APOSTOLATE 1967 One never ceases to marvel at the scope of the Roman Catholic Church nor at the variety of ways by which its vast lay constituency gives expression to their faith. A Protestant, accustomed to each denomination having a few "all-purpose" organizations, divided according to age group or sex or marital status, is continually amazed at the discovery of hundreds of national and international organizations among Roman Catholic laity. Most of these organizations had distinctive callings at least in the beginning. Dynamics became more complex when alliances among them were formed.[3]

Margaret Mealey, the executive director of NCCW, opened the way for me to be named one of the official North American observers to the Third World Congress of the Lay Apostolate, which met in Rome, October 11-18, 1967. Prior to the convening of the conference, over a thousand women participated in a meeting of the WUCWO. Dr. Lillian O'Connor, later elected a member of the Board of Managers of CWU, gave an outstanding address, opening up the issues of women in church and society.

The Congress itself had over 3,000 participants from 103 countries and several Catholic communities in exile. This number included 238 delegates from 62 international Catholic lay organizations and 89 non-Catholic observer-consultants. Only about 7% of official delegates were from North America. About one-third of the participants were women, with the highest percentage (48%) from Latin American countries.

There had been two previous Congresses of a similar nature where the clergy had taken the lead in the program. For this Congress leadership was in the hands of a lay committee which had worked since 1960 on its preparation. My special salute goes to Rosemary Goldie, a Grail member from Australia, who had worked for some years in the Secretariat of the

Laity at Vatican City. Her amazing organizing skill in world-wide registration procedures and in preparing documents ahead of the Congress and during the working sessions, as well as subsequent reports after the adjournment, deserve acknowledgment.

Their theme, "God's People on Man's Journey," called for an agenda in which any committed Christian would be vitally concerned. The Protestant and Orthodox observers felt perfectly at home participating in the working sessions on specific topics. There was an enthusiastic response to the recommendation that the next congress be truly ecumenical in character.

The Congress expressed its own opinions as laity. The Bishops there were urged not to assume the teaching role which they often exercised in their own dioceses, but instead to allow the laity the freedom to correct each other in debate and in discussions such as that on birth control. The findings of the working sessions and the workshops on Christian message, education, missionary education and ecumenics were forwarded through appropriate groups to the Synod of Bishops.

Mrs. John Shields of the USA, the only woman of the five-member presidency of the Congress, was chosen to address the Synod of Bishops and to present to them a memorandum approved by the Heads of the Delegations.[4]

Engraved in my memory was a climactic experience on Sunday morning. Gathered in the St. Peter's Basilica were the 'people of God' from many nations and parishes. The officials for the Mass were Pope Paul VI and twenty-four Bishops. Ten lay men and women read in ten different languages the invocations of the prayer composed for the Congress by the Holy Father.

After the celebration of the Eucharist by one hundred delegates from different countries, Mr. Rienzie Pupasinghe of Ceylon, president of the Young Catholic Workers, approached the high canopied platform where the Pope and four of his associates were seated. Speaking from the foot of the platform stairs, the young Asian expressed gratitude to the Holy Father for having celebrated this Eucharistic Service with the laity. He affirmed their identity with and responsibility for the peoples of the earth with whom they, as Roman Catholic laity, lived out their daily lives and made it clear that they were available to the Church in its work of salvation and service. In a clear voice he made known the desire of the Church's laity for further dialogue with the hierarchy as well as with the Bishops and the religious orders—all for the mutual edification of one another.

Pope Paul responded with an Allocution in five languages, the English and German being read by two Cardinals. Among his words were these:

> We say that this great unitive plan, still hidden in the heart of God, will be hastened by the efficacy of your commitment in the world, the ardour of your participation in the apostolate.

> His Holiness made it clear that the hierarchy, clergy, and contemplative orders had a distinctive, costly calling, symbolic of the nature of the Church, and that the laity are loved and trusted in their irreplaceable role in the Church.

As we left the service I noted that there was a difference of opinion among Roman Catholics about the import of the message of the Pope. However, I felt I had witnessed a dramatic encounter symbolic of the nature of the Church. Never had I seen a gathering of laity so representative of the earth's people; nor had I seen a hierarchy so impressive. The dialogue which they both seemingly desired may never be held on so large a scale again, inasmuch as a small appointed Council on Laity was appointed for world planning. Nevertheless, this Congress had made a clear imprint on us who were Protestant. We were glad to be on the journey with them as God's people.

ROMAN CATHOLIC SISTERS In the early 1970's, Church Women United became aware of our need to understand the calling of Roman Catholic Sisters as well as the changing situation in their American 'congregations' or 'communities' as they described their 'Orders'.

Perhaps this came about because both CWU and the Roman Catholic Sisters had some freedom from ecclesiastic structures, and both were finding new dimensions and new excitement in renewal programs. Perhaps it was because of a common emphasis on justice in society and a deep desire to share the religious motivation of others in civic pursuits. At any rate, Church Women United realized that our purpose as reconciling agents in the world could be more nearly fulfilled as Sisters participated in our movement. Some might even find comfort in the mutual discovery that some Sisters, like some church women, want to 'stay put' just where they were!

Therefore, we eagerly grasped an opportunity which came to us in the summer of 1971. Lily Badre, the president of Church Women United in Carbondale, Illinois, wrote to us that Sister Joan O'Brien of the faculty of Southern Illinois University would be coming to New York for the summer and would be happy to associate herself with our staff. Her field was theology and philosophy and we looked forward to what we might learn from her. In turn, she planned to learn about the dynamics and program of CWU. It was hoped that the end result would be a brochure which would introduce to Roman Catholic Sisters the background and program of Church Women United, as well as interpret to Church Women United something of the history, the program of renewal, and the different kinds of Catholic women's religious orders.[5] Such a brochure was prepared and mailed to each unit of CWU and in quantity to each motherhouse or headquarters of the four hundred congregations of religious in the United States.

During the six weeks in which Sister Joan shared our office, she led our staff in a study of some of the new theological thinking which had a direct bearing on the renewal and reform among the Orders of Women Religious. She emphasized four major thrusts of Roman Catholic thinking:

- the renewed emphasis on the Church as "the Pilgrim People" on the move toward the Kingdom, realizing that the totality of the reign of God is not now present either in the world or in the Church.
- the thrust toward ecumenism which would result in closer relationships with other Christian churches, as

well as with Jews and other believers.

- the reassertion that the Christian must always value persons above institutions and structures.
- the movement to recapture Christ's understanding of the unity of being which brings to an end any separation between secular and sacred.[6]

ROMAN CATHOLIC — In October, 1962, Cardinal Bea, Bishop
WCC COOPERATION Willebrands and Father Thomas Stransky were summoned to Rome by Pope John XXIII and requested to develop the administrative services and studies implied in the Vatican's new program in ecumenical relations. Nothing is more exciting than to create the job you have already undertaken to do! After buying a light bulb so they could see in the small office space to which they were assigned, they began to arrange for the formalities and courtesies to the many Protestant and Orthodox observers expected at the coming Vatican Council so as to use this occasion as a friendly platform to interpret the new climate for the growth of Christian unity.

The unique worldwide polity of the Roman Catholic Church would naturally restrict continuing relationships directly from the central body with any one of the hundreds of nationally based Protestant and Orthodox churches. Church to church relations could better be handled by regional judicatories. When dealing with issues that were worldwide in nature, it was natural that the Vatican should turn to the World Council of Churches, which acted as a coordinating base for its 161 member churches in 70 nations.

In 1968 the WCC and the Vatican created a Joint Working Committee, on which were two women. Feeling that there was an emptiness without the involvement of a greater number of women, Father Stransky proposed that a Women's Liaison Group be appointed composed of five women from the WCC and five from the Roman Catholic constituency.

Brigalia Bam of the Department of Cooperation of Men and Women in the Church and Society of the WCC, and Rosemary Goldie, staff member of the Council on Laity, were appointed to act as staff. The relationships with the Joint

Working Committee and the channels of communication to constituency groups were left vague. It was planned to alternate the place of an annual meeting between Rome and Geneva.

The five appointed by the Vatican largely represented international women's organizations. Four of those appointed by the World Council of Churches were representative of world church 'families': Reformed, Orthodox, Lutheran, Anglican, and I was the fifth.

No matter what we represented by way of experience or office, we could not claim that these conversations represented fresh insights from a representative world group. Nevertheless we did find it valuable to get acquainted with the points of view and activities of other members of the liaison group, particularly since it was during this period that we were all becoming conscious of expressions of women's liberation.

During the five years we had never been asked to meet with or report to the official Joint Working Group. There was a certain restlessness about the lack of significant relationship to women at large. The genuine encounter was happening regionally. So in 1972, we decided to sponsor a worldwide conference on the issues of world peace as an activity of significant involvement.

Brigalia Bam undertook the task of organizing the conference held at a hotel in Nicosia, Cyprus, May 1972. With the advice of a small committee near her office in Geneva, she was able to raise the funds, define objectives, invite participants, develop a program, and arrange for local courtesies, including a reception with President Makarios. The conference was financed from a common fund to which Church Women United had made a contribution. About 70 participants from 29 countries were present, of which the largest group came from the United States.

It was a real conference—meaning that we were able to confer with one another without being interrupted by outside speakers. Invitations had been issued to include women from various tension areas. All had some experience in peace activities and many were involved in some social or political arena. Each woman spoke with maturity about the issues without blaming other individuals for the policy or practices of their nations.

Our intention was to focus on ways through which women in their varied roles might work more constructively for peace and justice. Working parties developed tentative recommendations in three areas: Education for Peace; Social and Economic Development; Women's Involvement in the Peacemaking Task. Their findings were brought to the conference roundtable for extensive discussion and modification. With the assistance of a woman journalist, a daily paper kept us up with each other and gave some a chance at editorials. In the plenary sessions there was an interesting rejection of the feminine issue apart from the subject at hand. Yet our worship, our dramatized reports, our way of sounding out interesting people, and of expressing our common Christian commitments were relaxed and responsible—just because all of us were women.

CONSULTATION ON LAITY TRENDS A consultation of fifty persons to consider the direction of laity movements was convened in the Casa del Papa Giovanni in Assissi, Italy, in September 1974. It was jointly sponsored by the Council of Laity of the Vatican and the Department of Laity of the World Council of Churches. In order to give the participants some concrete basis for identification, they first divided into continental groups. Then the conference was divided into working groups on theological implications of laity formation, new woman-man relationships, formation for justice and cultural values, and tensions between institutions and community.

Of the seven in the North American Group, two were women: Helen Brewer of the National Council on Catholic Laity, and Elizabeth (Liz) Howell Verdesi who was named by Church Women United. The latter was elected chairperson of the Community on Men and Women United.

There were ten in the group and they were surprising in their unanimity of experience and viewpoint about the entire range of subjects from the ordination of women to the need for consciousness raising. At the plenary session over which Maria Vendrick of Holland presided, there was general approval of the reports from most of the working groups. When the report on "Women and Men" was read, there was silence. Marie Vendrick of Holland prodded them: "How come there is nothing but acceptance of everything this afternoon?"

At that point hands were raised all over the room and a heated, emotionally charged discussion followed. Liz kept wondering why Marie had not put the question before all this hassle started. Then, suddenly, an Orthodox man called for the question indicating he was ready to vote for the report. Later Liz discovered that Marie had purposely generated discussion for the purpose of consciousness-raising among the conference participants themselves. She was right.

Upon her return to the national office, our observer recorded some of her impressions:

As the days and nights passed, it became clear that it was not the theological issues that divided us, nor even questions of ecclesiastical organization and practice. Rather, the obstacles to our unity stemmed from national origin and the whole complex of socio-economic backgrounds that we represented. We discovered that those of us from North America (both Canada and the USA) were immediately suspect. The first words (and almost the only ones!) spoken directly to me by a Latin American participant were, "And what are you doing about the multi-national corporations in your country?"

As we worked we discovered differences of opinion, of course. But the astounding discovery I made was that these differences were *not* differences between Roman Catholics and Protestants or between Protestants and Orthodox. Rather, these differences were between individuals—each of us seeking to understand what obedience to the gospel means for us in this time. In this search we were ONE. But we had to listen to each other. We had to try new ways of articulating our ideas. We had to *want* to understand others as deeply as we wanted to be understood. Our unity became real only in the search itself. And the search led us to affirm each other as persons, to celebrate and enjoy our oneness of Christians. . .

WORLD CONSULTATION OF THE LAITY COUNCIL 1975 In response to the invitation to send an official observer to the World Consultation of the Laity Council, Edna McCallion, the coordinator of the CWU office at the United Nations and a member of our Assembly Planning Committee, was appointed as the Ecumenical Observer to represent Church Women United in the USA. Her report ably describes the make-up of the consultation and her own reactions as to its content and significance at this point in history:

As a Roman Catholic laywoman, I participated fully. My presence was a reminder to others that for the past 9 years Church Women United is a movement not only of Protestant women but also of Roman Catholic and Orthodox women.

The Laity Council was set up in 1967 by Pope Paul VI to work "for the service and promotion of the lay apostolate." Its experimental period of five years was extended to the end of 1975 in order to "make a contribution to the aims and activities of the Holy Year." The future structure and general functioning of the Laity Council are still under study but at present it is authorized to pursue its ordinary activities. The Council is composed of lay persons from around the world, although its chief officers are clerics.

There were about 250 participants at the Consultation who came from every continent. Participants represented a wide variety of involvement in national and international lay movements and organizations but all were invited as individuals. The composition of the group was very representative without being too large to allow for real exchange. The rich diversity of participants stimulated a wealth of personal contacts. The Consultation provided a milieu to realize the deep unity with our brothers and sisters who, although scattered throughout the world, share with one another in the communion of the Church.

The theme of the Consultation was "Towards the Year 2000 . . . Along the Way of the Gospel." The two major subthemes were "What the World Today is looking For" and "The Church as Communion, Diversity of Ministries and Unity of Mission." Like many meetings and conferences, too much time was spent in listening to prepared speeches and not enough on discussion. In the work groups, there was not enough time allowed to do more than scratch the surface of the assigned topic. Also, much of the richness and diversity in the work group discussions was sifted away in the final reports leaving the same tired rhetoric and platitudes. More conferences and meetings could profit by the personal witness, by the wisdom and insights of persons who are struggling workers and know poverty. Too often our conferences consist of the elite trying to decide what is best for others.

In the report about mass media, the exchange of experiences from different continents brought to the surface a common problem with differences owing to the national contexts. In most countries freedom of expression is confiscated, in one way or another, either by the State or by political parties or by financial groups. It was also noted that mass media are generally authoritarian in their action. A critical mentality must therefore be developed through education.

Another report said that "The Church must proclaim to the world by its words and actions its concern for the condition of man . . . We believe that at this time the Church presents an image of materialism, power and ritualism. We therefore resolve that from henceforth the Church in its teaching and practices must reflect totally the values in Christ of every human being."

The final report also stated that "the ecumenical possibilities in dialogue and in apostolic formation should always be kept in mind and the Laity Council is urged to continue its close collaboration with the World Council of Churches and other international ecumenical bodies and to encourage similar contacts at local levels."

It was difficult to dismiss the feeling of "deja vu" during the Consultation. What of all those endless discussions during the past decades of the vocation of the laity and the right of the laity to perceive and direct the Church? There are still too many church leaders unable to think of the laity as anything more than providing troops to march in the direction they might choose. I hope the Consultation will make a difference to the Church.

All in each place
. . . in a pluralistic society

A character in one of Israel Zangwill's plays cries out: "America is God's Crucible, the Great Melting Pot where all the races of Europe are melting and reforming . . ." This was an inhuman image and never was true. Even the immigrants from Europe and the British Isles hoped to gain personal identity in the new land—not to be poured into the same mold. The influx of peoples from every part of the world opened the many frontiers and vast resources of this nation.

If in the beginning they sought their own kind, it was often out of the need to find a home, earn a living, or share a friend. Their cohesion was due not so much to what they left behind but what they saw ahead for their children. The housing enclaves which resulted created the milieu for schools and churches and indeed gave rise to the possibilities of separate and unequal societies. The struggles of the Slavic workers in the steel mills and the protests of the Irish are woven into the fabric of American history.

Consider also the large importations for the labor force—the African slaves for the southern plantations, the Chinese workers who built the railroads in the West, the Mexican and Oriental farm workers whose labor made profitable large scale food production. Economically few had any options but to stay in the new land. Their incentive was that life would be better for their children and the first American-born generation grew up with the same loyalty and expectations as other young citizens.

By the middle of the 20th century, voices of a new and more sophisticated generation were being heard, and the media provided means to amplify the communications. The cries for justice came not only from the blacks and the native American Indians, but from Americans whose heritage was Puerto Rican, Cuban, Mexican, Filipino, and Chinese. It was a noisy public forum for each in his own way was speaking for the rights and contribution of every person to be fully realized. For any person to claim greater rights than another just because she was a member of the majority race was immediately labeled as white racism.

Official church bodies were confronted by leaders of the various racial minorities seeking "reparation" for many decades of discriminatory acts. Congress received delegations for "equal opportunity" legislation. Obviously the sharing of power—or even frustration across economic lines— called for learning new ways for all to participate in decision making. We became conscious of the fact that ours was now and always had been a pluralistic society.

The period was reminiscent of a county fair in my youth, with its flamboyant hucksters hawking their various wares. "Come one! Come all," each would shout. "Step right up. First come, first served!" The rhetoric and the realism did not need to match to assure the sale.

All of this is fine when the consumer at the county fair realizes she is buying spun sugar cotton guaranteed to leave only its sticky imprint after it has mysteriously disappeared. But if the product were a piece of "this nation under God," in which there is a life-long investment, it just hadn't worked out that the first come *got their choice of the goodies. The American Indian, the Spanish settler, the Afro-American were tilling the soil of this land long before the invasion of the Irish, the Swedes, or the Germans.*

However in this pluralistic market, the huckster with the loudest voice (and the greatest stockpile) was perhaps the white majority, selling his own brand of democracy. His words and manner were cordial enough:

"Come one!" . . . (We recognize you as an individual)

"Come all!" . . . (We'll accept your whole race—as customers)

"Step right up!" . . . (You are free to take the initiative)

"First come, first served!" . . . (Let the speedy be greedy)

Of course, we should add that not all the hucksters were white, and not all white persons were hucksters!

Yet the hot summers of 1967-68 in our cities, and the hot tempers within various institutions throughout the decade, created the intense heat of a new annealment in the life of the

American people. No other democracy in history had come from efforts of so wide a spectrum of people. This does not mean the United States is better or worse than any other nation. But it is distinctive in development; and this distinction makes us American. Our kind of nation-building will deteriorate when the seekers and sufferers of any race quit the common struggle to gain liberty and justice for all.

A corollary is the fact that any living church must nourish the roots from which it grows. One cannot appreciate the Lutherans without knowing something of the German history and papal policies in the Middle Ages, or understand the polity of the Church of England apart from the struggles of Henry the VIII. The transplant of the Christian churches to the New World meant changes as a result of their American environment. Although the many denominations which characterize American Christendom can be explained by the many migrations to new frontiers, the segregated congregations in each of them resulted from conditions needing' correction.

PLURALISM WITHIN CWU   CWU came into being in the United States after the nature of our society was clear. It was natural that this pluralism would challenge the reliability of our claims. At a staff meeting in the fall of 1968, I offered some unsolicited remarks on the subject, sounding like a huckstress!

CWU is called into being for such a time as this. Our bylaws say we are open to all women. But we must accept each for herself—not as a token of an ethnic group.

It is in the local community that segregated congregations exist regardless of the open policy of the national denominations. CWU offers a neutral place for all races and traditions to learn to know and trust one another. Every church woman is a member of one of the ethnic communities as well as a member of a denomination, and the racial mark is a more permanent distinction. Two American Indian women in Wyoming—one a

Baptist and the other a Roman Catholic—have more in common as Indians than either of them has with her white counterpart in her own denomination in a New York suburb.

To take our purpose seriously we needed to make pluralism in our fellowship as broad as that in the community at large. Women from many ethnic backgrounds coming 'together to affirm our faith in Jesus Christ' enhanced our witness in the secular community. Our declared intention to 'go out together as instruments of God's reconciling love' could hardly be fulfilled in most American communities without using the insights and experience of people of all races living there.

Furthermore, women had a lot of things in common which would be a touchstone into our understanding of each other and our influence on the community. There were a hundred possibilities for any one of us to find persons of a different race in the daily round of work, market, school, public park, restaurant, apartment house, or country road. Each interracial encounter could be filled with fear and chauvinism or with warmth, curiosity, and acceptance of another human being. Church Women United must be truly one, yet truly diverse to reflect God's rainbow of hope in this nation!

This eloquent conclusion was put in deep freeze by the quick response of one staff associate: "If CWU is its only hope, this country is in poor shape!" Despondently I rang up "No Sale" on my psyche register. It would take samples, not sermons, to sell a continuing commitment. Everything one says about a subject may be true, yet when it is all put together, it is not the whole truth. My eyes met those of Maza and Elsie, the two black members of our executive staff. Whether or not they agreed with my words, they had sized up the glint in my eye and were giving me Grade A for effort!

**CWU STATEMENT
ON PLURALISM**   As others, church women were confused
with the changing pattern in our society. It
is a bit awkward to be faced with a Cause in
a casual conversation at a shopping center or bridge game or
around the supper table, particularly if you are uncertain about
your position. By 1969 our Board recognized the need to
develop a common platform and issued a communication to
2300 local units of Church Women United, *A Statement on
Living Together in a Pluralistic Society:*

We are keenly aware of what it means to be alive in the
present age. We feel both the richness of a great variety
of peoples in our nation and in our world and yet we hear
around us the voices of separation.

WE REJOICE
- in the growing sense of identity and self-image
within each race that frees persons to realize their
full potential
- in the fact that the cries of many minorities warn us of
violations of human dignity
- in the expression of new freedom from binding social
pressures and age-long traditional roles

WE DEPLORE
- the growing evidence that we are becoming a nation
of separate societies
- the fear and confusion that has silenced many in our
society, including church women
- the failure among church women themselves to carry
forward their declared intention of being instruments
of reconciling love

WE AFFIRM our commitment to
- live according to our God-given conviction of the
worth of each individual
- recognize that our unity as a nation depends upon our
ability to work together in a society.

- discover the cultural contribution coming from every race and nation and become a responsible part of the interdependent world community

Therefore, WE RESOLVE TO
- *speak up* each time there is a violation of the rights of any individual or where there is a belittling of any race by careless generalization
- *act* to clear the path by which every person— younger and older, black, white, red and brown, female and male, Gentile and Jew—may make creative contributions to the life of all
- *press* for the elimination of poverty and the achieving of racial justice and peace
- *quicken* the movement of Church Women United itself to be in reality a community
     -where each can find her place
     -where leaders of all racial and ethnic backgrounds are recognized and their resources utilized
     -where our fellowship forms a healing community
     -where corporate action will show mercy and justice
     -where the new life in Christ may be visible in the love we have for one another

CONSULTATION IN ATLANTA In addition to developing a platform for our speaking on this subject, the national movement set some common goals for action. We sought advice outside our own circle of professional church workers, knowing that in our eagerness in activating our own programs, we sometimes become blinded to the realities that others see. So in the fall of 1970 we called a small interracial consultation in the Atlanta airport.

As the group of 10 women introduced themselves to one another, I marveled once again how a letter from the national office of CWU could induce women of this competence to give up their own work for a day to offer CWU freewill consultative services. Of course, it had something to do with identifying in common cause, but also a lot to do with the fact that CWU had a national grassroots constituency with an enviable record of getting something done!

Among others at this meeting there were *Amelia Betanzas,* the president of the Puerto Rico Development Corporation in New York City (Her news for the morning was that Mayor Lindsay had invited her to join his staff to direct youth programs in New York City); *Sister Margaret Traxler,* the able Administrator for the Catholic Council of Racial Justice; *Dr. Deborah Wolfe,* professor of Community Education in Queens College and formerly consultant for the Educational Committee of the House of Representatives, where for ten years her record for drafting legislation for quality education was unexcelled; *Coretta Scott King,* who was heading up the development program for the Center for Non-Violent Change in memory of her late husband (At this meeting her special cause was a concern for economic development for poor families in the rural south).

Of special interest to us all was the delightful sense of humor which came from the woman who represented a development program among American Indians. "I belong to the snap race," she said as she introduced herself. She went on to meet our puzzlement, "Right in the middle of most committees on economic development among minorities, somebody snaps his fingers and remarks: "We should have had an American Indian here!"

The consultants made a number of specific recommendations such as subsidy for a small industry, a bakery run by the rural people in the South, or encouragement of the ancient arts among Indian women. We pursued these possibilities as opportunity rose, but I was more interested in the discernable threads which ran through the discussions. Several times the assertion was made that "women are in transition," a phrase we picked up to use in our Calls to Citizen Action in 1971. Women are in transition going from rural areas to large cities, from elemental routine jobs to the next rung in the career ladder, from slumbering acceptance of their own fate to an awakening liberation of personal worth, from a sphere of influence limited to family, or clan, or local parish to an expanding social and political world.

Another thread running through the day's discussions was the longing for something new, a feeling coming from within their own ethnic cultures rather than being imposed from outside. It seemed easier to propose ways to help with economic development than to assist in the recovery of dignity and renewal of a racial heritage.

What was said that day had to be taken seriously by us if the movement were to venture into a journey toward wholeness. *All* women were in transition and *all* women were filled with longing for a more inclusive sisterhood. Where it was possible to ease the process without patronage we would gladly try. It would be a bit awkward to express for awhile, for so long we had treated an act of encouragement to Indian or Chicano women as an "outreach project" whereas in reality it was "all of us" accepting an invitation to join in a specific effort started by "some of us."

However, if we ever were to feel more natural on our way together, we must respect the distinctive marks of racial heritage. So we began consciously to act in the knowledge that our movement was open to very different Christian women who wanted to manifest their unity through fellowship, study, and cooperative action. Our national Board was strengthened by adding several American Indians, Spanish-speaking Americans, and Asian Americans. The Calls to national meetings and workshops accented the diversity of women who might be expected to respond.

INITIATIVES BY MINORITY WOMEN We answered affirmatively almost every request to give financial assistance to church sponsored projects where the initiatives came from minority women. Our experience was that these requests were always modest, always practical, and always well reported. They covered a wide scope of needs: educational opportunities for women, day care centers, self help projects in gardening, canning, handwork, and home industries; travel assistance for women to take part in decision-making conferences and to share in national and international meetings, special services for migrant families, subsidies for arts.

We were able to seize these opportunities for mutual service among women because money was available from the Intercontinental Mission Fund which was a portion set aside to carry forward our goals. Many races shared in these offerings so there was no feeling of patronage. Indeed *All-of-Us* were joining *Some-of-Us* in places where we could not all be; together we visited the sick, fed the hungry, and offered hospitality to the lonely stranger.

In the mid 1970's came three invitations with a R.S.V.P. to which *All-of-Us* were pleased to respond.

"Come, Dream with Us" opens a communication from Mary Pioche, a Navajo Indian and the director of a home for native Americans who are in transit from their reservation to a possible new location in Denver. She describes how her dream began with the dreams of others. "The Native Americans (Indians) come to Denver on a dream. Home for them had been a reservation—a place like Rosebud Reservation in South Dakota where the unemployment rate is 40% and where statistics show the highest percentage of alcoholism, tuberculosis and adolescent suicide in the nation." They come to Denver because they have heard that in that city were jobs, schools and opportunity. In Denver, so it was said, one can dream the big dreams the reservation stifles.

Often the dream bursts quickly. For instance when John Brave Eagle arrived with his family. One night in the relative's home made it obvious that the house was too small for both families. The next night they slept in a car. The rounds to the local pastor, the Housing Authority, the Welfare office were made. All but a barman in a local pub directed Brave Eagle to someone else. Defeated, the Brave Eagles returned to the reservation.

Another case in point was Toba Bahe, a recent high school graduate, who had come to Denver with high ambitions. She could find no job. No one befriended her except the young man who offered to put her up in return for favors. Nine months later she returned to the reservation carrying their child.

Then a group of Conservative Evangelicals with Social Concern stepped in. Gathering together other caring persons in the city, they dreamed their own answer to the nightmares of families like the Brave Eagles and single women like Toba. It was a half-way house with an apartment on the first floor where a family could live for a couple of months while locating a job and permanent home. Upstairs there would be several apartments allowing longer occupancy by single women. A board, half of whom were women, began to arrange financing and personnel. Church Women United joined the Christian Reformed Church, the Reformed Church in America, the United Methodist Conference, and the Church of the Brethren in assuring the purchase of the house. Two young women acted as staff, finding temporary homes and understanding friendship, helping them with jobs, offering counsel for emotional and spiritual problems.

Mary Pioche concludes her letter: "By God's grace, a dream has come true in Denver, and you are part of that dream."

Another invitation to *All of Us* began with lines from a poem written by a young Papago Indian: **Come, Join us** *Journey with us on a path lightly travelled but continuously eroding*

The next lines are similar to the purpose of a summer program of cultural awareness for 75 women from many tribes in northern Arizona, developed by the Traditional Indian Alliance of Greater Tucson.

We shall walk as rebuilders of the path,
adding a pebble here, turning a stone there, and

piling a handful of earth over there.
This path is the heritage of the Indian.

The preparation of leadership was part of the program itself. During April and May, 1975, twenty women were trained in the technique of pottery; ten other young women were taught dance and drama and sign language; ten others were learning the art of basketry from an expert, beginning with field trips to identify different kinds of Yucca used to make traditional Indian baskets. There followed workshops in all these fields during the summer. As their products were exhibited in various state and community exhibits, they developed pride in achievement and in the discovery of the meaning of the distinctive features which marked their tribal heritage. On one occasion, they went to the state prison to offer a program of varied arts for Indian Day. There was enthusiastic response. After all, in every person there rises the question of the struggle of life and death as told by a skillful Yaqui deer dancer.

More important than other results was that the summer program developed the will for the women to do other things together (such as nutrition courses, children's drama and youth activities.) The essence of any experience is the new understandings which smooth out the path toward wholeness. As Jean Chandhuri, the project director, said at the conclusion of her report:

With your support, you have excited us as Indian people to become aware of tribal and linguistic differences, whether we are Mohawk, Sioux, Seminole, Papago, or Yaqui.

We too have learned to respect and to appreciate each tribe's unique background.

Thank you so much for sharing with us our concern and common cause of preserving the American Indian heritage.

"Let us Go and Tell" echoes a conversation with women in the garden on the first Easter Day. They didn't quite understand Christ's resurrection, but they accepted the fact! They went quickly to tell the disciples, who found the news amazing

but reserved their opinions until they had collected evidence for themselves!

For those of us who have to strain all our ideas through committees in order to validate their inspiration, it is always refreshing to discover a spontaneous wellspring in an individual. Such was my experience in May, 1973, at the annual banquet of the Association of Hispanic Evangelical Women in the New York-New Jersey area. The Rev. Noemi Diaz, a member of CWU's National Board, was a counselor of this Association and had been helpful in bridging relationships with CWU. On this occasion there was a special festive atmosphere as hundreds of women and their escorts chatted gaily together in Spanish and enjoyed the featured musicians from South America.

Seated near me was Ruth Reina, a director of Planned Parenthood in Essex County, New Jersey, the president of Spanish Presbyterian Women in New York, and a regional director of COHAM, a movement of Hispanic Americans. During one of the intermissions, we began to talk. She told me of her hope that the Spanish speaking women in the hundreds of New York churches might become more competent in a person-to-person ministry aimed at making the Christian faith relevant to the present situation in their neighborhoods and places to work. In her mind it was a long range plan, requiring a theological course in Spanish to be offered in one or more seminaries in the New York area. To me it was an inspired idea since I had once dreamed of the same thing to be done by regions all over the country for CWU.

By coincidence, the next week at one of Dorothy Wagner's frequent supper parties for overseas friends, I fell to talking with Julia Campos, formerly of the Union Seminary in Uruguay. She was enroute the next week to some sort of summer job and was fascinated by my description of the hope within Ruth Reina. Within a few days my attention was called to a recent graduate of the Union Seminary in Puerto Rico, who was in the States for the summer. It began to seem that these various possibilities might mesh into a pilot project for the summer if we could find a sponsoring committee from the Spanish speaking community.

The team members were agreed on their approach and began by visiting Puerto Rican and Cuban churches, offering to be of service to their religious education programs, week night youth activities and vacation pupil assignments. In the process they got acquainted with women to whom they were able to explain their primary summer goal. The project proceeded quite smoothly with a series of evening classes held in the New York Seminary under Julia Campos's direction around the theme "Give account of the hope within you."

If I were to account for my reasons for hope, it would be in the sure faith that the same God who put hope in Ruth Reina's heart could add to it in other hearts and multiply it forever.

LOCAL CWU RESPONSES   The most important work of making "the visible fellowship" of Church Women United more genuinely pluralistic is done in the local community. It is there the opportunity can be seized more quickly for one to one relationships. Let me recount two meaningful examples.

During a free period in a workshop in the Dakotas, a casual conversation sent into orbit my pride in being part of this movement. Betty Litton, the president of CWU in North Dakota, was telling me about her Indian friends in Fargo who felt that racism was being inbred into children through derogatory allusions in their textbooks. A small delegation took the matter to the school authorities who dismissed the charge as super-sensitivity over simple semantics.

But the women were not so easily called off their concern. An interracial group went to work to document their case. Every textbook was read. The actual quotation and its page and line were carefully noted; in a parallel column was listed the reason why the reference was objectionable or untrue; in a third column was written an improved substitute. I leafed through the tabulated pages which covered only one history book, and marveled at the accumulated evidence. "What happened?" I murmured.

"Our committee was now loaded with ammunition, so we returned to the superintendent of schools. It was his suggestion that this documentation be sent to the textbook publishers. He ordered the material to be duplicated and given to every teacher. Although they had rejected our previous suggestion that teachers be offered workshops under Indian leadership, now the teachers themselves call on the Indians for supplementary information as the curricular topics come up."

Later she wrote that the superintendent himself was calling them to alert them on "bad movies." Program managers of the area educational TV were asking for advice and the inter-racial women's group was requested to re-write one of the scripts for local viewing. Yes, the sensitivity level had been raised in many, many ways. While it might take some time for text books to be changed, the school system of Fargo was offering their young students a corrected view of their pluralistic heritage.

Mrs. James Cooper had been one of the members of the first Board of UCCW and the first state president of Okla-homa. The spirit of CWU was in her blood stream. As one black school teacher said, "Well, Mrs. Cooper was our friend before it was legal!" Her folksy letters were always nourishment to those of us in the national office who were deprived of local rations. In 1968 she wrote these paragraphs:

> Today, I found another "gifted woman" that I am going to involve in CWU. She is new in my church, a darker than Georgia woman from Morocco, some kind of a technician in the medical field and married to a new doctor of Marietta. She talks with a most interesting accent and we aren't used to having anybody join our church with more than a Yankee accent. She followed me out to the door to open it for me and she said, "I have been watching you ever since I have been in this church and I have listened to you talk. I want you to lead me in the way I should go in my Christian experience.

> What an order! The first thing I will do is lead her into

CWU so I shall call her and ask her to go with me to World Community Day. She is as sharp as they come and is so enthusiastic about her life here. We must not disappoint her. We must make room for her alert mind and happy, joyous spirit.

You would have to know Marietta to appreciate what has happened in this town through Church Women United. To see our women actually in happy fellowship with Negro women over a coffee cup in Marietta is more than any of us even ten years ago could have dreamed of and now, to have our Catholic women so happy with us, calling us all by given name and actually being one with us.

Being-One-With-Us is another way of saying Church Women United in a pluralistic society.

TRANSNATIONAL WOMEN   A lot had been written about our world being a global village and international living becoming a way of life. Suddenly we realized that this was a person-centered phenomena, and that millions of persons were spending a great section of their adult life in countries other than ones in which they were born. The United States was a great exporter and importer of this transnational experience.

At the end of the 60's and beginning of the 70's, millions of Americans were living and working abroad. They were related to government posts, military installations, multinational corporations, educational and research centers in over 140 countries. They were technicians, news correspondents, educators, relief and rehabilitation workers, as well as international civil servants. Not to be overlooked in the situations where there was sustained employment abroad were the hundreds of thousands of American families who often remained in enclaves in places where they were in sufficient number. Whether they became ugly or beautiful Americans to the people in their host countries depended on a lot of things which the women in these families influenced.

Meanwhile, there was a reverse flow of persons from

other countries coming to the United States with their families. Not only were there great migrations of farm workers and technical laborers, but also thousands of white collar jobs in international business, professional jobs in schools and hospitals, as well as those related to their governments' consular posts in most major cities. With the exception of the director, several hospitals on the East coast were staffed by nurses and doctors all of whom were born abroad. Some apartment houses in suburban areas were chiefly occupied by families of Japanese businessmen.

Many of these new enclaves, like those of an earlier generation were overlooked by the established American community. Why this was true remains a mystery inasmuch as almost all families had a working knowledge of English and came with a cultural background which would have contributed much to any who took time to get acquainted.

Church Women United had much to gain and give by further association with transnational women. If their experience with a second culture could be put to use it would enrich all. If the gnaw of adjustment was eating away at their whole outlook and usefulness, then CWU might provide a healing community.

Gladys Naylor, the staff coordinator for International Community, accepted the challenge to survey some of the experiences which women were having as they translated their daily life into another culture. As always, she came up with an amazing array of organized data and new personalities. Her research included many volunteer associations such as the American Women's Club, Seoul, Korea, Association of American Wives of Europeans, United Church Women in Tokyo, the UN Wives Group, and the Association of Union Churches Abroad, to name a few.

We were interested in the driving motivations which held these overseas groups together. Some of them, like the Arab speaking groups in Washington or the Indonesian Women's Association in New York, were instrumental in helping women find their compatriots in a new country, as were many American clubs abroad.[7]

The Transnational Survey also brought out a great diversity of activities carried on by women living in a second or third culture. We also learned enough of their longings and frustrations to call together a consultation in the hope of developing some suggestions for their transnational sisters. To this gathering, held in June 1970 at a retreat center near St. Louis, 40 women were invited, half of them being American women who had recently returned from living abroad, and the remaining overseas women who were earning their livelihood and/or making their home in the United States.

Shahla Anand (India and New Jersey) acted as chairperson for the conference. Under the guidance of pre-warned stimulators (all transnationals), four topics were introduced: *Personal and Family Adjustment in Overseas Living, Participation in a Second Culture Community, and New Vocations for Women, Professional and Volunteer,* and *Clues for Creative International Living in the Future.*

Although many opinions on these subjects flowed freely, our best learnings came from the life stories which they told. By recalling several of them, we can suggest the nature of the adjustments which all faced:

Dr. Hermina Ruiz Cowley, an international lawyer from Paraguay, struggled through many disillusioning months trying to find suitable employment in her new country. She could not practice law among the people, for she had been trained according to another system. Personnel officers looking at her dossier kept trying to push her toward office jobs which could use the type of research which legal training implied. But this outgoing person "had to be me"—just because that was the reason she had come to this land of opportunity. As she told those of us at the conference:

> It is not enough for me to work on Wall Street to help the rich get richer, or push papers at the UN, nor just teach Spanish, so I am working on the lower east side in New York in a kind of a ghetto. There are Puerto Ricans, poor whites, poor European people, and old people. The situation is extremely, extremely dark. There is now a big growth of drug addicts, alcoholism, assaults and all

kinds of crime. This is where I must work. To be with your neighborhood is the way that brings to happen.

Dorothy Bapat, older, dignified, wise, and witty, had traveled from Ceylon to many homes in Europe and the United States with her husband, a career international civil servant in the area of social development. Their son was born and educated in the West, oriented completely in the same environment as his friends. Outside of occasional visits with his parents to Colombo, and his observance of certain cultural amenities at home out of respect to his parents, he had never developed any great feel for southern Asia. "So," his mother concluded at the consultation, "Someday he will marry a European or American girl, and what cultural heritage will my grandchildren have?"

Since almost everyone spoke on how Americans were friendly but seldom took time to be real friends, the matter of sharing real problems in a second culture often came up. To this question Dorothy Bapat proposed that overseas women initiate some practical efforts. "In my apartment house near the United Nations everybody says 'Good morning' in the elevator, but never 'Come in and let's talk', so I just volunteered to be a baby sitter for the young families and the doors were immediately open to me!" What a charming transnational grandmother she must have been!

Mary Baird was the wife of a competent senior officer of the AID staff, who had served in Indonesia, Ceylon and Pakistan. Mary had established households in all three places. Her warm sensitive nature, her uncommon curiosity and intelligent use of the language made her very much a part of the indigenous community. She had some helpful advice on how the two communities might mix:

> We have a tendency to go in and think that we're bringing something. But the fact is, we aren't. If you're in Pakistan for as long as two years, you can find out what the women are doing . . . just by going round where they are doing it. If you see some way you can help, just say 'What you're doing seems very important to me; can you use me?'

There are times when it is healthy to get back to one's roots with other Americans, and it doesn't matter if they are foolish Americans or wise Americans . . . But if it becomes completely absorbing so that all you know is the American community gossip, the fashion shows and other things that don't help your understanding of the job or the country, then it is bad.

We see the need of individual friendship on the one to one basis—a kind of extended family. But through all our differences, there is SOMETHING bigger than ourselves that is hovering over us in the world that needs to be tapped.

Our spirits were lifted and our age level lowered by the presence of three pre-school children who had come with their mothers. Catherine Mwanamwambwa, whose little two year old could be declared an American, had come to the United States from Nigeria for her college and graduate education in the field of anthropology. She married a staff person serving the Zambian delegation and was somewhat bored by social obligations. Later she served on the national Board of CWU and in 1972 went with her little family to a new homeland, Zambia, where she immediately developed her own life work with the rural women who labored in the unending food line— from planting to the meal on the table.

The young mother of the other two children was Zoreh S. Behbehani, whose home had been transferred from Iran to Shawnee Mission, Kansas, where her husband was in medical school. Zoreh told of a project developed by mothers of over 20 different countries for pre-school children called Mini Mundo: Her words are taken from the tapes:

When I first came to the U.S. from Iran, I thought I would climb my four walls. I had studied law and felt that I had something to contribute, but I had nothing to do and no way to do it. I was stacked up with diapers, and dishes, but needed the outside world to keep my sanity. So we started a *Mini-Mundo*.

A *Mini-Mundo* is a little international community in

Shawnee, Kansas, centered around families at the University of Kansas Medical Center. Mothers learn to drive, speak English, acquire skills, develop talents, all with the help of American women who baby-sit and free the overseas mother's time for participating in the community.

A *Mini-Mundo* is a little international community in facilities and anyone who comes in, whether foreign or American, pays 50¢. They come in and they put their children in different rooms according to age and they are sure that their children are taken care of. We employed professional teachers, raising the money ourselves.

The international children get to hear English from their peer group and in this way they learn English fast and so when they enter kindergarten or first grade they are not having language barriers or problems.

Women of such different experiences living together do not necessarily become an homogenized international community in five days. Opinions got fairly shrill by the third evening. So we all took a walk over the campus in silence and as we gathered again in the room, Shireen Subramanya was singing softly with her guitar.

By the next morning we were ready to bring our findings together to form the guidebook. We had the help of a professional cartoonist, Dani Aquila of Nashville and formerly of Manila, who created two charming little girl characters called "Mini-Mundo" and "Maxi-Mundo." They were distinguished by the 1970 skirt lengths, some of which were going up to the mid-thigh, and others dropping below the calf. We got the idea that in this rapidly changing world we could go both directions without contradicting ourselves. These findings, together with excerpts from the conversations of the week, were included in a brochure as a helpful aid to those departing from these shores.

All of us have our own "little world" and our own big world. And from each we obtain things of beauty and value which can readily transform the other. We would be spiritually stupid if we allow the Mini-Mundo *to become boring as life closes in on us, or the* Maxi-Mundo *to overwhelm us with its complexity. Both of our worlds are always waiting for the sunrise of ever new horizons—but, thank God, they never have to wait for long.*

**All in each place
. . . in the cities**

Church Women United claimed to be open to all
Christian women in each place. Yet we confess that in the large
cities where racial and religious pluralism converged, it was
not enough for us to open our arms to Roman Catholic and
Orthodox sisters and open our hearts to women long
separated by racial prejudice and discrimination. Damage
already done to stifle spirits must be repaired before any integrated social structure would be genuine. In the meantime
ominous changes in large metropolitan areas threatened and
thwarted any ecumenical development in the usual pattern
among church women.

What happens in an organization whose members
"represent" churches, when there is a flight into the suburbs—
thus leaving the 'key woman' dangling with no doors to unlock
in the downtown churches? Or what happens to the church in
the ghetto when there is an influx of rural black families not
used to the ways of the city and unwanted in the neighborhood? What happens to the morale of people when large
government grants are given for indigenous community
improvement in one year and withdrawn in the next? What
happens if schools, hospitals, garbage disposal and police
protection are found wanting while separate municipal
governments have mushroomed? What happens when active
church women move into a block of strangers and then seemingly cop out of former civic and religious concerns?
What happens to church women who had always counted on
friends to understand and speak with one voice, but within a
matter of a few months find themselves in a block of strangers?
And what happens when it all happens at once?

We did not anticipate the rapidity of change nor its
gravity: we were startled by the burning of the cities in 1967
and the subsequent wave of violence, drugs, and juvenile
delinquency. Even if we had anticipated these events, we could
not have altered them. Fear gripped some of us, replacing the
faith and courage we had demonstrated in 'normal times'.
Others saw God's judgment in the disruption of accepted

patterns and seized the opportunity to build a new and more just social order.

METROPOLITAN CONSULTATION 1966 In early July 1966, we invited a dozen women from large metropolitan complexes to come together for a couple of days to find out how the changing scene in their area was affecting Church Women United. The enthusiasm of the chairperson, Loris Coletta, had been aroused by a Southern California metropolitan planning commission that had involved CWU along with other community organizations in a goal-setting process toward conserving human values as technology transformed life of the greater Los Angeles area.

A subcommittee worked with Margaret Sonnenday of St. Louis to draw up a self study which would guide local councils to look afresh at how urban growth was affecting the program structure, volunteer participation, local relationships, and financial support of CWU. We secured Kim Andrews, retiring director of CWU in Brooklyn, as a consultant for one year to organize urban consultations and evaluate findings of the self-study which had been sent to 517 local units within the radius of 54 metropolitan centers. After finishing its own evaluations each local unit then chose three persons to meet with others in their metropolitan area.

Actually 48 of the 54 convenors held these metropolitan area conferences, and 304 local units went through the self study. The metropolitan areas had been identified by the latest U.S. Census Report and population maps. No structural changes were contemplated. Yet some units located in small towns may have felt these conferences an encroachment by their big neighbor unit in the central city. One real concern was what preparations should be made by outlying units to preserve the values of CWU if the present trends in central city units continued?

Deliberately we chose to hold the national metropolitan consultation in the Ecumenical Institute, housed though it was in a worn out building in one of the black ghettos of Chicago. We felt that it would bring a sense of reality into our discussions. There was an initial shock for those who taxied from the airport through the drab and dirty slum, but all was well as soon as they saw each other!

Out of fairness we should say that many were already adjusted to what they might find, for they had been around in their own cities. I roomed with Dot Dolbey of Cincinnati, the convenor of the task force on Urban Affairs reporting to the New Dimensions Commission. The first evening she dashed out into the neighborhood to get some fruit for breakfast. It was dark when she returned with her mission accomplished and some observations about the local shopkeeper catalogued in her mind.

"Weren't you afraid?" I queried, letting my own apprehension show. She replied, "Oh no, I often campaigned on streets like these when I was running for mayor of Cincinnati. That's what political life is all about—getting next to the people."

Her point was well taken. After all, 'getting close to the people' was a claim of Church Women United too. From the people came what I call the *Lessons-Learned-from-Life,* or *LLL.* My *LLL* in this case was: *Imagination behind a closed door generates more fear than a brisk walk in search of bananas on the city streets.*

The same evening, when the women introduced themselves by identifying with some significant local activity, I was amazed at the involvement of our city units. Of course, one *LLL* finding I discovered a long time ago: *Even with truthful intentions, some people away from home get carried away when reporting!*

Because we wished to focus our CWU programs on problems affecting women in the contemporary urban situation, we had previously gathered a group of women specialists for a two hour conference in New York City. They were selected because they had experience among women in minorities, teen age girls, welfare mothers, international students, retired persons, executive business women, volunteer women in the Junior League and in CWU, and the middle-aged (between 35-55) single woman. Since the research done on single women by Dorothy Payne was of concern to CWU in any city, we had invited Dorothy to share her findings with the Metropolitan Consultation.

Single women, which included unmarried, widows and divorcees, numbered in the millions and those who began working in their middle years were often caught in jobs of a fairly routine nature as typists, bookkeepers, administrative assistants, clerks and factory jobs and were accountable to someone farther up. The most experienced ones never got promoted because they were so essential where they were. They went home each night to rooms in a women's residence or to a one-room apartment. Unable to escape on weekends because they had neither resources for travel nor cars, they were caught in social ruts along with others in the same syndrome.

It was a self-defeating experience to try to make it in the city alone. Dorothy Payne illustrated the plight of many others from her own experience, the first response from the consultation participants was: "And what makes you think that the rest of us are not lonely too!"

In some ways we are all lonely and all needful. Nothing is gained by comparing one person or group with another. In fact the roles of 'being needed' and 'feeling needful' are interchangeable at different times within the same person. Life's experiences are great training programs; we are unprepared for the future only if we seek to shelter ourselves from the present.

WAKE UP As a result of this consultation and the work of her **SPEAK UP** own task force, Dorothy Dolbey introduced into **MOVE ON** the Commission on New Dimensions a set of sound urban goals and suggested skills which city women must develop to influence power structures of the city. After she was elected at the 1967 Assembly as the national president, she spoke widely throughout the country alerting women to the urban issues. Far more than a slogan were the words which called the women of cities to WAKE UP! SPEAK UP! AND MOVE ON! Translated into a program of action for the new form of society, the message was clear enough for all who wanted to hear. The dynamics of the words we had yet to learn.[8]

**CROSSING
ECONOMIC BARRIERS** Another task force reporting to the Commission on New Dimensions was concerned with how to keep open communication across economic and social barriers. The convenor of this group was Dr. Alice Young on the mayor's staff for human rights of Rochester, New York. She proposed a series of open "Worry Clinics" to be held on Sunday afternoons in a location accessible to those who had to come by public transportation. "Women are worrying about the same things," she would say. "Regardless of their race or their bank account, their agenda includes police protection, returning war veterans, the care of the aged, drug addicts, increased cost of living. If we would concentrate on the individual problem rather than putting all of the same race or wage scale into one category, we would be more compassionate."

She described how one of her proposals had been defeated by the City Council in spite of its support by the Mayor. When a crowd surrounded the City Hall carrying large signs of protest against the Council's decision, she stopped by the Mayor's office. "These people are on our side, so let's go out and join them." So, as private citizens, they picketed their official selves!

A member of our executive committee, Ruth Kodoni of California, was skillful in developing proposals for Foundation grants to finance a comprehensive urban program. Our timing and lack of track record were against us. So we had to begin where we were and take advantage of an opportunity that came our way.

**WORKSHOP
URBAN TRAINING
1968** Our first opportunity came when Elsie Penfield walked into our office to bring the glad tidings that United Presbyterian Women had a fund set aside for training of women in urban areas and suggested that the most strategic way to utilize it would be through a united effort. Claire Randall, working with a small committee of denominational staff, designed a Workshop in Urban Affairs which was held at the Center for

Continuing Education at the University of Chicago in 1968. In this instance we selected a number of cities and asked them to send several participants with the hope that an interracial team of leaders could effectively follow through upon their return. It was really at this workshop that I began to sense the wisdom of learning from life: *real people in real situations were our real resources.* There were three such findings at this meeting.

Lillian Anthony, a black woman from Minneapolis, had been invited to lead the WAKE-UP program. Using a carefully prepared sheet of multiple choice reactions, it soon became clear that we were "being wakened" to incipient racism among white women. Almost any response that wasn't already a dig at white women brought caustic remarks calculated to shock or subdue. This is a new Lillian, I thought. She had been a colleague of mine in former years and had always been comfortable with white women who affectionately accepted and admired her leadership. I had not seen her for a number of years and wondered what had happened. Perhaps she is playing a game with us, I thought. Maybe she had joined her own race while she was in Mississippi on the voter's registration drive. Or perhaps I am a racist. Or she is.

I felt a real sense of professional discomfort as the white women gradually withdrew from the discussion. There was nothing I could do at that point anyway, for the leader was closing with a summary, which, in reality was a defense of our accuser. The session was over. Lillian and I went into dinner together and she was her old friendly self.

Suddenly an *LLL* finding clicked in the back of my head! *We learn through experience how black women must feel when humiliated or overlooked.* In the years to come, many white women had the same reaction to efforts of being stabbed wide awake. The "in thing" was consciousness raising!

AVAILABLE   Another learning-from-life had to do with the
LEADERSHIP   natural leadership already developed in the
                  black ghetto. Among the competent women
leading sections on specific urban problems was Pearl Soil, who sparked the discussion dealing with unemployment

among black youth. Her gentle and good-humored approach to middle class women did not preclude her toughness in the best sense of the word in dealing with a program for hardcore jobless. While employed as an executive in the personnel department of one of Chicago's large department stores, she was asked to serve on a search committee seeking someone to initiate an inter-faith project aimed to encourage employment among young men and women in the black community. Her perception and skills were soon recognized by the search committee and she was pressured into service.

The interfaith project set up operations in a center in a vacant business establishment. Together with her associates, Mrs. Soil determinedly sought out the businesses, factories, and other employers who would assist in placing her applicants. She calculated the needs of the employers and classified aptitudes of the applicants. She arranged transportation to get them together. On one side she bolstered egos and on the other she nurtured receptivity. She helped applicants face such essentials as personal appearance, tenure, work attitudes and confidence. Among employers she asked for tolerance and understanding. She coaxed those in their first job to stay long enough to establish a record and extolled the employers for efforts in job placement and upgrading.

The track record? In three years time she and her team had successfully screened and placed over 25,000 young men and women. Today she remembers the real satisfaction and the gratitude of the many families who, through her efforts, enjoyed the privileges of a steady pay check.

At the conclusion of that first workshop in Chicago, Pearl and I sat in the lobby while I waited for the airport limousine. She was a Presbyterian elder so we had a common ground for a discussion of church affairs, as well as for a review of the tests and trials of her business encounters.

On my return to New York, Pearl telephoned very late one night just to share some good news with me relative to the previous day's work. After that our paths crossed several times during the next two years. Later she was to become an active member of CWU's Special Committee on Urban Program and was elected to serve on our National Board of Managers in 1971, and still later to become the chairperson of the Metropolitan Growth Committee.

My *LLL* finding: *Every leader needs her own supporting community—unlimited by geography or race.*

The chief speaker at the 1968 CWU workshop was Dr. Charles Spivey, the new director of the NCCC program on the critical aspects of American cities which at that time were experiencing rising crime rates, drug traffic among juvenile delinquents and destructive riots. It is not surprising that a director in an interdenominational agency like the NCCC would be encouraged by an enterprising group of women who were ready for action on the living level of the American people. His report provided hope for our urban plans.

Not long after, Dr. John Regier, the associate general secretary for the NCCC's Division of Life and Mission, asked us if we would be able to administer a sum of $35,000 which had been designated by the donors for work among women in the cities. During the 3 years since this money had been requested, the NCCC had been spinning off its service ministries to separate agencies, and accenting its role as a place for member denominations to plan together. The major denominations were channelling their funds directly to local urban coalitions, where the action was!

Perhaps it should be noted that the donor in the first place was Church Women United through their Inter-Continental Mission committee! So we pondered 'why not'? Women had always given money through their channels for mission. Was this not the time for women to be involved in mission themselves? By stretching our dollars through many hours of volunteer community service the scope of our witness would be enlarged. From this investment in time and money, we would gain some real lessons from real persons which could be shared with others at the 1971 Ecumenical Assembly in Wichita. My third *LLL* finding was: *Church Women United can act responsibly and creatively in the use of its own mission funds.*

PLANNING FOR 1969-71 The national president appointed a special Committee on Urban Program composed of 15 women from metropolitan areas in the 5 states adjacent to Chicago.

A national vice-president, Elizabeth Haselden, undertook the leadership of the committee and carried the administrative detail necessary from an office set up in her home in Evanston, Illinois. She maintained continual relationship with the national office through Elsie Jones, staff coordinator of unit cultivation and Claire Randall, staff person in charge of program development.

The committee was charged with defining pilot projects which, together with the experience of volunteer women in carrying them out, would offer guidelines to CWU in metropolitan areas.

The probing of two questions was considered essential to significant survival of metropolitan units:

1) How could a cluster of local units located in a given metropolitan area maintain their jurisdictional independence and yet act together in developing strategy or facing the demands of sudden crises?

2) In a period when large funds, both from government and church agencies were being used to employ many staff personnel to carry on the service and education programs in cities: what function, if any, was the volunteer church woman to fulfill?

METRO 71 In a search for an answer to the first of these questions, a program entitled *Metro 71* was made available to three selected metropolitan areas surrounding Denver, Baltimore, and Minneapolis-St. Paul.

A flying squadron of church women with experience in other metropolitan areas performed a catalytic function in each workshop. The participants talked together about how the new features of the movement (listening teams, planning groups, forums) could be useful in meeting the needs of the city units. Then two sessions were spent on choosing an "umbrella problem" which was faced by all in the region,

(Education, Children, and Hunger were chosen) and planning together how the various units in the area could work on a common goal.

The experience of *Metro 71* led to the development of a pliable structure called a *Metro-Gro-Group,* a plan which was discussed with ten other large urban centers before it was refined and offered as Guidelines in the revised *On-Book* published in 1972.

The *Metro-Gro-Group* is an arrangement which brings suburban and central city units of CWU into equal partnership for the purposes of agreeing on specific goals and operational procedures needed to realize some change in the area. A *Metro-Gro-Group* is intended to be complementary to whatever CWU organizational structure already exists; it can usually operate creatively since it can utilize the human resources of all units but is not required to undertake consuming functions by officers of each unit.

PILOT URBAN Judging from the record, the women who made
MINISTRIES up the Special Committee on Urban Programs
must have had a very satisfying experience in initiating pilot urban programs during their two year assignment. There was no effort to decry the traditional activities of community service or advocacy in these cities. These ongoing ministries might have been described by some as "muddling through" the crises, yet, in times of change, there are values in keeping up relationships or fulfilling obligations. After all the big, bold, 'relevant' crash programs had their share of casualties too!

The Special Committee on Urban Programs focused its ingenuity on relevant urban ministries which volunteers conceived and carried out. They were good stewards of the limited funds available for seed money in approved local ventures. They seemed to realize that those entrusted with stimulating new national programs must be able to describe specific projects in terms of *What, When, Where, How Much—* and the very important *Why!*

A person from each unit which sponsored a pilot project was included in the committee to assure a genuine support community. Even their minutes were exciting reading! After each progress report made by a person involved, the recorder would comment "This is important, because . . . ."

There was no elitist separation from the rest of CWU. For them the city was a setting in which the holistic program can be visible and inter-related. Each project had its special thrust but those who worked on it knew how it meshed into the whole.

There follows a brief description of the specific projects undertaken to test the processes necessary for church women to penetrate urban society in the 70's. The special committee initiated and evaluated them all according to specific objectives, reporting in person to the Ecumenical Assembly in Wichita and to the general constituency through a printed brochure entitled "Church Women United in Urban Ministries—1969-1971."

COMMUNITY DECISION MAKING—1970 The purpose of the Pilot Project in Grand Rapids was to provide exposure to the ways in which decision on vital issues of concern were made in the city and to help church women to become more knowledgeable in attempting to move into local centers of power. By June 17 women had committed themselves to the project. All summer they kept busy with a reading and research project including the use of a clipping service. In September a two-day institute gave them some on-the-job training. Part of their orientation was interviewing members of the school board, the staff of a newspaper, the officials at city hall, and leaders in the black community. One of the black leaders, obviously fed up with merely answering questions about the situation, was quoted as saying:

> People have forgotten how to feel. They say I didn't make the rules, but they don't want new ones. Grand Rapids is not really ready for significant change. Priorities of human needs are not the priorities here. If women really wanted to make some change, they could. With this challenge to their lethargic city, the task force

tackled the specific problems of the plight of the aged, the school lunch program, civil service policies and open housing.

When a local issue became 'live', as in the case of the school lunch program, all groups mobilized for action. The school lunch task force circulated petitions in area churches and thereby tipped the scales toward favorable action by the local school board.

The two-member task force on "the aged" became so involved in research in the Grand Rapids community that they became co-authors of a book on the subject with 32 organizations assisting in the project.

The civil service group, working on methods that would insure fairness in selection of civil service personnel produced a model for the personnel section of the new City Charter then being written and asked permission to testify before the commission regarding such changes.

The open housing group reflected the frustrations and rebuffs of any involvement by remarking: "Facts are hard to come by and power plays further complicate the problems." But they did not give up! Working with the head of the housing department of the local Urban League, they began to understand the obstacles to progress in their community. It takes time and dedication to establish continuing relationship with the people who are in the midst of the daily experience, whether it be city hall or a rundown housing development.

BLACK COUNT There has been a strong affinity between the **1970 CENSUS** National Council of Negro Women and Church Women United not only because of common goals but also because the women's organizations of the black church are integrals of both movements. Therefore, when the Chicago chapter of the NCCW initiated a project to get an accurate black count in the 1970 census, CWU was pleased to be involved. It was particularly important to alert black people to the importance of honestly reporting the number of people living in their over-crowded neighborhoods, for these statistics affect housing and city services as well as representation in electoral districts.

Under the aegis of a planning group of ten women who

met in January 1970 in a field house of a housing project, a caucus workshop was held in February 1970 to teach the procedures of the census and discuss the relationship of the census count to community concerns. A $4 registration fee was charged to defray expenses and provide a kit to the 142 participants. The convenor of the workshop explained the need for further financial assistance:

> All women assisting in this project are volunteers. Understandably we will need financial assistance to encourage the indigent recruits. Thus far this project has been promoted on a goodwill basis. Obviously the financial assistance is needed for lunch, carfare and child care.

Impressed by this grassroots volunteer effort to ensure an "Accurate Black Count," CWU made an encouraging grant and offered supportive services that were requested.

Action mushroomed. Locations for 53 Help Stations to assist the public in completing census forms were secured and 300 volunteers were recruited and trained to run the Help Stations. In the course of the census period over 2500 people were helped.

Esterfina Jones, the effective public relations chairperson of NCNW, generously gave Church Women United co-sponsoring status. Some 4000 brochures on the census and 10,000 folders on the Help Stations were printed and distributed. Radio stations carried news and facts, and other volunteers wrote letters, spoke before organizations, and mobilized neighborhood training sessions. *The success of this tremendous volunteer undertaking indicates that women will respond as volunteers to a 'felt need', if convinced of the validity of the plan.*

Among busy employed women, it worked better to recruit for a specific number of hours and to offer good materials in training for the job. Volunteers get tired more quickly when they feel ineffectual!

SUBURBAN RACISM   *White Racism—Myth or Reality?* described the scope of a self study of 42 women in Dupage County, Illinois on six consecutive Mondays in the fall of 1970. Jointly sponsored by the West Suburban Branch of the YWCA of Metropolitan Chicago and a task force of leaders from several suburban units of CWU. The project attempted to move from talking about racism historically to an examination of racism within the persons and its subtle effects in everyday life when working on the local school board, or in the church, club, or market. Almost all of those enrolled finished the course, and at its conclusion remained together as a core group to stimulate action among others in the various suburbs.

One of the primary goals of the CWU Urban Program was to explore ways in which women might better understand and support other women in the urban complex. The special committee on Urban Program had difficulty defining specific projects and finally selected two—one which was stimulated in an all white area through a Friday morning discussion group and the other which rose spontaneously among church women in the heart of a black ghetto which they named *Reaching People Where They Are.*

FRIDAY MORNING   A specific area in Southwest Chicago was
DISCUSSIONS   selected where there was bound to be
                     traumatic social stresses which challenged
the established patterns of life. The neighborhood was all white, largely from Lithuanian and Polish background, 90% Roman Catholic. Men worked hard in jobs dubbed as "blue collar" and were vigilant in protecting their immediate neighborhood.

Three women—a Roman Catholic nun, a Protestant minister's wife, a local YWCA secretary—invited a few women to meet in a church in early May just to talk together. From this informal beginning, the *Friday Morning Discussion Group* began. Elizabeth Haselden drove across the city to be one of them each week. She describes in *Urban Ministries* the mood of their concerns:

> The discussions during the early weeks reflected the impact of the turbulent events of 1969-70, for the island of a homogenous neighborhood was no longer 'secure.' Other mothers in the community were picketing to

protest mobile units in schools, i.e., "integration". "Law and Order" was the theme, yet student violence, police violence, racial violence flared. The protest of the Vietnam War was vividly portrayed on TV which invaded every mother's home. Meticulously organized Block Clubs covered an eighty-block area of this one community, the goals of which were confusing and often divisive, splitting families and alienating neighbors. There was practically no opportunity for children or adults to know people of other racial and cultural backgrounds. Policemen's wives, who were part of the group, freely admitted daily fear for their husband's safety and said it haunted them.

So the fears and uncertainties, the concerns and convictions about all these things bubbled up, and the group had no difficulty in setting the direction of the Friday morning discussions.

As mutual confidence was established, conversations began to include invited guests from the surrounding enclaves whose way of life was quite different from their own.

One Friday morning a young black mother was invited to share in the discussion. All were uptight as the discussion started on the changing neighborhood. Then the black woman began to talk about her five children and some of the tough daily decisions this forced on her. The white women had something to say about theirs too! The discussion was on! Several white women shared their feelings of fright as their husbands went out on police duty. The black woman identified with the feeling, for her husband's life had been threatened over and over again. Once strangers, they became women together in a violent world.

Another time two members of a women's liberation group came over to talk—which must have been a mutual education. Still another Friday morning a young woman from the Catholic culture movement was invited. On another Friday, a black community organizer from the Cabrini-Green area responded to their invitation to tell them in very human terms of the desperate people he talked to on the streets. He spoke of the alienation he found among families. The defense mechanism of the group was lowered because he didn't blame white people for all their trouble. The next time any one of them picked up her paper and saw a picture of a bomb disaster in the Cabrini area, she remembered his stories of the frustrations and the courage of people who lived all their lives there.

These experiences were meant originally not only to open doors to what was transpiring in their city, but to open windows to inner reactions on subjects they had never before talked about together. After each discussion they came to view themselves less and less stereotypes of a wife, a Protestant or a Catholic, a mother, or a girl friend. As a result they discovered themselves as persons growing with each encounter with their neighbors in the city.

REACHING PEOPLE
Reaching People Where They Are was the way in which an interdenominational group of black women described a project which aimed at the stabilization of their immediate community. The planning committee of women from the Methodist, Baptist, Presbyterian, Roman Catholic and Seventh Day Adventist Churches held two common convictions; that they should carry responsibility for the well being of the children in the blocks of their immediate neighborhoods and that this was the church's business.

Their specific intention was to enable mothers to set up and work on the kind of program they saw as meaningful. They planned to include unemployed mothers for duty at specific times; to develop a mother-to-mother relationship as each in turn related to her child and her neighbor's child. Since the parent-child involvement was primary, they limited their activity for the summer of 1970 to 100 children in the blocks near one of the churches which offered rooms for their activities. They spent Sunday afternoons canvassing the homes, enrolling the children and involving the mothers (two adults for each child were recruited).

It was arranged for one adult to take all the children from a particular housing unit across the city to a free clinic, thus saving many who would have to give up a day's work. The kind of records clinics might require in diagnosing an illness was explained to each co-operating mother. A day camp was organized in a vacant church facility, enlisting 15 neighborhood youth corps workers as well as the volunteer hours of many mothers. The Department of Human Resources furnished luncheons, equipment, buses for field trips, and specialized personnel. Throughout the summer, events were planned for the adults and youth to share, and the program closed with a tremendous "bash" over Labor Day weekend. The outpouring of volunteer hours, and of material and personnel from sources available in the community showed what can be done if channels are opened and goals recognized.

Even volunteer efforts require some overhead money, so the planning committee went about the job of financial support toward which CWU contributed some from its urban program budget. A program coordinator for the summer day care and help for carfare and baby-sitting service were thus provided for with business-like competence. Yet no one would deny that the real result was a neighborhood being stabilized by *Reaching People Where They Are.*

These two mini-communities, which still exist as operating identities, now recognize themselves as expressions of Church Women United in Chicago. An informal group of church women coming together to do a specific job develops initiative and leaders. Their experience together adds meaning as they identify with a wider fellowship.

The encouragement of cooperative projects is valuable for its own sake. It can also be a viable way for Church Women United to penetrate parts of the city where they have had no previous relationship.

Acting as a network among various ethnic communities, CWU assures its own inter-racial character and fulfills its reconciling purpose.

ONGOING Although its report to the 1971 Ecumenical
URBAN Assembly completed its assignment, the Special
PROGRAM Committee on Urban Program had proved the
value of a group from a compassable region coming together
for stimulation and consultation. We were also convinced that
a continuing inter-racial staff team familiar with the complexities of urban life could render valuable service to
volunteer women by uncovering resources, keeping alert to
radically changing situations, making objective evaluations,
and enlivening flagging spirits.

It was our dream that we might put such a team in each
of the eight regions of the nation where the Department of
Labor already had established resource centers for urban
development.

But in spite of the valiant efforts on the part of our
finance committee to secure a major grant from some foundations for this bolder plan, we were forced to settle for what we
could do by ourselves. Fortunately, the United Methodists and
the Episcopalians made generous gifts to our 30th anniversary celebration which gave us courage to begin with one staff
team to coordinate the National Urban venture. If you are in the
business of making dreams come true, here is a helpful
*Lesson-Learned-From-Life: Never give up a small gain just
because it is not larger!*

A natural choice for one member of the permanent team
was Elizabeth Haselden, the coordinator of the special
program for the experimental period. Her knowledge of the
program and structure of the national movement, gained from
her years of service on national committees and as one of its
officers, would be used to the full as she transferred that experience to other metropolitan areas. She set up the CWU office in
a family room of her first floor, where, with the assistance of
Kayo Suzukida she carried on the correspondence necessary
to set up the field schedules and leadership training program
envisioned for the next period.

For the second member of the team we sought a black person with demonstrated ability to mobilize women in the inner city into significant action. We turned to Katie Booth who had an enviable record in real achievement with volunteers in community service in Chicago. Katie Booth earned her living in research at the Chicago Medical School, but the work she loved best was done in the evenings when she returned to her home in West Garfield Park. It was a district in Chicago with a high crime record and an unusual number of transients which brought about much neighborhood instability. One summer she borrowed a microscope from the medical school to meet a group of little boys in the basement of a tenement apartment house. Without fear of being scolded for the 'living dirt' under their nails, they placed their fingers under the lens. Theirs was the excitement of pioneer scientists fighting the war against germs!

As a friend and neighbor, Katie Booth could easily organize the mothers in a block for a health delivery system. As an active church woman, she was among those who came together to form *Reaching People Where They Are,* and to help them tap the community resources which supported their summer program for children. She was among those women who organized the program for an accurate census among black people. She revealed a shrewd sense for the dynamics of the political system in city and state. She dispensed this knowledge discreetly.

It was in the home of Katie Booth where Coretta King met with an inter-racial group of women who were deeply concerned about racial justice. The meeting resulted in the movement "Women Mobilized for Change!" This movement was an alerting system whereby women could inform each other of a crisis of any threatening proportion before it could grow beyond control. The office was an old converted school bus which could be dispatched to any part of the city, and without further ado be a meeting place for a small inter-racial consultation. Yes, Katie Booth had the experience we so badly needed on the staff if we wanted to be on speaking terms with black women of the inner city.

I sent her a job description and asked if she would talk it

over with our personnel committee. When she arrived I told her quite frankly that we would not be able to meet her present salary within our present wage scale. She replied: "Whatever you offer me, I'll take. I have already accepted the job. It fulfills my dream of community service. I have had my fill of huge crash programs with their pile of paperwork and high administrative costs. The people themselves are the real hope for the city's future."

INNER CITY PROGRAMS It was agreed that Katie Booth would be available as a consultant to CWU in inner cities and she would carry a field program upon invitation. However, we hoped also that she would keep close to the realities of the people in West Garfield Park where she lived. She was free to initiate programs when the local leadership of the community would be the sustaining force. Let me illustrate with three of them:

An available store building was used by church women to set up a place for voters to register. A mock voting booth was set up and church women trained to teach people how to use the voting device in a real election where each could register a preference among the candidates and proposals on the ballot. Buses were made available on certain days to carry the young 'first time' voters down to city hall to register. When I asked why they didn't register out in their own community, Katie said something about a 'wake up' program for the Mayor to let his associates know the next generation would soon 'speak up'.

A summer program similar to the year before was enlarged to involve twice as many children and adults. In addition to the crafts, special classes and field trips, the program was augmented by some expertise offered from other parts of the city by persons wanting to be part of it. Dr. Jean Unsworth, Associate Professor of Fine Arts of Loyola University, came over frequently so that she and the children together could uncover elements of beauty in materials that had been discarded as rubbish. Church Women United came into high visibility when sweat shirts with our insignia were ordered for all the boys as well as girls, who then went through the blocks of the ghetto selling subscriptions for *The Church Woman* magazine.

In addition to funds which were solicited locally, some of the overhead costs came from the Asia Conference of Church Women in a surprise grant from the Fellowship of the Least Coin. When Katie told the mother assistants about the world movement of prayer supported on an equal basis by rich and poor women with the 'least coin of their own realm', the women caught the idea instinctively and became one with women all around the world.

FAMILY CENTER   At the graduation exercises on Labor Day, Katie Booth began to cogitate on an old question: Is graduation the end or the beginning? What the summer day camp proved in terms of new horizons for both young and old, should not be an 'on-again-off-again' affair.

What was percolating through her mind was a community-based family center. It could be located in one of the inner city churches whose many empty rooms were readily available on week days. It would need a sponsoring board, a few business managers and program directors, a continuing means of income activities for mothers (like a Clothes Closet), interest groups for working women, in addition to a whole range of continuing programs for children and youth. The *Booth Survival Kit For Families* listed the following basic needs: a decent place to live (housing), a balanced diet (nourishment), substantial clothing, adequate health, a basic education, religious and cultural meaning. "Anything less will add to the mounting problems of delinquency and broken homes," she said, "It is in the family unit that caring and sharing begin."

The family center came into being in 1972—simple in equipment but extravagant in imaginative and joyous activity. Their program flexed to the needs of the city. In the summer of 1975 when all cities were revising their programs and their budgets, a 'children's city' became the central involvement of the children. They elected their own Mayor, City Council and Board of Education, operated their own police and sanitation department, planned their own cultural and religious experiences. Of course they had field trips to visit with those who actually were working in these city services in Chicago, and then came back to the family center's city to set up processes which would assure that their own little citizens would be healthy, wealthy and wise—and live happily together at least all summer.

An inner city ministry is not only offering a program facility where children and adults can create their own community as they work and play together, it also consists of surrounding individuals with loving security and some informed guidance as what can be done to work themselves out of their predicament. Only one of many examples in the confidential records of the Family Center illustrates the point.

A young woman despondent over the fact that her baby would be born out of wedlock came in for counsel. Through the activities of the center during the next months, the father and mother of the new baby were brought together and married. In another state where the father had a job, a home was established for the family and both parents completed their education. From despair to hope because pastoral care was available in a crucial time.

As soon as the experimental period was over, the Family Center was established with its own church and community connections and it was transferred to its own board, some members came from the local community, and others from CWU units in the immediate area. In a letter appealing for financial help, this paragraph describes the continuing need:

The Family Center is here on the west side. We see youth becoming more and more confused and frustrated because of unemployment, drug abuse, alcoholism, abortion, school drop-outs, etc. We know the experience of helpless people because of hunger, lack of education, lack of adequate housing and employment. Our purpose here is not to *make change happen,* but to create a climate that will encourage the community to become so aware of the problems that their involvement will bring about change.

On the bottom of the letter that came to me speaking of its special significance, Katie Booth scrawled a note:

> We are in the midst of so much poverty in this area, perhaps it seems to some people we are not making a dent. We who are here know what it means to touch one life and give a ray of hope. CWU has been introduced to this part of the city via Family Center.

What a wonderful introduction as hand touches hand!

Ongoing cultivation of a program cannot be measured in the same way as milestones of a pilot venture. We cannot catch glimpses of the 48 metropolitan area stations along the Urban Program Express! Every metropolitan area differs in complexity and those who live in each place must plan their own entrance and exit to action proposals.

There is reflected in our experience through the years from 1966 to 1975 the dramatic changes going on among city planners and in the urban departments of major denominations. In the mid-sixties bold city planning for the future metropolis was at its height and simultaneously there was great concern over the explosive frustration among the black people in northern cities. All this signalled change and the churches wished to be part of it, investing large sums in urban priority programs.

By 1975 all major cities openly admitted their serious budget predicament and their people felt the general deterioration of public services. In projecting another national Urban Consultation in 1976, Elizabeth Haselden said to the Board, "Obviously the urban program of CWU cannot rebuild the cities before they collapse on us, but Church Women United can continue to involve the Roman Catholic, Protestant, and Orthodox women who form its natural constituency in the cities, and challenge them

- to probe the problems and their causes
- to be sensitive to the needs of persons in the inner city
- to adjust the operating practices in order that Christian women might have a greater impact on

the life of the Cities

- to penetrate neighborhoods where women can minister to one another."

Church Women United in metropolitan areas are, of course, part and parcel of one national movement. The problems were not all that different from those reflected in towns, counties, and small cities. BIGNESS was what was baffling—the size of the predicament, the density of the population, the complexity of municipal government.

Just because of an understanding of the Christian calling in our time, Church Women United in metropolitan areas will remain flexible and friendly, purposeful and prayerful. You will find them along the unsure streets of their own cities, sharing the fiestas and the folkways of their multinational homing place and perhaps shedding a tear with those whom so many have passed by without knowing they were there.

FOOTNOTES TO CHAPTER 8

1. *All in Each Place* is the title of a brochure on local ecumenicity published by the World Council of Churches in 1966.

2. As Archbishop of North America between 1931 and 1949 Athenagoras had done much to consolidate the Greek Orthodox Church in a new homeland. When he departed in 1949 to assume the highest office in Orthodox Christianity, Ecumenical Patriarch of Constantinople, he left a Church with 375 parishes across the land, the Holy Cross Theological Seminary, and a reorganized highly effective philanthropic federation for women—the Philoptochos.

3. This complexity could be illustrated by the World Union of Catholic Women's Organizations, the board of which is made up of one representative of each country. If there is more than one large organization, they must agree on that person. At present, Lillian O'Connor represents the United States and is also the world treasurer. In the United States there are about 15 women's organizations affiliated with the National Council of Catholic Women—such as the Catholic Daughters of America, and The Daughters of Isabella. The NCCW consists of 8,200 local organizations from 32 archdioceses and 135 dioceses in the USA.

4. The substance of the memorandum seemed to be in line with those working Sessions of the Congress whose findings on Racism; Fight against Oppression; Peace and World Community; Development; Mass Media; and the Handicapped were similar to those in other international gatherings of the time. In addition the Congress made statements on the status of women and mixed marriages which were significant to have come from a congress of this nature as early as 1967:

Women in the Church

"The Third World Congress for the Lay Apostolate wishes to express its desire that women be granted by the Church full rights and responsibilities as Christians, and a serious doctrinal study be pursued on the place of women within the sacramental order and within the Church."

—from Lay Apostolate Bulletin 1967 No. 3

Mixed Marriages

"Men and women from all over the world realize the pastoral failure of the present regulations . . .

1. The validity in principle of unions contracted before a minister of one of the main Protestant communions should be recognized, as has been the case for unions contracted before the ministers of the Orthodox Churches. (The refusal to recognize this validity in principle harms the charity and peace developing between the Christian communions.)

2. Responsibility for the Christian education of their children belongs jointly to the two parents, who share in the grace of the marriage sacrament, with the help of qualified representatives of their Churches.

3. All efforts toward common pastoral care, that is to say, concerted at every level between the ministers of the different communities, will be welcomed with joy both by the partners of mixed marriages themselves and by parents and families."

—from the Workshop on Ecumenism, ibid, p. 18

5. In answer to our questions, Sister Joan showed some of the practical ways in which the Roman Catholic Sisters were changing in response to these accents in theological thinking:

What about the abandonment of the traditional dress which identified their Orders? Although the habit was a sign of religious dedication in the past, it was developed in a time when its style was such that their separation was not conspicuous. A growing number of Sisters now feel that the "sign of Christ's presence" among them in today's world must be their identity with others who are open to the struggle for human rights.

What about the freedom of Sisters? Sisters must proclaim their right to be themselves which means they will restructure their communities to give appropriate expression to their freedom and feminine talents. Some large congregations offered their sisters a wide variety of choices: some choose to live in the traditional lifestyle in convents; some choose to live in small units in apartments near their place of work (such as in a ghetto or on a campus); others choose to live as recluses, making their chief contribution the life of contemplative prayer. It is too early to predict which of these new lifestyles will survive. If the groups are too amorphous, they will hardly stand the test of time; if they are too structured, they may stifle the inspiration of the Spirit. One can only hope that those which survive will best embody the pilgrim nature of the Church.

6. This information is from the brochure, "Roman Catholic Sisters and Church Women United."

7. From the point of view of its origin and its contemporary program, one of the significant overseas movements is the *Tomo-no-Kai* whose membership comes from among the readers of the FUJIN-NO-TOMO (The Women's Friend) The FUJIN-NO-TOMO, the oldest women's journal in Japan, was begun in 1903 by a remarkable Christian educator, Mrs. Y Motoko Hani. Today 171,000 subscribers enjoy each month a 200 page slick color pictorial magazine with articles on education, health, literature, current social issues, Bible studies, and newsworthy happenings from the Christian community worldwide . . .

 Tomo-no-Kai (The Friendly Association) began in 1930 as a separate organization from the magazine, although they perform mutually supportive services. In 1976, there were 176 chapters all over Japan and a few in North and South America. The purpose of these volunteers is to forward goals in modern society based on a Christian spirit: love, freedom and cooperation. Some of their activities are: study groups on home and family life; development of consumer's cooperatives; establishment of long-term and short-range program for women and girls in farm villages as well as baby-clinics and centers for pre-school children. As occasion demands, their chapter members respond with other civic organizations in flood and famine relief and world peace.

 The distinguished editor-in-chief of the FUJIN-NO-TOMO, Yoshiko Waturi, is a longtime friend of CWU having been one of the overseas members of the 1967 CAUSEWAY and a participant in the consultations ahead of the Ecumenical Assembly.

8. In an article in *The Church Woman* interpreting the May Fellowship Day theme on *Human Values* the following plans were outlined:

 WAKE UP—and find out what is happening and what you want to happen. Organize Search Parties to discover facts, hold interviews, compare notes, establish goals.

 SPEAK UP—but learn how first! Set up a training program with resources in your community. Find out how to isolate the issues and how to identify "power structure" such as city council, school board, churches, industries, chamber of commerce, unions, community organizations. Find out what they think is important and what decisions they make that affect the life of the city and its long range goals. Encourage groups affected by discrimination to speak for themselves.

MOVE ON—and change a situation! A definite target is needed here (such as open housing) which has been agreed upon by the executive committee. Let us be sure that we have the facts, that we have made them available, that we are able to indicate why we as church women are interested.

chapter 9

Offer gifts God has given

On a Sunday stopover in Aukland, New Zealand, I listened attentively to the pastor of St. David's Presbyterian Church present an overview of the Gospel according to St. Luke. The pastor surmised that the material for this Gospel must have been collected by Dr. Luke when he accompanied the Apostle Paul to Jerusalem, and the latter got caught with time consuming legal processes.

As the only gospel writer who had not known Jesus during his earthly ministry, Dr. Luke must have been especially interested in asking questions of those who did! Many people questioned were women and what they remembered tells much about human sin and sickness, of daily living and dying, as well as of the joy and peace that filled their faith in their Lord.

A line from a stanza of an unfamiliar hymn sung at the end of the service caught my imagination. It went something like this: *"Offer back again the gifts that Thou has given."* (It was this phrase I remembered the night of my fantasy on the Cathedral and wrote "All in Each Place May Offer Gifts God Himself Has Given.")

I recalled the day before in Australia when I had talked with a woman once of the Hungarian aristocracy, who remarked: "The women in the West have sold their freedom too cheaply."

And then I remembered a conversation with Anna Hedgeman the year before. She had gone to India with a delegation from The Seaman's Institute and was the only one who had interviewed Nehru, then the Prime Minister. When they returned, all the men were asked to speak on radio and TV, but she was not. "Was it because you were black or because you were a woman?", I asked.

"Because I was a woman," she snapped back. "I'd rather be a Negro, a Puerto Rican, Catholic and a Jew all rolled into one than to be a woman when it comes to getting in the media."

I told her I had been approached for a job with United Church Women but hesitated to give up my present one where there was a satisfactory arrangement with men on a policy making level. Her astute reply was *"One* will make no significant difference."

Still pondering on these things as the plane landed at sunrise in Fiji, I began to think of many women I had known whose God-given gifts ought to be taken out of the original tissue paper and put to everyday use. The church and the world were being bogged down by boxed up personalities waiting to be untied . . . and united on their way together. By sunset, it had become clear to me.

I had not been back in my New York apartment twenty minutes when the phone rang. It was Edna Sinclair again with the same question that she had been posing for months. This time I had a different answer. In fact, I'd be glad to come to work with United Church Women!

Two years later I would have had to explain what I meant by gifts. Do women have different gifts than men? Then I was only convinced that whatever gifts women had, all of them should be put to use. It never occurred to me then that words like "potential" and "consciousness" and "liberation" would take on a feminist significance. Although their meaning was vague (as was true of the word "gifts"), they served as a sort of shorthand communication among many diverse groups of women. The decade of the 70's saw the rise of "women's liberation" springing from such widespread sources that it defied organization by conventional leadership.

LIBERATION Since we were in an era when many churches
VOICES were abandoning their women's organizations in
favor of groups for both men and women, our
staff found the articulation of women-for-women in secular
groups something new. Stirrings among women's groups were
rising quite independently of each other.

In the fall of 1967, I was invited to a Park Avenue apartment to meet leaders of women's organizations interested in
mobilizing for a peace march on Washington in the name of
Jeannette Rankin. All were younger, sophisticated women -
with the exception of 80 year old Jeannette Rankin and me.
Much of the time was spent in voicing the frustration of women
not being heard. "I don't like women," shouted one young
lawyer, "but the only way we will get peace in this male-
oriented country is to organize a women's party and elect our
kind to the power structures."

In 1968 we convened a black women's consultation to
consider current demands on Church racial practice but it was
the women's issue that captured the agenda. At the initial
meeting of the Special Committee on Urban Program and the
meetings of the Executive Staff Conference (women denominational executives) the often repeated protests were voiced
at length before a chairperson could get to the subject at hand.

Meanwhile certain events in the wider community were
appearing as feature stories in the newspapers. In an Eastern
university town, a tavern designated "For Men Only" was
invaded by irate females who tossed a few bras around. This
and other similar incidents created hostilities among some
women who wouldn't have done it that way. Even though
satisfied with their own situations, some women were
supportive of the general movement. In others, there had
always been a kernel of protest which, tossed on the hot
griddle of submerged feeling, was soon popping into a
women's liberation movement. Eventually we would all be
involved one way or another!

1968 NCCC   Just two days before the opening of the General
ASSEMBLY   Assembly of the NCCC in Detroit in October,
1968, one of the staff members of the NCCC
phoned to inquire if women would support a black caucus
bringing in a nominee for president of the NCCC. This was
rather an academic question since as yet the black caucus had
not been able to come up with a nominee; even if they did, 95
women among the 786 official delegates would hardly be
decisive, given the unlikely possibility that they would vote as a
bloc. I inquired if he knew that the candidate being presented
by the nominating committee was a woman and, if chosen,
would be the first woman president of the NCCC. He was
aware of the fact. I was fairly sure that with a nominee as highly
acceptable as Cynthia Wedel, the women wouldn't miss the
opportunity.

It was a friendly exchange of opinion between two staff
members, for neither of us were voting delegates. At that time
the NCCC and its member churches had made racial justice a
priority, and there was no real consciousness that a women's
movement was rising.

We had set up a briefing session for women delegates
and the background of various prepared position papers to be
introduced at the plenary session was to be presented by the
chairmen of the sponsoring committees. It was discovered that
with the exception of the nominee for president, all other
members of the executive committee were scheduled to be
men. The women decided that a forceful statement must be
made from the platform to alert the churches that the era of
tokenism was over. Other meetings of what amounted to a
women's caucus were called to talk about concerns which
were incorporated into a statement presented on the third
afternoon of the Assembly.

It was a moving moment when President Arthur Fleming
recognized Peggy Billings, one of the United Methodist
delegates. As she spoke, all women delegates stood silently to
express the seriousness with which they regarded her
remarks.

Peggy Billings deliberately began by identifying the group who had endorsed it:

> We are an informal group.
>
> We are members of churches represented here.
>
> Some of us are voting delegates.
>
> The statement that is to follow is not unanimously consented to in every part by those who are standing, but it is a consensus of the group.

She continued by affirming:

> We begin our statement with an affirmation of support for the movement to liberate women in the United States. This movement is a part of the spirit of the 60's which will continue, because it is raising crucial issues and pointing to new possibilities for humanity.
>
> Women's oppression and women's liberation is a basic part of the struggle of blacks, browns, youth, and others. We will not be able to create a new church and a new society until and unless women are full participants. We intend to be full participants.

She went on to say that women were rising to demand humanity for "ourselves and others." The churches cannot seriously undertake the quest for meaning and wholeness unless they are willing to deal with the role of women. She presented facts to show the inequalities in salaries, representation, and other matters on the national level of the churches and warned the Assembly that they would be hearing from women all during the 70's.

In the meantime the black caucus had presented a nominee as President of the NCCC. Later that afternoon I was approached on behalf of the black caucus to select 10 women to join them at dinner that night. The purpose was not to discuss the election but to discover whether the two movements could work together in the months ahead. It sounded like a good idea. I asked two questions: Will there be any black women in your delegation? (Answer: No) Will the other candidate be present? (Answer: Yes) Then I indicated that there would be five black women and Cynthia Wedel among the ten whom I would like to invite.

The dinner was in a private dining room. The two candidates happened to be at the same table. Evidently the word had gotten around that we were going to talk *only* long range strategy. The opening speech concerned the crucial election of a black president. The point was made that since Cynthia Wedel had not been placed in nomination by a women's caucus she was really a candidate of the establishment. Inasmuch as the other candidate had been nominated by a black caucus, we should show our understanding of liberation by calling a meeting of women delegates to demand that Cynthia withdraw her name from the election ballot. Feeling for all the world like a minority of minorities, I replied: "Had we nominated a candidate ourselves, we could not have done better." Then I risked a thrust: "Anyway, even if the women delegates did demand her withdrawal, I doubt that Cynthia would comply!"

Cynthia's instant reply sounded like the veteran liberated woman she was. "I surely would not," she said with a smile, "for the simple reason that I think I would make a better president of the NCCC."

Claire Randall was in charge of a delegates luncheon the next day. No program had been planned, thus giving the delegates a chance to exchange views. However, with the consent of all, both candidates were given seven minutes to present their reasons for wanting to serve the Council. Each spoke honestly and well. The next day Cynthia Wedel was elected to succeed Arthur Fleming and became the first woman president of the National Council of Churches.

Before the close of the NCCC Assembly, I flew to Europe for the second annual meeting of the WCC—Vatican Women's Liaison Group. On two separate occasions, I had the opportunity to talk with long time friends about the stirrings among women in church circles in the United States. Each listened intently. When I finished, one of them, Dr. Buhrig, a well-known Swiss woman theologian, replied slowly, "I wouldn't have done it the way those women did, but I know exactly what they were talking about." The other, Dr. Nolde, a leader in the World Lutheran Federation, turned to her associate and said: "I'd hoped it wouldn't come during my lifetime, but it is here. Translate anything coming on this subject from America so all our women will know."

I have taken time to narrate conversations and events which spoke of various aspects of what we came to call "women's liberation"—just because we must remember that it started spontaneously *within* women and was first articulated in small groups. This was a different dynamic from that of former feminist movements for voting rights, or the prohibition of alcoholic beverages, or the abolition of slavery, or even the promotion of missions. The earlier movements started with a few strong minded women at the top who believed that women should be mobilized around a common cause in order to be effectively heard. This time the *cause* was the *woman* herself. Well over half the world's population were women. Naturally with so many able to speak with "authority," there would be countless words uttered about oppression, repression and depression.

It was a natural calling for Church Women United. In 1966 we had affirmed principles of releasing the full potential of every person, and of seeking creative and healing encounters in the human community, and of working toward the wholeness of woman and of society. We claimed that our religious faith was a part of, and essential to, the other parts of the whole person. We were developing appropriate relationships with "third world" women who were bound to have different and more concrete agendas.

It is of the essence of the women's liberation movement that women break out of their cocoon of conformity, but it was not within the cultural tradition of every woman to know how or where she wanted to fly on her new wings of freedom. *If* we women could remain generous about the beginning attempts of many kinds of groups to articulate their innate ideas, we might not break into many parties. *If* we could develop ministries to and by women, we might avoid the permanent hurts of the transition experience.

These were big IF's. The phases of women's liberation came so rapidly and spontaneously that no one had any way to count the cost. Once the wounds of experience were inflicted there followed long periods of loneliness in the process of healing. It was part of the process that each wife, each mother, each daughter, each organization, each employee, and the women of each denomination spoke for themselves. For too long we had "been told" or "told each other" what was expected; the art of becoming a supporting community to another person had yet to be developed.

THE WOMEN'S ERA   Although I never felt I needed to decide whether "feminine characteristics" were a result of cultural heritage or were the inate distinctions of sexuality, I was exhilarated by conversations with Dr. Jean Houston, who having researched the issue, was convinced that mental facilities were somewhat different in men and women. She had taught philosophy at both Columbia University and Marymount College, and with her husband had published a study of the social and religious implications of LSD on young people. She was presently engaged in research on expanding the potential of the mind. A spell of flu had prevented her coming to our consultation on Women's Participation in a Futurist Society, so one Saturday morning several months later we got together in her studio to get acquainted. A beautiful woman in her early 30's, she quickly exhibited a warm human zest for all that was happening around us.

Within five minutes I had defined the turf, and she raced around on it for hours. My questions concerned the development of the forthcoming Assembly in Wichita: What was the relationship between the extraordinary claim that God in Christ made a breakthrough into history and the unprecedented technological breakthroughs of our own age? How could we focus on the breakthrough in technology without overwhelming ordinary church women?

Her immediate response offered basic insights into the significance of the present era. "Three breakthroughs are going on simultaneously," she said. "The Christ breakthrough, the technological breakthrough, and the Woman breakthrough." In abbreviated form, this is what I understood her to be saying:

1) *The Christ breakthrough.* The resurrection power is more relevant today than in the first century. Amazing, transcendent empowerment is in evidence today in many persons and movements.

2) *The Technological breakthrough.* A whole new way of life is opened by technological advance, and it challenges the linear social system. A linear system (which is seen in big business, government, military, church, and education) is operated through a responsible chain of command having various departments and bureaucracies. Since these systems are either adjusting or collapsing, there is no point in women flexing their muscles to climb up the ladder just to put men down. Rather, women should realize the great potential in the horizontal social and political patterns of the future. By participating in the development of a new social order (where all races and nationalities are learning to give and take from each other like an extended family) women will both define and hold leadership roles.

3) *The Woman breakthrough.* Although she safeguarded herself by stating that the differences between the sexes were only relative and varied greatly from person to person, Dr. Houston said that her research seemed to prove that there are two important characteristics of the feminine mentality. (A) Women have the capacity to conceive ideas and situations as a whole; that is, rather than viewing the separate parts, they see the whole pattern. (B) Women have *textured hearing*—the ability to hear more than one voice on different levels at the same time.

These general gifts of men and women are complementary rather than competitive. It is true that the present linear society is dominated by men or by women who have learned to "think like men" in a logical sequence of relationships. But it is likely that in the new inter-related society of the future, men will need to learn to "think like women" in order to comprehend their own piece of the whole. However, admittedly, there will always be some fields such as scientific development, where linear gifts would have an advantage. In other fields, such as social planning, the whole "pattern gestalt" will have to prevail.

During this interview, Jean occasionally sent a sideward glance (through a smoky glass) toward the sun which was being eclipsed on that very day in 1970. But as for me, the glow within had an ever enlarging circumference. Not until mid-afternoon did I soar sunward right out of the studio oblivious to any block maneuvered by the man in the moon! Like any new convert, I immediately called a friend, Claire Randall, and bubbled my ecstasy over the phone.

Five years later when I reflect on this four hour conversation, I feel Jean was right. Women might well have spent their time kneading the dough of a fresh social system where we would have been part of the leaven—rather than try so hard to get to the top of a stack of bread already baked.

COMMISSION ON WOMEN IN TODAY'S WORLD Since CWU needed some reflective group to advise its Board and the women of the denominations who must think through these issues in company with others, the national officers created a *"Commission on Women in Today's World"* which was established for the remainder of the triennium in 1969. Its functions were described as identifying the primary issues that concern the full participation of woman as a person in church and society; gathering relevant data and current information on developments to be shared with the national denominational leadership; making recommendations for action that enables church women to utilize their power to achieve their full and responsible position in both church and society.

In addition to a liaison woman from each denomination there were other individual women making a priority of Women's Studies such as Nelle Morton, Associate Professor of Christian Education of Drew Seminary; Pauli Murray, of the faculty of Brandeis University; Sarah Bentley Doely, then editing a series of essays for a forthcoming book on *Women's Liberation and the Church;* Helen Southard, developing a resource library on women for the YWCA; Charlotte Weeks, activist in women's liberation. Claire Randall, around whom an informal denominational caucus had developed following the NCCC meeting, was assigned as its staff executive.

We were fortunate that Thelma Stevens who was just retiring as executive director of Christian Social Relations of the Women's Division of the United Methodist Church was available to give it full time leadership. If CWU ever issues a series of stamps for outstanding contributions, the portrait of Thelma Stevens—a pioneer in human justice—would be in the first series. Not only was she confidently sure of her goals, but she had the ability to articulate the issues. Her judgment on the persons to be trusted, the appropriate strategy, and the necessary compromises in specific situations was always good. Like other women who had been active throughout their careers in the field of human rights, she was eager to concentrate on opening possibilities for women to claim equal opportunity for themselves.

In an article in *The Church Woman,* Thelma Stevens expresses the basic philosophy on which the Commission developed a sound program:

We are Women.
*WHAT WE ARE AND WHAT WE SHALL BECOME DE-
PENDS UPON OUR CONCEPT OF:*

- the history, both 'religious' and 'secular' that has molded us for better or for worse,
- the structures of society into which we were born,
- the images of ourselves that have been given us without our asking,
- the meaning of 'freedom and equality and all persons' in a man-oriented world,
- our own potential to effect change in relationships and structures and our responsibility to do this,
- the basic meaning and power of Christian commitment in a troubled and segmented world,
- the wholeness and universality of Christ's Church living and working among us today.

Within such a framework of challenges, limitations, and hopes many of us have combined our efforts, united our strength, and tapped the depths of our inner life to seek together, as Church Women United, ways of generating the power and developing the skills which can produce the changes in church and society that the new age demands.

The Decade of the Seventies may well be a span of time in which the power of women—'over half the world's people'—becomes clearly visible in those areas of society's greatest need. The traditional concept of woman's *'place'* and woman's *'power'* will be replaced by a growing understanding of God's Creation and the real meaning of human dignity for both men and women of 'every race and clime.'

Thelma Stevens brought the Commission's recommendation for regional workshops on women's identity to the Board of Managers in 1970 and with it a personal gift of $10,000 to assure an interracial team to develop models for this purpose. Dr. Nelle Morton and Mrs. Harvey Winn (Tilly), a vice president of the United Methodist Division and chairperson of the section on Christian Social Relations, were selected. Pilot workshops with different designs were conducted in Westfield, New Jersey, Kansas City, and Pittsburgh. The leadership team was used in the Executive Staff Conference and in the development of materials subsequently used in CWU state and local workshops with leadership resources from the area.

Another concrete effort of the Commission was in the field of theology. It was clear that male theologians had formulated statements relative to the church's doctrine, some of which were offensive when applied to women. The Commission was not only concerned with theological statements about women but how to encourage "theologizing" by women themselves.

EQUAL RIGHTS AMENDMENT Upon the recommendations of the Commission, the Board of Managers at their annual meeting in March 1970 approved two resolutions concerned with women's rights: One urged adoption of the Equal Rights Amendment and the other was a statement of

Christian concern for women desiring to terminate unwanted pregnancies.

The proposed Equal Rights Amendment was passed by the House of Representatives in 1971. That amendment was a simple sentence of twenty-four words:

Equality of rights under the law shall not be denied or abridged by the United States or by any State on account of sex.

Upon its referral to the state legislatures for ratification the Board of Managers again urged "elected representatives at every level to support and vote for it."

It was on the state level where the struggle was to continue for several years inasmuch as it would require the approval of thirty-five states if it were to become an amendment to the constitution. There was a rude awakening among the proponents of ERA when they were confronted by other women aggressively opposing them. In many cases the organized opposition read into the general words of the amendment their own imaginings of how it would work out in practice. One of the state presidents telephoned me in chagrin when her state legislature had failed ratification by only one vote. "The women who oppose it are very emotional, pointing out that women in the army will have to use the same facilities as men." This line of argument would have grounded most travelers years ago, since airlines have always assumed that privacy could be guaranteed to either sex by a bolt on the washroom door.

However, there were those among our own constituency who could not support the amendment, feeling that the struggle would be academic and heated and that energy could best be conserved by using Title VII to back individual cases of alleged discrimination.

The struggle for ratification still continued in 1976. When specific issues, like the ERA and the abortion issues result in factions in our own units, Church women need to remember that reconciliation and righteousness go hand in hand. We are not asked to agree on every issue, but to understand what fears and facts are of serious concern to our sisters.

In a Biblical study, *Wellspring 3,* Dr. Winsome Munroe wisely suggested this guideline: "It is important for the leader to affirm those women who express ambivalence or even negativity. Any move to larger freedom is fearsome, even painful for those who make it, from the Exodus to the Equal Rights Amendment."

UNWANTED PREGNANCIES An even more sensitive issue was the 1970 statement of Christian concern surrounding women who had strong reasons for terminating an unwanted pregnancy. This was not a statement for abortion any more than a statement for prison reform is a statement for crime. It was a statement for the right of the woman and her physician to decide; a concern to protect the woman from unsafe techniques or dangerous situations; a call for counsel from family, doctor, and spiritual advisor; a statement for understanding and support for differing conclusions; a call for further ethical and theological study.

I doubt if any Board statement had ever been more carefully studied or worded, and yet it was destined from the beginning to be shriveled into hard-shelled words: FOR or AGAINST.[1] Other forces were moving through the nation which made the statement a divisive force rather than an instrument of healing.

The meetings of the Commission on Woman in Today's World also became a retrieval center for stirrings among women working in other contexts. Important was the development of women's centers, particularly those connected with graduate theological schools and others meeting immediate needs in some local communities.

Also within the denominations, women's task forces were being formed, and some national agencies staffed offices to focus on the "woman issue." The Commission was helpful in these efforts particularly in their formulating stage. As consciousness was raised in the national staffs of the denominations, specific efforts to challenge the power structure was reported at Commission meetings. Although each woman was in a situation peculiar to herself and her Church, there was camaraderie in the freedom of exchange of experiences.

At the close of the triennium in which its members had been asked to serve, the Commission on Woman in Today's World presented its recommendations for an ongoing program. The proposals called for a special committee within the Board of Managers to focus on the women's issue and a staff person assigned to carry out its program and keep in working relationship the denominational executives with similar goals. The program was to be aimed at a broad constituency offering women a chance to gain confidence in their own potential, and to accept responsibility in today's liberating movements. This final report particularly called attention to programs for local and regional workshops on the changing image of women, and pointed out the need to offer a religious orientation to them.

ONGOING EMPHASIS Dorothy Barnard of St. Louis was named the chairperson for the Board Committee which carried forward these emphases plus some of their own.

The priority set for the triennium at its Ecumenical Assembly in 1971 reflected the continuing goal:

Our priority in this triennium is the expansion and deepening of Church Women United as a national movement which finds expression in every community.

For this movement to be dynamic, it must involve us . . in a growing comprehension of our faith as Christians and of ourselves as women, and . . . in a unity characterized by creative and flexible relationships.

The staff assignment for the priority continued with Claire Randall who had the editorial assistance of Sally Doely in the preparation and updating of a women's packet for workshops. Thousands of these were widely used by leaders in workshops during the next five years.

It is an axiom in administrative circles that every vacancy is an opportunity, but few would have put many odds on a woman having an opportunity to assume the top office in the NCCC.

When the Search Committee for the new General Secretary of the NCCC began its considerations there were over 40 applications. Anxious to have a woman applicant, some denominational women put their personal pressure on Claire Randall to be one of them. As she rose through the process of elimination to become one of two possible choices, she realized that she must answer affirmatively to a question: "If you were nominated by this committee and elected by the General Board, would you accept?" So five years after women alerted the Assembly of the NCCC, its General Board elected Claire Randall to be its General Secretary. She assumed her new office in January, 1974.

What turned out to be a loss from the staff of CWU was a gain for the prestige of the NCCC, whose staff and General Board were willing to accept a feminine style of administration in this established body of Protestant and Orthodox communions. The publicity which surrounded this election made a positive impact on the public as well as the churches— and the cause of women was to be the winner.

Although it is hoped that church women were supportive of the many manifestations of the wider women's movement in the 70's, it was appropriate that Church Women United focus its program on building in the religious dimensions of women's liberation, and emphasize in its activity the equal and responsible roles of men and women in the churches. Just because the complete story can never be written, we shall try to describe here certain projects: our intent, our procedure, and some of the substance of our learnings.

WOMEN AND THEOLOGY If words could describe the week-long experience of 63 women gathered in the Grail Center in Loveland, Ohio, they would have the quality of a reversible coat. In retrospect, this conference could have been "woman exploring theology" or "theology exploring woman." And in 1972 both "woman" and "theology" were many-splintered concepts.

It is no wonder that the words "wholeness" and "holiness" came through as one underlying satisfaction of this particular June conference. However much the phrase "women theologizing" was a puzzlement to male theologians, it proved to be no dilemma to the women themselves at Grailville. Theology as a general term is like food as a general term; neither has meaning unless specifically tested, digested, and put into energy.

Those who previously attended Schools of Theology in order to confirm, clarify, or codify their Christian doctrine found this a new happening. Those who were wearied but not exhausted by daily realities (sighing, swearing, sorrowing, laughing, hurting, praying, keeping on, copping out, bruising, bluffing, feeding, suffering, birthing, dying, resurrecting) were amazed that their contributions were especially relevant. Those who were in between or 'middle class' discovered that active church women had something to learn from those who were present, rather than those whom they wished had been around!

"It is well nigh impossible to capture, especially via the print media, what happened to, with, and among the women who gathered together," was how Sally Bently Doely explained her frustration as she compiled the findings into a usable packet for others. Yet in reading the evaluations of one of the younger women, it is clear that there was a healing experience of many inner splits—the splits between women and men or between generations, or splits between what happens in theological circles and what happens in real life. This healing was a result of being surrounded by a caring trusting community, as well as what was happening beyond their own endeavor—which was described as "the grace of God."

WOMEN IN CHURCH POLICY-MAKING Dorothy Barnard convened a Planning Group of women who, like herself, were elected members of a church board or agency, to explore whether there was a felt need to increase competence as they served their churches in policy making capacities. Regardless of whether they themselves felt this need, there was general agreement that their female colleagues could use some assistance!

Women board members would never have been elected had they not been leaders in their own regions. In their local judicatories or organizations, they had been aware of the beginning, development, and reasons for terminating projects. Now they had landed in an ongoing enterprise that had all the complexities of national and worldwide programs carried on by a professional staff. Desiring to be as good as the next "man", they were baffled by the great accumulation of data which an executive staff had been compiling for months, on which they were to act responsibly in the course of a few hours. They wanted to keep quiet until they understood a question, and often, when they did speak, their comments seemed peripheral to the line of reasoning being used by their male colleagues.

Not wanting to be like the 'Board types' who were on "ego trips", they sometimes failed to bring out their special insights. In a mixed meeting how is one supposed to handle other women with whom one disagrees, or support effectively those whose ideas one would like to endorse?

They resented the gallant remarks that men leaders used to dismiss them; they resented even more the backlash from men still smarting from some "women's lib" encounter who took it out on the next woman before she had done anything to deserve it! If the same thing had occurred on a local board, they would have had the time and background to deal with the situation, but how could their tempo be increased in a three day meeting to handle position papers of a thousand words, budgets involving millions, and nonchalant chairmen whose decisions were influenced somewhere else than in the plenary sessions? Many a woman lost confidence in herself or felt her only use was to second intelligently the motion and interpret enthusiastically the larger work of the Church when she got back home!

As a result of these common concerns, it was readily

agreed that women members of boards, where there were men majorities, would welcome a workshop on Women in Church Government. Subsequently two workshops were held, one in Michigan in 1972 and the other in Oklahoma in 1973. A dozen major denominational agencies selected the women participants and paid their expenses. CWU acted as a convenor and secured the process consultants. At the workshop the participants helped each other realize their place and their power in mixed company where male dominance for over a hundred years had established an approved process. They talked about their own role in this transition period, awaiting the time to come when both men and women would more nearly understand each other's gifts.

Three years later one of them said to me: "We all have changed and there's more listening to both male and female voices; there's more give and take on an individual basis; we think more about what's being said than who says it; we are satisfied if the product as a whole is good enough to be tested by the entire church."

INSTITUTE OF WOMEN TODAY When Sister Margaret Traxler first proposed that CWU join the National Coalition of Nuns and the American Jewish Committee in an ongoing program called *Institute of Women Today,* I hesitated. We were short on staff time and money; any new programs would likely require both. "Why Church Women United?" I asked. She responded that the cooperation of Church Women United was essential:

One of the crucial reasons for beginning the Institute is to bring church-related women and their values into the women's movement. The call for women's equality is in need of values related to faith and this is our reason for seeking Church Women United first and foremost. In my experience CWU is the strongest and broadest-based group of women in the world. I know of no group as large, as representative, as well organized at grassroots levels as Church Women United!"

Her proposal was a timely one, Community Institutes on Woman Today sponsored by church-related Protestant, Catholic and Jewish women's organizations would search for the religious and historic roots of women's liberation. Her formula for curriculum and faculty were sound. She reasoned that most problems resulting from questions raised by the liberation issue could be classified as legal, psychological, and theological. On these kinds of questions the middle class woman not now involved wanted some authentic answer. An academically qualified faculty panel would be selected within reason of schedule and location. Each would be asked to give her time for one or two institutes a year.

Sister Margaret would assume fulltime administration and would be responsible for raising the funds from foundations and interested individuals for office and program expense. She asked that CWU's office receive and disburse the monies until the institutes got started, and that we assign a liaison person for counseling them on approaching local units.

Initially the workshops would be composed of an equal number of Protestant, Catholic and Jewish women invited by a local sponsoring committee who would also analyze the specific questions being raised locally.

The Institute established a base in Chicago with an advisory committee, and Sister Margaret followed through on her administrative responsibilities. She secured her "faculty-panel," a list of professional women, which no doubt was one secret of the many calls for these institutes. Thirty workshops were held the first two years all across the country. Invitations came from college campuses and regional meetings of church, civic, and professional organizations. The press was always interested and usually helpful in quoting their speakers and thus spreading the message. For instance, the pre-Institute publicity relative to the Lawton-St. Sill papers gave what amounted to 194 inches in feature stories relating to the substance of the Institute. Always the underlying religious purpose and the sponsorship of Church Women United was mentioned.

The tone of the workshops was constructive, for they could not afford the luxury of anger. Because their leaders had a breadth of experience, their questions were answered in that context. In Cincinnati when one of Paul's oft quoted phrases about the subjection of women to their husbands was brought up, the Biblical leader pointed out that not only were they taking his words out of a first century cultural context, but they were overlooking the fact that other Biblical passages from St. Paul were fully supportive of liberation, wholeness, and justice, which applied as much to women as to men.

During the Bicentennial observance, fifteen women historians were added to the leader's panels and offered realistic channels for all women to search for their cultural roots. The anomaly here is that historians of our day are finding what the women of the last century "researched" and found, just as Nineteenth Century women had to find what the Eighteenth Century scholars had created and amassed. That this has happened each century gives us pause because there is not likely to be an on-going flow of history unless we establish archives, bibliographies and a continuing growth of the discipline of women's studies.

Another dimension of the Institute of Women Today was opened in 1975 for women in prison, centering pilot programs in the Federal Prison for Women in Alderson, West Virginia. The opportunity came while the director of the Institute program was visiting one of the residents (inmates) and had occasion to tell the wardens of some of her activities. When the warden pointed out that the prison women needed the help of such professional women, it was explained that the Institute's curriculum would not be of value or use to women thus incarcerated.

However, the faculty panel was available, and a series of weekend workshops were set up. In each there was made available at least four lawyers who were experienced and compassionate women, one or two clinical psychologists, and one or two professional educators.

The response was far beyond what anyone could have guessed or hoped; the programs were well-received by administration, staff and residents. The Alderson Federal Prison for Women had 575 residents and a staff of 250. There were 72 Hispanic women and not one prison employee who spoke Spanish. The population was 60% black and yet the staff had only three blacks in administrative positions. All of these factors delayed further the rehabilitation process and made them less ready to cope with normal society on their release.

When Sister Margaret was asked, "What do you do there," she replied:

On a given weekend we are given freedom of the entire compound and the Warden sends a memo saying that every resident who wishes is to have access to our faculty. We are housed in the Little Theater and in the adjoining rooms. Our lawyers speak briefly about the Parole Board, about things like the classifications of offenses and the rules regulating federal parole, naturalization rights, etc. Then each goes to a separate room and conducts interviews the entire weekend. It may be that they write a writ of habeas corpus or that they give the person forms to fill out for obtaining the court transcript for appeals, or they simply listen and tell them that it seems that all was fair and square.

Incredible though it may seem, they have found women who never talked to their court-appointed attorney or for whom no Spanish speaking lawyer or interpreter was found. Attorney Mary Sfaciatti, who for ten years was with the US District Attorney's office as special assistant, joined our faculty to serve the Spanish speaking since she was an expert on naturalization laws. Attorney Ralla Klepak, a criminal lawyer, headed up the lawyer's assistance program and has special empathy with the residents.

The Institute's education specialist, Dr. Judith Schloegel, is head of the right-to-read program in Atlanta. Out of 575 women residents, less than 75 are involved in the education program. There are problems here, especially since there is no income for women who study and they can earn from 25¢-45¢ per hour in prison industries, i.e. the garment factory, or punch cards. The education staff is open to new ideas, especially in that almost all teaching is done on the individual progression method.

The psychologists had a hard time at first because of the experiences of the residents with other psychologists. They discovered however that many women were keeping prison diaries and this as a therapy was highly esteemed by our psychologists.

When asked about the future of this pilot program, Sister Margaret replied:

We want to nurture these plans and help them grow into a design which can then be given to all women's prisons and women's divisions in prisons where both men and women are housed. We have been invited to many other prisons but we first want to do something well:

The institute performs the extra services which enable the residents to initiate activities of their own choice. For instance, choir robes and expense money for traveling to churches were provided to the choir. On one memorable Saturday in April, 1976, Coretta Scott King came to spend many hours. She sang with them for music is one extracurricular activity in which many wholeheartedly participate. The black residents accompanied Coretta to the gates singing all the way. As a farewell they presented her with two dozen American Beauty roses.

WCC CONSULTATION ON SEXISM — 1974 "Why, in heaven's name, is the World Council of Churches running a conference on sexism?" queried a male colleague of Pauline Webb, a Christian educator in Great Britain and a member of the Central Committee of the WCC.

In the opening session of the Consultation on Sexism in the 70's sponsored by the WCC's Committee on Education in June, 1974, Pauline Webb gave her considered answer as she expressed for 160 women from 50 different countries the purpose of their being together:

'IN HEAVEN'S NAME'—that's the first reason. The WCC is primarily concerned with the proclamation of the wholeness of the Gospel ... The Savior came to offer us all—women and men—a full, abundant human life; the Spirit brings into being among us all a new community where Jew, Greek, bond and free, male and female are all one in Jesus Christ.

That's the good news and yet so much of our experience in the world today denies that reality . . .

By sexism, I take it that we mean any kind of subordination or devaluing of a person or group solely on grounds of sex . . .

It's not just a matter of acknowledging the physical differences between men and women . . . Rather it's recognizing that alongside these differences there has been a different history, expectations, sense of identity; and an association with the structures of power that has created a male-dominated order in almost all human society and certainly within the church, making it impossible for the church to foreshadow the truly human community.

So it is FOR THE SAKE OF THAT COMMUNITY that we Christian women come now to examine the heresy of sexism and explore the ways of overcoming it that shall liberate both women and men for a new partnership in the Gospel.

As was true of the other delegations, the Americans had been chosen by a WCC committee in Geneva from lists submitted by an international committee. The women coming from this country tried to prepare themselves for possible misunderstandings, since the "American liberation movements had been somewhat misrepresented by the media." They agreed ahead of time that they had better remain low key when participating. Some of them learned that being quiescent also caused suspicion. Sally Bently reported in *The Church Woman* (November 1974):

Over a late-night sandwich one of us sighed: 'Today I was confronted by the Third World, the Conservatives, the Liberals, the Socialists, the Capitalists, Single Women, and Radical Women.' Asked what she had done

or said to elicit such a reaction, she replied philo-
sophically, 'I was just standing there.'

Often to find an American 'just standing there' was
enough to provoke a discussion, but as the week went
on, we all learned that staying with a conversation
begun in this way ultimately led to a new communication and understanding, if not to agreement.

Communication came about partly because they were
together as women and as Christians. Dr. Nelle Morton spoke
on the theme "Whole Theology"—defining it as a full human
experience which is possible when all the peoples of the world
speak freely out of their own experience and then reach out to
touch one another to heal and be healed. Annie Jiagge of
Ghana spoke of the maturity of women which comes when
they can cope responsibly with the daily struggle.

In a fascinating blend of reflection and interviews at the
Berlin Conference, Margaret Wold captures in her book, *The
Shalom Woman*,[2] a new concept of wholeness and well being
in a woman fully alive to her own capacities and her Christian
calling. She points out that the "Shalom woman cannot claim
the blessings of health, happiness, and peace at the expense of
others. Therefore those who maintain the American way of life
while most of the people of the world are impoverished are
under God's judgment, for the greedy will not inherit the
kingdom of God!"

Toward the end of the conference, a small group
gathered to reflect on how they had grown together during this
week in June 1974, and they came up with the following points
of consensus:

*"The specific meaning of liberation for a woman
depends upon her own life context."* Judge Annie
Jiagge of Ghana put it this way: In Africa, 80% of the
people live and work in rural areas where starvation is
not far away . . . And in that struggle, men and women
participate equally: that puts a completely different
conception of their relationship.

*"Achieving one's own liberation and that of others
presumes that a woman has the freedom to work*

effectively for change in her society."

After listening to the realities of women who were living under repressive governments or who came from countries where the great majority of women had not even had access to basic education, even the Americans were willing to admit that liberation of women is meaningless unless it is linked with liberation from all kinds of oppression.

The awareness of our interdependence, no matter what kind of oppressions are involved, was possibly the most hard-won and basic agreement which emerged at the consultation:

"The liberation of women all over the world depends on mutual understanding and support of each other."

We realized that it is not enough to 'understand' and 'sympathize' with each other's situations; we must learn to make specific the connections between our lives and, whenever possible, declare our solidarity with each other across the lines of race, nationality, and economic status . . .

Finally, all agreed that as Christian women we recognized that *"Liberation is both freedom 'from' and freedom 'for'."*

A liberated woman is one whose eyes have been opened to see oppression in the whole world, to see all kinds of oppression and then to do something about it .

When we talk about world peace, bringing about shalom—justice and well-being for everybody— imagine what women could do if we would hold together! . . .

INTERNATIONAL WOMEN'S YEAR In 1972 the United Nations designated 1975 as International Women's Year, as it would be the midway mark in its "decade of development," and the 25th anniversary of the creation of its Commission on the Status of Women. Probably the officials did not guess that the momentum generated by the involvement of women themselves around this theme would be greater than all the other annual developmental slogans combined. *Equality, Development, Peace* were their program goals. Even though the women of the West may have given priority to the first, their consciousness as women had raised their concern about the social and economic oppressions of their sisters of the third world calling for development. And there are few women in any country who are not concerned with the human cost of violence and war.

The IWY Conference in Mexico City, June 19 - July 3, was the first worldwide gathering of governments to be called for the specific purpose of considering women's issues. There were more than 1000 delegates from 133 countries; almost 75% were women. Helva Spivila the UN Secretary-General for IWY and the highest ranking woman in the UN Secretariat, should be credited with handling the tensions which emerged during the planning of so diverse and complex an effort, and at the same time projecting an international conference which could develop goals and action over the years to come.

The official delegates had all the prestige and limitations which representing an establishment usually entails. Yet they did hear enough from the platform to take seriously the issue of women in policy making decisions and to recognize that there was emerging an international force of great proportion. Said Mary Anne Krupsak of the United States delegation: "Let us begin to see our strength as women together . . . not competing, not matching achievements, not being choked by the dishonesty of unfulfilled egos. Let us bring the politics of humanism to foreign policy. Let us set new agendas for the future!"

More important, the Conference did what only official delegates could do. They asked their governments to give priority during the next decade for development among women. The World Plan of Action authorized by the Conference was to be undertaken by member nations of the United Nations over a ten year period, 1975—1985. By the end of the first five year period, 1980, it was hoped that at least these seven items could be achieved:

1. Marked increase in the literacy of women—especially young women.
2. Extension of vocational training in basic skills,

including modern methods of farming.
3. Equal (or certainly proportionate) enrollment of boys and girls at the primary level of education.
4. Increased employment opportunities for women.
5. Establishment of broadly based social structures in rural areas.
6. Enactment of legislation giving women equal rights in the areas of voting, eligibility for election, and legal affairs, and equal pay for equal work.
7. Increased participation of women in policy-making positions at the local, national, and international levels.

TRIBUNALS A series of tribunals for women meeting simultaneously with the official conference were arranged in Mexico to provide an international forum for women at large. Church women were not surprised that Esther Hymer, who had done so much to establish sound relationships for CWU at the United Nations, was chosen as the chairperson of a committee of NGO's that initiated the project. Working with the full cooperation of Helva Spivila, these tribunals were designed to give representatives of women's organizations and others the opportunity to face the specialized issues such as education and health and to offer opportunity for women to air priorities of their own.

Plans were made optimistically for 2000 women; arrangements were cheerfully adjusted when 6000 turned up. The many simultaneous meetings with agendas from the floor confused the press, who were used to fifty word summaries of two-thousand word speeches. But with the "textured hearing" of women, millions of words were heard on scores of subjects important to some of their number.

Deborah Partridge Wolfe, the official observer for CWU at the United Nations, was the representative of CWU at the Tribunals and played a real leadership role. When I telephoned from New York our concern over press reports of angry women, she assured me that things were lively but the spirit was free and congenial. I told her that a coalition of 70 women's organizations had met and drawn up a "national women's agenda" and that they had asked Virginia Baron, a staff member of CWU, to present it at a press conference in New York, and to arrange for the same in Mexico City. The cooperative and competent Debbie Wolfe knew how to set up this press conference, a feat that would have taken those working through protocol a week to accomplish.

Although the participants in the Tribunals came from many countries, those representing the Americas were most numerous. According to Leah Margulies, the frank encounters which went on between those of the North and South Americas may have been the most significant. Those from the United States got the message that Latin American women feared that now that the Vietnam war was over, there would be available to reactionary governments vast military and economic resources from the United States. But the American women had "joined the world" and were able to see the different forces playing upon their neighbors in the southern hemisphere. In fact, during the last several days of the Tribunal, as more Latin American women spoke, there were agents and police present. Many were concerned about the repression that might be brought to bear on these women, many of whom went straight into exile.

ENCOURAGING OTHERS The International Women's Year Conference named a set of priorities to be achieved within the decade. The women of the USA now could urge that this government take its full share of financial grants-in-aid through the appropriate agencies of the United Nations. Church Women United had through the years given millions of dollars through Christian agencies to similar programs among minorities in the United States and in many of the countries of the so-called "third world."

RURAL WOMEN The International Women's Year goal "to estab-lish broadly based social structures of women in rural areas" would have had little meaning for me had it not been for a conversation with a retired Scottish missionary in Jamaica who was concerned about the housing and livelihood of families in the central mountain area. When asked what they would most like to have in the way of housing, women from that mountainous region almost unanimously replied, "an inside stove, running water, a separate bedroom for our daughters, a garden plot, perhaps chickens for eggs and a pig for the market."

By experimenting on a model house using native materials, the canny Scot figured out how the same torrential rain which put out the fire on the "outside stove" could be contained in a roof reservoir and channelled indoors by a hand pump. A three-room house patterned after this model and built by the families themselves, together with the seeds for the garden, the money to buy the hens and the pig would require an investment of $5,000. CWU provided a fund sufficient for the first five houses. As families completed their houses and repaid their loan, a revolving fund for others was established.

ASIAN WOMEN'S   One satisfaction about being with this move-
INSTITUTE   ment for many years is seeing what the
                 change in the generations of leadership
signifies and demands. Church Women had shown a vital interest in higher education for women in Asia since the founding of colleges under Christian auspices. Several generations of women graduates had come out of them.

For the first time on Asian soil, the presidents of nine women's colleges were meeting together in Seoul, Korea in 1972. "This is a history-making occasion," said the convener, Dr. Eva Shipstone, president of Isabella Thoburn College. The consultation had been facilitated through the Association of North American Cooperating Agencies for Overseas Women's Christian Colleges, and a grant from Church Women United. The administrators had asked for an American consultant experienced in college administration. Elizabeth Luce Moore, then president of the United College Board, flew to Korea to join the Asian administrators gathered to fulfill their obligation to future generations of Asian women. It was not the fact of the meeting to share common administrative problems that was history-making; it was the birth of a new endeavor appropriate for their times and yet in harmony with their founding purposes. It was proposed to work together on an international system of women's studies and research in the Asian setting.

No good idea is born in one place at one time. There were further meetings of Asian representatives of these colleges at the time of the Ecumenical Assembly in Wichita and also a Colloquium of 80 Asian educators following the Memphis Assembly where ideas generated into further development of an Asian Women's Institute.

By 1975 the Asian Women's Institute was established with an international office in Lucknow, India. The enterprizing Dr. Eva Shipstone is the coordinator of its program aimed to assist the women of Asia in their striving for fullness of life. In the United States, a committee of 75 prominent American women under the leadership of Phoebe Gregorian committed themselves to be their supporting community.

The original idea of a women's center in each of the colleges has taken root and most of them have a full time director. In each center there is a reading room where an extensive library is housed on subjects of special concern to women of the area. A faculty-student committee is at work on an interdisciplinary curriculum aimed at helping women realize the potential of their own gifts.

The centers aim to increase understanding and concern of a growing number of women in their whole area who are enmeshed in the problems of poverty and illiteracy and enable them to cope with their rapidly changing times. Mrs. A.K. Dass, the director of the Center for Women's Welfare and Development at Isabella Thoburn College has the enthusiastic support of students and faculty for a program among underprivileged women in rural villages and urban slums. These projects are snowballing into multi-dimensional community services and building a base for meaningful research rooted in the realities of human experience.

Even the political stress and upheaval in Lebanon was used by Dr. Julinda Abu Nasr, the director of the center in Beirut. She had flown to Cairo for a weekend and found that her return was delayed because of the closing of the Beirut airport. She used the time in Egypt to set up research scholarships which would be of value to the whole Arab world.

The Asian Women's Institute will be worth watching as some of their dreams are fulfilled: meetings of Asian women scholars, a publication program, increased among educated women leaders, the well-being of all Asian women. In an age when any institution is tempted to survive for its own sake under pressures exercised by nationalist govenments, this venture of cooperation among colleges in six different countries may be a forerunner of the way in which the spirit of dedicated women moving within their own cultural traditions will influence a future global society.

CHURCH LEADERS During the International Women's Year itself, CWU provided a number of one time grants to allow for church women to get together for mutual encouragement. Here is a quick snapshot of three of them:

Eighty women from Argentina and Uruguay came together from a variety of church backgrounds; they included housewives, doctors, lawyers, maids, grandmothers, mothers, and teenagers. Their agenda was to think and pray together about their responsibility in the world of violence and struggle in which they lived. It was envisioned that out of these seminars a network of communication might develop among women with common concerns.

A Pan-African Women's Leadership Course at the Mindolo Ecumenical Center in Zambia was designed to provide advance professional training for women employed by churches, other voluntary organizations, and government. Participants came from various African countries to receive training in the theory and practice of leadership and to explore the skills needed and provide leadership for women's programs in their countries.

The Conference of Caribbean Church Women in Barbados provided an opportunity for the coming together of women from widely scattered countries and islands of the Caribbean—with diverse racial, cultural, and historical backgrounds. As they planned for the future of their work, there resulted a new awareness of Caribbean identity and a movement of Caribbean Church Women was begun.

A colorful handmade banner was presented to Church

Women United in the USA which had stood with the Caribbean women during the three years of their self-development. It bears the inscription: "Let me be free to dream, and to plan, and to aspire."

CONTINUING   Although CWU could not carry the primary
AGENDAS   role in the struggles for the ordination and fair
                  employment practices within the separate denominations, these issues were of prime importance to all that we stood for.

Rights and laws do not establish a practice. Many seminary trained women in churches which do permit ordination are offered very few options for employment. Their acceptance becomes a part of a continuing agenda. A European woman theologian once remarked about the short-sightedness of the church in its "non-use" of the theologically trained women. "The Church lost its intellectuals, then its artisans because it could not find within the Church ways to use their gifts. It would be a shame if it lost its best women for the same reason."

At the conclusion of the International Women's Year we were asking "How far have we come?" A National Forum on Women was held at the Riverside Church in New York City on November 18, 1975, sponsored by the National Board of the YWCA and 11 additional organizations, including Church Women United. Speaking to an overflow audience, Gloria Steinem, much-publicized editor of *MS* magazine, sketched what the struggle for recognition was doing to the nation's women. She was not oblivious to the women's lib backlash or the traditionalists among women. "Powerlessness corrupts" she paraphrased as she outlined the stages which led her to be an exponent of women's equality. She told of a study which had shown the tendency of men to demolish the weak among them. She suggested, "Perhaps we women demolish the strong among us!"

One thing had become clear—both the "fly by night" extreme advocates and extreme opponents of women's liberation were proving to be faddists. But there had come into being a core group of women who understood each other and those who steadily move on even though the way is rough and uncertain. Said Betty Friedan: *"The only test of our movement is whether it opens real life to real women."*

As for Church Women United itself, Ruth Weber editorialized in the January 1976 issue of *The Church Woman:*

>   With regard to the question of social change and women's part in it, Church Women United has a history of long and deep-seated concern. *As the most pluralistic of movements, we must constantly deal with the tensions that variety forces upon us, and this may be an important strength.*
>   Extremes and excesses are the pitfall of every constructive social program and the tensions of pluralism may well rescue us from these. The definition of 'real life' and 'real woman' cannot be a sudden or immediate achievement; it must be a process, tempered at one point by creative and daring motion, at another by the warnings and hesitancies of the more cautious.

As we look to the future, let us listen to the voices of the prophetic women among us and those with the courage of great convictions. There will always be some women, oppressed by their own trivia, who bitterly oppose those who break with the established custom of what women can becomingly do.

How well I remember my inner response at hearing Dr. Lillian O'Connor address a thousand women at the Assembly of the World Union of Catholic Women's Organizations in Rome in October, 1967. With careful evidence from three case studies of women in other centuries who dared to have ideas which today are accepted better than the women who uttered them, this brilliant American Catholic lay woman challenged us all with the priorities of women of any era:

>   What that World of Tomorrow must have is the participation of women in the realm of ideas—ideas that center on the conservation of life, the improvements of living

conditions, the channels through which to reach order in the world without use of force.

. . . In our lopsided world women accept passively the great advances in methods of communication, effective control of epidemics, improvements in sanitation, health measures, modern facilities for household chores. We accept these changes having barely lifted a finger to bring them about and do not lift our voices in the great humanitarian causes which would bring about the rights of the weak as well as the powerful. Why are we fearful of each other? Why unwilling to take the risk of our own best thoughts?

FOOTNOTES TO CHAPTER 9

1. Because the matter of abortion became such a controversial subject in the years that followed, it may be useful to quote the whole statement as passed by the Board of Managers in 1970. (It was agreed at that time that the majority and minority reports would be circulated together and never separately.)

VOTED to approve the following with the additional signed statement to be appended to the Resolution as a Minority Report signed by those listed:

Our Christian concern for the human rights of all persons, whether as individuals or as groups, compels us to support the right of women to make the final decision about termination of an unwanted pregnancy in which a woman has strong reason for not bearing a child. Therefore, we believe the current abortion laws that deny this fundamental human right should be repealed.

New medical techniques make abortions safe, but current laws force women into dangerous situations and discriminate particularly against the poor woman. Whereas there are a variety of opinions about when life becomes human, laws of the state should not bind all women to one view. A woman does not make a decision for abortion easily or lightly and every encouragement and support should be offered to avoid this extreme solution. But this recourse must be open to her and she must be free to make the final decision with the help of her family, doctor, and spiritual advisor for she is the one who is required to go through the pregnancy and childbirth and will be expected by society to be primarily responsible for any child that is born. We also believe it is important that those who counsel and support women not be restricted by legalities.

We urge that serious work be done by the church on the ethical and theological aspects of abortion and that the results of such studies be made available so that women may find adequate understanding and support.

In speaking on this issue of urgency to women, Church Women United recognizes that within our constituency there are some women who belong to communions who do not agree with this statement, but we believe that our unity is strong enough to contain varied opinions.

(The above statement was approved with two voting in opposition.)
Minority Report:

We, the undersigned, recognizing the human motivation of the Resolution on Abortion, and recognizing furthermore the reason that we as women united in a movement would feel the need to take a stand nevertheless ask that, because we have not resolved this issue as a matter of personal conscience, and because we belong to communions opposed to such a stand at the present time, we be listed as abstaining from the vote on the Resolution as worded and we be recorded as so doing in any report of the Resolution.

We do, however, associate ourselves enthusiastically with the study recommended in paragraph 3 and with the objective of reforming inequitable laws which do not recognize the rights of women.

Signed by: Lily Badre   Abigail McCarthy   Brenda Wilking
            Sister Mary Luke   Clara Nickolson

(A motion that the word "repealed" be changed to "revised" in paragraph 1 of the Resolution was lost.)

2. *The Shalom Woman,* Margaret Wold, Augsburg Publishing House, Minneapolis, Minnesota, 1975, p.

Church Women United
1966-1975

It is a rare churchman who, having come to years of retirement, can offer his accumulated wisdom with a relative ease of conscience inasmuch as he intends to let the next generation respond with their own *Yea* and *Nay.* Roswell Barnes was such a churchman. Retiring from the World Council of Churches in 1964, Dr. Barnes became an advisor to the Ecumenical Relations Division of the United Presbyterian Church of which I was serving as staff coordinator.

Our divisional staff marvelled at this human reservoir of information about ecumenical affairs. On every activity we undertook—relationships with ecumencial organizations, Roman Catholic conversations, ecumenical studies, or the movements of youth, students, men and women crossing denominational and national lines—he displayed wisdom collected from having been there before.

Dr. Barnes gave me two concepts which served me well in Church Women United. One was that the tension between church structures and church movements is inevitable, given their nature, and healthy for both. The other was a phrase, *integrity of the church* which he often used where others spoke of Christian unity.

Integrity had a root meaning of one-ness, of wholeness, but also carried with it a quality of soundness. Our goal in sound relationships is reached through oneness in spirit and accomplishment. Integrity requires that each party in the relationship be recognized as having her own character and gifts; thus in giving or receiving, the identity of each is undiminished while the work done together is enhanced.

The real integrator is the Holy Spirit. The fruits of the Spirit—joy, patience, kindness, love—naturally nourish personalities that are diminished by artificial additives and enable people to get along with one another. Because the Spirit brings about integrity among persons of diverse gifts and functions, something new happens. The result is creativity rather than conformity.

Ongoing relationships are somewhat taken for granted among church bodies inasmuch as their overall purposes are already the same. Yet special occasions give opportunity to express our common loyalty. Accordingly a national officer of CWU is likely to be a participating observer at Assemblies or international seminars of the World Council of Churches or the Board meetings of the National Council of Churches, or at a Consultation on Church Union. CWU is able to respond to invitations for special occasions sponsored by sister organizations in the United States or overseas. Our representative reminds those gathered of the wider dimensions of Christian integrity while she is enriched by sharing other expressions of the Christian fellowship. For instance, CWU had representatives meeting with a thousand Reformed Church Women on board the S.S. Queen Mary in the San Diego Harbor, with the 10,000 women at one National Baptist Convention, with 3,000 Roman Catholic women in the aftermath of a Florida hurricane, at the annual meeting of the Federation of Evangelical Women in Mexico and at the quadrennial meeting of the Asian Church Women's Conference.

Through action of its national board, CWU makes commitments as an integral part of associations which have their own identity. Women in Community Service, Inc., is such a relationship as are the International Committee of the World Day of Prayer and the Fellowship of the Least Coin. In all these cases Church Women United carries an essential role as the largest participating movement and takes seriously this role inasmuch as our withdrawing from any one would change the nature of its entity. In order not to dissipate our energies, we limit the number of these commitments to those which we can responsibly carry.

THE ANDERSON INTERNATIONAL CONSULTATION The commission on New Dimensions received advice from special consultants before making its recommendation on the continuing and new program of Church Women United. Because the movement needed to discover its own identity before moving toward its ecumenical relations worldwide, the Consultation on International Relationships was delayed until a week before the Ecumenical Assembly in July 1967.

Appropriate relationships between a movement of our nature and Christian women in other countries requires flexibility and sensitivity inasmuch as there is no uniform pattern of women's work or of their role in the Church. Just as Church Women United would always be in the process of becoming, so would its relationships need to grow by taking into account the variety of ways in which women had been nurtured by the several Christian traditions within their national or tribal cultures. As each in her own way affirms her faith in Jesus Christ, we are mutually strengthened. For relationships are never one way. We do not relate to them unless they relate to us!

Arrangements were made to hold the conference at Anderson College (Indiana) from July 6 to 12, and to transport the 125 members of the Consultation to Purdue University from the Assembly by bus. Our hostesses were the officers of the women of the Church of God whose headquarters were located in offices on that campus. Anima Bose of New Delhi who was teaching at Stephens College in Missouri at the time was chosen to be the chairperson of five international women on the planning committee for the International Consultation. Gladys Naylor was assigned from the staff to be their executive secretary—which fact, I might say, assured a smooth running conference.

Of the 125 women who accepted our invitation, less than 20% were Americans and the others were members of churches located in 42 countries. In my experience, Americans always have a new experience and respond to it differently if they are in the minority. Anderson was no exception.

The planning committee, as had been anticipated, put the program immediately into the hands of the participants. The worship each morning was led by a woman from a different continent; the planned dialogues on family life, community projects, human rights, urban problems and team leadership from two different regions. Luz Bacerra saw to it that a cultural program came spontaneously from the different regions at tea time each day. Coretta Scott King and other leaders surpassed our expectations for evening vespers. Audrey Sorrento of the Grail Community assisted the group in singing together informally throughout. It was in Anderson that we began to sing "They will know we are Christians by our love."

One period, called *Thinking Aloud,* gave opportunity for a critical look at the day and for points of difference to be clarified. Anima Bose commented that all the 20th century issues seemed to be wrapped up in the persons present. "Each of us has looked into the face of at least one of her enemies at this conference and found she was loving her."

One American wrote afterwards of the conference's integrity:

> We parrot a lot of things about Christian concern and honesty and mutuality, but how often do we really see these qualities in action? In modern America, one is tempted to suspect that no one in her right mind ever expects them to be real. But at Anderson, there was an indefinable sense of friendship, of caring, and I think the reason for this lay in the directness, the simplicity, and the complete frankness with which we approached each other. I returned home with a new serenity, a new hope and a new zeal.

But the participants never lost sight of the fact that their primary task was to be consultants and they worked hard each morning in one of three workshops (International Community, Ecumenical Encounter and the World Day of Prayer). Each workshop worked under the leadership of a team, one of whom was an American. After refining the extensive papers of drafting committees, each workshop presented its findings to the plenary sessions for final review.

Walking across the campus one night to see whether the drafting committees would be ready to report, I was startled to see a fire truck enter the campus, the long ladder extended to the third floor directly to the window of one of our distinguished participants from the Netherlands. While the fireman climbed up the ladder, I dashed up the stairs to see what had happened. Her door had jammed shut so she had called out the window for help.

Meanwhile just outside her door in the third floor lounge was the drafting committee of the workshop on International Community (all in dressing gowns and several in curlers) getting ready for the next day by eagerly refining their paper, totally unaware of their sister in distress.

The next day when Turin Ehteshami (Iran), Margaret Flory (USA), Luz Asejo (Philippines), and Shahla Anand (North India) presented their paper, and spoke with competence to the issues it contained, we knew that this kind of cool on the part of Christian women could put down a lot of commotion caused by fires of world crisis.

Because their recommendations showed vision as well as practical vitality and were basically acceptable to succeeding national boards, CWU was able to "live into the policy" for many years to come. All reports were written into extensive position papers from which we record some key paragraphs:

The *Workshop on International Communities* looked with expectation at the new social phenomenon in the world created by the mobility of persons and families who are spending part of their lives in countries not their own for purposes of study and work. We have taken notice of the way the mass media have made possible widespread information; we have noted significant steps toward the development of a world culture. We have looked at the international communities created through the presence of the following types of persons who go from one nation to another; church, academic (students and faculty), business, diplomatic, UN personnel (international civil servants), military, migratory labor, refugees, and tourists.

We see emerging international community as a major frontier of our time. We have rejoiced in the depth of community we have experienced in this International Consultation. We know that similar resources in persons and leadership are available locally in all parts of the world, and we trust that church women everywhere will have the willingness, imagination, creativity, and faith to work steadily in the certainty that God will use them abundantly in the new global community being brought into being.

There followed recommendations particularly geared to what responsible church women might do: i.e., preparation of laity for overseas involvement, reconciling alienated people by encounters in the academic community which would be difficult to arrange in their own countries (as Japanese and Koreans, Indians and Pakistanis, or Greeks and Turks, among others); long-range programs for students studying in other countries and international faculty exchanges; practical help for the families of international labor communities and advocacy for their legal rights; exploring the cultural wealth of tourism; encouraging responsible journalism and mass media to hasten people's awareness of the currents of change; ministries in foreign military observations; assistance in overcoming the potential difficulties and frustration that may be experienced by persons reentering their homelands.

Under the leadership of Shanti Solomon of India and Laura McCray of Tuskegee Institute in Alabama, the Workshop on Ecumenical Encounter prefaced its report by words of motivation which in part reads:

Rejoicing in the reality of belonging together in a world-wide family of believers;

Grateful to God to be living in a time when we can be mutually encouraged and strengthened by each other's faith and experience for ministry in the world, and

Desirous of serving one another with the particular gifts God has given each of us as faithful stewards of the grace of God, the Workshop on Ecumenical Encounter presents the following recommendations:

1. That *The Church Woman* magazine be used as a forum for international exchange on issues of common concern to Christian Women in all nations.

2. That a Christian Causeway be planned to Latin America and Caribbean; including women from Spain, Portugal and Rio Muni, which share common languages.

3. That since the World Day of Prayer is the only ecumenical experience of Christian women in some areas, suggestions for related Bible studies should be included in resource material.

4. That the Fellowship of the Least Coin be furthered with emphasis being made on genuine prayer as well as acts of reconciliation.

The Workshop on the World Day of Prayer included women from Europe and Latin America who had come at the expense of their own committees. The correspondence with overseas national committees and translators previously carried by the Division of Foreign Mission of the NCCC had been tranferred in 1965 to Church Women United. We were particularly anxious to fulfill the expectations of our sisters in more than one hundred countries. As Americans, we were one of the peer organizations and anxious not to become dominating at a time in history when the World Day of Prayer was the most universal expression of local Christian unity and one which had been initiated and carried on by women.

Under the co-chairmanship of Esther de Saenz of Argentina and Ruth Zimmerman of the United States, the workshop brought the basic recommendation for the creation of an international committee to develop policy and an annual program. In the spirit of mutual trust, they developed practical steps so that many women shared the responsibility. In their report they prefaced their recommendations:

> We live in an era when God has planted the Church in every nation. Each church bears witness in its own situation on behalf of the whole Church of Jesus Christ, and at the same time enters into the ecumenical responsibility of bearing one another's burdens. We are grateful to God that there has grown up a world-wide expression of this mutual concern in the World Day of Prayer. In each of the 127 countries this observance has emerged with its own history. Its meaning is enhanced by the realization that lay women on every continent have made possible this manifestation of Christian unity and obedience.
>
> Therefore, Christian Women from 42 countries, with communications from many others, gathered informally at Anderson, Indiana, July 6 -11, 1967, would like to make the following recommendations of their sisters in other countries.

There was designated an official World Day of Prayer Committee in each country or national unit, as representative as possible, taking into consideration the multi-racial nature of its society and the diversity of the several Christian traditions. The new International Committee was to be composed of the official correspondents of the national World Day of Prayer Committees, plus six members at large chosen from the various continental areas of the world. To insure the presence of the at-large members, a fund was set up of voluntary contributions from several national World Day of Prayer Committees. It was at this time that it was decided to recommend that the administrative responsibility for the International Committee be carried by Church Women United in the U.S.A.

The conference also made a plan for a provisional committee, composed of six members at large and, ex-offico, the Executive Director of Church Women United. This provisional committee was asked to convene the first International Committee for World Day of Prayer in Europe, in July 1968. The Provisional Committee was elected by the Anderson

Consultation of representatives of the various regions of the world. Rathie Selveratnum (Ceylon), Sylvia Talbot (Guyana), Turin Ehteshami (Iran), Jean Jolobi (South Africa) and Edna Sinclair (U.S.A.) were elected to the Provisional Committee.

It might have seemed to some that CWU had abdicated responsibility before it had exercised it. However, by being willing to give up a smaller base we had gained one much larger. Likewise, the new plan safeguarded the world community from being dominated by the American administrator inasmuch as the International Committee at its regular meetings must either vote for the continuity of this arrangement or provide for an alternate one.

The choice of CWU to be administrator was made with genuine insistence, inasmuch as we were the only movement with sufficient staff to carry the amount of correspondence required in a world movement of this dimension. But our office would have been overwhelmed had we not had the dedicated and effective work of Gladys Naylor up until her resignation in 1973. She began immediately clearing files, checking and updating a mailing list of over 900 names, making arrangements for the first meeting of the International Committee scheduled to be held in Sweden following the Assembly of the World Council of Churches in 1968.

Integrity in relationships
   . . . with International Committee of World Day of Prayer

The coming into being of an International Committee for World Day of Prayer was for me a sure sign of God's integrating action bringing the parts into the whole. In practice the plan called for each national or regional committee to name a liaison officer through whom the committees could be alerted and consulted about the annual materials. These materials were prepared by one of the member committees and sent also to hundreds of local committees and translators in countries which had no central committee. Every committee was invited to participate either in writing or by a delegate, even though it was not expected that all could be represented.

It took a great deal of faith to call meetings of the International Committee in Sweden in 1968, in Thailand in 1970, and in Mexico in 1974; yet the results of each showed the continuing work of the Holy Spirit. Women from 58 different national committees participated in one of these three meetings, many committees had someone at two of them. Eight national committees were represented in all three meetings: South Africa, Canada, U.S.A., Germany, Philippines, Australia, New Zealand and Guyana. The plan of regional locations made it possible for member committees in Asia to participate in 1970, and those from the Caribbean and Latin America in 1974. The composition was appropriate to the nature of the World Day of Prayer. The presence of the Executive Committee assured both continuity in planning and participation from other parts of the world.

Not only were these meetings more representative of the worldwide constituency than most international ecumenical committees, but the mutual bearing of administrative cost of preparing, mimeographing and mailing Contributions from national committees met the entire adimistrative cost of preparing, mimeographing and mailing the materials to a vast constituency, and the travel expenses for the Executive Committee and the Administrative Secretary to the international meetings. CWU contributed staff services necessary, and agreed to keep the other expenses within the budget available. The ingenuity and quality of those coming to the meetings as well as the hostesses in Europe, Asia and Mexico enabled us to fulfill significant purposes with integrity. When a general secretary of another ecumenical movement heard of our arrangement, he muttered, "Incredible!". We women murmured our praise to God for each other!

1968 MEETING Just because one reason to write this story is to
IN SWEDEN include many of you in these historic experiences, come sit in the corner of my heart and together let us go into the big reception room of a renovated medieval castle, Hasselby Slott, in Vallingby, Sweden on Saturday evening, July 20, 1968. As my eyes met those of thirty-three women gathered around the hollow square of conference tables, I would have muttered to you, "How is it possible?" And you, having read the registration list, would have whispered back: "From twenty-three countries!".

With gracious dignity, Rathie Selvaratnum, the chairman of the provisional committee, convened the meeting with a worship service filled with thanksgiving. She remembered all those who had in faith brought us to this day; those women pioneers in the United States over eighty years ago who had issued the first call; those in many other countries who had taken the initial steps; those who formed the prayer fellowship on the six continents on the occasion of the 75th Anniversary; those at the Anderson Consultation the year before who had made the plan for this committee to come into being; and many greetings from national committees who could not send representatives but were joining us in prayer, and surely those present whose official action would be confirming the hopes and dreams of all the years. And, if you had asked me how she knew all of this history, I would have shaken my head. I didn't tell her! I even wondered if any of those women who had carried on full of faith in previous years would ever have imagined that one day an international committee meeting in Sweden under the leadership of an Asian woman would be entrusted with "this most precious heritage."

As each person in the room introduced herself, the

global family came into view through the "windows of the world," a phrase used by a participant from East Germany describing the World Day of Prayer. Its spiritual genius was expressed by Dr. Nopitsch who had seen the beginnings of the World Day of Prayer in Germany following a visit to America after the Second World War. She had been asked to begin the encounter between two former enemy countries. "In this painful situation, I was asked to be a sister among sisters, a Christian among Christians. The World Day of Prayer was the greatest gift I received. More than food, more than clothing, is the gift of Christian forgiveness and love."

Then Gudrun Diestel opened a discussion on the "crisis of prayer" which was in reality a crisis of faith pervading the modern scene. She spoke of the questions of younger women as to the relevance of days of prayer, of the call of youth for integrity in worship forms, and for understanding the ways that God is acting in restless and violent times.

On Sunday morning, our worship service used the 1969 theme of the World Day of Prayer, "Growing together in Christ." The message was in the form of testimony as to what growing together meant: Sylvia Talbot describing growth in husband/wife relationships; Edna Sinclair on racial tension; Luz Bacerra on the growing fellowship among churches in ecumenical encounters; Frau Basusova and Frau Krause on the deepinging fellowship among Christians overcoming political and social barriers. An offering was taken and later designated for Near East relief.

On Sunday afternoon our Swedish hostesses arranged a bus tour of the famous city of Stockholm, stopping for awhile to walk leisurely through Millisgarten and have tea in a nearby restaurant.

By Monday morning we knew enough about each other to begin profitable discussion of the business of organizing the international committee. These discussions took place in a setting of corporate worship, led by: Gwen Petch (New Zealand), Afifie Dabaghie (Lebanon), Clara Piernaar, Ana Cordova (Philippines), Laura Burnett (Canada), Jean Jolobe (South Africa), and Marjorie Stanhope (Australia). Dr. Marga Buhrig of Switzerland led us in a series of Biblical studies on questions raised for life today by the parables which Jesus told his disciples.

The report of the administrative secretary itemized several general communications sent on behalf of the provisional committee, and pointed out the problems of updating extensive mailing lists of individuals and translators and of identifying the national committees. The report indicated that the expenses of this first meeting had been covered by contributions of $6,612.77 made by the Asian Church Women's Conference from the Fellowship of the Least Coin and seven national committees. Of course, the national committees had also enabled the attendance of their own representatives.

A committee under the leadership of Mrs. Violet Williams of England presented the "rules" of the International Committee which precisely defined membership, the election and responsibilities of the executive committee, the criteria for national committees, and the responsibilities of the International Committee.

The committee on the Administrative Operation, chaired by the capable Miss Sibenda Holsteijn presented recommendations which were adopted by the plenary session: 1) that the next meeting be scheduled to take advantage of the meeting of the Asian Church Women's Conference. 2) that a total budget of $12,000 for the two-year period be approved toward which all national committees be asked to share on a voluntary basis; 3) that Church Women United in the U.S.A. be asked to continue with the administration. Dr. Buhrig expressed appreciation to CWU for the work which it had undertaken. Dorothy Dolbey, representing the U.S.A. responded that the work had been rewarded by genuine spiritual satisfaction.

There was discussion of the setting of a specific permanent date for the World Day of Prayer. The current practice of holding the service on the first Friday of Lent was different each calendar year and this added to the confusion because the Eastern Orthodox celebrate Easter on a different date than Protestant and Roman Catholics. The first Friday in March was proposed. In the discussion it was brought out that the weather was still unpredictably bad—too cold for the northern hemisphere, too hot for the southern! The Europeans pointed out that the growing practice of long holiday weekends was cutting attendance on Fridays. Not being ready to change tradition too drastically, the committee voted that the World Day of Prayer be celebrated on the first Friday in March each year.

Relationships were considered with other prayer movements—such as the World Week of Prayer of the YWCA and the WSCF, the Week of Prayer for Christian Unity, the Fellowship of the Least Coin. Greetings were sent to each of those movements with the declaration of common concern as well as mutual understanding of the identity and distinctive purpose of each.

Edna Sinclair, on behalf of a subcommittee, presented future themes. For 1970, the theme proposed was "Take Courage!" But someone reminded her that in England, "Courage" is the name of an alcoholic beverage and this slogan was already advertised on all the buses! It was conceded that in some cases the theme had better stay with the King James version, "Be of Good Courage."

The themes for the next two years were selected and assigned to committees in the Caribbean and West Germany to develop. We should note that the theme, "All Joy Be Yours," rose from the spirit and experience of the two women from the German Democratic Republic who had added so much to our gathering.

The nominating committee which had been elected by ballot brought in the following slate for the Executive Committee: Gudrun Diestel (Germany) Chairman; Esther Coker (Sierra Leona); Mariko Imai (Japan); Amal Halaby (Lebanon); Laura Burnett (Canada); and Sylvia Talbot (Guyana).

Alternates were also selected and when it was impossible for the Reverend Mrs. Imai to serve, the Reverend Mrs. Margarethe Lie Dharma (Indonesia) replaced her. When Amal Halaby moved to the United States with her American husband, she was replaced by Mrs. R.S.C. Dingle (Australia).

1970 MEETING The next meeting of the International Commit-
IN BANGKOK tee was in Bangkok, Thailand, September 20 -
24, 1970. The hospitality of the Thai Christians
began as soon as planes touched down at the international airport in Bangkok, where incoming members of the
International Committee were welcomed by the local
committee headed by Lydia Mojdara and Sucon Chaloryoo.
Many friendships had already formed inasmuch as some of the
women had just spent ten days as participants in the Asian
Church Women's Conference held in Sukabumi, Indonesia.

A reception held in the garden of the YMCA, the place of
the meeting, was attended by over a hundred civic and
religious leaders of Thailand and there was wide coverage in
the local papers. On two other evenings the fifty overseas
guests were received into the hearts and homes of the people
of Bangkok, and a special tour of the ancient royal buildings
and Buddhist temples will never be forgotten. As needs in
shopping, health and visa problems came up, someone was on
hand to be of assistance. Not until the last guests were at the
airport ready for their departure did the gracious local
committee take time for rest.

Gudrun Diestel, with the backing of her own national
committee, had given herself wholeheartedly to the development of this prayer movement, having visited many places in
Africa, Europe and the Americas in trips of friendly cultivation. Her letters to the National Committee were always
thoughtful and her agendas included items which gave a
broader understanding of the cultural context in which a
Christian woman makes her witness in today's world.

Four Thai leaders from the university and government
interpreted the whole question of peace building in Southeast
Asia. Since there had been an expressed desire to have an
opportunity for greater understanding of Buddhism in a
country where most of the people embraced Buddhism, the
local committee arranged a lecture by Princess Poon Pismai
Diskul, President of the World Buddhist Association. She
charmed the whole company by her concern both for world
peace and for prayer. There followed a question period in
which she was asked, "Do you count as authentic Buddhists

the young people in the West who seem to be devotees of Buddhist practices of meditation?" This revered person of eighty years answered: "We have no way of counting Buddhists since it is a matter of the heart. But my experience is that the reason young people want to change their religion is because they do not understand their own. Or perhaps it is their way of protesting the hypocrisy of their parents!"

Adelaide von Guttenberg of Germany submitted on behalf of the wider group of Europeans the preliminary draft of the 1972 World Day of Prayer service on the theme, "All Joy Be Yours." The service had vignettes of problems which the European women had proposed as subjects of concern and prayer, such as migrant laborers, youth and the aged. Then we were divided into groups to discuss how these problems affected our own countries.

At a plenary session other prayer concerns were shared. Florence Mahoney of The Gambia spoke of the need for dialogue between Christians and Moslems; Grace Aaron of India spoke of oppressive poverty; Oo Chung Lee of Korea spoke of human dignity; Michiko Okuda of Japan made a moving appeal on behalf of the people of China and spoke about the need of Christians of her country to relate to all people, not just to other Christians. Vilma Dube of Trinidad spoke of the disillusionment of youth in the Church whose leaders have acquiesed to the practices of oppression; Mrs. Ang Kim Kiat of Singapore added her concern about youth. Sylvia Talbot of Guyana focused our attention on another group—the young, professional people returning from study abroad disillusioned by the church leaders in the countries where they studied. Elisa Ocera of the Philippines and Lidia Mansilla of Guatemala both mentioned the need to be more open to Roman Catholics in the World Day of Prayer. Rose Catchings who represented the U.S.A. spoke about the needs of full participation of ethnic minorities. It was pointed out by Adelaide von Guttenberg that this kind of discussion should go on in national committees in order to introduce petitions for prayer of greatest concern on the Day of Prayer. I made a mental note that Christians feared becoming a closed sect in countries where they were a small minority. I wished there had been more discussion of how this problem might turn into an opportunity.

Shanti Solomon, who had just been elected the Executive Secretary of the Asian Church Women's Conference at the meeting in Indonesia, made a statement about the relationships of the Fellowship of the Least Coin and the World Day of Prayer.

Some of the members of the Planning Committee of the Asian Church Women's Conference met with the Executive Committee of the International Committee for World Day of Prayer and both agreed that the Fellowship of the Least Coin and the World Day of Prayer were movements that involve women through prayer and both are ecumenical and international in nature. Each has its own identity and meets a need.

The monies of the FLC were all sent to one source without distinction of country, and the ACWC was responsible for distribution, whereas the offerings of the World Day of Prayer were reserved by each national committee for distribution. The two committees agreed to interpret and promote both movements. The two committees had agreed that in 1971 we would sponsor several joint teams into various parts of Latin America and the Caribbean to include the stories of both movements of prayer.

It was agreed at this meeting to co-opt two persons from the World Union of Catholic Women's Organizations to be designated by them. Jacqueline Stuyt, the ecumenical chairman of WUCWO, and Dulcinea Rodrigues, President of the NCCW of India and Vice-President of YWCA, were subsequently named. It was felt that this would provide the world committee with necessary counsel during the period in which Roman Catholics were being recognized by the national committees. Indeed, the correspondence with these two women was delightful during the next years, and they proved real promoters through their channels for the World Day of Prayer. Gudrun Diestel was re-elected chairperson of the International Committee, and Esther Coker (Sierra Leone), Michiko Okuda (Japan), Eileen Sheard (New Zealand), Margaret Sonnenday (U.S.A.), and Sylvia Talbot (Guyana), were elected to the Executive Committee.

Thirty-two national committees were represented in the fifty women present, which included several from Indonesia whose islands are so far apart that it was necessary to recognize several independent committees. We were particularly glad to have the opportunity to welcome Akaiti Ama of Cook Islands and Ha Britaia of the Gilbert Islands, for they had come by ship as far as Australia and had been weeks on the way. In addition, observers had been invited from the YWCA, the World Catholic women, the East Asia Christian Council, the Asian Church Women's Conference, and, of course, the Executive Committee which sponsored the conference. Greetings from dozens of other national committees were posted on the wall as the roll was called of the one hundred and fifty-five countries or islands known to have shared in the World Day of Prayer in 1970.

The concluding dedication service took the form of an Agape Supper. At each place at the table was a small Thai lamp and a silver pin representing the first century ICHTHUS, which each pinned on her neighbor as the sign of our faith in Jesus Christ. As we shared food, we talked of the love of Christ we had ourselves experienced during the week. Our concluding time together was spent in sharing our prayer concerns as we sought strength to face the torrent of problems unleased by the crises of our world.

1974 MEETINGS IN MEXICO Four years later, on September 26, 1974, sixty women from thirty-seven countries gathered in the beautiful Nuestra Cabana, an international Girl Scout Center near Cuernavaca, Mexico, for the third official meeting of the International Committee for the World Day of Prayer. Many took advantage of this opportunity to dip into the cultural heritage in Mexico City where the museums, architecture, murals and drama speak eloquently of the ancient Indian civilizations—the Maya, the Aztec, the Toltec, among others—as well as many aspects of the modern renaissance of Mexican art and music.

We were fortunate that Sylvia Ortega, a brilliant young sociologist and the daughter of Sra. Guadalupe de Ortega, the gracious president of Union Nacional Interdenominacional de

Sociedades Femeniles could be present throughout the meeting to give some interpretation of the social changes brought about by the coming of the Spanish *Conquistadores,* the subsequent submission of the Indians, the exploitation of the *mestizos,* Indians and other peasants by rich landowners, the social revolutions, the coming of the foreign investors and tourists, and the annual exit of a million agricultural migrants across the borders each year! To many who had overlooked these countries previously, these experiences were excellent background when the special committee of Mexican women presented the problems of Latin America as the basis of the 1976 theme, "Education for All of Life."

From the point of view of an international prayer fellowship, a meeting in Latin America was bound to be important since many Protestant women belonged to churches whose leaders discouraged interdenominational movements. The World Day of Prayer, first observed through denominational channels, later formed an opening for women to pray with one another. We were gratified to have present women from ten countries from Central and South America and six countries of the Caribbean. We welcomed several Roman Catholic women among the participants. The strong autonomous committee in Puerto Rico sent its own delegate. For the first time there were representatives from Austria, Haiti, Spain, and Uganda. Claudia Pillipuk of the Union of Evangelical Christian Baptists of Moscow in the Soviet Union had hoped to be present. Passport difficulties also prevented the participation of Mrs. Duk Kwee Kong, chairperson of the World Day of Prayer Committee in Korea, and of Miss Lee Oo-Chung, President of Korean Church Women United, as well as the representative from the Philippines, Mrs. Noemi Navarro. Mrs. Ruth Bond of Washington, D.C., represented the U.S.A.; but Margaret Sonnenday, as a member of the Executive Committee, carried responsible parts of the leadership. There were a great many visitors who participated freely upon the ruling of the Executive Committee. All had been invited to be at the Ecumenical Assembly which was convening two weeks later in Memphis.

For the first time, it was necessary to conduct the

plenary session in two languages. Gudrun Diestel exhibited cheerful patience while slowing down the eager discussion to allow the hardworking Spanish/English interpreters to catch up. Yet it was good to be on a continent where so many nations had a common language.

The committees worked diligently in producing the proposals later accepted by the plenary body. Olga R.T. Noguerira (Brazil) headed a committee which developed a plan for the development of responsible central committees and also proposed that the international office put out a series of short news bulletins to keep interest alive all year round. Prakai Nontawasee (Thailand), on behalf of a committee on new themes, offered five subjects (and recommended authors) and brought them to the plenary body with the development of their basic content.

Alder Hall of Australia, on behalf of the administrative committee, proposed a number of recommendations which were accepted:

> . . . the next International Committee meeting be held in Africa in 1978. (It was subsequently determined that the Committee would respond affirmatively to an invitation from the Christian Council of Zambia to hold the meeting in Lusaka. If the political situation did not permit this meeting in Africa, an invitation to join in a 50th Anniversary celebration of the Women's Inter-Church Council of Canada remained open.

> . . . national committees take seriously their responsibility to extend services to new places and study ways by which their committees could become more representative of various racial and religious traditions.

> . . . additional official delegates be recognized by the Executive Committee in situations where there was a strong minority or majority which needed to speak for itself at the meetings of the International Committee. (This committee had the very valuable help of Mrs. Jean Walker of South Africa who reported the hope that one result of negotiations now going on in South Africa among black leaders would be included in the central committee. It was noted that unresolved pluralistic

situations might exist elsewhere, particularly in areas where the Roman Catholic or Orthodox were a majority in the population yet the committee by tradition had developed as Protestant. At this meeting, Egypt had three persons, one a Coptic Orthodox, one an Evangelical, and its official representative, Roman Catholic Sister Nadia Bishara.

. . . a greatly increased budget in order to allow for leadership development in certain areas, and also take into account the unusual expense of the African meeting.

. . . CWU be asked to continue the administration, and that Dorothy Wagner be named as the Administrative Secretary (replacing Margaret Shannon who would be retiring in 1975!)

The Nominating Committee, chaired by Esther Coker, presented the following proposal for the Executive Committee, which was unanimously elected: Prakai Nontawasee (Thailand), Regina Addo (Ghana), Hildegard Seidel (Austria), Guadalupe de Ortega (Mexico), Mary Fadel (Egypt), Avanell Tuttle (Canada).

From this list the nominating committee presented the name of Prakai Nontawasee as chairperson of the International Committee through its next meeting. She was elected unanimously. I was sitting in front of her as her name was read and heard her soft cry of protest. If she had been given a chance to reflect on the invitation, she might have found plenty of excuses not to accept the responsibility. Yet with the enthusiastic applause, she had to accept this decision as a call of God for her time and talents. Prakai Nontawasee, whose capacity as a Christian educator and administrator was recognized when she was elected the first woman president of the Thailand Theological Seminary in Chiangmai, was known to us as an understanding woman with a loving regard for what all other women were facing in this kaleidoscopic world.

I often remember this circle of friends and reflect on why this ever-changing committee had been such a lasting satisfaction. Perhaps it was just because genuine prayer cannot be measured or its worth advertised or its value judged by others. How many committees are wrecked in spirit by evaluations of end results that focus blame or give credit to someone? Prayer is a democratizing experience and only the arrogant go away empty-handed.

Perhaps it was the integrity of the many women I had known through this committee. I was always grateful for members of the older established committees who gave such undergirding strength yet each representative entered into the life of the committee as one among many peers. Perhaps their hunger, like mine, was fed by the realism of the Asian and African Christians whose prayer agendas were so much of this world. The elitists deserve to get lost in poetic phrases! The depth of the cry to God is still conditioned, as it has always been, by the intensity of the human struggle. I noticed that often those of us who were at ease with many material things, and living in relatively free democracies, seemed to be the ones to echo "vain repetitions," while those whose spiritual sensitivity had been sharpened by living under repressive regimes expressed their longings as genuine originals.

But as I look back over the years, we were not divided by country at all; we could not separate ourselves from nor generalize about, "third world women." After all, it was our Lord's prayer that we might become perfectly one!

One of my memories was the last morning at Cuernavaca when I had gotten up at dawn to pack. There was a committee praying together on a side porch as they got ready to give the finishing touch to their report before an eight o'clock breakfast bell called them to join the sleepy disciples.

The World Day of Prayer began as a movement among Western Christians who met to pray together for their missionary movement. Now the women of the world are calling each other to further understand the prayer for the mission of the universal church—which begins with each person where she lives. The next generation will inherit a most precious possession—a prayer movement of global dimensions. Along with our sisters in 160 countries or islands, we are an indispensable part of the whole. As we are partners in petition, likewise all of us have a significant part in God's answer to prayer.

Integrity in relationships
. . . with Fellowship of the Least Coin

Just because I saw a longing give birth to the *Fellow-ship of the Least Coin,* I could later write, "A Cathedral is being built as heart responds to heart, enabled by the Spirit *"to . . . long for . . . one another!"* Lest the founder, Shanti Solomon, become only a legend, let me tell you about Shanti Solomon who touched other persons in very human ways.

We met in 1956 on the way to Alaska where we both shared in a Women's Fellowship Mission to Christian women in some of the countries surrounding the Pacific basin. Three women from the United States were joined by Shanti Solomon of North India, Teriko Ohashi of Japan and Ellen Lang, a native Alaskan Indian.

The immense beauty of the snow-capped mountains in Alaska were impressive even to the two who claimed Mt. Fuji and the Himalayas as their own. But more amazing to Teriko and Shanti was the sparcity of the population. We went from one fishing village to another by float plane to be welcomed by a handful of people at the wharf. When Ellen would point out an unusual peak enroute, Teriko and Shanti would laughingly shout, "But where are the people?" Mt. Fuji was hidden in clouds when we landed in Tokyo, so Ellen was able to make a comeback, "Where is your mountain?" Teriko and Shanti waited until we got on a crowded subway platform where droves of polite Japanese were pushing each other like the rest of the world's commuters. The two Asians turned to point out to their Alaskan friend: "Look! People!"

It was the people we had come to see in Alaska, Korea, Japan, Hongkong, and the Philippine Islands. The agreed upon pattern in each locality was to study a new chapter of the Gospel of Mark. This kept our team fresh and our hostesses knew that no preconceived selection of Scripture was aimed at them.

It was after the Bible study in Juneau that I began to discover Shanti's philosophy of prayer and action. We had focused on a selection in Mark where Jesus claimed that prayer could remove mountains. During the refreshment hour, an older woman came up to comment: "The trouble with that statement is that it just isn't true." She had come from a church in Iowa where mission study was the heart of the women's association. Finding none in her new church home, she pursued the matter regularly with the program committee. Finally they agreed that the next month she test out a mission study! She worked and prayed, and prayed and worked, but when she gave the program it was a flop! Later, I told Shanti about my failure to explain the dilemma satisfactorily. Shanti said, "She should have kept on praying but let someone else give the program!"

On the long trip across the Pacific, I gave Shanti the window seat. After all this might be her only trip across the Pacific! But she was not so much interested in the distance between clouds as in closeness among people. Shanti talked about the dimension to her own life which had been added by her brief touch with women in Alaska. She kept remembering that this privilege would never come to women in the villages of India where she and her husband worked. Imagine what would be added to the dull, daily routine of village women if they could have friends in another place. Prayer and imagination might link them, but how to feel the reality of it? In prayer we are equal. Money is what divides us. Money buys education, travel, jobs, pictures, books; yet these things can also separate us from those people too poor to share in the same pleasures.

Even the doing of good works was a barrier. If all the money that the village women in North India could muster were gathered together, the result would not amount to anything they could talk about. Americans could build hospitals, send missionaries, provide scholarships. In Christ, could women become one—even those who were the "poor-in-some-ways-and-rich-in-other-ways?" My hand reached over and touched her. "Perhaps the way will open to you in Asia," I whispered. Years later, I wished I had not said "perhaps!" It was as if I didn't believe that prayer could remove mountains!

When the Korean government refused to give a visa to a citizen of India, we sent Shanti to the Philippines to share the Bible study there while the rest of us carried out the original schedule in Korea. Two weeks later we were all together again attending a church service in Tokyo. The crowd was unusually large. It could have been because the Emperor was due to pass the church in a motor cavalcade about the time of adjournment. We were on the church steps on time! The Emperor and Empress passed within a few feet of the curb on which were standing hundreds of school children with gaily-colored flags. As royalty and subjects waved and smiled at each other, I recalled that only a few years before Japanese tradition had venerated His Highness as divine. If some political systems could change in a decade, why are we cast down about others?

As soon as we could find time alone, Shanti told me about the happenings in the Philippines. They even had agreed on a plan. Any woman could communicate through prayer if in her heart she included a woman in a faraway place. As a token, she would set aside the "least coin" of her country—a centavo, a penny, a peso, a yen. "Tell it here," I murmured as we joined the Japanese women at luncheon, served so tastefully in beautiful lacquer boxes.

The next week in Hongkong, Rayann Ma, who had substituted for Shanti in Korea, acted as interpreter. Her enthusiasm about the "Fellowship of the Least Coin" assured another international transplant. Who would have dreamed that ten years later, the Fellowship of the Least Coin would be a blooming reality in nearly seventy countries, all coming from the seeds scattered by some woman's enthusiasm!

I was pretty sure that the least coin was one answer for participation of Asian women, but I doubted that it would appeal as an idea to Presbyterians at home. I wondered if any would bother with a penny a month! To this doubt the dauntless Shanti replied: "If you Americans can't do something like the rest of us, then you deserve to be more and more isolated from the common people of the world!" Even in 1956, I could see this was a likelihood. One of the Fellowship Mission, Amy Carl, agreed to present the idea to the national executive committee of Presbyterian Women. With each woman knowing she was being asked to vote in faith for an idea that could never be proven until tried, the enabling process was approved.

A year later the executive committee dedicated the few hundred dollars that had come in response to the idea. The national president, Grace Salsbury, read the Beatitudes and fifteen members of the committee prayed in silence for women they knew outside their own community. Then each took a penny from her purse and laid it on the table as Grace Salsbury swept the whole Christian family into our circle with earnest intercession. She prayed with special care for the right spirit among American women:

> Forgive us for trusting in bigness. Help us to discover the blessings which come to the meek and humble minded and those who are poor in spirit.

In 1958 the Asian Church Women's Conference was organized in Hongkong, and it seemed appropriate that the responsibility of interpreting the Fellowship of the Least Coin should be undertaken by them. It was hoped that there would be an appropriate group of Christian women to sponsor the idea in each country who could find the way to forward the least coins to a central place.

In spirit, join this fellowship-in-the-making during the beginning years:

> —Laugh a little with the women of a Pakistan village for they may be describing someone like you as they mould small clay pots. Each pot will later be plastered on the wall of an adobe home ready to receive the year's contributions of least coins.

> —Go with a woman in Lebanon on a special trip to South Sashaya where native pottery is made while she orders a large vessel to be used for the annual collection of coins. On it is written in beautiful Arabic letters, "Fellowship of the Least Coin."

> —Imagine yourself with a professional woman from the Cameroun who was in this country as part of a Causeway team and was being entertained in Pittsburgh between meetings. At the breakfast table reference was made to some special trouble in the life of the African guest five years before. Slowly it dawned on the hostess that this was the person whose problem had been shared with her by a missionary. She had prayed

for this woman through the years, while she would scrounge through her drawers looking for a one-cent piece, which was a game she played with herself. Now in her own home, she was touching the very African woman whose inner hurt had been healed by prayer.

—Read a note from an American resident in Manila soon after she shared in a dedication of three large woven baskets full of least centavo coins:

"Last Sunday I participated in a meeting of women of the Manila Conference at their dedication of the Least Coin. I want to share with you the glow of belonging that swept over me as I sat there. It was indeed an inspiration that Shanti Solomon left here. We of the West know nothing of the poverty of the East. To have an opportunity to share our least coin with Christian women of the world is a rare and wonderful privilege."

—Share the surprise of another American visiting with her friend in Yugoslavia. At daybreak one morning, a small group of faithful women in an isolated church gathered to welcome this visitor. Through an interpreter, she told the story of the Fellowship of the Least Coin to these women with their attentive faces framed in black babushkas. A woman slipped quietly out of the gathering and in a moment returned with a small box filled with least coins. Remote and cut off as these women once were, they found themselves already part of a worldwide family of faith.

The administration of any funds collected had been given to the East Asia Christian Council, a body with a knowledgeable staff and financial facilities. Dr. D.T. Niles, the General Secretary of the EACC, was a widely known ecumenical figure. Since these funds came unsolicited from all over the world, Dr. Niles felt it was a good idea to make the gifts in the same spirit. Thus unsolicited grants were offered to encourage responsible programs while not encouraging their getting caught up in continued support.

Unexpectedly in 1958 a number of worthy projects on five different continents each received a gift of $1,000.00 from the EACC through the courtesy of the Fellowship of the Least Coin. One recipient was a church in Harlem. The gift would be used for their summer youth program. Another grant went for the expenses of a Cameroun pastor to work among African students in Paris. Other gifts were made to South America and Africa and several to Asia.

The gift to CIMADE, a French Aid Committee which sponsored the Cameroun pastor, came to the attention of Madeline Barot of the World Council of Churches. In 1961 she attended the meeting of the EACC in Madras and noted that the women who were accumulating the money were not getting much credit. So when it came her turn to speak, she started out by thanking "the women" of Asia for the gift to the Cameroun pastor in Paris. She then continued to point out what "the women" of Asia had done in other parts of the world through their prophetic way of financing ecumenical mission. The headline of the newspaper the next day read something like, "WOMEN OF ASIA MAKE POSSIBLE WORLD SERVICE." The leaders of the EACC read the newspaper, and belatedly rejoiced in the fact that among them were certain amazing women.

At the second meeting of the Asian Church Women's Conference in Petburi, Thailand, in 1962, Madeline Barot, Dr. Niles and I were all present. Dr. Niles convened a consultative group to discuss the policy and practices which should assure continuity of the Fellowship of the Least Coin. This plenary body of ninety Asian women agreed to the following recommendations:

> . . . that the prayer aspect of the movement be emphasized and that a symbol and a brochure be developed to focus on this primary purpose. (Later the CIRCLE OF PRAYER was published bi-annually and the symbol, a circle of praying hands forming a lotus flower, was adopted).
>
> . . . that all national groups send their funds designated for the Fellowship of the Least Coin through the EACC account of the WCC in Geneva;
>
> . . . that a person on each continent be chosen to become a member by correspondence of the committee

which approved the expenditure of funds:

. . . that all correspondence and acknowledgment of gifts should come from Asia;

. . . that grants continue to be made in all regions of the world;

. . . that the Asian Church Women's Conference be authorized to save a portion each year toward its quadrennial meeting;

. . . that the accumulated funds be used primarily for ecumenical participation of women in world planning or objects of relief, reconciliation and evangelism;

. . . that individuals be urged to use no more than the least coin of their own country as a symbol of their prayer activity; that national or regional channels avoid publicizing the total gifts in order not to look or be competitive.

The new chairperson was from Thailand and so was able to work closely with the Asian Conference of Churches whose business office had been moved to Bangkok from Burma.

In 1966 the Asian Church Women's Conference meeting in Tokyo celebrated the tenth anniversary of the Fellowship of the Least Coin which by this time was in sixty-six countries. Rathie Selvaratnum was elected chairperson of the ACWC for the next quadrennium and gave herself wholeheartedly to the promotion of the FLC. She traveled in many countries, answered hundreds of letters promptly and received and recommended projects for the ever increasing funds. These were reported to those national organizations which were acting as channels, although it should be emphasized that not every country in the world has such national offices and there- fore the needs of individuals and single groups were met by individual correspondence.

The Executive Committee of ACWC had begun to take more responsibility in screening projects and recommending to the Asian Conference of Churches (formerly EACC) the distribution of the funds. Church Women United received its first grant from the Fellowship of the Least Coin early in 1966 for a leadership training conference at Fisk University, and later many more grants for work it was doing on behalf of American minorities and for its ecumenical teams. In 1966, the Executive Committee voted that CWU should become an official channel for the promotion of this idea and for liaison responsibilities with the Asian Committee.

By the time of the fourth meeting of ACWC in Indonesia in 1970, the work had so grown that the executive committee recommended to the Conference that an executive be employed to coordinate the general work of the Conference and give continuing and consistent policy and practice to the Fellowship of the Least Coin. At the invitation of the executive committee, Shanti Solomon was a participating observer at this meeting, speaking on the early dream of the Fellowship of the Least Coin. She had dropped the leadership after 1958 because of the extended illness of her beloved husband. Later she was elected national secretary of women's work of the United Church of Northern India. To her surprise the delegates of the ACWC elected her as their executive. It was an excellent choice. She had accumulated considerable administrative experience in her professional work with the Church of Northern India and had been active in ecumenical work of that country. In addition she offered an authentic interpretation to the FLC and its values.

Shanti was the chief speaker in Bangkok in 1970 at a church meeting of English-speaking women whose husbands were serving in government or business. *As I listened, I noted especially her emphasis on reconciliation as a necessary prerequisite to prayer—and an essential component to world peace. But the least coins were taken up like a collection! Too often this public collection among American groups seems to result in emptying the purse rather than pouring out one's heart for another in prayer. How much better it would have been if we remembered that both the prayer and the mite of the widow were offered in sincerity and in secret!*

The Fellowship of the Least Coin grows with the integrity of praying individuals bound together by reconciling acts. Its reality is symbolized by a simple token which makes kinfolk of rich and poor. Integrity—Reconciliation—Community coalesced by prayer become instruments of peace in a world of increasing hostility.

Integrity in relationships

... through Christian Causeways

The term *Causeway* was officially adopted by the executive committee in March 1966 as a sort of "trade-mark" of a style of relationships that interprets the distinctive purpose of Church Women United in a global context. *Causeway* does not replace or supersede other forms of international encounters in which we participate along with other civic and religious organizations, nor the traveling seminars under program directors which are educational in nature.

The aim of the *Causeway* is to encourage common understanding and mutual motivation between Christian women in other lands and those in the U.S.A. Participation in *Causeway* is not defined by travel, study, or hospitality, although it may require one or more of these elements by some of those who engage in this experience together. It is evaluated by the enlarged scope of Christian faith and practice which we discover in ourselves as together with other human beings we transcend differences.

We are on a journey of faith on a highway already built by God through the tested faith of the faithful of many generations in many lands. The destination has been determined by the Designer and Builder although there are many lanes both going and coming. In this speed-driven era, we can, of course, cause a congestion which slows down and immobilizes the other travelers; or we can drive off the bridge into some boggy social dilemma; or we can have the exhilarating spiritual experience of being on the WAY together.

So we called this venture *Causeway*—a term with meaning to those who traveled on American highways, even though it turned out to be difficult to translate into other languages! With proper acknowledgment to the editors of recent dictionaries, the term was defined:

A CAUSEWAY is a modern road rising above marshy ground bridging a gap which otherwise would mire us down and keep us from finding each other.

Wanting to have a single set of the mind, we described this venture into a common care for integrity as follows:

Across the races
across the nations
across the generations
women walk together
on a CAUSEWAY
FOR US
Christ is the CAUSEWAY
It is his CAUSE
It is his WAY
and therefore we are unafraid
to walk together down new paths
into a new day.

ALONG THE WAY
We discover life is a sacrament
as common as daily bread
which is broken to be useful
to build up the body of the CHURCH

We face
the rising Sun of Righteousness
which exposes
all that is sordid and sinful
and brings God's judgment upon us
and God's healing among us.

Therefore we shall not turn away
but shall press on together
WITH OUR FACE TO THE RISING SUN—OH LORD,
HAVE MERCY ON US

Generally speaking participants travelled in small inter-racial teams so more intimate encounters were possible. It had once been conceived that the women would actually work together on some project for a period of several weeks, but the understandable longing of women going abroad for the first time to have a touch with more than one area postponed this part of the plan. At the conclusion all teams and a representative of the host groups were convened at one place for a summary and evaluation experience. They often made recommendations to the church women of all the "home" countries involved.

Between 1966 and 1975, women from forty countries had opportunity to walk the *Causeway*. It would be beyond reason to think that the sum total of their experience could be expressed. However, for the record let us summarize here the general scope and features of six *Causeway* experiences between 1966-1975 and then some reactions of the participants in two of them.

Twelve international women were selected from those coming to the Ecumenical Assembly to explore in depth the situation in which Christian women make their witness in local communities. Divided into pairs, they were received in six states where they were able to observe the everyday involve-ment of women as wife and mother, teacher, nurse and cook,

Dateline: Christian Cause—Direction Africa—Summer 1966.

After attending a conference sponsored by one of the agencies of the United Nations in Addis Ababa in May 1966, Kitty Strong, the national director of International Affairs, took a circular trip around the African continent in order to interpret our desire to have a person-to-person encounter with Christian women there. She shared our need to reinforce our Christian faith and to learn from each other about improving living relationships between black and white races. She discovered able African church women who were willing to set up the circumstances for *Causeway* experience and welcome a small inter-racial team into their homes and churches.

Since the African women had only a couple of months to make these plans and CWU had only that length of time to recruit the *Causeway* participants, a lot of credit needs to go to Kitty Strong for her ability to follow through with administrative details. A strong inter-racial team, well fortified with introductions, went to Ghana and Nigeria, another team to Malawi, Kenya, and Uganda. Another team went to South Africa and were received by both black and white church women there—even though an American black woman was not able to get a visa to enter the country. Each woman also did some travel in other countries in Africa and all were together in Zambia at the concluding conference at the Mindolo Ecumenical Center, where they shared facilities and program with an all Africa Methodist conference of church women.

Dateline: Causeway—Direction U.S.A.—Summer 1967

Twelve international women were selected from those coming to the Ecumenical Assembly to explore in depth the situation in which Christian women make their witness in local communities. Divided into pairs, they were received in six states where they were able to observe the everyday involvement of women as wife and mother, teacher, nurse and cook, community worker and chauffeur, and employed in many vocations. It was assumed that they would question the factors which make up our society—our segregated churches, city ghettos, suburban provinciality, rural communities, and welfare programs, and social systems which seem to separate the generations. The plan was to meet with Americans to discuss their mutual concerns as Christians, climaxing at a special session. Among their observations was one that Americans were so busy being gracious hostesses that there was no time for discussing how witness is made in differing cultures and circumstances.

Dateline: Causeway—Direction Latin America—1968

A *Causeway* together with women of Colombia, Ecuador, Peru, Argentina, Bolivia, Uruguay, Brazil and

Venezuela was set forward by Emily Gibbes who made an exploratory visit to South America in the late fall of 1967. Emily Gibbes was a sort of one-woman *Causeway* herself, being able to communicate readily with a woman of another culture. Having sounded out the natural leaders, she brought back the places where invitations for a *Causeway* might be forthcoming. In the spring of 1968, CWU commissioned three teams, each of which undertook to find common cause with Christian women of a different region of that continent. At the conclusion, a woman selected by each host group in Colombia, Peru, Bolivia, Uruguay, met together with the participants from CWU in Guatemala to evaluate their experience together. At that time suggestions were made for a return group of participants to visit Church Women United in the U.S.A. during the next year.

Dateline: Causeway—Direction Spanish-Americans—1969

Church Women United had a "problem-opportunity" and we sought a group of 11 women from Latin America to help us! The Spanish-speaking American is the second largest minority in the U.S.A., yet we were embarrassed that so few of them could be found in the fellowship and service projects of Church Women United. Language barriers! Cultural differences! Economic classes! Yet we needed each other in order to be practical about ways to overcome these factors.

There was also the invisible barrier: our reluctance to give enough time or even to care enough, to understand these warm-spirited persons in our midst—among which there was also so much diversity.

The women who came from Argentina, Bolivia, Mexico, Uruguay, Colombia, Chile, the Dominican Republic, and Puerto Rico were also individually quite different. They were Pentecostal, Anglican, Roman Catholic, Evangelical, Protestant. There were hospital administrators, pastors, teachers, lawyers, social workers. Yet they had a common mission—to be a catalytic agent to help so that Spanish-speaking Americans might be involved more fully within CWU.

Since there needed to be an opportunity for the *Causeway* participants to get acquainted in their own language, they began this process in Puerto Rico. Then a short seminar on Inter-American affairs was planned for them with resources of the United Nations.

Their orientation into the historic and present situations of Spanish-speaking Americans was planned by a specially gifted group of professional women of Hispanic background. Through the careful preparatory work of the Manhattan CWU, every one of the Spanish-speaking churches in the area had been visited and the women invited to come to the opening reception. More than a hundred did! Then South Americans flew to Austin, Texas, where the Reverend Jorge Lara-Braud assisted them in theological study and explained the historical background of the Mexican American.

In pairs, they went to their assignments in 22 states where women in local units had set up forums, making every attempt to include in them the Spanish-speaking minorities in their vicinity. The visiting participants kept diaries of their reactions in Spanish, which they later permitted to be translated, with excerpts put into *The Church Woman* (April 1970).

The round-up sessions were held immediately after World Community Day under the auspices of CWU in Wilmington, Delaware. We were able to discover in those two days a great deal about the Spanish-speaking woman, her daily life and her goals. There were some general recommendations as to how we could continue to stimulate the concern of the *Causeway.* One had a feeling that the Latin Americans were as baffled as were we, for obviously in their home territory they were in a different situation.

One also had the feeling that the device of the Forums was good to provoke discussion but that the time was too short to develop a kinship among Christian sisters across cultural lines. Perhaps that is why in our last hour together in Wilmington, Heydee de Benzo proposed we follow a custom of her church in Uruguay by having together *a time of the open heart.*

We had been eating a late supper together by candlelight. The shadows on the wall and the light on our faces had the mystical feel of the early catacombs. On behalf of CWU, I had presented each with a gift of a silver fish pin to indicate our central bond as we parted was Jesus Christ, Lord and Saviour, the Greek acrostic of which spells "ICHTHUS" - fish. We had formed prayer partners by each drawing one of the two curves which outlined a fish.

After many of the women had expressed their deep feelings, Hilda de Yanez, the Pentecostal from Chile, signaled her interpreter and quietly said, "From time to time I have wondered why I had come here without English and feeling so inadequate everywhere. Now I know. (And she pointed to the double elliptical line which forms the fish). "My American sister is the top line. I was needed to be the belly of the fish. *Together we are the sign of Christ.*"

Helen Gangwer, an artist skillful in the medium of finger painting, told them that the sign of ICHTHUS—fish was in each person's hand. With skillful movements she created the background of a blue sea in which there were coral shells and seaweed ferns. Then she encouraged each of our guests to make her sign by a sharp chop of the side of her palm on the wet blue paint. In a few minutes, the imprint of each had placed the "ichthus" into the center of the painting. With a few finishing touches by the artist, the painting was presented to CWU in the USA where it still hangs on the walls of our national office as a reminder that the sign of Christ is a living bond among Christian women of the Americas.

So *Causeway* had a further interpretation—Christ in my hand. My hand touching another hand. There was a mood of quiet communion lighted by a kind of celebrative glow. We are reminded by all who come from all over the world that Christ-in-the-hand of each of us can become for others a series of living beatitudes.

Dateline: Christian Causeway—Direction Asia—February 1974

The World Day of Prayer for 1974 had been prepared by the Women's Committee of the National Christian Council of Japan on the theme, "Make Us Builders of Peace." An informal inquiry was made as to appropriate ways that the Christian women of Japan and the U.S.A., two industrialized nations, could take the theme very seriously. Michiko Okuda, a member of the International Committee for the World Day of Prayer, flew to New York to plan with us a consultation. It was agreed that it be held at the close of a *Christian Causeway* encounter in some countries of East Asia affected by the wars of the last three decades, with representatives of each of these countries present in the peace consultation itself.

Forty-eight participants were chosen from more than a hundred applicants to travel together for orientation in Hawaii and Hongkong and from there to divide into four Peace Caravans to visit Thailand, South Vietnam, the Philippines, Korea, and Taiwan. At a Retreat Center near Tokyo women gathered for the Peace-Building Consultation. The American and Japanese delegations were approximately equal in number and both included minorities living in their countries.

A moving experience for overseas participants was the journey to Hiroshima where they participated with the local community in the World Day of Prayer service, talked with some of those who had survived the explosion of the atomic bomb in 1945, and sent a message to the 8,000 World Day of Prayer services being sponsored by CWU in the United States. They visited the Peace Memorial Park and paused for acts of remembrance, reflection and repentance at the cenotaph—a memorial to the Japanese who died in the bombing, and at the memorial to Korean victims of the bomb. The testimony of the survivors spoke of the hope that is found in reconciliation, one of the undergirding spans of *Christian Causeway.*

Dateline: Christian Causeway—Direction Caribbean/USA September 1975

Mutuality in planning should always be a characteristic of *Causeway,* and in the case of the one planned for the Caribbean that was possible. Dr. Thelma Adair, a member of the Board of Managers, with wide experience in the Caribbean, flew to Trinidad to meet with women planning for a Conference of Caribbean Church Women, to determine what would be valuable both to the participants from the Caribbean and from the U.S.A. The bonus from this planning was an invitation to those coming from the U.S.A. to attend the first Conference of Caribbean Church Women. The Caribbean Church Women and CWU discovered they were working on a similar priority, so there was immediate agreement to make "The Child Indivisible" the mutual concern for the *Causeway.* The visitation teams included both Caribbean and North

American women. Each team visited one or two areas in the Caribbean (St. Croix, Barbados, Curacao, Belize, Grenada, Trinidad, Jamaica, St. Vincent, Guyana, the Dominican Republic, St. Lucia, Surinam, Aruba) and on the Eastern Seaboard in the United States (Tampa, Charleston, and Washington, D.C.). Alice Leppert, Director of Community services of CWU, met with state and local committees in Florida, South Carolina, and the Capital area, to involve them in the planning. Special exposure experiences were arranged to visit Headstart programs, children's centers, as well as to see the needs of the children of Seminole Indians and agricultural migrants and among families in the inner city.

Fortunate were the participants to have two of their planners experts in early childhood development. Dr. Dorinda Sampath, of the University of Trinidad, was a President of the Caribbean Council of Churches and Chairperson of the Women's Advisory Committee. Dr. Thelma Adair, Professor of Education at Queens College in New York City, presided over the final sessions which assessed the *Causeway* experience and developed a set of key recommendations regarding program development, as well as guidelines for advocating reforms which should be carried out by their governments. Then they made ten suggestions which answered the primary question of this *Causeway:* "What can women—wherever we are—do about "The Child Indivisible?"

I did not actually participate myself in any of the ventures along the *Causeway,* but I had many aspirations for those who did! In the case of our first effort on *Christian Causeway:* Direction Africa, I would have been satisfied if only a few came to feel at one with some African women as they shared their faith and hope with one another. As I reread the issue of *The Church Woman* (April 1967) written by participants in this *Causeway,* I found this had been the experience of many. Reading their words, I, too, was on the *Causeway.*

Our West African Causeway team often used words like these: 'We come to you from America with our imperfections: we know you recognize yours. We dream not of what we are separately, but what we shall be when we are together.' The response from the assembly was usually three distinct claps which mean, 'Very good, we agree.'   Laura McCray—Alabama

There is no doubt—the Causeway was already there—and we who have opportunity and responsibility were able to look into each other's faces and speak together.

I count with real joy the number of African women who walked over the Causeway toward me—and whom I now call friend. I know that I shall gain much more from those friendships as often these committed, eager women in their discernment and conviction drive me back from the superficial to the heart of the issue, and thus help my decisions to be basic ones.

Emily Gibbes—Pennsylvania

Traveling a Christian Causeway in South Africa was a shattering experience because you are torn by the predicament of the oppressed and are also wrenched by the dilemma of the oppressors.

. . . Few outsiders with a different orientation to Christ's message are able to accept their view of the gospel . . . The chasm, created by fear, resentment, rationalized statistics, and deeply held religious convictions which might have kept us apart, was closed through Christ. Now we must go forward, reaching out in deed and spirit, keeping the Causeway open, praying and working so that we may forever find in his Cause the way of walking together.

Patricia Young—Pennsylvania

Likewise I would have been satisfied had there been only one whose commitment to Christ and His Cause had been enlarged by the Causeway experience. Olive Tiller bears this witness:

While our new Christian friends across the sea may not have been aware that they were instilling within us lasting values and teaching us new truths about the Christian life, that is exactly what happened. I will mention four lessons that I learned from the women of East Africa.

1) Most outstanding was the lesson of simplicity . . . There is a quality of freshness and earnestness in the faith that is planted in Africa . . . Unfeigned joy is not masked by polite restraint—it is expressed without inhibition!

2) Their faith is relevant to their daily life . . . There will be no time for the teachings of Christ unless they have specific application to the problems of national building and the everyday lives.

3) Being a Christian makes a difference in how one lives.

4) Christianity is not equivalent to any one culture—either African or American . . . The kind of mutual scrutiny in which we engaged with our African counterparts made it possible to sort out those things which are basic to our faith from those which are extraneous.

When all of the trappings and window-dressings have been removed, that which remains can be reduced to two simple truths on which our Causeway has been constructed:

> God, in His love, sent Christ, who may be received by each person, whoever and wherever she is.

> I am more like every person I meet than I am unlike her.

Elizabeth Hartsfield (Kentucky) describes a worship service at Mindolo:

> Suddenly, in the moments of worship, I realized that I was in Africa. But more important, I recognized a kinship with these people because of our common belief in and commitment to Jesus Christ. The communion service that followed found me on my knees as I thanked God for the experience and the privilege of a Causeway.

Martha Kiely, venturing from her home in Buffalo, New York, on the spiritual pilgrimage over the Causeway in South Africa, shared her experience as a white woman:

> South Africa is a seductive nation. I had come not so much as a tourist as a pilgrim. I was determined to see how and where God was working in this nation so notorious for its elaborate system of legislative dividing

walls erected to keep apart her people of various races.

I was impressed anew with the extravagant ends to which all go to cover the scent of our sin with the perfume of selflessness and purity of motive. The explanation of apartheid is so clear and clever, so filled with philanthropic and religious overtones that one does not wonder that so many Christians accept the package.

Some days in South Africa I caught a nightmarish vision of America as she might become if we falter in receiving the brothers God has given to us. All of us have played at this little game of expediency. That is why we recognize it so quickly. From sad experience, we also know that God is not taken in by our propaganda.

Gathering for fellowship or worship across inter-racial lines is strongly discouraged and almost universally prohibited in South Africa. Yet this experience is still possible for persons with sufficient ingenuity, conviction, and courage. I shared in such obscure gatherings of concerned Christians, and I can testify that in these catacomb-like clusters, people are experiencing a quality of comradeship heretofore unknown. Loyalty to one's colorgroup fades and obedience to God takes priority. Eagerly they draw together, though a calculated risk is the price of admission. The Presence in their midst makes the fellowship of kindred minds well worth the cost . . .

A black South African woman described for me the intricacies of the cruel trap in which her people felt so helplessly caught. Then I had to put to her the questions foremost in my mind. 'How do you see that these conditions are ever going to be changed?' 'From the human point of view I see no hope at all,' she said. 'But at night as I walk past rows and rows of tiny Bantu homes and hear them crying out in prayer to God, I know that as sure as there is a God the future will be his and our deliverance will come.'

Another significant experience of *Causeway* is when all lanes of separate movement converge close to the destination! By its very nature those who travel and those who receive them are both participants. Obviously the hosts will have involved more people and the traveling teams will have covered more miles; therefore the conclusion is always a round-up experience when the size of the two groups are more nearly equal. The Consultation on Peace Building was a climactic experience for *Christian Causeway:* Direction East Asia.

PEACE BUILDING IN ASIA — 1974 Early in 1972, Clairie Harvey flew to Bangkok to participate in a consultation on education being sponsored by Committee III of the World Council of Churches of which she was chairperson. She stopped over in Japan wearing her "CWU hat" to confer with Akiko Yamaguchi, executive secretary of the Women's Committee of the NCC of Japan as to the possibilities of our jointly sponsoring a consultation on peace building in Asia in 1974. As citizens of the two powerful industrial nations bordering the Pacific, they agreed that Church women should plan responsibly for action.

A consultation of 100 women had an equal number of Americans and Japanese and some invited Christian women from other countries of Southeast Asia. Michiko Okuda flew to the United States in 1973 to work out the details of the program and procedure with Sister Luke and Dorothy Wagner who would be among the 48 women from the USA on the *Causeway.*

The careful planning did not exclude some issues spontaneously bursting from the floor of the conference when it convened in late February 1974. There were grievances of the economic imperialism aimed at the two rich nations who were hosting the consultation and a protest of Korean born minorities in Japan of discrimination. The Japanese committee had thoughtfully included eight members of the Korean Churches in Japan among their number. Learning that Koreans early in the century had been brought to Japan as forced labor suffering the loss of cultural identity and still facing discrimination in housing, education, and jobs, the Americans felt they had been there before!

A reporter from the National Council of Churches of Japan caught a revealing set of impressions in the published summary of the consultation proceedings:

For the 48 American women, the consultation was the culmination of nearly three weeks of direct exposure to social, political and economic realities in Taiwan, South Vietnam, the Philippines, South Korea and Thailand.

Drawing from these visits, the U.S. delegates confessed their shock and surprise about the levels of poverty, injustice and censorship. 'We hadn't heard that South Korea was under martial law and that Christian pastors were being imprisoned,' said one American woman. 'We had no way of realizing how terrible the situation is in South Vietnam,' said another.

The Japanese women also had their series of awakenings during the consultation which was held at the YMCA Tozanso Center February 25-28. Several of the 19 non-Japanese Asian women appealed to the Japanese women regarding economic exploitation. 'Since you have captured the markets,' said a Thai participant, 'you think you can capture the people.'

'You lent us money before,' said a South Korean woman, 'then, when our government couldn't pay, you took over the country. Now we see large (Japanese) investments and loans being made again, and we are afraid of becoming an economic colony of Japan.'

Although most of the consultation was done in small groups (focusing on international relations, the family, the community and education), there were two major addresses, by Sister Luke Tobin, Associate General Director of CWU in USA, and the Rev. John Nakajima, General Secretary of the Japan NCC.

Sister Tobin cited the energy crisis as 'dramatizing the interconnectedness and interrelatedness of nations and peoples today' and said that no one can deal with problems of peace, energy or pollution from a national vantage point any more.

Nakajima emphasized that 'peace is not just a fringe task for the church, but the very thing for which the church exists.' He said that all peoples must learn to work together in order to 'achieve the unity of all things which is our peace.'

The consultation was designed to be this kind of 'working together.' Instead of seeking to pass resolutions or approve strategies for peace, the women concentrated on dialogue across the barriers of language, culture, race and nationality. An American participant said that this dialogue—'the unburdening of each other in a spirit of mutual trust'—did more for her consciousness about peace-building than a dozen resolutions. She reflected the remarks of Tobin and Nakajima, saying that 'peace begins with global awareness which begins with person-to-person sensitizing as we have done here.'

But if the plenary and group discussions were person-centered, they were still issue-oriented. Both the U.S. and Japan were repeatedly accused of applying economic and political pressures in ways detrimental to the self-development of the Asian peoples. The accusations included: excess profits and low wages paid by the foreign firms; aid that bolsters dictatorial regimes and rarely reaches the people; treaties that benefit the powerful; and the exportation of pollution.

There were some tense moments during the consultation when eight Korean residents of Japan laid out the pain they feel in their struggle to gain human and legal rights in Japan. There are 600,000 Korean residents in Japan.

Some of this discussion centered on Chong Suk Park, a Korean who was denied a top income post with the Hitachi Company after his nationality was discovered. The case is now pending in Japanese courts, and women at the consultation vowed their support for both his defense and for the larger struggle of Koreans in Japan.

The women expressed urgency in dealing with the 'appalling conditions of political prisoners and civilian detainees' in several Southeast Asian countries and said they would seek release of such prisoners, including the imprisoned pastors in South Korea.

The Japanese women explained the conservative Japanese government's pressures on the educational system, including a 'playing down' of World War II in approved textbooks which, the women fear, may lead to a revival of Japanese militarism. The Japanese also outlined government plans to nationalize Yasukuni Shrine, a Shinto Shrine dedicated to Japan's war dead. They explained their Christian and pacifist opposition to the bill, and some sought support from their American sisters to stop President Nixon from visiting the shrine when the President makes his promised visit to Japan soon.

Some delegates suggested the need to abolish nuclear weapons and to develop non-violent methods of problem-solving. They felt that one key means to building peace would be to establish local Christian peace centers which would cooperate with secular groups.

Because of cultural differences, the American women tended to be much more frank and outspoken than their Japanese counterparts. However, the Americans in no way dominated the consultation. The Japanese took a number of initiatives—including making most of the arrangements, insisting that Japanese be an official language along with English, and speaking out on their own.

Although a number of Asian women were impressed with the willingness of the Americans to listen, some were baffled by the American tendency to take immediate action.

'Maybe it just indicates a different stage of social consciousness,' said an Asian woman, 'but I want to relate problems to myself more than calmly before taking social action.'

On other occasions the eagerness of the American women to 'help' was countered by the Asian women saying, 'this is something we must work out by ourselves.'

In a greater measure than is usual at international meetings, the participants of this consultation were determined to act as well as talk. A case in point was their concern over the fact that the Hitachi Company had dismissed a Korean employee, whose family had been in Japan for three generations, when the Hitachi Company discovered his ancestry. But what could a multi-national group of 100 women do in the face of a huge multi-national corporation?

It seems to be a universal pattern that women begin with what they have in hand. Returning to their own home territory where they had influence, they took up the case of Chong Suk Park and the Hitachi Corporation. A single achievement has often set the precedent for advance in the whole human struggle. After all, the civil rights movement in the United States was keyed by the action of one Rosa Parks sitting on the front row of the bus in Montgomery.

There is a sense that when participants of consultations separate to go to their own homes, each will bear her own burden and yet each will also feel the burden of others. The Americans cannot bear the burden which Koreans must bear; nor can the Japanese carry the responsibilities laid on the hearts of the Americans. Yet these are sometimes all part and parcel of the same cause . . . and each must do what is possible within the scheme of particular limitations.

So Dorothy Wagner summarizes what happened:

On their return to Korea, church women urged a boycott against the Hitachi Company there. In Japan the Christian community was active in the struggle for the human rights of Chong Suk Park (who was not at the time a confessing Christian). In the USA women urged representatives of several church-related groups, including CWU, to visit the Hitachi office in New York. An official of Hitachi listened carefully and then sent a long cable to the office in Japan telling of the concern of the Christian community in the U.S.A. over this issue.

This visit, added to the weight of pressure in Japan and from Korea, seemed to tip the scale. Miss Akiko Yamaguchi, of the National Christian Council in Japan, who had shared in the Peace Consultation, wrote:

'Since Chong Suk Park has fought this long struggle not for his own purpose to get better earnings but for the liberation of his own people, we required Hitachi to change their policy about employment . . . The company had refused to continue the talks with us after the court decision, but they changed their attitude after your visit in New York . . . And, finally, after meeting for nine times they agreed to change their employment policy . . .'

After a three-and-a-half year legal struggle, the Hitachi Company not only re-employed and reimbursed Chong Suk Park, but established a non-discriminatory employment policy. On September 1, 1974, a Victory Rally was held in Japan to celebrate the agreement of this giant industry to institute new non-discriminatory employment practices.

A later letter from Miss Yamaguchi brought the good news that Chong Suk Park proved to be such a valuable employee that other Koreans were being recruited by the Hitachi Company. She also shared the news that in December 1974, this young man was baptized as a Christian believer.

A *Causeway* is not a visitation which at some point in time must end. The *Causeway* is always there. Just because of the work of the Great Integrator, those who begin to walk together in any one journey will continue to do so even if there is a space in their togetherness!

All that were in the Consultation of Peacemakers grew in appreciation of the leadership of Lee Oh Chung, president of Korean Church Women United, and the chairperson of the World Day of Prayer Committee, Mrs. Duk Kwee Kong. They knew of the deep concern of Korean Church Women for those victimized by poverty, of their work to protect young women from prostitution in the thriving tourist trade of large Korean hotels, of their action to humanize the working conditions of the thousands of girls and women working in large factories, of their advocacy on behalf of student and Christian leaders imprisoned because of their stand for democratic freedoms.

In the months following the *Causeway*, Miss Lee was taken by the Korean CIA for questioning in relation to her activities and on behalf of Korean victims of the atom bomb. When word of her detention reached the USA thousands of letters went from church women all over the country to Korean authorities and to Congressional leaders. Miss Lee and Mrs. Yun were scheduled to be at the International Committee of the World Day of Prayer in Mexico in September 1974, but were denied travel documents allowing them to leave Korea. Miss Lee had been invited to speak at the opening night of the Ecumenical Assembly in Memphis.

As I sat on the front row of the Civic Auditorium in Memphis Dorothy Wagner tiptoed in and whispered in my ear. It was during the final business session of the Assembly on a Saturday morning and Margaret Sonnenday was presenting the plan for goal setting in the area of a global community. I muttered to Dorothy, "Now is the time."

I walked to the platform as Margaret finished a sentence and whispered in her ear. Without a moment's hesitation, the incoming national president introduced me to make an announcement and quietly said, "Will the members of the Asian Causeway join me at the foot of the platform steps?"

"God has given us in this Assembly our own miracle," I said to the Assembly. "In the middle of the night Dorothy Wagner heard a knock on her hotel door. Upon opening it, she found the person we had given up hope of ever seeing, Lee Oh Chung." By this time Miss Lee had arrived at the podium and spoke quietly of her confidence in God and her commitment to stand by those who were oppressed. She did not hide the actions of a repressive government and requested supporting prayers.

She probably did not notice forty women walking toward her from every part of the huge auditorium, and could not hear the doxology they were singing in their hearts. But when she turned to go down the steps, there they stood, her sister-travellers on a *Christian Causeway*. Their radiant faces, outstretched arms, and brimming eyes proclaimed the glory of a Causeway continuing forever.

Integrity in Relationships
          . . . Conference of Church and Synagogue Women

As had been true for many years, Church Women United continued to work actively with the National Council of Jewish Women in matters of common social concerns, particularly in the field of race relations, the School Lunch Program and the Women in Community Service. A vacuum in national relationships needed to be filled with the major women's organizations related to the Synagogues. As would be true of Church women and the YWCA, for instance, many Jewish women were active as members of both the NCJW and their particular branch of the Synagogue. In local communities Church and Synagogue women were most readily identified as having religiously oriented programs. In the secular age through which we were living, we all had much to gain by closer association on a national level.

Leah Treiger, the executive of the National Women's League of the United Synagogue of America was my near neighbor and so, as we walked to work together, we began to talk about normalizing official relationships. Through the peace movement we had recognized the leadership of Jane Evans, the executive of the Temple Sisterhood related to Reformed Judaism, and found her responsive to greater cooperation. Miss Evans also was instrumental in getting an affirmative response from the Women's Branch of the Union of Orthodox Jewish Congregations.

Leaders of all three organizations were invited to meet in our conference room in June 1969 to talk over areas of mutual concern. There were so many, but our enthusiasm was dampened by subconscious reservations of women who were already too busy. In order to sort out priorities and to formalize some continuing relationships, Jane Evans proposed that three representatives from each organization and ex-officio staff, come together at another meeting in the House of Living Judaism where the Conference of Church and Synagogue came into being on May 25, 1970.

Through these conversations we learned something of the program and dynamics of each of the four national organizations. And we were able to come to agreement on some common effort. Most of all we learned to know personally some remarkable women. One of these, Norma Levitt, the national president of the Temple Sisterhood, wrote down some of the highlights of the Church and Synagogue Women and gave them to me upon my retirement as a sort of living reminder of our journey together. There could be no better resume of this relationship than her notes:

> On June 2, 1969, a small group convened at the head-quarters of Church Women United, to join in 'A Dialogue of Women Who Believe in God' and to explore possibilities of further relationships and mutual common concerns of women of faith. An agenda for the 70's was proposed which included consideration for action on such subjects as: the role of volunteers, the generation gap, youth, drugs, the plight of minorities, Christian-Jewish relations, women's liberation.

> In May 1970, the group met again. The group adopted the name, 'Conference of Church and Synagogue Women', and agreed to meet at least once a year for the purpose of exploring issues and perhaps reaching agreement on mutual concerns which, hopefully, might lead to joint actions.

> The rising expectations of many repressed groups, among them women, were noted as well as the increased appreciation of the unique contribution which women make in their multi-dimensional ways of awareness and problem-solving. 'Women of religious groups are supportive of all women,' it was said. We have a network of communication throughout this country and around the world. What are some of the ways we can cooperate?'

> Their first tangible answer came in *A CALL TO CONSCIENCE,* a statement which protested against the deliberate violence practiced against children both in war and in peace. It was adopted, released to the media and widely distributed in the name of the signatories who were members of Church Women United; Women's Branch, Union of Orthodox Jewish Congregations;

Women's League for Conservative Judaism and the National Federation of Temple Sisterhoods—the four organizations which comprise the Conference of Church and Synagogue Women.

The third meeting of the group in May, 1971, found itself immersed in speculation about the spiritual significance of such crises of the human spirit within our own generation as Hitler's holocaust; the Vietnam war; the crimes of My Lai and its civilian counterparts. The responsibility shared by religious women for the failures of our Western World was recognized and the question was asked: 'What can we do about it?' Creation of an open letter designed to encourage conversations between women of the church and synagogue in local communities on seminal issues of mutual concern was suggested.

In December 1971 a fourth meeting of the Conference included a Chanukah party. A draft copy of the OPEN LETTER to our Christian and Jewish Co-Workers in Local Communities was used as a base for dialogue, to 'discover the variety of spiritual understandings and how we may work together'. It was to be a call to action to use the concerted power of women of religious faith in the struggle to achieve freedom and responsible social order in a global society of benefit for all people.

By the next meeting of the Conference of Church and Synagogue Women in June, 1972, the final OPEN LETTER was ready for free distribution by the Conference's four national organizations to selected groups. This letter urged Christian and Jewish co-workers in local communities to acknowledge the sharing of a common faith in God and to initiate local dialogues on matters of social concern, such as: *Human Rights*—at what point did we make our mistake? what can we do now?; *Social Institutions*—what is happening to family life? the neighborhood? the church and synagogue? to the nurture of children and to the educational system? in what does our security lie—both nationally and internationally?; *Forces of Liberation*—what do we hear from the voices of the young? from women? from blacks, Chicanos, Indians? from the peoples of the developing nations? How can we have freedom as well as responsible social order in a global society for the benefit of all people? *Ecology and the Environment*—what does a move from seemingly impending disaster require?

At a meeting in May, 1973, the theme of the meditation, 'Shalom'—Peace—was interpreted through readings and scripture from the traditions of the respective groups. The original purpose of the Conference was reiterated: 'To discover common concerns of religious women, to enter into dialogue, and to extend to their constituencies the benefits of the conversations'. It was said that Sisterhood is not simple, but Sisterhood is powerful. The topic for discussion was 'The Question of Amnesty'. Each organization presented the way the subject was being dealt with by their policy-making bodies, for it was felt that the time was immediate to lay the groundwork for education on this controversial issue. It was recognized that the change on the national political scene might have some bearing on the willingness of the American people to deal with the issue of amnesty with more sympathy and rationality.

At the meeting in November, 1973, reports were given from each organizations. For Church Women United, Margaret Shannon spoke of their planned and on-going projects, including the annual World Day of Prayer, which is localized in communities all over the world. The service for 1975 is being prepared, she noted, by the Women's Ecumenical Fellowship of Egypt. CWU was concerned that this be understood by Jewish groups. There are no political overtones and the scheduling was done long before the recent terrible Arab-Israeli Yom Kippur War.

Norma Levitt reported for the National Federation of Temple Sisterhoods. They had just completed their Biennial Convention, November 9 - 13, 1973, celebrating their Sixtieth Anniversary. A new award, 'Or Ami—Light of the People' was presented for service to the community based on the following criteria: Did the program raise the consciousness of the Sisterhoods? the community? Is the program unique? Resolutions were passed which enunciated the stand the delegates took on various issues. The most heated one, which involved parliamentary maneuvering by delegates, was on amnesty. In the ensuing discussion, it was pointed out that in Reform Judaism, women had long been the forerunners of liberal positions on social justice. But in the last decade it is the men who have become far more liberal than the women. Women are becoming more conservative.

Evelyn Henkind reported for the Women's League for Conservative Judaism, which had sponsored a Conference Tour to Israel and had conducted its biennial Social Action and United Nations Conferences. Most recently the efforts of Women's League have been heavily devoted to the emergency needs of Israel. Leah Stern, Executive of the Women's Branch, Union of Orthodox Jewish Congregations, spoke on the P.O.W. issue of Israeli prisoners held by Syria and the violations of the Geneva Conference by Syria. She asked that Church Women United raise their voices in protest. Edna McCallion indicated that she has raised the question at various times in the United Nations. Church Women United sent a letter to the International Red Cross expressing their concern and urging that everything possible be done to secure from Syria the names of the Israeli prisoners of war.

In December 1974 there was some change in the conversationalists and a spirit of friendly endeavor about the future. Yet each organization was eagerly involved with the impetus which their own organizations had received in recent national meetings—an excitement we all shared! There were four new presidents: Deborah Turk (Mrs. Samuel), of the Women's Branch, Union of Orthodox Congregations; Ruth Perry of the Women's League of Conservative Judaism; Betty Benjamin of the National Federation of

Temple Sisterhoods; and Margaret Sonnenday of Church Women United. Each organization had well developed Bicentennial plans and they were well worth sharing with our broader constituency where interfaith impact might be made in regional celebrations.

May, 1975, a leaflet, "Frontiers of Understanding" was approved to suggest the part which women of faith should take in pioneering today. The four areas which were proposed for community consideration where joint Bicentennial plans were feasible were: Understanding Ourselves, Understanding the Family Today, Understanding Our Society, and Understanding Our Faith.

Just because we learned to know each other through the Church and Synagogue women, all of us were able to facilitate other projects of common concern. An informal group of Jewish and Christian women attending a professional conference on the effect of drugs, including alcohol, on mental health found themselves talking informally about what could be done in the educational program for children to counter the effects of the drug culture. The Jewish women already were engaged in relevant research and invited us into a working relationship.

From this informal beginning there developed the Committee of Combined Concerns sponsored by the Synagogue organizations the NCJW and CWU. This action-oriented committee sponsored many symposiums in neighborhood and drug therapy centers in the greater New York area and recommended joint action on appropriate legislation related to this field.

In 1975 the five parent bodies published a brochure entitled, "DRUGS/ALCOHOL" which contained guidelines and resources to encourage analysis and action in local communities on this problem as well as an excellent preface on why women with religious convictions must be concerned with the quality of individual and community life.

Traumatic events among Jewish people in Eastern Europe and the Middle East were continually recurring. At such times CWU tried to come alongside our Jewish colleagues and share some of the stress and tension which they experienced. Here are two examples:

In 1970, the Leadership Conference (National Jewish Women's Organizations) mounted a program called, "Women's Plea for Human Rights for Soviet Jewry". Target cities were selected for educational demonstrations. In New York City, a group from the national board of CWU joined with the program of education on universal human rights and walked with our Jewish sisters to the wall of the United Nations for appropriate ceremonies. I joined in a press conference to indicate that human rights were the concern of us all. Similar displays of solidarity were made by CWU in other cities across the nation. These Human Rights Days were repeated annually in the following years.

On Yom Kippur (Day of Atonement) in 1973, a short bloody attack on villages in Israel had particularly tragic overtones because Israeli people and soldiers were in the midst of their holy day observance. CWU sent a personal letter to each of the women with whom we had been working in the Church and Synagogue Conference. Death and destruction are terrifying no matter where one's sympathies. It should be said that there had been no attempt throughout the five years of conversation to press the issue of Israeli State in our conversations. We were moved that each woman wrote back by hand. Each in her own words stressed the human and spiritual issues as if to make clear that she had not assumed that our heartfelt sympathy was necessarily a political bias. This was the tone expressed in different terms in each response:

> Your thoughtful, sensitive expression on the tragedy of war again in the Mid-East is most deeply appreciated. We can only hope, pray and strive to achieve a cessation of hostilities to be followed by a just peace that shall protect the security and development of all the peoples and nations of the Middle East. Meanwhile, we join you in profound regret over the loss of human lives and the agonizing pain of their families, whether Jew or Arab. We also pledge with you unswerving devotion to the translation of the concepts of our respective religions into service to all races, nationalities and creeds.

AFFIRMATION OF JUDAIC ROOTS   Just because we wished to affirm our Judaic roots on the opening night of the Ecumenical Assembly in Memphis when we were interpreting the Christian faith with all its time and global dimensions, we asked Norma Levitt to lead the opening service. Her creative genius and her sensitive nature are amply shown in her interpretation called "The Gathering and Scattering of Light." Her original prose poem illumined the God-given components of the faith revealed in her scripture and traditions of the people of God. Because her description of her own experience offers so much an understanding of the journey toward wholeness, let us continue with her words:

The invitation from Church Women United filled me with awe, excitement, trepidation. But could I do it? Would I be worthy? I consulted with various lay and rabbinic leaders, who encouraged me to accept the responsibility.

A day of theology was held in June, a day of sharing of ideas about 'wholeness' and an honest airing of questions, differences, and search. What a privilege it was to participate in this day of conversation and belief led by Dr. Paul Verghese. We spoke of fragmentation and the urge to wholeness, of our search for unity and goodness, of the individual and the community, and of conflict and justice. How do we find the 'we-ness', how do we keep lively the hope within us, how do we share the way and find fulfillment in the journey? These were the questions which led us, through dialogue, to our work for the Assembly, 'Journey Toward Wholeness.'

Now came the time to face the sharpened questions, questions which involved the community of those who believe in Judaism as well as me, the individual: what do we believe? what do I feel? what do we do? Head, heart, and hand. Through the ensuing months, these questions accompanied me, guiding my pen over the yellow paper wherever I went. On a plane traveling to England for another Conference, the central theme shone forth: Light, the Scattering and Gathering of Light. Then the structure, the basic ideas of Judaism emerged: *Continuing Creation, Revelation of Oneness, Community,. Redemption in the World.* And as the past years and days fed into my writing, the outreaching epilogue came clear, an *Affirmation of Life and Hope.* Flying high above the clouds with no sense of time, I wrote the poetry of each section and then in a leap of the imagination forward to the opening evening of the Assembly, the concluding sonnet,

'Gathering from all parts of the earth
We come together to listen and to speak.'

A big suitcase of reference books was packed, Bibles, Rabbinic Anthology, Haggadah, Commentaries, Thesaurus, and off I went to an island to look at the sea and to write what would have to be the clear explanations of each basic idea, long hours to enunciate, clarify, and simplify. The first draft was ready for typing.

Many people helped. No work is ever done alone: careful editing, typing, checking footnotes, proof-reading, one rabbinical scholar advising about the core meaning of 'Shechinah' (in-dwelling radiance of God), another rabbi reviewing recent Christian-Jewish dialogue, a third helping with Hebrew transliteration. Finally, I was ready with a fifth and final draft, and there was the shining acceptance, for which I was so deeply grateful . . .

On the evening before the Assembly opened, there was a tight time schedule and the need to condense for the presentation on the following night. If difficult rehearsals presage a good conclusion, we had a sure promise and hope. Sitting under dim auditorium lights, I cut lines. Then the artist, Sister Gabriel Mary Hoare and her assistant, Sue Bostwick, arrived and we chose slides.

Anxious and jittery, I went to lunch in the cafeteria. As I sat down, my name was called, 'May we join you?' 'Yes, yes.' We lunched together, Edna McCallion, a colleague among NGO observers at the U.N. and a woman from Egypt, who would be participating in the service from the World Day of Prayer, which would open the program that evening. Many strands came together, the mention more than a year before of the Egyptian women preparing the World Day of Prayer.

Soon Edna excused herself to complete her work on the UN booth, and the Egyptian woman and I were alone. She asked a frank question which had long worried her: 'Is it true that the Israeli government has desecrated the Christian holy places in Jerusalem?' My answer of assurance came that all holy places of all religions were carefully protected. I then asked her about the creation of the Palestinian state. There was such instant trust in each other that she invited me to her home the next time I was in the Middle East. An Arab and a Jewish woman who wished that problems could be solved in peaceful ways were friends forever at the end of twenty minutes . . .

The Opening Service was a radiant evening. 'One in Spirit' . . . 'Let us now stand to cross the threshold of worship' . . . Music. Lights. 'Our Heritage: The Gathering and Scattering of Light.'

'Yes, we speak together from the roots of our faith—of our questions and our differences, as we share our longing and our search.'

Biblical Voice, quiet, reverence.

A radiant evening. Archbishop Iakovos, a choir from Memphis' Annunciation Greek Orthodox Church, testimonies of hope under the title 'Our Horizon: The Global Diaspora Today'. The clear voice and music of Sister Jane Marie Richardson.

This part of the evening is not mine to tell but it is mine to hold enduringly in my mind and heart, for it filled me with the spirit of an age-old tradition and of luminous individuals. Is this a universal story? No, it is one person's experience. But one and one make a community. A young woman kindly said, "You have given us much." I felt I had gained more than I could give, that I was filled and fulfilled. Said Sister Jane Marie, "In the silent meditation I thought I would like to pray with you."

One person's experience may be unique, yet it may at times converge with the experience of others. This is only one part of a great and noble plan of a "Journey Toward Wholeness." We are at the end of one section of the road we travel. Where we will go on the road I do not know. I know only that companions along the way have become friends, that we are part of each other's lives. And there is a far horizon ahead.

"Together we affirm our hope,
Together we seek the way."

Church Women United
1966 through 1975

Chapter 11

Joy and Peace in Faithfulness

Stunning in a white slack suit, Mary Louise Rowand entered the Concert Hall on the opening night of the Ecumenical Assembly in Wichita (April 22, 1971) and walked briskly down stage. She always commands attention and in this instance the 2500 women were anxious to hear the program interpreted by the person responsible. She started out enumerating the extraordinary claims of Christians. In a few minutes she was sitting on the edge of the stage talking with someone from a bygone age who turned out to be Martha of Bethany whose brother Lazarus had died. Martha felt she had sent for Jesus in plenty of time, but he had taken his own time in coming. Since it had not previously occurred to her that Jesus could claim power over death, she was now recalling the incident with some embarrassment.

Martha:	O-oo, if only I had not run down the road to scold him. "Why didn't you get here?" I cried. "If you had been here my brother would not have died . . ."
Mary Louise:	That's when he made the BIG claim: "I am the resurrection and the life . . ."
Martha:	You stand on the other side of the Resurrection. No wonder you're so sure!

Mary Louise: (modestly comforting her new friend) Oh, I keep everything safely regulated, so its sure to come out all right. I pray for the POSSIBLE: I venture into the POSSIBLE!

Martha: Just like me. When Jesus said, 'let's go down to where Lazarus is buried, and open the grave'. I just couldn't let him embarrass himself right before all our neighbors. So I just pointed out that if we opened that grave, there would be an awful stench.

Mary Louise: We are 'holy sniffers', with a capital H . . . Holy Sniffers of days gone by . . . We don't dare inhale the breath of fresh power that is bringing in something that never happened before. Imagine seeing a dead man come alive. Everybody that saw it must have become a believer . . .

Martha: Seeing isn't always believing. It doesn't work that way. We can't co-opt a little faith from other people . . .

But Martha, her scriptural sister, was anxious to press advantages—having been there in person.

Martha: Jesus was never in a hurry. It was his compassion that slowed him down. He stopped to take Peter's mother-in-law by the hand and helped her to her feet; He listened to the paralytic on a stretcher; he even touched the leper all covered with sores.

Mary Louise: Ugh!

Martha: Jesus wouldn't say that. He'd say 'Shalom'. But more importantly, he did something. He healed them.

Mary Louise: Do tell!

Martha: And he always had the kindly word. Remember the woman-who-crashed-the-party with a gift? It wasn't done that way! Or the unpopular tax collector whose curiosity had him up a tree.

Mary Louise: Do tell!

Martha: Or the thief hanging beside him when they were both on crosses. It was a criminal who said, "Remember me, Jesus." Immediately he was invited to share Paradise that very day.

Mary Louise: Do . . . . .

Martha: (interrupting) Really all that is necessary is "to do." The other person does the telling. Remember the blind man who came seeing—after Jesus healed him? The neighbors couldn't believe what they saw. But a man who once was blind now could see!

Mary Louise: Now I see. Faith makes healing possible, yet healing makes faith plausible! We must accept the whole package—or deny it all!

So it was that Church Women United from across the nation and the world in a visible fellowship at the 1971 Assembly together declared their faithfulness:

We affirm that all power was given to Christ
We are enabled to act through the Spirit.
We are able, by God's grace, to feel with those who are hurt, the alienated, the hateful and self-seeking.
We can love them all as we love ourselves.
We are called to find ways to make visible God's reconciling love . . . in every relationship, in each neighborhood in each nation.
We are instruments of reconciling love.
God enables us to be creative, to be courageous, to be constructive . . . overcoming the powers and principalities of darkness. Jesus said to his followers:
Greater things than this will you do.
Greater things we will do.

In the epistle by James it is written that faith without works is dead. In fact, a faith in God that compels good works is fully alive. There are two marks of God-given work: joy and peace. A vertical shaft of light enters the horizontal plane of service—and there is joy. When everything has gone to pieces and the puzzle comes together unexpectedly, the faithful know that a promise of peace is fulfilled. This chapter can only tell some of the happenings along the way as Church Women United journeyed in faithfulness down the paths of human need in the years that followed 1966.

The joy of work is in the doing of it which means that church women in each local community have all the fun and deserve the satisfaction of sharing in a nation-wide movement of like-minded women.

The national office assumes a supportive role to those who carry the action in local communities. Current issues are highlighted in publications and the Celebrations. Channels are provided where needed for such action programs as that on Hunger. Regional and national workshops are offered for more effective planning in selected areas of action such as Health Delivery Services. Advisory services are kept updated through continuing relationships with other national agencies in the same field.

In general there are three ways by which Church women are effective in ecumenical action: 1) in mobilizing programs which meet human need; 2) in volunteering for significant services in the community; 3) in participating in the life of the nation and the world as citizens. In the pages which follow we will be able to illustrate briefly some of the ways in which the national movement was able to proceed during the decade 1966-1975.

Joy and Peace

. . . in meeting human need

Millions of victims of drought, of earthquake, of war, of dire poverty have received a "telegram of concern" which expressed in some concrete way the following sentiments:

"Inasmuch as I saw you hungry, and thirsty, and sick, and in prison, I am doing something to meet your human need. Faithfully yours."

The signature could have been any one of many women who purchased a Gift Certificate.

GIFT CERTIFICATES It all started when Kitty Strong visited New Windsor, Maryland to see the warehouse used by Church World Service for the collection of clothing for overseas use. During lunch with the staff, the conversation began to move around to the sudden emergency needs which often hit CWS unprepared. When a typhoon, earthquake, or famine hits a country, food, blankets, medicines are necessary immediately. These were not being met by the carefully planned sewing projects or huge amount of clothing being collected for which church women sent "poundage money" to ship overseas.

Kitty knew that Church women not only were aware of the amount of energy and money the processing of material aid cost, but also had the good sense and good will to respond to more realistic schemes. Kitty's practical nature felt that the ordinary church woman would give over and over small amounts of money about which she doesn't have to make a major decision providing she trusts the administrative agency; also she would likely give more often if the plan makes it easy for her—no letters to write, no address to find.

As they returned to New York, Kitty Strong and Mel Myers (the director of Material Aid for Church World Service) talked further. Blankets were always needed and CWS estimated that by bulk purchases they could get them for $3 apiece. Jim MacCracken, the able Director of CWS, recognized that CWU could do something which CWS could not do—

appeal for and meet domestic needs—so he suggested that this be one option offered on the gift certificate.

The details were worked out with Church World Service for purchasing and shipping. Dottie Nosset, the caretaker of CWU's financial integrity, insisted on serial numbers for the coupon books—so that the local collectors were accountable. Church World Service cooperated fully in helping us work out specifics.

The response was the second real surprise which Church Women United gave to the national office—the other being the tremendous number of peace ballots following the first World Community Day. The first year (1967) the gift certificate money reached more than $219,000. Church Women United was able to supply enough blankets to meet every validated request of Church World Service that year.

Our auditors were very particular in checking to see that designated money, such as blankets, was restricted. They were also impressed with how money called "where needed most" was able to answer emergency requests. One day in the midst of an annual audit, the phone rang to ask for $1000 to get temporary housing, food, and water to hurricane victims in a small town in the Southwest. Our word assured the planning of the relief program and a check was on its way within the hour.

Because our grants are made to agencies or groups who really care about the people themselves, a dimension of caring is added to the value of the gift. For example, men and women were hurting badly when unemployment was at a peak in the neighborhoods of the Chicago area. Families were actually hungry and morale was low. So a grant for the purchase of basic food was made to the CWU Family Center in West Garfield Park.

A giant food pantry and distribution center for certain bulk basic foodstuffs was set up. Representatives from thirty-two neighborhoods over the metropolitan areas came on designated days to get supplies. They were met by cheery volunteers who made up the Family Center 'staff' for this purpose. Overhead was a sign saying *"Come in and get your faith lifted!"* That's what it's all about!

SCHOOL LUNCHES In the summer of 1966 Jean Fairfax, director of the Division of Legal Information and Community Service of the NAACP Legal Defense and Educational Fund Inc., came into the office to talk over her BIG CONCERN.

During the course of her work she had become increasingly aware of the numbers of children who were going to school hungry in spite of the common belief that the 1946 National School Lunch Act had made provision for them. Some study by a group of national women's organizations with religious orientation was called for. She had made preliminary inquiry of the Field Foundation as to their interest in funding the study if the proper sponsors could set up the commission and endorse its recommendations. By fall five such national organizations had agreed: Church Women United, the National Board of the YWCA, the National Council of Jewish Women, the National Council of Negro Women, and the National Council of Catholic Women.

Each organization appointed two women to the national committee and Jean Fairfax agreed to be chairman. All ten committee women were highly qualified with special skills in nutrition, home economics, consumer interests or experience in other government programs. The committee worked on the following assumptions:

> . . . adequate nutrition is as essential to good education as an adequate curriculum and both require standards and good administration.
> . . . the millions of people living in poverty can no longer be concealed by statistics proving the highest living standard in the world or statistics which blot out the human problem of families, black and white, living on bare subsistence.
> . . . Out of 6 million school-age children from families in the rock bottom of poverty, fewer than 2 million children receive free or reduced price lunches. Hunger makes a child inattentive which leads to poor learning, and leads to drop-outs, which is a factor in juvenile delinquency.
> . . . the method of determining those eligible for free

lunches varies according to local administration, and federal help in food subsidies does not take into consideration lack of kitchen equipment in older slum schools in the city or in poor rural areas where hunger among the young is prevalent.

The Committee carried on its survey over the next 18 months. Out of 50 communities selected where there were local units of the cooperating national sponsors, 40 communities responded with a local study committee. A Community Study Kit was prepared with background explanations of how the National School Lunch Program operates, questionnaires for the local school lunch director, public health officials, teachers, and parents. The whole kit was submitted to the Director of the School Lunch Program to scrutinize for accuracy before sending it to the local communities. Since the interviewers were women of the community, their reports documented many "living examples" to the statistical record.

The Committee sought extended interviews with the State Directors of the School Lunch Program and 39 of them cooperated by contributing data on administration and facts which indicated only a partial success in administration of the Program during the twenty one years of enforcement after the Federal Act had been enacted.

The committee delved into the records and the experience of administration of the School Lunch Program on the federal, state, and local levels and senses a profound feeling of inadequacy and defeat; in fact, some communities were beginning to drop out. In at least seven states there was evidence of organized community protest either because there was no program available or the cost had outpriced those who needed it most.

The committee's findings and recommendations together with a wealth of interviews and charts were published in a book called *Their Daily Bread*. A copy of the book was sent to each member of Congress. Then it was circulated among their various constituencies of the sponsoring organizations. The report prefaced its recommendations by recognizing that adequate financing depended upon the general public's acceptance of the National School Lunch program as a "means to provide education and health to present and future citizens." The report continued,

> Too many legislators viewed the program primarily as a convenient market for surplus commodities; too many school administrators as a welfare burden rather than an educational responsibility; too many school principals as a headache rather than a way to raise academic performance; and too many people disliked and distrusted poor people in general. There were more white, poor children involved in the free school program than black but all were recipients of stigma similar to that imprinted in racial discrimination.

The recommendations themselves showed great practical understanding of administrative problems and of the reality of the present situations. The immediate improvements called for a reduction in the price of the individual lunch, uniform standards for those eligible for free lunches, increased federal funds and state funds for communities with a high proportion of very poor. Local school districts (and not the individual school) would be the unit of administration. Local districts would pay for basic labor and equipment as is done generally for the rest of the school system, so that children's fees and local charity donations could be applied to food, and the cash value of donated commodities be kept at a dependable level.

The long range proposal recognized that nutrition among children of parents who could easily afford to pay also was neglected. Continual education of general health requirements must be included within the overall curriculum, and eating together should be done in a way to encourage congenial community relationships.

Specifically the report stated:

> The Congress, USDA, Boards of Education, state legislators, school lunch administrators should begin planning now for a universal free school lunch program as part of a coordinated plan for better nutrition for all children.

It further recommended that Congress provide incentive grants to school districts who develop model nutritional and food service programs for children and youth and that the President appoint a National Commission with a mandate to design a federally sponsored free food program.

The facts were released at several press conferences. "The odds are 3 to 1 against the poor child getting a lunch whether he goes to school in a small rural southern county or a large northern industrial city" reported the *New York Times.* "If he does get one he is usually singled out from his fellows and humiliated by having to stand at the end of the cafeteria line or by presenting an identifiable token." Editorials picked up these themes with comments and moves were made for a reform bill in both houses of Congress.

Our special Committee on School Lunch also made proposals to their sponsoring organizations on how to implement proposals. The facts in the report formed a basis of testimony before Congressional committees and for advocates of legislative reform, as well as a basis of monitoring local school lunch programs and citizen education.

In May, 1970 Congress sent to the President a bill which was, in the words of Senator Herman Talmadge, "an important bench mark in the Nation's fight against hunger . . . the first major antihunger bill to come out of the current national concern with eradicating hunger and malnutrition."

In presenting a report of the conference committee which had reconciled differences between bills passed by the House and the Senate, Senator Talmadge also stated that:

> Prior to the consideration of the pending bill, there has never been an overall reform of the school lunch program, and there has never before been such a concerted effort to see that a free or reduced-price lunch is provided to every needy child in the Nation.

Speaking for the bill, Senator George McGovern, who played a decisive role in its development stated:

... (The school lunch program) has come to be one that serves some better than others, and some not at all. It is a program where that old saying, 'Them that has gets' is all too true. Two-thirds of our poor children receive no lunch because they or their schools cannot afford it . . .

Three years ago the excellent study, *Their Daily Bread* brought this situation to our attention and made us aware of this need for legislative change in the national school lunch program. That started us on the road that led us to this day. Along that road many came to the assistance of the Nation's children.

The bill incorporated practically everything recommended in *Their Daily Bread* except the completely free school lunch program, a high tribute to the competent work done by the Study Committee and the follow up work of Jean Fairfax with the sponsoring organizations.

1969 WHITE HOUSE CONFERENCE ON FOOD During the first week of December 1969, some 3,000 men and women met in Washington, D.C. to grapple with a basic factor of life in all of its aspects — food.

President Richard M. Nixon had called the White House Conference on Food, Nutrition and Health "to put an end to malnutrition and hunger among the poor, to make better use of our agricultural bounty and nutritional knowledge, and to ensure a healthful diet for all Americans."

Goaded by the urgency of the subject, Dr. Jean Mayer, of Harvard University, Chairman and Special Consultant, succeeded in getting the Conference off the ground in six months and he was able to involve persons from all walks of life. It was said to be the most diverse group of Americans ever gathered for common purpose under any auspices.

Dr. Mayer himself came to New York City two months before the conference to meet with representatives of about eighty organizations. He seemed to be eager for the ideas of the group and they did not hesitate to express themselves! It was a liberal education to hear representatives of the Welfare

Mothers, the YMCA, the NAACP, and dozens of others make their contributions to the planning. On the way out of the meeting, a young man asked what organization I represented and then commented: "They all made a lot of noise in there as national organizations, but yours is the only one that can deliver at the grass roots!"

On this issue we did our best through a coalition of women's organizations on which Pat Young of Scranton, Pennsylvania, represented CWU and was the Chairperson of the Task Force on Voluntary Action by Women. She must have made several hundred long distance calls to rally women of all ages, economic backgrounds and races, and as a result, nearly half the Conference were women who added a personal and compassionate dimension to the proceedings.

The Coalition decided to hold a series of rallies in major cities by way of stirring up interest in the findings. CWU was assigned three cities and Jean Frye of Evanston undertook the job of mobilization. By December one participant called the project "the greatest exercise in adult education I've ever witnessed."

The White House Conference produced a significant document containing hundreds of substantive recommendations. This document formed the basis of our nation's nutrition policies for many years, reflecting a consensus on the moral imperative of immediate action on hunger.

Pat Young commented, "The chemistry of being together, the cleansing force of honest dialogue, the drama of the many confrontations, produced a unanimity on at least two points:

1) Hunger in this country is real and totally unacceptable and must be eradicated now, and

2) The only permanent answer with dignity is money, not food stamps or commodities.

In addition there was a call for reform in the present food programs, a national free lunch made available to all children regardless of income, and the transfer of all hunger relief and nutrition from the Department of Agriculture to the Department of Health, Education, and Welfare.

Six persons including Pat Young presented the recommendations to President Nixon who received them with apparent concern. On Christmas he made a statement promising free or reduced price lunches to every needy American school child by Thanksgiving of 1970.

On Monday, November 23, 1970, representatives of seventeen national organizations including Dorothy Dolbey, the president of CWU, sent the President a telegram reminding him of the unfulfilled promise.

DECADE OF DEVELOPMENT Simultaneously, a study program was launched to widen interest in the growing number of hungry families in other parts of the world. In 1970 Betty Johns organized a series of four seminars at the Church Center at the United Nations majoring on the hunger problems in Asia, Africa, South America and the Middle East. This series with their recommendations for local action was one way in which Church women entered the realities of the UN Decade of Development.

In 1974 the same priority came out of two conferences of church women meeting on different continents. In June the WCC Consultation on Sexism in Berlin said a statement was futile when talking about women's rights in the third world unless there was a commitment to work toward making clean water available for every woman in the world.

COVENANT COMMITMENT 1974 - 1977 In October of that same year, Church Women United in Ecumenical Assembly heard Catherine Mwanamwamba describe the African Path to Food with women walking every step of the way — from planting to harvesting to preserving to preparing and serving the daily meal. There were many Hunger Programs already launched in this land, and one more would not meet the need. The imperative to identify with those who were hungry was an *imperative.* One resolution came from the floor calling for simplified living on the part of all Americans and the creation of a Hunger Fund to be forwarded in amounts not less than $100.00 to meet immediate needs in starving areas.

All joy belongs to those who responded promptly to this Hunger Fund for it enabled CWU to put into the hands of Sister Susan enough money to purchase a month's supply of milk for several thousand infants in Christian orphanages in Vietnam. (Each little baby abandoned on the doorstep of the orphanage was given a distinguished name such as "Jackie Robinson, Mary Luke, etc. Many babies did not survive; those who died were buried with prayers and his or her own name on the grave. Later I received a snapshot of the orphans' burial place. On one marker I could read *"Margaret Shannon d. Mar 1975."*)

Other funds which came in the early weeks went into the Emergency Food Pantry administered by the Indian Division of the Council of Churches of the Greater Minneapolis Area, and the Mother & Infant Food Program administered by the Intertribal Council of Nevada.

As they broke bread and shared the native catfish around the breakfast table on Sunday morning, 2200 women responded to the request of their new president by making a covenant to assure available clean water and a source of protein to other women in some needy areas each year.

To carry out this commitment, CWU through its Mission Committee made it a priority for funds for the next three years; this became a source of blessing in three destitute areas:

Niger, located south of the Sahara, had experienced one of the worst catastrophes of modern times — a drought which had turned the area into a wasteland. Starvation and malnutrition had become a daily fact of life. Working through Church World Service, Church Women United sent funds to assist in the cost of drilling new wells and improving old ones. The result was safe drinking water for some 100,000 people. In order to make available a more adequate source of protein, CWU committed resources to a project to stock the lakes of Niger with fish and to train workers to process fish for the local markets.

Malagasy, one of the world's largest islands, had a very serious water problem. Church World Service, in cooperation with Catholic Relief Services, was involved in a service program in which local leadership played a vital part in planning. When a village requested a water supply, an agency team was sent to talk with the villagers to see if they were willing to do their part of the work and to accept a financial share in developing the water system. If the village people agreed, a volunteer was sent to live there as an advisor. The villagers provided the labor and raw materials such as sand, gravel, stone and planks.

At the same time, CWU gave the initial impetus to the program which provided home-grown sources of protein as an alternative to importing foods. Enroute to the WCC Assembly in Nairobi, Margaret Sonnenday visited three of these villages and wrote of her satisfaction in this fulfillment of the Covenant Commitment:

> What a change in the life of the village! No longer must the women walk six to eight miles each day to carry water for all their family's needs. No longer are the children (and most adults) constantly sick from intestinal parasites which live in the polluted water they often used.
>
> In each village the leaders met us and walked with us, proudly showed us the water facilities, and tried to let us know what pure water means in their lives.

Bolivia has two-thirds of its five million people living in rural areas, but only a little more than three percent of these people have clean potable water; less than one percent of these rural homes have latrines. These conditions cause upwards of 90 percent of all adults and children in the rural areas to suffer from intestinal parasites. Church Women United, responding to their commitment, channeled funds to Bolivia through UNICEF whose program included health training of the village people and was supervised by a Swedish engineer expert in water systems.

Had we misused a sacred term in applying the word covenant *to this program? Surely, if we value the program only in terms of dollars or bushels of wheat or new wells in a desert land, we have indeed missed its significance.*

*Let us remember that in Scripture the covenant relation-
ships were expressed by the faithful when, in hopeless situations, they were yoked to the promises of God for a brighter
future:*

> *. . . a family safe in the receding waters of a devastating
> flood seeing the sign of their future livelihood in an olive
> leaf in the beak of a dove.*
>
> *. . . a nomad and his barren wife together in an alien land
> longing to people a God-fearing nation.*
>
> *. . . prisoners of war dreaming in captivity of a restored
> Jerusalem and Temple built to the glory of the One God.*

*Many died in faith — having instilled a song of hope in another
generation who someday might see their God faithful to his
covenant promises.*

Should the rainbow of hope arch the heavens in the 20th
century and touch down to save the sight of a child in
Bangladesh or the livelihood of a family on the edge of the
Sahara, then joy and peace will keep company with all the
faithful who see God's covenant being fulfilled among the
earth's people.

When a cup of clean water or a soybean sprout becomes
a sign of a new tomorrow — *the Covenant brings joy.*

When a little food every day for their children makes
bitterness and resentment between adults disappear — *the
Covenant brings peace.*

Joy and Peace

. . . in community service

**JUST BECAUSE
WE'RE INVOLVED** Marge Gross was on her way to Sioux Falls
to speak to the wives on ordination of
women when the president of CWU in
Yankton called to ask what some of the other units were doing
by way of community services. Hastily picking up a few case
studies from a stack of *Church Woman* magazines, Marge
swung by the meeting for coffee with the Planning Group on
Ecumenical Action. After her presentation, a Roman Catholic

remarked, "My priest tells me that the greatest need in Yankton is for a clothing center that stays open."

"Why don't we raise the question at a forum on May Fellowship Day?" asked Marge, on her way out to her speaking appointment.

Questions and answers came from all parts of the room on the first Friday of May. The advertised questions were:

What does this community need most?
What can CWU do about it?

Yankton, South Dakota, is a county seat with a population of 14,000. In 1975, the town was surrounded by a drought disaster area — and there were a lot of hurting people. The women who were attending this forum readily admitted the need for a well-run clothing center where purchases could be made with dignity. Church women knew that it was the kind of project which would easily gain support from others. So, within a few months, a clothing center started by volunteers was making enough "non-profit" income to employ a manager and to finance all the emergency situations which the County Ministerial Association was receiving daily.

The success of this project stimulated the leaders of a number of civic organizations to meet for further planning. Out of these meetings there was published a Referral Directory which answered questions people were asking: where to get medical service, inoculations, lung tests, and food stamps. Like most handbooks, it was out of date before it got off the press. However, out of it came a 'committee of five', which sought a more human and flexible way of responding to the ever increasing list of citizen needs.

Soon there came into being a Contact Center where most anyone could get most anything from advice to artificial teeth. The Lutherans housed it; various church and community organizations funded it (including a contribution from the County itself) and various groups specialized in the collection of requested articles such as eyeglasses. The Food Pantry in the Center became a special service provided by CWU.

Working with the extension department, the Food Pantry offered demonstrations in cooking for dietary needs for newly married women. Others organized a way to handle specific services as the need arose. A young blind man needed a seeing eye dog. A sick boy had to be driven to Sioux City. Soon a mutual assistance program had been developed with the discovery of an ever-growing number of people who could be counted on for caring what happened to their neighbors.

Church women acted as individuals in each project whatever the manner in which they were recruited. They were wise enough never to fall into the trap of possessiveness. Besides they discovered early that one necessary contribution was the 'gift of encouragement.' The townspeople were all so busy they didn't notice that Marge Gross, who had taken such a large part in the initiation of this community effort, was off doing something else. "How come, Marge," inquired one of her friends, "You're always in on the beginning of these community activities, then you seem to deal yourself out?" Marge might have answered "Just because . . ." except she was already on her way to an Indian Jurisdiction Study and a leadership training class for the pre-retirement program of the bank.

When involved in developing a community project, church women meet other likeminded women and thus uncover new growth potential for Church Women United. With so many pressures and expectations surrounding them, women are glad to find other free spirits who want to choose how they use their valuable time and skills. The spin-off of a project initiated by CWU to a community based sponsor is an important way to stabilize the effort. It also leaves each generation of church women with the self-imposed responsibility of working creatively on other needs emerging in the community. This kind of involvement is not only a rewarding kind of personal experience with other sectors in the community, but a way to bring a religious point of view to civic enterprises. Without any 'special interest' label, volunteers very often carry much weight in community affairs if their goals are clear and their concern genuine.

Participation in community service requires that a volunteer be knowledgeable, skilled, and motivated. There are odd jobs such as addressing envelopes or answering the phone which many women are glad to pitch in and help with in order to get a project rolling. But Church Women United, under the professional leadership of Alice Leppert, chose to work toward the increased competence of the volunteers in selected fields.

Church women have always been concerned about these fields as citizens and, with adequate background, could make a personal contribution. Three different types of volunteer roles are outlined in *Guidelines for Health Care Volunteers* by Ann W. Fales of Rutgers University and Alice Leppert of CWU.

The first is the *direct service role* which could be a variety of functions such as first aid training to assist a scout troop, assembling family medical histories, translating a physician's instructions to a Spanish speaking patient, giving one-to-one attention to an institutionalized child. The second role is *administrative* in which a volunteer might be the director of a hospital fund raising function. The third type of volunteer is the *policy setter* who might serve on the Boards of a neighborhood health center for instance.

All three types of volunteers need exposure and reflection in the field, but require different gifts and temperaments. All must learn how to work side by side with professionals and paraprofessionals respecting each of their roles. Each must be reliable in her use of time and materials, as well as cooperative and helpful during staff conferences. The volunteer has a "bill of rights" also. She should not jump into the job until she has an opportunity to see what is involved, has some training in her job, knows the policy of the institution and has the skill and time required to perform the required work satisfactorily.

The role of the national movement, according to Mrs. Leppert's plan, was to examine thoroughly the present trends in each field and to seek the interest and cooperation of professionals in the field, to organize national workshops for the training of state leaders, (each of which was partially financed by grants from the New York Foundation and the Lilly by grants from the New York Foundation and the Lilly Endowment, Inc. Foundation) to assist the state leaders in getting local units involved, to render on-the-job counsel through an active field program, and to use these experiences to publish guidelines and resources in each field.

In order to carry effectively this national responsibility, Alice Leppert needed to develop relationships with private and government agencies working on each area. She was proud of the contribution of her constituency and had no difficulty in getting the interest of professional groups or foundations in the same field.

One at a time CWU selected an arena for action in the field of community services. The cycle of resource, experience, training, and publication was utilized for each. Once the publication was available, local leaders in communities had adequate guidelines. As Alice discovered local groups at work, she would keep alive their interest in development along with the pilot projects in the current Arena for Action. The arenas chosen and the years which they were developed by the national office are as follows:

ADULT BASIC EDUCATION   The 1969 *U.S. Bureau of the Census Report on Level of Education* pointed out that there were over 4 1/3 million white adults over 25 years who had completed less than 5 years of school (and over 1½ million black adults). Adding to the total number of undereducated adults were the million dropouts from schools each year, many of whom have serious deficiencies in reading and arithmetic skills, as well as immigrants some of whom arrive without being able to speak or read the English language. These adults have difficulty in finding suitable jobs and keeping them, in maintaining stable family life and in reading signs and labels which protect their personal health and safety. Psychologically many are in a state of deep frustration, so discouraged are they by repeated failures.

A great many people are working at the problem through businesses, libraries, correctional institutions and national associations such as Adult Education Association, International Reading Association, National Reading

Association and National Association for Public and Continuing Adult Education. All of these resources may be available for teaching skills to tutors or may want volunteers who supply an important element in their concern about the individual student. There are two general types of volunteers. Those called instructional assistants or tutors help the adult learn specific skills such as communication skills of reading, vocabulary idioms and phrases used in basic health care, trades, or shopping, and the skills of basic arithmetic. The others are program aides who help in recruiting, record keeping, conducting educational tours or guides to hospitals, museums and factories.

We often pointed to the models called Literacy Volunteers of America, Inc. located in Syracuse, New York and with a network of many affiliates. Started by Mrs. Ruth Colvin, an active church woman, the program maintains a headquarters, co-opts reading specialists from universities, develops materials and techniques, and includes evaluation and adult diagnosis systems. In one year (June 1969 to June 1970) their records showed that 1,203 adult students received instruction amounting to 40,286 teaching hours. During that period of time, 6,812 new volunteers were trained in 23 different communities or institutions. With this kind of record, television and other media cooperates fully which helps in recruiting students and tutors and the funding of the program.

The U.S. Office of Education maintains 8 regional offices which have special interest in community programs, and CWU's original plan called for eventually activating supportive services in each of them. CWU began an adult education pilot program in 1968 in Region II (New York, New Jersey, Delaware and Pennsylvania). The satisfaction of establishing a community-based program was great among the women themselves, and their competence prompted public awards from the U.S. Department of Health, Education and Welfare and from the U.S. Adult Education Association.

Realizing that the proportion of black disadvantaged adults was nearly four times greater than white, CWU next focused on Region IV (North Carolina, South Carolina, Georgia, Florida, Alabama, Mississippi, Kentucky and Tennessee).

A workshop held at Florida State University in March 1970 brought together interracial teams of volunteers from the Southeast. Co-chairing the workshop was Alice Leppert, CWU's program specialist for adult basic education, and Dr. George Aker of the faculty of Florida State University and president of the Adult Education Association of the United States of America.

Workshop participants studied the psychology of the disadvantaged learner, the role of tutors and aids, the use of educational technology, and how basic education is presently structured through the schools, agencies, unions, and business firms. They learned how to relate to state education departments and to existing community programs of Adult Basic Education through which Church women work in supportive roles.

The 1971 CWU "Right to Read" Workshop for Adult Basic Education was held in the San Antonio, Texas area on the campus of Incarnate Word College. Leadership teams chosen by CWU in Louisiana, Arkansas, Oklahoma, New Mexico and Texas made up the participants. Learning from exposure and observation was featured as the teams visited the highly successful volunteer program carried on by Margarita Huantes, the San Antonio Literacy Council, the Reading Clinic in the Katherine A. Ryan Center, and the basic education program at the Job Corps Center in San Marcos, Texas. They visited the classes for WIN (The Work Incentive Program), CEP (Concentrated Employment Program), and migrant programs in the area. Their discussion of the factors inherent in the Hispanic cultural areas of the South Central region were thus informed by their observations of the many kinds of programs in the community.

While reinforcing the efforts through the South with regular field trips during the next two years, Alice Leppert was engaged in the background exploration of the opportunity in ABE among American Indians in the West.

OREGON A workshop on Indian Adult Education and the
WORKSHOP Volunteer Sector was sponsored by CWU at
Oregon College of Education in October 1972
with participants from both the white and Indian communities. The demonstrated cultural contribution of Indians in that
area delighted the entire group.

Dr. Helen M. Redbird-selam, Professor of Social
Science at Oregon College burst the balloon into which some
would like to lump all minorities when she pointed out that "not
even Indians could be seen as one people, much less one
problem."

No one Indian speaks for all Indians and natives about
their ways and their way of life. If you're going to work
with native population, to me, that is the first thing you
must internalize. That the Bureau of Indian Affairs does
not speak for the tribal people. That no *one* Indian
speaks for the tribal people. And this you must internalize and you must internalize it first, because everything
else falls into place after that.

Her words went far beyond her own community when
she went on to say:

I want to deal with you in relation to cultures, the ways
of the people and how they might influence the learning
that you deal with. Culture influences every aspect of
learning; how an individual feels about himself, what
influences him to learn and what influences him in his
behavior.

Once again we learned that minority leaders were
already there. All we could do was help to build a higher
platform from which they could teach us.

In guidelines for *Adult Basic Education Volunteers*
published in December 1970, Alice Leppert summed up the
learning of the church volunteers in many localities who had
ventured in a new way into the educational needs of their
communities. Church Women United is particularly grateful

that its consultant was wise enough to get counsel and encouragement along the way from a host of leaders in the adult basic education field which she incorporated in the Guidelines to offer a resource to those who value excellence of performance in their contribution to the welfare of the community at large.

HEALTH Among all citizens there was a growing awareness
DELIVERY of the relationship of health to other aspects of
SERVICE human development and the need for health ser-
vices to be available for all segments of the population. Current trends in health care opened new opportunities to the volunteer who wished to channel her energy in constructive ways in this field.

Here were some of them: Federal government financing was moving away from funding only enormous programs of research and toward funding for comprehensive health planning and care. Under various sponsors there were coming into being Health Maintenance Organizations, Family Health Centers, and the National Health Service Corps. There was a trend in support systems for the overworked medical special- ists in new types of health professionals such as physicians' assistants, nurse practitioners, and dental therapists. The number of nurse-midwives tripled in ten years making possible adequate care for mothers throughout the normal pregnancy and birth of babies in many urban centers and rural counties. Comprehensive emergency care networks with the use of computerized lists and helicopter service made better use of "high skill" facilities. There was new attention to advanced cancer treatment centers and to legislated programs for venereal disease, alcohol and drug abuse.

But how can the poor citizens make use of these services as long as 64% of those with family incomes under $3,000 are uninsured and the growing number of senior citizens increases the common responsibility for maintaining normal health? Could volunteers help deliver the health services available to those who have health needs?

Sentences from the introduction of "Guidelines for Health Care Volunteers" answered these questions and became the basic reasons which made the National Board in 1972 call for this arena of action:

> Concerned response to personal and community health needs flows as naturally from the life of the person of faith today as it did when Christ ministered to the pressing needs of the sick . . .

> Any action should be labeled pure dreaming, however, if it does not result in the actual delivery of the health services which are needed by all segments of our population. The church-related volunteer has a tremendous opportunity to help bring idealistic theory out of the sky and put it to work for health programs which truly serve all the people—promptly, effectively, and compassionately, and with a measurable degree of permanence.

Two CWU sponsored Health Services Workshops were projected in 1972. Considering the medical facilities and professional leadership available, Buffalo, New York, and Boston were choice locations. Among the most valuable resources were two knowledgeable members of the national board who had enough prestige to mobilize leadership. In February, Miriam Minkser, chairperson of the Buffalo committee, secured medical resources for participants from states in the north central area.

In the workshop held in The Children's Inn, Boston, September 28-30, 1972, Patricia Nelson, Director of the Health Education Department of the Children's Hospital and a member of the state and national Boards of CWU, challenged the church women to consider Health Education as the next frontier. Able and authoritative leaders coming from the professional training centers and clinics of the Boston and New York areas echoed this concern.

The Health workshops had three main elements. The first provided *exposures to actual conditions* and actual people. On-the-spot visitations were made to drug therapy program sessions, crisis intervention centers, mental health programs of inner city schools, neighborhood health clinics, nursing programs for minority women, school nutrition and health education programs, hospital services, etc. Opportunities were provided for church women to talk with the "consumers" of health services in many different types of neighborhoods and to doctors and program directors who were the "providers" of the services. In this way, a "feel" for the needs and the problems of real people emerged.

The second element featured in the workshops was an *intensive updating of current knowledge on the trends and developments* in medicine and health care, outstanding professionals from the Boston University and Harvard Medical Schools, the State University of New York at Buffalo, regional medical organizations, the National Health Service Corps, all contributed their analysis of health insurance groups, maternity and infant care programs, and community action projects. Various proposals for national health insurance were also analyzed and discussed. This section of the workshop made it possible for the participants to have an overall view of the total health care situation before deciding upon any particular form of local action for their own community.

The third part of the workshops featured a training session in goal-setting skills for health action by local units of Church Women United. In both workshops Dorothy and John Wagner from the Joint Health Venture in Hollywood, California made extremely useful evaluations.

In the evaluations participants listed many things to do when they returned home. It was apparent that women had an insatiable interest in the whole issue of health care which matched their eagerness to find their own responsible piece of action.

WOMEN AND PRISONS   Nothing jars the sensitive woman so much as the facts about women in prison: what—or who—put them there? What happens when they get out? And who cares? Nothing jars more than the facts—except knowing the women offenders themselves.

One of our national consultations held in November 1973 in Washington, D.C. concentrated on the issues which must be resolved to find humane solutions to the problems of women and the prison system. Judge Margaret Haywood of the Superior Court and the first woman moderator of the United Church of Christ, answered the question "Who and what puts women in prison?" In part she said:

> Who are the women who are arrested and go to jail, and for what? . . . In 1968 only one of every seven persons arrested was a woman. In 1970 the pattern remained about the same . . . It would appear that there is a far greater willingness to institutionalize girls for far less serious offenses than boys. For example, in 1965 over half of all girls referred to juvenile courts were referred for conduct which would not be criminal if committed by an adult . . . As a result of the statutes' imprecise language, minors, usually girls, may be (and are) institutionalized for acts that are neither criminal nor violent—for example, running away from home, staying out late, or having undesirable companions.

> What are the acts for which women are arrested? This is a most significant question since its answer has forced me to ponder another one: Is it really necessary at all for most women offenders to be incarcerated?

> The crimes for which women are arrested fall largely into two categories: crimes against property and what essentially are crimes against themselves—prostitution and narcotics.
> · · ·

> A disproportionate percentage of women offenders are from minority groups. . .Women's prisons have increasingly been receiving more disturbed, aggressive, younger women. Clearly a young inmate population will continue to be a distressing problem unless our institutions for rehabilitation manage to do their job.
> · · ·

> The majority of women in prison have small children. Thus there is a double problem, the fact of incarceration and its immediate effect on the women and the necessity of finding some kind of care for the children.
> · · ·

Given these facts, i.e., only routine chores in prison as jobs, what does life hold on the outside for one who is about to be paroled or released?

                              • • •

Let me quote some remarks by the present warden of the Women's Detention Center in the District of Columbia: "Look," she says, "There's an emotional need to obtain money in this society. There is nothing more important. We're all money-oriented. Television, magazines, billboards, they all advertise things. All of a sudden we're supposed to tell these women. "Don't grasp for money; it isn't as important as high moral values . . . You expect a woman who can make her own schedule and earn enough money to survive and pay no taxes to take a factory job for $1.65 a hour? Society has taught that everyone has a right to have things and that everyone should have nice things. They don't give these women any respectable way to get them, and then when they go out and get them the best way they know, we tell them it's wrong.

The community has just got to make up its mind about what it wants. They're punishing these women for the very values they taught them!

Since women offenders are so few in proportion to men, who are apprehended, they are frequently crowded into the top floor of a county jail or a wing of a state prison. Since they are no "big problem," their access to community or educational services are overlooked. However, increasing attention is being given alternatives to imprisonment, for the jails are an expensive way to handle people—some of whom don't belong there to start with. Community-based correction facilities give an opportunity for the concerned citizen to act. Some judges will delay the sentence and assign a woman to a homelike residence, where there are supervised living conditions and some counseling services are available. This gives the offender an opportunity for education, training, recreation and even a job during this very difficult period of her life. Sometimes judges now offer a pre-trial release to the offender or a "work release" where the offender is confined only at night or weekends. In some states hospitality in individual homes is offered to the offender providing her the security of a friend or a home in which to re-orient her life.

HORIZON HOUSE   A workshop held in Milwaukee, Wisconsin July 26-28, 1973 focused on ways women could begin to shape new social structures that would result in judicial and penal reforms. Participants from six states gathered near Horizon House. A successful effort on the part of CWU in Wisconsin to offer women a needed opportunity for normal community living after serving their sentences. CWU in Waukesha and Milwaukee had done an excellent job of planning and financing the project which was appropriately called Horizon House. In selecting the neighborhood in which they finally purchased the house, they also were sensitive to the reactions which the neighbors might display. So teams of church women called on each family and explained their new project and asked for cooperation. When CWU sponsored an openhouse to welcome the staff and first residents, all the neighbors were invited—and came!

RELEASE   The story of Horizon House was featured in a film called *Release.* This 28-minute color film documented one young Chicano mother's re-entry into society after a four year prison term and her relationship to Horizon House. *Release* was made by Ms. Susanne Szabo Rostock and Lauren Stell for Church Women United in the U.S.A. and was awarded the 1974 CINE Golden Eagle for social documentaries. It was widely used in organizations and community groups, in government offices, and in college classrooms.

Release presents the special problems that plague a woman prisoner when she is released. What about her three very young children who were put in foster homes? What about getting a job and making a home for them? In the film one sees the supporting role of the volunteer who drives the children to the state prison to see their mother, and also the counseling work of a man and a woman, both social workers on the staff of Horizon House. It is the kind of film, says an anthropologist at New York University, that calls forth empathy seldom experienced in a social science classroom.

Along with obvious human needs like feeding the hungry and clothing the naked, why did Jesus say 'visit the prisoner'? No doubt it is partly because these are inter-related problems and the guilt of being an accessory to the cause of legal offense is shared by us all. But more importantly, it was for our own sake that Jesus, in outlining the criteria for the final judgment in Matthew 25, specifically mentioned this frequently broken spiritual law of compassionate under-standing.

Something happens to my faith when I love a socially ostracized person as my friend. Does she realize that Christ sat beside her at her trial? Was condemned with her, went to prison with her, shares her social bruises, her bitter regrets, her longing for her children? Does she believe that God is love—and forgives? That God is Hope and goes with her into the future? Do I?

THE CHILD While Minnie Gaston (Mrs. A.G. Gaston) of Alabama, was chairperson of the national committee on Community Services, we all looked forward to her report to the Board. In a businesslike way she got through the recommendations of the approved national program which were always limited to what was administratively feasible. Then she would launch into a lively and good-humored tirade about what church women ought to be doing. Her theme was always the same: What about today's children - tomorrow's citizens? She was doing a lot about the next generation in her educational and health programs in Alabama and in the consultations with national service agencies, but this did not lift the burden from church women.

In my heart, I knew she was right. So I am grateful that by the time of the 1974 Assembly we were able to lift into priority the needs of American children. In the meantime, this general category was an effort to stimulate global awareness among children in elementary schools.

GLOBAL LIVING   The opening paragraphs of a leaflet, "What In The World Is Happening" were aimed to challenge Church Women to undertake a survey to stimulate global awareness:

> Church Women United invites you to participate in a nationwide effort to explore how much Global Living is going on in your community and what is happening in the education of children under twelve to prepare them for this exhilarating possibility.
>
> In this decade, which is decisive for all of us—old and young, American, Greek, Brazilian, Chinese—what will happen?
>
> Some say that the world will self-destruct.
>
> Some say it will be a great new world transformed by technology.
>
> We say that we must look at the world through God's eyes, seeing every person as important and deserving the loving care of all others.
>
> We say that human beings can learn to work together in an interdependent world. We need a new loyalty, recognizing that all nations are under God. If we are alert to our times, we must become strong in new values which we practice right where we are.

Children in this pluralist country are fortunate in that they can begin right where they are to discover how people of different backgrounds exchange gifts of fair play, equal opportunity, and greater cultural enrichment for everybody. When people learn that they really do depend upon each other for health, clean water and air, beauty and fun, trade and ideas, they are becoming global citizens.

Unfortunately not every American child was interested in looking around; not every ethnic group was concerned about sharing or even preserving its own cultural heritage. Then there were other factors such as older textbooks, general reading books, the romantic TV movies, and some teachers and parents, whose point of view mirrored the children as limited as themselves. Even friendships seemed impossible as long as the stereotypes of 'the little barefoot brown child' persisted.

So Gladys Naylor began through quiet consultations with educators and publishers of children's books. Finally CWU sponsored a national consultation. These experts were far more aware of the situation than we had imagined and were helpful in pointing out the newer resources in which they were trying to overcome isolationism. We then launched a national community effort to discover what was happening in schools, churches, synagogues, homes and neighborhoods which either encouraged or hindered global consciousness.

A leaflet was prepared to suggest ways of organizing, some conversational hints, and a guide for feedback. A training program on how to interview was included in the *Response-ability Workshops* during the summer of 1973.

In the fall the interviews began with the hope that as questions were asked, we would find allies for a stimulation of an action program in the local community.

In her report from the Champaign-Urbana community, Louise Leonard comments on the local phase of global awareness: "One of the first things we realized, however, was that you just couldn't walk into a school and say to people, 'I want to interview you.'" We went to the League of Women Voters who knew the school officials. The field director of the Survey Research Laboratory at the University of Illinois became interested in the project and he helped us to formulate the questions and led a training session for interviewers. We concentrated on the fourth grade. Who has told you the most about people from other countries? In children with a high or medium awareness of 'global consciousness,' this was invariably their immediate family. In low-awareness children no definite pattern emerged. Television was as important as you would expect. But I was astonished at the programs they mentioned. For instance, *Hawaii Five-O!* They were impressed by the sea, the palm trees, the beautiful flowers. Imagine!

We also discovered in our community a fabulous multi-lingual school program. Champaign-Urbana is very cosmopolitan and there are a sufficient number of foreign-born children to form the majority of the students. Three classrooms are dedicated to the foreign-born child; lessons are conducted in Hebrew, Hindi, Spanish, French, Japanese, and German, and the children take English as a second language. Parents going abroad with their children can request that the youngsters participate.

The children in these classes are very proud of their source of origin and are most open in sharing their kind of food, songs, and way of life in general. On the other hand, children from overseas who are not in these classes were less open.

The librarians all seemed to feel that the American Indian is the most stereotyped of all ethnic and racial groups in this country.

One of the questions, "Do you find that the textbooks or books available in your library are biased or silent on the subject of other cultures? Almost everybody said, "If you had asked that five or six years ago, we would have had to say 'yes,' but in that time we have done a tremendous amount of work, going over all the books and getting rid of those that are perhaps cute but not truthful."

Many parents in Champaign-Urbana and certainly most teachers were more concerned with a true understanding for and appreciation of the various cultures within the United States rather than how we portray people in overseas countries. Once we are globally aware, the recognition of cultural diversity in our midst is seen as one of our national assets.

IT'S ALL US   As a natural outgrowth of this arena for action, CWU developed an educational tool for us in study groups and public television. *It's All Us* is a 28-minute, 16mm documentary film in sound and color on the multicultural aspects of global education for children. It was produced by Susanne Szabo Rostock and Lauren Stell, and filmed at the Emerson Primary School in Berkeley, California.

The film grew out of the experience of Virginia Hadsell, a reading specialist in the Berkeley Public Schools, who was coordinator of the on-site filming. In 1964-65 she lived in Ibadan, Nigeria, teaching in the staff school at the University of Ibadan. She has since returned to Ibadan for shorter visits—one for sabbatical study and again as leader of a study tour.

It's All Us is a documentary which invites the viewer to share in the experiences and understandings of a group of children in the third grade as they learn about the culture of the Yoruba people of Africa and compare it with their own way of living in Berkeley, California.

The Yoruba are a major tribe in southwest Nigeria, centered in several major cities, the chief of which is Ibadan, the largest all-African city south of the Sahara Desert. According to Yoruba myths and legends, the ancient capital of Ife is "the place where the world began."

The study of the Yoruba people is part of the third grade social studies curriculum at Emerson Primary School. The film makes it possible to observe, through the eyes of children, one section of the total multicultural educational program as it unfolds and is comprehended by a class of eight-year-olds.

Emerson School draws children from all ethnic communities in Berkeley as it is part of a completely integrated school system. Emerson children, therefore, are from the upper, medium, and low income groups of the city and have parents whose educational backgrounds range from the elementary school dropout to the doctoral recipient.

The professional and support staff of Emerson is also multiethnic, providing a natural setting for interracial, intercultural education.

The film compresses into 28 minutes more than a month of classroom experiences. Special materials for the study of the Yoruba came from books, films, artifact collections, and from experiences of various persons familiar with Nigeria. Yoruba music, food, and clothing were utilized in the classrooms.

A high point of the film is the reenactment of the traditional Yoruba "naming ceremony" for a newborn child which takes place one evening with the entire school community present.

CHILD INDIVISIBLE In our Journey Toward Wholeness, we planned to stop long enough at the Assembly in Memphis to form some signposts for 1975. It was clear the *Child* was one of the victims of kaleidescopic times and that our own tomorrow would be in their hands before the year 2,000.

Eleanor Craig of the staff of a child guidance clinic in Connecticut described what was happening to children as adults concentrated on trying to mend their own broken lives. Stories of child abuse and child neglect filled the daily newspapers. David Burgess, a senior officer of UNICEF, spoke about the children all over the world where even survival was a problem. Being part of an interdependent world carried some grim responsibilities.

It was with these things in mind that the participants of the *Causeway* in the fall of 1975 used the theme, "The Child Indivisible." Forty women (half of whom were from the Caribbean Islands) held a major conference on this theme with specific programs which could be undertaken by church women both in the United States and in the islands of the Caribbean. The answers will come slowly as families, neighborhoods, communities all over the world realize that we cannot say to children, "Wait until tomorrow." Their minds, bodies, and spiritual outlook are being formed TODAY.

Joy and peace

. . . through citizen action

CITIZEN ACTION is

walking into life with an open agenda
stepping alongside our sisters to find the way together
jumping into the center of the sick society to discover
causes
pouncing on issues that can produce creative change
running for office once we are ready
stopping only to catch our breath and give thanks to
God for creating us

CITIZEN ACTION is

learning what the problems are and trying to solve
them
searching out injustice in our social structures
declaring our advocacy for the powerless and
helpless
proclaiming the value of every human being on earth
affirming our belief in the oneness of human family
committing ourselves to become instruments of the
fulfillment of God's promise

Virginia Baron wrote these words during the brief months that she worked in the national office following the sudden death of Betty Johns. Virginia was puzzled by the tone of some letters that asked: What do *you* mean by *citizen action?* For Virginia, citizen action was a life to be lived, not a definition to be struggled over. Responsible behavior would have a quality of excellence if you really believed that this nation was *under God.*

Let us not pass judgement on the women who raised the question for it did represent a change in point of view for Church Women United. For many years the issues affecting our common life with other people through social and governmental structures had been defined as subject matter for departmental committees on Christian social relations and world relations. The emphasis on the role of the person as citizen was more flexible, more feminine, and more forceful than a single focus on subject matter determined by national committees. The next decade was to see fewer pronouncements and more participation. Calls to Citizen Action were to shape the directions of the national movement and decision-making about action was shifted largely to women where-they-lived in the hope that mutual trust and readily available interpretation would be more effective.

1970 SEMINAR ON CITIZEN ACTION One hundred women from thirty state units arrived in New York on April 13, 1970, for briefing at the Church Center at the United Nations Headquarters. They then proceeded to Washington by bus to spend three days in a rewarding program arranged by Abigail McCarthy and Betty Johns. Special occasions had been planned to provide opportunity to know personally many of those carrying national responsibility in government. The Christian concern of the leadership could be discerned throughout the whole seminar. There were special field trips to the Office of Economic Opportunity, the World Bank, and to the congressional offices on Capitol Hill. There were seminars on local, state and national political involvement. Participants felt some alarm with their own lethargy as they saw how some of their Christian claims were weakened when translated into legislation when they had failed to support a stronger position at strategic times.

Let me select a few quotes from the speakers at the Seminar which will give the tone and indicate the high calibre of the leadership. Mrs. Mark Hatfield, the wife of a Republican Senator from Oregon, set the basic tone in her opening prayer:

Cleanse us from worshipping our own comforts,

privileges, and good fortune. We know that our preoccupation with ourselves has eliminated our concern for others. Forgive us for giving priority to our welfare. Break down our insulation from the need of our neighbor . . .

The keynote address on *The Gospel and Political Action* was given by Honorable Walter F. Mondale, U.S. Senator from Minnesota. (In 1970 Senator Mondale was chairman of the Select Committee on Equal Educational Opportunity; chairman of subcommittees on Migratory Labor; on Social Program Planning and Evaluation; on Production and Stabilization, on Retirement and the Individual).

These were areas in which church women looked to their government for affirmative action, but Senator Mondale let us know that some responsibility lay on the Christian citizen. He spoke frankly:

> Unless Christians become actively involved in politics, I do not know if this country . . . is going to survive in the form we want it to survive. My observation is that where you find a people unable to stand up in the power structure . . . you find a desperate people, often the object of our discrimination and hatred.

He illustrated from his own field trips:

> There were 22,000 migrants in this county. The chairman of the county board did not think it was legal to feed the hungry. He said, 'These are not our people; they are federal people. They are gypsies; they like to roam. If you give them anything, they destroy it.' He was the official spokesman of the county dependent on the labor these farmers supplied.
>
> ▪ ▪ ▪
>
> I'll never forget visiting a pathetic little shack in Nome, Alaska, in the frozen tundra. I noticed there were no high school age children around. I asked where the children went to school. The mother said, "In Oklahoma."
>
> ▪ ▪ ▪

We have a policy of sending over 1,300 junior and senior high school Alaskan children by airplane to Oklahoma to a military-type environment in a desert-like area. They do not see their families for nine months of the year.

On the Navajo Reservation, we have a system of elementary boarding schools. Every year, 35,000 Navajo children, many five years of age, leave their parents and are put in military-type barracks where about half as much is spent as in a regular boarding school. Psychiatrists have recorded anxiety levels beyond anything they have seen in their lives. The children are without emotional support, without the strength parents can bring them, away from parents for months at a time. This human tragedy in the lives of thousands of Navajo children continues today despite the outcry of mental health specialists. The results are shown in the suicide rates. Two children froze to death trying to escape this winter. There is a highly sophisticated truancy program . . .

Then he returned to his opening theme:

When I look at my mail, I look at those who involve themselves in the political process and very few come forward with the issues we are discussing today.

Hunger, education, health, emotional support, human values, and the dignity of the human being—these are the issues being starved in America today, possibly because women are too neutral, too remote from the political process . . .

I give these examples not because they are unique but because they say as much about the problem as they say about us. If the ideas we so often express are what we really believe, how can this continue? If it does continue, our society is in profound danger.

Our institutions seek to want to protect themselves from the problems they are set to solve. Our courts are among the institutions which must be responsive to these problems. This is why I feel so strongly about equal educational opportunity. This is why I feel the Church must bend at the joints and become a part of these human problems and their solutions. We must change institutions that bend, fold, mutilate individuals, but keep IBM cards immaculate.

Cynthia Wedel responded on behalf of the participants in these words:

I hope we as Christian women, looking at this world through God's eyes and seeing the hunger, the despair, the tragedies in our own country and in every country of the world because of a lack of political activity on behalf of the deprived will be filled with righteous indignation and say, "This can *not* go on."

Other speakers pointed out the indifference of women to seeking public office. In looking at the electoral process, it was noted that in 1959 there were 17 women in Congress whereas a decade later there were only 11 (and in 1959 there were 18,000 in elective county posts over against 3,862 ten years later).

Therefore it was fitting to honor Senator Margaret Chase Smith. For a generation she had been calling forth confidence and loyalty from citizens everywhere, as Dot Dolbey pointed out in presenting a citation at the luncheon which paid her tribute.

Unlike most groups who come to Washington to put pressure on Congress to act in their own interests, Church Women United were there to get material to put pressure on the people back home.

CALLS TO CITIZEN ACTION By the time that Betty Johns had the mimeographed report of the Washington Seminar ready, she was able to add a preface indicating the number of workshops, newsletters and forums which had already been organized by the eager participants. Clearly once church women got the idea, they found ways to make a difference in their own communities.

Capitalizing on this momentum, a task force began to work on a fresh approach to the whole process of effective citizenship. A working paper was prepared for the consideration of the participants at the 1971 Ecumenical Assembly, entitled, "Calls to Citizen Action."

The Calls to Action were general areas of concern which formed the framework for action on specific issues. The national office planned to alert the state chairpersons for Citizen Action on pending legislation and special events which had some relevance to the issues. After appropriate study and reflection, each local unit should come to its own decisions on specific issues.

The Calls to Action proposed to the Assembly in Wichita in 1971 were three:

I. CALL TO SHARE IN SHAPING NEW SOCIAL STRUCTURES

Scope of Problem

To attempt to evolve social, economic and political patterns which take account of global communication and the knowledge explosion; to see the need for consumer distribution in the interest of greater justice and fulfillment of all; to deal responsibly and imaginatively with the elements causing serious disorders in our society; to utilize discoveries in technology for the creation of community rather than for its destruction.

A Christian Perspective

As Christians, we declare our oneness as a human family under God. We accept our responsibility in gratitude to God to live out our affirmation that in Christ *"there is neither Jew nor Greek, there is neither bond nor free, there is neither male nor female."* The prophetic call is to let justice and righteousness roll down like a mighty stream. As we claim this heritage we recognize that the God of the future is pulling us forward to a New Age and a New Humanity. Because we respond to this vision we reject present exploitation and oppression. God's judgement and forgiving love frees us to enter into community and to discover together how to become instruments of the fulfillment of God's promise.

Action Issues to Explore

1. *Envisioning the new social patterns* — encounters between the generations to discuss human values in a very mobile society; creative centers for children of all classes to grow together in enriching experiences; quality education preparing all to use new knowledge for constructive purposes and challenging the assumptions of our life style in a nation with 6% of the world's population consuming 40% of its production.

2. *Areas of constructive change* - guaranteed basic adequate income for all citizens; assurance of health care delivery systems for all; housing and human settlements which allow individuality and privacy but also include socializing structures; expansion of social, intellectual and spiritual communities that transcend national barriers; exploration of structures and sub-structures for systems control and responsible sharing of resources of the New Age as planetary citizens; conservation of resources and just distribution of consumer goods and services such as electrical energy; assurance of sound ecological practices.

3. *Treatment of social evils* - elimination of institutional racism; prevention, treatment and rehabilitation of drug addicts; judicial reform for equal justice and rehabilitation of prisoners.

II. CALL TO OPEN OPPORTUNITIES FOR WOMEN IN TRANSITION

Scope of Problem

To raise the consciousness of women, changing their image of themselves to one of full personhood, and to recognize their particular contribution in the reordering of values now dominated by false competition and consumption; to enable women to help one another to participate fully in society; to rectify the injustices so as to eliminate the educational, economic, and physical handicaps.

A Christian Perspective

In the Bible we are told that God made humankind both male and female, and that he affirmed his creative act as good. Part of the good news that Christians proclaim is the worth, dignity and potential contribution that might come from any person. The realization of our oneness in Christ does not deny the diversity among women and men, but encourages their full and unimpeded development. As we accept the judgment of our failure to witness to justice and fulfillment and to the release of the oppressed, we give thanks for God's mercy and his constant call to bring the promise of abundant life for all into reality.

Action Issues to Explore

1. *Heightened consciousness of woman's situation* - awareness of the tremendous waste of human potential; participation in policy-making and planning for the new future; the creative new tasks the New Era will demand in the work and leisure fields; encouragement of women to seek public office and other leadership in community life.

2. *Struggle for rights of women* - guarantee of economic growth and protection for low-income jobs now held largely by women; freedom for upward mobility in careers; elimination of legal inequalities; adequate child care services; equal rights in home, church, work and community; recognition of oneness with women in other lands and working with them for opportunities and justice.

3. *Assistance of women in transition situations* - housing and jobs for families moving into cities; provision for moving from poverty to control of adequate incomes; opportunities for transnational women to enter fully into economic, social and civic life; needs of women in transition from one age to another related to careers, volunteer work and personal problems; re-entry problems of those handicapped by physical or mental illness, drug addiction or alcoholism, or prison records.

III. CALL TO ENGAGE IN PEACE BUILDING

Scope of Problem

To explore together how to act innovatively and courageously to fulfill our calling to peace building in our own communities and then in the community of nations and international structures; to engage in peace making tasks in local communities and to perceive the inextricable relationship between local issues and their global dimensions.

A Christian Perspective

The prayer that "Thy Kingdom come on earth" calls us to bear witness to our love of God by showing reverence for all persons serving as advocates of those without power and privilege. In a time of such resources and possibilities for human life we are all the more vulnerable before God as we see polarization of races, class stratification, widespread violence and conflict among nations. We are called to a ministry of love and reconciliation, which must be rooted in justice. Witness to the Christian faith implies a radical reordering of our personal habits and of communal structures. Since we claim that Jesus Christ is the Lord of life, we deny our faith when we wantonly destroy a life or deter its full development.

410   *Church Women United 1966 through 1975*

Action Issues to Explore

1. *Priorities* - examining the moral basis of political decisions; reordering of national priorities; reassessment of U.S. foreign policy; prompt planning for reconversion from war to peace-time economy.

2. *Practice of peace making in local communities* - self-determination of cultural groups in communities; skills for bringing alienated people together; elimination of hunger, prejudice, ignorance, and psychological blocks that prevent inter-group relations.

3. *Exploration of international cooperation* - study relationship between liberation, justice and development; influence of world trade policies and international financial structures; opening up relationships with China and other estranged nations; dialogue among women in areas of international tension; increased U.S. support of international structures.

4. *Restraints for limiting conflict* - limitation of armaments; control of Federal military budget and aid; alternatives to the draft; education and action to end war; policies and practices related to atrocities in war; responsibility for reparations and restoration; violation of Christian principles and all moral order.

This plan was presented to the Assembly by Abigail McCarthy. In her introduction she commented on our general **motivation as Christians and as women:**

> To live in this world and not to love its people is to view oneself and all other persons as less than human. 'It takes too much energy not to care,' cried a person in one of Lorraine Hansbury's plays. This is undoubtedly one reason why any church woman keeps on trying.

> Our calling as Christians is to find the way to say 'God loves you' to every person on earth. Sometimes this means just standing beside a person until the next step becomes clear; sometimes it requires lending a helping hand; and more and more it is figuring out *with* someone what causes the problem and what the possible answers might be. This requires some corporate answers—some new kinds of structures and institutions which relate to the new needs.

We are in danger of exhausting ourselves trying to fulfill limited and self-centered goals. We are tempted to criticize and label others because of our own frustrations. We are prone to paralysis caused by situations which are seemingly beyond our control.

In every age freedom must be defined in terms of the longings and aspirations of the people of that time. We must see that to love ourselves may be the new liberation. 'Love your neighbor as yourself' is our means of releasing liberating forces for all people.

1972 WORKSHOP ON CALLS TO ACTION Following the Ecumenical Assembly of 1971 when the Calls for Christian Citizen Action had been issued, it was felt important to have a national Workshop to center in on the problems which these issues presented. It was held in Washington, D.C. on January 31—February 4, 1972, and opened with a briefing for the capital visitation by Elsa Chaney of the Department of Political Science of Fordham University, Dorothy Stimson, formerly League of Women Voters' Legislative Chairperson and Dr. Deborah Wolfe, the Legislative Affairs Consultant for CWU.

The opening luncheon was held in the new senate office building and featured relationships with Latin America with addresses by Charles Meyer, Assistant Secretary of State for Inter-American Affairs and Senator Frank Church, Chairman of the Foreign Relations Subcommittee on Western Hemisphere Affairs. Later Senora Pedad de Sura, immediate past President of the Inter-American Commission of Women spoke on the Status of Women in Latin America and Dr. Chaney spoke about a new approach to the urban problems of Latin America.

The section on domestic action continued to consider the problems of poverty and hunger. Senator George McGovern, Chairman of the Select Committee on Nutrition gave a major address and John Wilson, Director of the Office of Family Benefits Planning of HEW spoke of the crucial planning in the field of Welfare Reform. A number of women formed a panel on issues where Voluntarism and Government meet, speaking from their experience in CWU.

A major address on *Ecology—the Balance Between the Future of Man and His Immediate Needs* was delivered by Senator Edmund Muskie, Chairman of the Subcommittee of Air and Water Pollution. The informative discourse was of tremendous interest to women, somewhat distracted by the amount of TV coverage he was receiving since he was at that time seeking the presidential nomination on the Democratic Presidential ticket.

But the recurring question of why there were so few women in political office was faced one night by two women who had been elected to the House of Representatives. Both felt that church women who chose this arduous road could offer a spirit of moral purpose sorely needed in American politics.

The practical Shirley Chisholm said it in a straightforward way:

> Forget conventionalism. Forget what the world will say, whether you are in your place or out of your place. Think your best thoughts. Speak your best words. Do your best deeds looking only to your conscience and to God for approval.

> As we think in terms of a new spirit of morality needed so desperately on the American scene, it is going to have to come from church women. If you believe in the Judeo-Christian doctrine you will be prepared to stand up and be counted because you know you will receive the energy, the strength, and the guidance, if you will, to help you carry forward the struggle.

> So my charge to you is that all of us, including me, have to reassess our roles from time to time. We have to reassess our priorities. And one of the priorities right now is the need for Christian women to run for political office.

Representative Lenore Romney of Michigan was equally forceful in her challenge to women for political involvement and reminding them of scripture which warned of tepid, lukewarm works (see Rev. 3:5 ff). Among the things she said were these words:

> If you and I don't get involved in the tremendous problems of our present-day society, we are going to turn over these important problems to someone else. Somebody is going to be deciding the great issues of our day.
>
> It will be bruising, but it will be an education and you'll be making the path easier for somebody else to come along and follow you.
>
> And when your children say to you, as I'm sure mine will, "Where were you when all these things were happening to our country?", you can say, "I was fighting. I was working. I was doing everything I could to turn this country around."

Women are desperately needed—we can't sit back any more. We can make the difference, and if the next generation goes down the drain the world will never forgive us. If we don't live up to the opportunities we have, if we don't embrace all beings in brotherhood and sisterhood, we are not fulfilling our obligations.

PEOPLE'S PLATFORM FOR A GLOBAL SOCIETY Since 1966 we had been talking about becoming global neighbors. This was not just a cozy phrase for world planning. We used the word neighbor to imply that we cared and that we were all in this together. We knew that every family in the global neighborhood—including our own—was in trouble. We were beginning to have an inkling that happenings in our local community did have some bearing on what was happening in other sections of this country and even in other regions of the world.

Whether we liked it or not, we were part and parcel of the same world at the same time. And what was more serious: the future society would grow out of the present. The young, at some magical moment, do not take over and start anew. Greediness and disillusionment as well as cooperation and vision are ingredients of the soil producing the quality of life for tomorrow and tomorrow's tomorrow.

Furthermore, we must live with friend and foe on the same destructable planet and build for the future of all. Some friends and some foes are within a telephone reach, and others are living in every nation of this world. By friends in a global neighborhood, we mean any with a sensitized conscience about the welfare of every human being and who are therefore under obligation to work toward the common good.

To be effective, action muscles must be flexible and coordinated. Would we be able as women with diverse points of view to unite on some common convictions? Would our corporate conscience leave the mark of a loving Christ still suffering midst the agonies of the earth's people in our day?

Of course such talk was going on everywhere and the tragedy of talk without effective plans for action still haunts us. This became more clear as we met with various committees set up by both the government and private agencies to plan for the right projects about the past like Bicentennial Minutes and gala occasions for the present.

A look at our Colonial past reminded us that some immigrants in adverse circumstances forged the ideas which were to call for self-government. If there were any need for the colonists of South Carolina to compare notes with those in New Jersey, it would take months. Yet it was in these times that among the common people, the farmers, the merchants, the lawyers, the teachers, a vision of a new nation arose and with it some convictions about what it ought to be. Many put their ideas into pamphlets and spread them among their near neighbors. The grammar was sometimes faulty and the readers were uncertain, but these pamphleteers continued for fifteen years and generated enough common feeling to produce a Declaration of Independence and a bill of rights for the citizens of a new nation under God. It took thirteen more years after 1776 before the first government came into being. Genuine convictions have two companions—perseverance and perception!

So it was proposed that we sponsor the development of a *People's Platform for a Global Society,* as our contribution to the Bicentennial Celebration. We would begin by getting together as diversified a group of women as could come to a 'Forum on Wholeness' sponsored by Church Women United.

The term 'Forum on Wholeness' was uncovered by Barbara Hubbard in one of the mini-communities at the Memphis Assembly. When she had explained that we had no vehicle by which we could channel our ideas to the government, a welfare mother interrupted and said, "Oh yes, we do. I'll start when I get home to get everybody I know into a Forum of Wholeness!"

At these Forums we would raise a question which in the course of human events in the 20th century had to be aired: What On Earth Do *We Want Now?*

Out of such talk, if people were not afraid to be honest, would come other talk wherever women went in their communities. After a few months they would come together again, hopefully with some others who had caught the spirit, for good ideas seldom arrive when you punch a time clock. A second Forum would then surface some consensus of what issues were important from the point of view of the community. And then the practical Marthas could dig in: Is This Dream Possible?

As task forces began to discover resources, define obstacles, latch on to possibilities, and explore the worldwide ramifications, there would be proposed plans for the platform which of course called for a third Forum on "How shall this plank be formulated as a part of a Platform for a Global Society?"

We invited local and state leaders committed to spark a People's Platform to come to Washington in May 1975 for training sessions after a seminar at the CCUN in New York on the global dimensions of International Women's Year. The leadership was not as diverse as we could expect it to be in a local community, and we had to compress our pamphleteering into fifteen hours! Nevertheless we saw ourselves as Synergistic Saints.

Synergy is a word used to express correlated force or united action. Synergy is possible among the believers in God whose will and inspiration moves us toward unity in the world as well as the Church.

At the end of three days working in Forums of Wholeness, Barbara Hubbard, a prime-mover of the Committee of the Future, presided in a summary Panel which came out with some significant "planks!"

A Guidebook for the People's Platform for Global Society was developed out of this experience. There were outlines for the three Forums and resources galore. It was mailed to 2,200 local units well ahead of World Community Day 1975. It was our plan that women in local units would do their work in Forums and report the results to World Community Day 1976. A committee from each state would make a preliminary review and analysis in December and send a report to the national offices.

As the year closed, the nation was in the midst of political campaigns. Margaret Sonnenday wrote to each presidential candidate explaining about the involvement of church women during the bicentennial year, and indicated the desire of our officers to present priorities coming from this process to the new President after his inauguration. Both candidates answered. For the record, we quote a memorandum dated October 5, 1976, addressed to our national president.

I really appreciate your informing me of Church Women United's "A People's Platform for a Global

Society." There is a great need in our country for a mechanism through which people can make their proposals known to their government. Church Women United's program is especially important because of its ecumenical nature and its reflection of local opinion. If I am elected, I would welcome your proposals."

It was signed by Jimmy Carter.

The People's Platform was only a means to involve American women in global planning. We, the people of the earth, will continue the unfinished agenda.

PEOPLE UNDER REPRESSION One of the curious facts of this decade was the way governments and political parties adopted for themselves labels which defied any traditional interpretation. While using in their official names such terms as Socialist, Democratic, Christian Front, Free World People's Republic, the realities appeared quite different from what these concepts have come to mean. In many cases governments established by military cliques were likely to have opposition from citizens who value the right to speak and act with freedom, particularly if they were advocates for the poor. Some, finding their situation intolerable, fled their native land and became political refugees; others remained to take their stand against the repressive governments and frequently ended up by becoming political prisoners.

Church Women United could often reinforce the efforts of Councils of Churches abroad who were in position to come alongside political prisoners and their families. In 1966 financial assistance was offered to church women in Indonesia to work among women who had been imprisoned because of political activity. Getting to know a person on a one-to-one basis assured understanding relationships. Soon the Indonesian Christian women were bringing the prisoners supplemental food and clothing and materials for making products which the visitor then could market to provide a little additional income to the prisoner's family. Upon request, arrangements were made for worship services in the cells, resulting in some new life happenings and renewal within the Church itself.

Similarly, grants were made for a ministry to families of political prisoners in South Africa where often a young black man paid for his struggle for racial freedom by being kept incommunicado for months and even years.

In the wake of the overthrow of the Allende government in Chile, thousands of persons were put into jails and prison camps. An unusual proportion of them were women. At great personal risk, the exiled widow of the assassinated president, Hortensia Allende, became an effective international advocate for them. CWU was asked by her sponsoring committee in the United States to arrange a meeting in the InterChurch Center in New York for persons in the vicinity. Her purpose was to get petitions signed by several million women from scores of countries to press for the release of women held solely because they were accused of some relationship to the former regime. Her presentation also engendered concern and understanding for the continuing repressive situation continuing in Chile.

In the spring of 1974, a telephone call from two units of CWU in the greater Miami area alerted us to the dire situation of some 900 Haitian men and women who had come to this country to seek asylum and protection from the Haiti dictatorship headed by Jean-Claude Duvalier. Some had arrived by open boat without permits and were in Dade County Jail. Practically speaking, all were excluded from any employment covered under Social Security and there was a limited amount of menial work available. The daily food ration required in the Haitian Refugee Center cost more money than they had been able to raise locally.

The national office sent CWU in Dade County on behalf of their sisters in other states several thousand dollars for emergency food. Sister Luke Tobin, together with several men representing various denominations flew to Florida to visit the Haitians in the jail and returned to the nation's capital to apprise the appropriate government officers of the predicament which oppressed black persons found in coming to the 'land of the free!'

In 1974 and 1975, Church Women United were continually alerted to arrests and hasty trials of those who were speaking in opposition to the repressive measures of President Park Chung Hee. The concern for human rights in Korea reached a critical point when in April 1975 eight men accused of being Communists were summarily executed following a secret trial. Korean Church leaders, believing that the charges against the accused men had been fabricated, sought an open trial. Led by their president, Oh Chung Lee, Church Women United in Korea was on the forefront of the efforts to insure basic human rights. Whenever Oh Chung Lee was taken into custody for questioning, a telegram was sent from our national office directly to the Korean government making inquiry as to her welfare.

A call went out from the national president to CWU units in cities where there were Korean Consulates, asking them to cooperate in plans for services to be held in front of the Consulates. The liturgy used at the services was entitled, "That Scaffold Sways the Future." It included excerpts from documents on the human rights situation, a litany, and a prayer of a Korean mother whose son was in prison.

Cora Sparrowk, then president of the CWU in Northern California-Nevada, who had been on the Causeway, wrote of the meaning of this experience for her:

> The service was held yesterday at noon in front of the Korean Consulate. Two Korean ministers participated in the service and several students. I was asked to read the "Mother's Prayer," which I did. I found this to be a very moving experience and could not help but think as I shared in this way of our two dear friends in South Korea.
>
> This was a 'first' for me to participate in such a protest, and while I had counted on attending, it was something else to be asked to speak. There was a deep soul searching as I asked myself, "What does it mean to stand beside people?" and "What does it mean to really become involved in another's struggle?" I thought of

those days when I roomed with Mrs. Yun in Japan and what a beautiful Christian she is. Our lives became strangely interwoven with the women of Asia on the Causeway. It was a life- changing experience.

On March 1, a day of special significance in Korea's struggle for independence from Japan, Miss Lee read a statement at an ecumenical service in the Roman Catholic Cathedral in Seoul. It was called, 'A Patriotic Declaration of Democracy' and was signed by a number of leading Christians. Miss Lee was taken into custody immediately after the service and interrogated for several days and nights. In the days that followed, other signers of the Declaration and opposition political leaders were arrested. In May all received sentences from seven to fifteen years. In the case of Miss Lee, the sentence was suspended.

Joy and Peace

. . . in peacemaking

THE VIETNAM AREA As long as any of us can remember, American church women have been officially calling, "Peace! Peace!" Yet for them there has been no peace. During their lifetimes the nation has been almost constantly involved in military conflict, albeit not always with clearcut declaration. American involvement in Southeast Asia dominated our concern for over 20 years.

The United States had grown rapidly to its position as a big power which in itself made her actions vulnerable and her critics many. American capital developed its own opportunities to the mutual advantage of many areas of the world where there were underdeveloped natural resources. Multinational corporations expanded without an appropriate international body of control. For the sake of national defense, military bases were maintained all over the world. This called for special treaties and large payments for the use of the land to other governments, some of which were repressive in their internal policy and practice, thus giving the impression of American alignment with non-democratic forces.

The Cold War, a descriptive term of the power struggle between the western nations and the Communist bloc, reached worldwide proportions. As colonies and territories won their independence, internal divisions and power struggles broke out on their way to becoming unified nations. All of these factors had some bearing on the long American involvement in Vietnam.

For almost a century the peoples of this area had been governed by France. After World War I, nationalist movements rose and gained strength during the Japanese occupation until the end of World War II. The efforts of the French to regain colonial power and of the Americans in following decades to keep the area from "falling to the communists" were to prove tragic and costly failures.

The refinements of guerilla tactics and of technological warfare served but to raise the toll of human suffering. "Destroy to save" was more than a slip of military tongue in a time when words and values were confused and debased. The commitment of American troops for combat duty in Southeast Asia in 1964 brought the reality of war into the heartland of American communities without any unified conviction among the people. Millions were to die and millions of others to return disillusioned to a baffling new problem of livelihood before there began the groundswell to end the hostilities.

It is no wonder that during the decade from 1966 to 1976 the word "peace" became too tired and complicated a term around which church women could rally. But the question remains: What did the advocates of peace do during this decade? What motivation made them keep on trying to be heard? I asked these questions of one of the most valiant church women of our times—Sister Mary Luke Tobin. She agreed to write down the sequence of her experience as a peace advocate during the Vietnamese struggle. I urged her to include all the channels which she used. One was through her own religious community, the Sisters of Loretto, which she has headed for years, and through the Leadership Conference of Women Religious, of which she was president. She was also identified in the activities of Clergy and Laity Concerned, a group of Christian men and women who already had come to a clear position on this issue and therefore were ready to act. Because of Sister Luke's prominence, she was frequently the woman chosen to join their advocacy teams.

Sister Luke was also involved in Church Women United—as a member and officer of the National Board and later as staff Director of Citizen Action. In all of these roles she acted out the courage of her convictions, but also wisely recognized that others might carry different roles. Her leadership as an advocate of peace will be recognized by those who read her simple record:

THE CHRONICLE OF   A number of influences helped to shape
SISTER LUKE TOBIN   my consciousness about the war/peace
1964-1975   issue and to lead me to peace-advocacy.

One cannot seriously reflect on the Gospels without being convinced of Jesus' call to peace-making and to love, to non-violence and to justice for the oppressed. That realization is one that grew in me.

The Second Vatican Council, in which I participated in 1964 and 1965, spoke out in opposition to nuclear arms. One of the questions dealt with by the Council's Commission on the Church in the Modern World, on which I served, was the problem of war and nuclear weaponry. The pastoral constitution which that commission drew up took a strong stand against the arms race and urged the total banning of war: "The arms race is an utterly treacherous trap for humanity, and one which injures the poor to an intolerable degree. It is much to be feared that if this race persists, it will eventually spawn all the lethal ruin whose path it is now making ready . . . It is our clear duty, then, to strain every muscle as we work for the time when all war can be completely outlawed by international consent." (Sections 81, 82)

After the Council, back in the United States, I became gradually more sensitive to the war and to the military buildup question. As early as 1967, my community, the Sisters of Loretto, made a strong declaration of opposition to the escalating war in Vietnam, appealing to the U.S. government to negotiate at once to end it. This stance against the war was reiterated by the Loretto community's general assembly (legislative body) in the succeeding years. (Examples: In August, 1971, the assembly passed a resolution to request that President Nixon stop all U.S. military involvement in Southeast Asia by December 31, 1971, and withdraw support from the Saigon government. This call for withdrawal was repeated in August, 1972, when assembly delegates also condemned the continued bombing of Vietnam.) With my community's consistent stand for peace and with their voices raised in dissent against U.S. policy in Vietnam, I felt an increasing responsibility, in the late

1960's and into the 1970's, to speak out in opposition to the war and to engage in the anti-war activities.

Another influence that raised my consciousness in the late 1960's was the thought and work of the Christian poet-mystic, Thomas Merton, who strongly opposed the Vietnamese war, even with the result of alienating some of his followers. The urgency of taking a position against the escalating war compelled persons such as Merton, Daniel Berrigan, and others to turn from their art and the pursuit of the inner life to engagement in the harsh task of confronting the war-making establishment. There was no stopping one's ears to their compelling words.

One reason for my initial attraction to Church Women United (with whom I first became associated in the late 1960's) was that CWU took courageous stands in facing social justice issues. This was certainly true of the race question and also true of the war/peace issue.

At my first meeting as a member of the Board of Managers in Atlanta in November 1967, the Board was asked to endorse the Jeanette Rankin Brigade which called for women from all over the country to assemble in Washington to appeal for a cessation of hostilities in Vietnam. The organizing committee had chosen to rally around the name of Jeanette Rankin, a Republican representative from Montana during two separate terms. She voted against the declaration of war against Germany in 1917, and was the only member of the House to vote against the declaration of war against Japan in 1941.

The debate on the floor of the Board was not so much on the intention of the proposal as to the advisability of CWU endorsing this particular means. The ambivalent position resulted in a tie vote. The president, Dorothy Dolbey, appointed a committee to work out a statement that might be more generally satisfactory. Later, the Board voted unanimously to inform its state units of the plans and purposes of the Brigade with the understanding that individuals would respond as their consciences dictated.

A delegation headed by 85 year old Jeanette Rankin ascended the steps (several thousand women did gather on the Capitol steps in Washington, D.C.) to deliver their message to the congressional leaders. Although somewhat disappointed by their reception, the leaders had arranged for a friendly Congressman to call to the attention of the Congress that women were waiting on the steps outside to address their grievances to the elected representatives and he requested that their statement be printed into the Congressional Record.

In January, 1969, for example, CWU urged President Nixon to pursue negotiations to end the Vietnamese war, based on "the widest possible representation by the parties involved." CWU also urged no further use of napalm anti-personnel and defoliation bombs, and stated that as American women they were willing to accept any "loss of face" as "the price of peace."

In 1969 also the CWU Board of Managers opposed the anti-ballistic missile system; opposed further testing of the MIRV; urged the creation of a U.S. Department of Peace and a Joint Committee on Peace and Cooperation in the Congress; and urged the ratification of the nonproliferation and nuclear weapons treaty and a comprehensive test ban treaty.

In 1970, I became chairperson for citizen action of the CWU board. That related me directly to work on social justice issues undertaken by the CWU staff. This connection reinforced my conviction the CWU was willing to take the kinds of positions that indicated their commitment and willingness to risk, to take the "cutting edge" position even if this meant "losing face."

It was in 1970 that I was initially involved in formal anti-war activities. From July 5 to July 13 of that year, I was in Saigon as a member of a fact-finding team, sponsored by the Fellowship of Reconciliation, whose search was to determine if peace initiatives existed in South Vietnam and, if they did, how they were expressed. From visits with many persons—lawyers, professors, farmers, publishers, groups of women, students, social workers, Buddhist monks, Catholic priests, etc.—we learned that while many peace desires existed, attempts to express them resulted in severe repression and sometimes imprisonment and torture. I was very moved by our conversations with the "grass-roots" Vietnamese people—including women whose husbands or sons had been imprisoned, students still bearing the scars from torture they had endured, and Taoist monks at a floating "peace monastery," where they prayed for peace at least six hours a day and where many conscientious objectors lived.

Our little group, joined by many Vietnamese students, walked to the American Embassy to present a petition stating our objection to U.S. support for the repressive Thieu government—a peaceful and non-violent march. However, we were teargassed by the police, and about 30 students were arrested. When we returned to the U.S., we met in Washington to speak with several Congresspersons about our findings.

The Saigon experience, with its first-hand contact with people so immediately affected by the war and by a repressive U.S.-supported government, continued to sharpen and clarify my efforts to work for peace. Many of these efforts were undertaken in conjunction with the Catholic Peace Fellowship, which I had represented on the Saigon mission, and with the Fellowship of Reconciliation and Clergy and Laity Concerned, on whose national boards I served for several years.

In March, 1971, I participated in the Citizens' Conference on Ending the War in Indochina, which convened in Paris for six days, and which included meetings with leaders from North Vietnam, and with delegates from Saigon, the U.S., Cambodia and Laos. This conference, organized by the American Friends Service Committee, Clergy and Laity Concerned, and the Fellowship of Reconciliation, was aimed at preparing concerned people (about 165 attended) from all parts of the U.S. to be more effective in creating support in their own communities for the necessary steps to make peace a reality. Both this meeting and my Saigon trip became the focus of many speaking engagements and interviews after I returned, in all of which I urged others to continue to work for ending the war.

Church Women United, through its board of managers, meeting in Wichita, Kansas, in April, 1971, adopted a statement of "Concern for our Continuing Involvement in Indochina." Excerpts from this resolution illustrate CWU's steady stand against the Vietnam conflict and determination to heal the wounds of war:

As Christians, we are called to love all humankind. We must share the guilt for the killing and suffering of people, and for the destruction and defoliation of their lands which have been inflicted by our nation . . . We acknowledge the fact of American atrocities . . . We know that any death perpetrated by violence anywhere in the world diminishes us and our families. We cannot accept the system of Vietnamization which substitutes Asian casualties for American and provides people with weapons to kill their own countrymen and women . . . We bear the burden of what this war has done in making one-third of the Vietnamese people refugees, in destroying their homes and hamlets, and in breaking down family life. We are horrified at the billions being spent for death, so urgently needed for causes that enhance life . . . Because we value life, we believe a military solution to this war is neither possible nor desirable . . . We call upon church women at once through every means available to them to persuade our government to end this war through complete and total United States withdrawal by December 31, 1971, and to engage in those means that will assist citizens in Indochina to build a real peace.'

It was at that Wichita Ecumenical Assembly that Church Women United first met Sister To Thi Anh, a Catholic sister from Vietnam who spoke with quiet conviction of her people's strong desire for peace: 'For our part, we choose life . . . Everyone who is killed is someone's beloved.' Anh's association with CWU, her beautiful embodiment of the unity of East and West, continued to be an eloquent call to peacemaking in Vietnam.

I remember well a church woman standing in the sunlight at our peace demonstration in Wichita, with the television cameras playing the crowd. I heard her say, "This is my first peace demonstration. I'm here because I believe in this. But I hope the folks back home don't see me on TV!" That statement perhaps spells out the courage and the commitment of many church women as they moved toward a stronger stand against the war.

My work for peace sometimes involved direct actions that resulted in being "detained" by authorities. In November, 1971, I was among a group of Clergy and Laity Concerned (including Harvey Cox and the Rev. David Hunter) who went to the Air Force Academy in Colorado Springs to participate in a silent witness of concern over the mounting deaths in the air war over Indochina. We were detained by military authorities for distributing—to air cadets and others attending a Sunday Chapel service—leaflets containing an order of worship which focused on prayers and Biblical readings on peace. The group hoped that its action would raise the consciousness of military personnel and other citizens about the horror of the bombing deaths in Indochina.

In January, 1972, as a prelude to a four-day international, inter-religious peace conference in Kansas City, CWU held a two-day peace-building workshop, January 12-13. Women from other countries, and from the Jewish, Buddhist, Muslim, and Christian faiths, gathered for this, united by our desire for peace and our commitment to work for the cessation of military hostilities in all countries. At this workshop, the U.S. participants pledged themselves to continue working for U.S. disengagement in Southeast Asia, to boycott products of war-related industries, and to encourage programs of peace education. Sister To Thi Anh was again with Church Women United on that occasion.

At the larger "Ecumenical Witness" following the CWU peace-building workshop, I was with many members of the national and international religious community, all concerned with witnessing against the immorality of the Vietnamese war. At that conference, I chaired a session on organizing peace centers.

In April, 1972, I went again to Paris as one of a small group of Americans who met with a delegation of North Vietnamese to explore the possibilities for peace negotiations. This mission, sponsored by the People's Coalition for Justice and Peace, a network of anti-war groups, occurred after the Paris peace talks had been officially discontinued by the U.S. government. Its purpose was to help re-open and to keep open the lines of communication, at least informally. We met with groups from the North, with Madame Nguyen Thi Binh's group, the Provisional Revolutionary Government, from the South, and with some neutral groups (Catholics, Buddhists, others opposed to the Thieu regime). All were eager for war's end and for self-determination for the Vietnamese people. I felt that this unofficial exchange with the Vietnamese delegates reassured them that indeed there were people in the U.S. who were pushing for the cessation of hostilities. Also, our reporting about it when we came home was one more effort by the U.S. peace movement to urge the American public to protest the war.

One way in which peace advocacy was exercised during the Vietnamese era was through challenging the war-connected activities of major corporations who held military contracts. A number of church-related groups, through stockholders' proposals presented at annual corporation meetings, tried to raise the consciousness of other stockholders and of the public about the complicity of big business in the destruction of Vietnam. Several times I was involved in visiting company executives in an attempt to dialogue with them about their military production. In late April, 1972, with Dr. Robert McAfee Brown, Rabbi Balfour Brickner, and Roman Catholic Bishop Walter J. Schoenherr, I led a prayer service at the Honeywell, Inc. stockholders' meeting in St. Paul/Minneapolis. Honeywell was involved in producing anti-personnel weapons for use in Vietnam. We felt that silence about this was betrayal, and tried to convince such corporations, through visits, leaflets, and stockholder pressure, that they should cease their military production.

Another important phase of peace advocacy was, of course, the efforts to lobby Congresspeople and other government officials to push for an end to the Vietnamese conflict. I participated in such activities on several occasions. During the spring of 1972 a concerted move was launched to have religious leaders join in continuing visits to Congressional offices, urging that funds for the war be cut off.

As part of this organized drive by Clergy and Laity Concerned to spur on Senate-House action, over 100 religious leaders were lobbying the Hill one May day in 1972. When informed that there would be no anti-war legislation until after Nixon's visit to Moscow, we gathered in the Capitol rotunda for a prayer service. Rabbi Abraham Heschel, Dr. Robert McAfee Brown, Dr. William Sloan Coffin, and I were leading these prayers for peace. When our group continued to remain in the rotunda, we were arrested and spent the night in a Washington jail.

The link between the Vietnamese sister, Sister To Thi Anh, and Church Women United was further strengthened in late spring/early summer of 1972, when CWU and the Leadership Conference of Women Religious jointly sponsored a speaking tour in which Anh met with many inter-faith and women's groups across the country. As chairperson of the LCWR's Justice and Peace Commission, and because of my CWU role, I coordinated the arrangements for this endeavor with Virginia Baron, staff citizen action director. Anh's message was always the beautiful one of seeking peace for Vietnam, and the unity of different religions in desiring that peace. She herself seemed an integral embodiment of deep faith and peace.

When Anh returned to Vietnam in late summer, 1972, having completed her doctoral studies in the U.S., she opened the House of Peace, a center for reconciliation in Saigon, the purpose of which is "to promote the capacity of cooperation among people." Church Women United helped purchase and furnish this lovely oasis for peace and strength, where many war-worn Saigon women went for thinking, meditating, and getting in touch with themselves. Later, just after the Paris peace agreement was signed early in 1973, CWU saw the House of Peace as a concrete way to help with the reconstruction of Vietnam. A special collection at the World Day of Prayer that spring went to Anh's project as one way of giving church women an early opportunity to share in the reconciliation and rebuilding after the war.

The week end of October 6-9, 1972, an international Assembly of Christians in Solidarity with the Peoples of Vietnam, Laos, and Cambodia convened in Quebec. This was an opportunity especially to learn first-hand about religious conditions in North Vietnam. Several Catholic priests from the North assured the participants that religious freedom existed in North Vietnam and that several priests were ordained each year. The priests described their journey to the assembly: 'We have come half way around the globe. But the hardest part of our long trip is some hundred miles from our diocese to the frontiers of our country. We had to drive by night over craters newly created by bombs. We had to cross rivers by means of pontoons since bridges as well as highways were seriously damaged by U.S. bombs.'

I was very much impressed at that conference by Madame Masie Bui Thi Cam, a lawyer and member of the North Vietnamese general assembly. A beautiful and very knowledgable woman, she spoke regretfully of the way in which Vietnamese children were now being trained to violence because of the continuing war. "Children who have been taught to kill," she said, "need a completely new education for appreciating life's values." At this gathering, Madame Cam was interviewed on videotape by president Clarie Collins Harvey.

In January, 1973, just before I began my work as director of citizen action on the CWU staff, I went again to Europe on a peace pilgrimage to officials of various European churches. The small (six members) ecumenical group, organized by Harvey Cox, urged the church leaders to exercise their moral and religious leadership to bring the Indochina war to an end. Our delegation, which included Methodist Bishop James Armstrong, Episcopal Bishop Robert De Witt, Dr. Robert McAfee Brown, Rabbi Leonard Beerman, and Harvey Cox (I was the only woman), visited church leaders in Holland, Germany, and England, and met with the Pontifical Commission on Justice and Peace at the Vatican. We took with us a letter of Pope Paul, part of which read: 'We realize that a word of love spoken on behalf of the Vietnamese will necessarily be a word of judgment spoken against our own nation, and yet we ask for that word of love and judgment, for here the pastoral and prophetic roles coincide.'

Our letter to the Pope urged him to visit Vietnam and report to the world about the war and 'the devastation we have wrought.' Asking him to condemn the stepped-up bombing of Hanoi at Christmas tide 1973, we implored, 'If you do not do so, we feel that our leaders will continue to destroy both the lives of the Vietnamese people and the moral conscience of the American people.'

Work for peace did not, could not stop with the signing of the Paris peace agreement in late January, 1973. One of the issues which especially surfaced during the aftermath of the war was that of amnesty. Church Women United organized a task force on the question. In my work as director of citizen action, I included information on amnesty in our news-briefs and alerts sent to citizen action chairpersons.

In the spring of 1975, CWU sponsored a Christian Causeway to Asia in which 40 American women crossed the Pacific to meet and talk with their Asian sisters from various countries. Their conversations concerned the problems of injustice and violence and explored the possibilities of new patterns of international living. I was very moved by this experience especially by our observing the World Day of Prayer at Hiroshima and our participating in the Peace Consultation held at the foot of Mt. Fuji. The Causeway was a concrete example of the ability of women of different languages and cultures to work together for peace. However, it became clear that the Asian women from all the countries we visited had one urgent message for us Americans: 'Ask your government to stop supporting the repressive regimes of Asia—Indonesia, Korea, and the Phillippines.'

In January, 1975, I was among 36 religious leaders who issued a 'Pastoral Letter to the Religious Communities of the United States,' calling on the U.S. government to live up to its pledged word made at the Paris peace agreement two years earlier, and to cease its current military presence in Vietnam. At that time, American bombs were still being dropped from American planes on Vietnamese targets, and the U.S. was giving massive military aid to the Thieu regime. We objected to these violations of the peace agreement. To enlist support for a wider protest, we urged American Christians and Jews to attend the Assembly to Save the Peace Agreement later that month in Washington, D.C.

CWU established its own group to deal with the aftermath of the war when, in April, 1975, the Board of Managers set up the Committee on Swords to Ploughshares. Its stated purposes include exploring the root causes of armed conflict today, encouraging women to take part in peace-building action, and providing information on U.S. military spending and U.S. foreign trade and aid policies.

One of my most recent peace-advocacy projects has been co-authoring—with Michael McIntyre and Hazel T. Johns—the book *Peaceworld* (Friendship Press, 1976), in which I treat violence, non-violence and values.

The subject matter of that book is perhaps an indication of the vast area that is peace advocacy. While it is true that some of the "high" points of my own peace-advocacy work occurred during the thick of the Vietnam era, and while peace missions abroad, anti-war witnesses, and contacts with other peace activists made up the bulk of that work, it is also true that the place for peace efforts is in the ongoing building of a human community that holds the promise of liberation for all peoples. It is in this building that I feel CWU, with the strength of its leadership and the richness of its ecumenical dimensions, has played and will continue to play a significant role.

As was stated in one of the papers at the Quebec International Assembly of Christians in October, 1972: "The Gospel cannot be neutral. We are convinced that Christ is always present where men and women are struggling for justice. It is for this reason that we reaffirm that Christians must be artisans and conscious agents of Liberty.

> —*Sister Mary Luke Tobin*
> *March, 1976*

RECONCILIATION   In order to give full opportunity for
IN INDOCHINA   reconstruction to be based on the
                         judgment of those most concerned, in 1972
the World Council of Churches established the Fund for

Reconstruction and Reconciliation in Indochina. This Fund had its own board and its own bylaws. It was made up of fifteen people—five from Indochina, five from other Asian countries, and five from other countries around the world. The Fund received money from the churches throughout the world and from some neutral governments seeking ways to demonstrate concern without political involvement on the side of anyone of the parties to the conflicts still raging in all of the countries of Indochina. In four years more than nine million dollars was raised for work that involved Buddhist, Catholic, Protestant and representatives of the Indochina governments.

Church Women United and the International Committee for World Day of Prayer also channeled funds for relief and reconstruction in Indochina through this Fund.

In early February 1975 an unexpected opportunity was offered to CWU to name one of the Americans to a Consultation called by the board of the Fund for Reconstruction and Reconciliation in Indochina to be held in Vientiane, Laos, February 22-26, 1975. We were fortunate that Olive Tiller (Mrs. Carl), as chairperson of our standing committee on Intercontinental Mission, was able to get leave from her job and to depart on short notice. She needed no orientation for her life concerns had been one continual series of reconciling acts both in the struggle for racial justice and in informal conversations with women of Eastern Europe.

Enroute to Indochina, Olive stopped over for a visit with the Christian women of Burma, whose contribution to international conferences had been significant until the political situation prevented them from making outside contacts. She arrived on Valentine's Day—and was just the right symbol of love to impart the affection and esteem we have held in our hearts for them.

There were 30 people invited to the Consultation, 16 from all the countries of Indochina. Others came from America, Japan, Germany, Hong Kong, Thailand, New Zealand, Indonesia, India, the Netherlands, the United Kingdom, and the United Republic of the Cameroun.

The purpose of the Consultation was not to make resolutions or statements or even recommendations, but simply to talk, to hear each other, to learn and make suggestions to the Board of the Fund for further steps that might be taken to bring about reconstruction and reconciliation. All but one of the study papers had been prepared by Asians. It was felt important that those from outside the area should have some exposure to different parts of Indochina before the actual meeting, and a plan was made for teams to go to North Vietnam, South Vietnam, Laos and Cambodia.

Olive Tiller went to Cambodia with a team of five which included two other Americans—the Rev. Boyd Lowry, Director of Southern Asia and Operations Director, Church World Service; Dr. Robert McAfee Brown, Professor of Religious Studies, Stanford University; as well as the Rev. John Nakajima, Executive Secretary of the National Christian Council of Japan; and HansOtto Hahn of Germany, Director of Bread for the World.

Arriving back in the United States in time for the meeting of the Board of Managers in Kansas City on February 28, Olive was able to report to her sisters on the Board her first impressions. Her spirit moved all who heard her. Some of the sentences which were recorded may suggest to the reader why:

The team met for the first time the night before we left Bangkok for Phnom Penh. The program was set up by a South Vietnamese staff member of the Fund for Reconciliation. Although he made all the arrangements for Cambodia, he didn't want us to go in for he felt we would be in great danger. The news from Cambodia was very grim. The airport was under attack. The opposing forces—the Khmer Rouge—were getting closer.

We faced several questions such as: (1) What if one of us is injured? (2) What if the government falls while we are there and we are guests of the government? (3) What if the airport is captured while we are there? It is now the only means of getting in or out of the country. The river is closed off. All the roads are closed. There is no railroad. We didn't have answers, but we wanted to be aware of the possibilities. We formulated three purposes for our team:

1. To express solidarity not only with the Christians but all the people of Cambodia—the victims of war.
2. To experience the war ourselves and see what was happening to the people.
3. To seek some means of bringing about reconciliation.

The airport at Phnom Penh is almost like a fortress. There are barricades where the planes come in. When you get off the plane there are barricades about seven feet tall, a sort of zig-zag wall built of American gun cases stacked on top of each other and placed at an angle to each other to form a wall all the way around to give protection to disembarking passengers. Not too comforting. The rest of the airport, in fact the whole city is sandbagged. I've never seen so many sandbags.

We had an impressive reception and were treated like VIP's the whole time we were there. We were not viewed as representatives of a certain country, but rather as an international group of people of faith who had come with an intention of finding a way of bring about peace.

The chief effect of the war on the country is to have made a nation of refugees. Many of them are in camps around the fringes of the city, which is certainly the most vulnerable part of the area. It's where the rockets come daily. This is where the artillery fire comes and you can hear it any time of day or night. Near the airport there are tents, all around. In many of the Buddhist pagodas the refugees are now lodged. We were much impressed with the ministry that the Buddhist monks performed for these refugees. The camps seemed to be pretty well run. One of them in particular was actually a showplace. They have established craft projects and agricultural projects for the refugees for some self-help. There are well-run feeding programs. Schools have been established for the children. There's every effort to keep families together and there's evidence of beautiful family life. These are people who have not been wealthy people but they've had a good living on the land and the only thing they want is to get back to the land and resume the type of life they had known.

The hospitals are filled with both military and civilian victims of the war. The hospital I visited was in the heart of the city. There were many refugees in it. There were also many injured soldiers in it while we were there. A badly shot up soldier was brought in and carried right past us. It was not a pleasant sight, but it was something we felt we needed to know. They're not hospital rooms, there's just one big hospital room with mats on the floor.

I saw one young woman lying on a crude cot with a child of perhaps three or four sleeping beside her. She was covered except that her right arm was on top of the cover. I was the only woman in our group and I particularly related to the woman I saw in the refugee camps and in the hospitals. This particular young woman had a lovely face, and I could tell she was in some pain. I reached for her hand that was on top of the blanket— just to take her hand. We had no common language except the language of the heart. Instead of taking my hand, she pulled the cover down and instead of the left arm, there was only a bandage. The doctor who was taking us through the hospital didn't know the patient, but he saw her condition and he spoke to her and asked her if it was the result of the rockets and she said yes. This is just one of so many thousands.

At the official reception we were met by all the important government officials—the President, Prime Minister, Minister of Refugees and Community Development, Foreign Minister, Minister of Health. The ministers are young people. The average age of the Cabinet is thirty-four. The minister working with aid-giving agencies was our principal host.

It was significant, I think, that never once in any of our conversations with any of the government people was there any request for aid—for military aid or material aid of any kind. The only request was, Help us find peace.

And it was reiterated again and again that offers to negotiate had been extended to the enemy without any preconditions. They had made an offer in July, 1973 with some preconditions, and then restated in July, 1974 an offer any kind of talk with any person in the government and with no preconditions whatsoever.

I think that the leaders of this government wanted us to know that 1) they are very sensitive to the fact that the people who are suffering most are the innocent victims of all that's going on, and 2) the aid that's coming is only serving to prop up a falling government that can't possibly win . . . It seemed to me that they were hopeful that this impartial group might be helpful as a channel of unbiased communication.

—Olive Tiller
March, 1975

Olive Tiller became a prime communicator. Her home in Maryland was near enough to the Capital for her to make the rounds day after day through the Congressional office building in an effort to talk to the staff who briefed those who cast the votes on the floor. She talked with many members of Congress, including her own Congresswoman, Gladys Spellman, Paul McCloskey from California, Donald Fraser from Minnesota, Senator Hubert Humphrey from Minnesota and Senator Charles Percy from Illinois.

She also received a very friendly reception by staff members of the special subcommittee of the House Foreign Affairs Committee dealing with this special issue. Since the rules did not permit public testimony at the Committee meeting, she was urged to prepare a written statement describing the experience of her group, what they had done, and her own conclusions on the situation. The statement was submitted and entered into the written record of the Committee. When it came to faithful follow-up, no wonder that Olive Tiller was rated by her male colleagues as TOPS!

In the New York Times of December 4, 1976, Richard Hughes, who spent eight years in South Vietnam founding and running hostels for street children under the Shoeshine Boys

Project, writes of his Christmas dinner in 1975 with an official of the new national Government. During the course of the meal, Hughes expressed concern for the future of these home-less children. The official broke into the conversation: "If you love them, you can do everything. Without it, you can do nothing."

I was reminded that upon their return from Vietnam, our Causeway team had spoken of the joy and peace pervading those hostels of boys who had never known a home. CWU had sent an unsolicited gift to the project by way of saying thank you for the hospitality.

Then my eyes fell on another paragraph and my heart responded to these words:

> *"I owe the people of Vietnam so much. They have reordered my life by teaching me simplicity, brother-hood, how to touch, and a reason for carrying on . . ." As hand touches hand . . . just because . . . .*

VIETNAM ERA WOMEN   One day in the fall of 1973, Richard Killmer, staff director of the NCCC department dealing with special ministries to war veterans and draft resisters, dropped in to explore the possibility of a jointly sponsored consultation of women involved in the Vietnam war.

When I asked how big a problem it was, he pulled out an amazing set of statistics: 91,000 women war veterans, 6 million wives and mothers who have been directly affected either due to men missing in action, killed, wounded, or in serious postwar adjustments. He proposed a small conference of wives of veterans in the middle west. He agreed that among them there would be women who were black, Chicano, American Indian and white. He readily agreed that in the planning and follow up Virginia Baron, then on the staff of CWU, should be completely involved.

Virginia was just the person. Sizing up the twenty-four women who gathered in Chicago, January 13-14, 1974, she sensed their initial mistrust of each other and of the sponsors but she saw the signs of their growing appreciation of both during the meeting. They had come together from a wide spectrum of educational and cultural backgrounds, but common problems are implied in the following sentences that Virginia recorded from statements made by women present:

> I may not have engaged in hand-to-hand combat but I feel like a vet, too. We never had any counseling about our problems when he came back from Korea or Vietnam. I never did understand why we had problems because I was doing my best.

> Can I just let him drown or do I have to keep trying to hold him up? I don't want to feel guilty, but I can't carry the burden alone. He has to hold his end up, too.

> His family didn't like it when he said the medals were bullshit, that he didn't do anything positive as far as his values were concerned and that the war shouldn't have been fought. His biggest hassle was his mother—she didn't want to hear how bad it was in Vietnam.

> My cousin is a vet. He's from the island (Puerto Rico) and he doesn't speak English. How do you think he feels fighting for a country that isn't even his own and they don't bother to translate anything into Spanish?

Before they left Chicago they formed themselves into the Network of Vietnam Era Women and vowed to keep in touch with each other and to work toward some services for the vast number of women like themselves. They couldn't quite get their idea off the ground; their problems were too 'daily'; their means too little; their future too uncertain; their homes and livelihood too mobile.

CWU felt their story, and the lessons we all should learn from them, were too valuable to lose. With some funds coming from American Lutheran Women and the NCCC, we urged Virginia Baron to spend a year in traveling among them and to use her skill for sensitive writing to let the story be known. Articles were printed in *The Christian Century, The Church Woman* and other journals. *The Stars and Stripes,* a veterans biweekly publication carried a series of reports. Her forthcoming book, *Women in the Wake of War,* offers documentation of this particular era of women's history.

As we might expect, Virginia Baron White offered her own spontaneous and sensitive ministry while she gathered material for her book as this quote I found in the newsletter of the Gold Star Wives of America will testify:

> You just don't know what you missed by not attending the meeting with Virginia White of Church Women United. What a delightful, warm and caring person she is. Although I was hesitant when communicating with her via the mails, I am so glad it was decided to hear her out. We may never have met this newly found friend who really cares how we think and feel. It took her four hours to drive here and the meeting didn't break up for almost five hours. A small group, but so much was said and I guess we all really let our hair down. What a relief to be able to talk without fear of offending someone or feeling that protective, transparent shield most "civilians" wrap themselves in when we mention our husbands or widowhood.

I asked Virginia to write down what her listening and learning had meant. Her answer implies something of the cost to women of the Vietnam Era:

> For almost a year I traveled around the country, to cities, towns, suburbs, rural areas, Indian reservations, veterans' hospitals, military bases, to talk with women, and some men, about the way the war in Southeast Asia affected their lives and the lives of their families. I have talked to the wives and mothers of men who are Vietnam veterans, deserters, recipients of 'other than honorable' discharges, resisters within the military, incarcerated veterans, physically and/or psychologically disabled veterans, released prisoners of war, and women related to veterans who never came home, those who were killed inaction or whose status remains 'missing in action.'

I have talked to wives and mothers of men who were conscientious objectors, draft-resisters, draft-evaders, those who served prison sentences for resisting and those who are living outside the country as political exiles. I have talked to an abandoned Vietnamese war bride of an American serviceman, Vietnamese women whose lives are now devoted to locating and recovering custody of their own children who were evacuated to the United States as part of 'Operation Baby Lift'—and were adopted by American families. I have talked to women veterans, including a nurse who built her own hospital in a peanut field in CuChi and another nurse who was courtmartialed for her anti-war activities while on active duty. I have talked to a Gold Star mother whose son was killed in 1968 and whose step-son left for Canada in 1969 as a draft resister.

I have been welcomed into some women's homes and lives, and I have had to talk my way, cajoling, persuading, even nagging, to convince other women to meet me. The name of Church Women United has been my banner. I have used it to open doors in some cases. In others, my credibility arose from my having written several columns which appeared in *Stars and Stripes,* the national veterans' newspaper.

I have learned to listen, too, and I have become more sensitive to the feelings of people whose lives are rooted in philosophical and ideological convictions worlds apart from mine. I have become more aware of some of the deepest themes of life, including the ambivalences and contradictions that are characteristic elements of all our lives.

As a result of my conversations, I have grown more eager to discover, and nourish the *links* between human beings, to concentrate on developing those possibilities in spite of the vast differences that must exist between individuals and groups (in a complex society). In a midwestern suburban community, I talked to the mother of a draft resister whose much publicized case caused his family emotional, financial and social hardship. Across town, I met the mother of two sons who served in the marines in Vietnam, one of whom was wounded. The first mother said her friends of twenty years had dropped her, one by one. The second said her friends didn't want to talk about the war or be reminded of it since none of their sons had gone into the service. For both, there was an overwhelming feeling of loneliness and isolation. They represented the two opposite political poles of the longest war in U.S. history which may have left families even more splintered and damaged than the Civil War.

I have learned how much people feel deserted by one another. Perhaps that is why almost every woman thanked *me* after it was *she* who had given *her* time and related *her* experiences and feelings to me. The women were grateful to be asked the questions. It was a sign that someone cared.

I have learned how very much there is to do—to bind up souls, not only wounds, in order to build a moral unity in the nation, to rededicate our energies to bring about justice in areas where we have failed. As an Asian-American mother of a Vietnam veteran said to me, 'It is not communism that will, in the end, destroy this country, but racism.' I learned how much there is still to learn about the consequences of our military policies, about the price that must be paid by nations full of victims, the 'little people' of the planet.

But mostly I have learned about the indomitability of the human spirit that is able to overcome obstacles, to rise up over unspeakable pain and hardship, to push its way through, like the tough and fragile wildflowers that each spring break through the hard earth, to signal hope to anyone who is there to see.

—Virginia Baron
November 1976

FOOTNOTES TO CHAPTER 11

1. During the two years following the 1974 Assembly, well over $100,000 designated for the Hunger Fund was voluntarily sent to the national office. By agreement with the Intercontinental Mission Committee, this entire amount was transmitted through recognized agencies for foodstuffs in areas of need. The actual listing of those who benefitted from the Hunger Fund and the agencies which served them was periodically reported through the pages of *The Church Woman.*

2. WICS (Women in Community Service, Inc. in 1965) remained the community service most generally participated in by CWU. Its record during this period is included in the story of its beginning on pp.

3. Grants from the Lilly Foundation made possible the Workshop on Adult Indian Education and the Private Sector; two Workshops on Health Delivery Services; two Workshops on Women and Prisons; as well as the documentary films RELEASE and IT'S ALL US.

4. The Washington Post editorial of April 18, 1970, sensed this unusual spirit:

CHURCH WOMEN AND THE WORLD

Without a lot of noise a group of 100 women has been meeting in Washington this week to pull together their power and ideas. Church Women United, a two million member arm of the National Council of Churches, believes that religion must do battle not so much with the devil and the flesh, but with what St. Paul called "the world rulers of darkness," among whom the ladies would indeed include power-obsessed bureaucrats and politicians, impassive businessmen, the indifferent average citizen. This conglomerate, or some combination of it, is often the cause for social change being so slow, the reason why so many millions are kept poor, powerless and ignored. Or so the leaders of Church Women United believe. Their conviction is that religion must confront this enemy, or else be swept into irrelevancy.

In taking this course, the group is getting involved in a struggle that will be long, slow and often without immediate results. But this is what going into the secular city means: not becoming radicalized but becoming informed—in this case, informed about the ways of using politics, social agencies, churches, businesses in defending the helpless and powerless.

Church laymen are notorious for taking up the popular "cause" of the day—last year hunger was big, this year a theology of ecology is already being talked up. Next year, it will be something else. "This may give the activists good feelings for a moment," says Abigail McCarthy, an officer of Church Women United, "but what is really accomplished after the excitement fades?" Nothing, usually.

The hundred women leaders meeting here this week will return to their home regions and churches and attempt to re-activate the local group. This is the solid work of reforming society—learning how to penetrate and use local power—being as kind as doves but as wise as serpents, to use the expression of Jesus. If some Christian churches have become increasingly irrelevant as a practical force to deal with real problems—and many believe they have—it is largely because in keeping their eye on the next world they have ignored this world. Church Women United is not only trying to correct this tactical error, it is teaching its members, through this week's leadership meeting, that once in the world, they had better know how to act and think as shrewdly as those powers St. Paul talked about. Otherwise, there are just more good feelings, not good results.

**Church Women United
1966 through 1975**

chapter 12

Far more than we can imagine

When I finished my graduate work in the heart of the Great Depression, I knew I would never find employment in the field of my choice. In 1933 even experienced college teachers were losing their jobs. So I welcomed a letter offering me a teaching job in the Beirut College for Women, then in its beginning stages.

This decision triggered another happening which was to give an upward bound to my life for the next twenty years. It began in a letter from Ruth Hyde of Memphis, Tennessee, a bedfast polio victim since her high school days. Having learned through a mutual friend of my going to Lebanon, she explained that she was the self-appointed president of an 'international company' of 8 or 10 workers in different countries. Her role was intercessory prayer; her working partners were to be her hands and feet in places she could not go in person.

In the years that followed I always looked forward to her letters and its 'company reports'. She had a rare sense of humor about her peers as well as a sense of divine resources of energy. Her letters always concluded with a statement of the 'company' policy which was really the benediction in the epistle to the Ephesians. Using a variety of translations she underlined different words each time, which always offered me current relevance. For instance:

> "<u>Now</u> unto him who by his <u>power within us</u>, is able to do <u>far more than we</u> ever dare to ask or <u>imagine</u>—to him be <u>glory in the church</u> through Christ <u>Jesus</u>. Amen"
> Ephesians 3:19-20 - (Phillips Translation)

Although Ruth Hyde died several years before the 1966-76 chapter in the life of Church Women United, the Ephesian benediction remained central to my working faith. All of us were submerged during this decade with the writing of the futurists, whose dire and wonder-filling predictions for the year 2000 were mind blowing. The results of actual explorations of both inner and outer space were beyond my conception of the universe as was true of many other earthlings who shared this planet.

The decade proved to be a tremendous test of the quality of our religious belief. Admittedly we had confined our faith to bit-size pieces which we could handle ourselves without embarassment in case God failed in bringing his will on earth. The writer of Ephesians was convinced that God's power, manifested in such a surprising degree in the Resurrection, could be internalized as a tremendous resource of human energy. The height and depth and breadth of our calling thus expands beyond imagining.

We were living in an era when the futurists were getting the headlines. Groups of scholars in every discipline were predicting what the world would be like by the year 2001. Modern technology would change many things—education, business management, energy and environment control, even the use of oceans and the outer space for mankind. Without moral values to control these developments dire disasters were predicted. The time table was perhaps the most overwhelming. 'Before your grandchild of 4 finishes high school' . . . or before you die a normal death of old age, life would be radically different. We felt we were on the rim of destruction or on tiptoe of a bright new age. Shirley Anderson, the headquarters chairman, said one day: "A third possibility is that we are about to go through a period of social and political anarchy." As it turned out, a little bit of all three were to be true by the end of the decade. The grandchild graduating from high school took it for granted. Her grandmother was getting used to it.

OPTIONS OF TOMORROW The Planning Committee for the 1971 Assembly decided to focus the thinking of church women toward the options of tomorrow. Under the leadership of Julia Piper and Mary Louise Rowand the program design looked at the implications of the breakthrough in technology for those with a faith that God had broken into history through Jesus Christ. It was decided to invite 30 women of various disciplines whose careers were future oriented to a consultation in November, 1969. A member of the Planning Committee, Edna McCallion, agreed to search for women of the calibre to be invited. She organized a set of questions which challenged their response when the invitations were sent out. Every one accepted, although illness kept a few away when the consultants gathered around the felt covered table at the Villa Cortona in Maryland. The Planning Committee, with pencils poised, sat nearby listening and learning.

Much was said in those two days. Particularly in some field of research there was a call for a "U" turn to allow our social responsibility to catch up with what was technologically possible. Yet in several fields the consultants alerted the church women to begin to shape their future.

The life style would change very rapidly. It was of crucial importance that "church women not fall into the trap of ineffectuality at the local level by agreeing on words and not on realities." There was need for a theology of hope. Often people are more available for thinking through options in times of polarization and alienation and therefore we must work for creative relationships with the community at large.

Children of tomorrow might have a brighter future since they would absorb more readily the new learning than their parents could re-learn. Housing patterns still allowing for the privacy of the nuclear family would be adapted to allow for a natural extended family. Thus all children would have a variety of adult relationship basics by the time they were ten under a new educational process. Children would consciously learn how to share in a global family and therefore should be taught at least five languages.

The natural gifts and resources of women would be fully used. Women could play an important role in conceiving of new images of themselves, of men and of children. They could do a lot of the 'nitty-gritty-difficult types of reorganization' of our technology as well as new social patterns and ways of thinking. The next 20 years are of special importance if we are to avoid social disaster. There was need for sharing deeper inner resources to enhance the quality of living and to enable people to live more helpfully with one another.

Many were unwilling to share in the birthpangs involved to bring forth something new in the midst of an era of anarchy, totalitarian repressions and chaotic confusion in the democracies. They somehow wanted the assurance of what the 'new baby' would be like before they were willing to deliver! Others, like Mary of old, pondered the image of a new era of righteousness in their hearts—in the hope that faithfulness to truth and justice will be used by God for the making of a new earth beyond the expectation of any of our present dreams.

FUTURE OF CWU ON THIRTIETH ANNIVERSARY　On the cover of the January, 1967 issue of *The Church Woman* is a photograph of a six year old black girl dressed in her perky Sunday best dress. Her foot is on a shovel as if she were turning the earth over for a cornerstone (which indeed she was) and her eyes were focused straight ahead. The caption read, "Dig in where you are with an eye on the goals ahead!" The Spirit of '67.

It was, also, the Spirit of 1971! The same little girl, now ten, stood beside her beloved cousin, Clarie Collins Harvey on the platform of the Ecumenical Assembly in Wichita. The newly elected president was about to give the keynote address opening the celebration of the 30th anniversary of Church Women United, calling the women to "dig in" at a crucial juncture in history:

One age is dying and another is being born. You and I are the in-between generation. Ours is an age that has struck its tents and is on the move . . . Ours is an age characterized by super-normal rates of change.

She knew full well that people were weary, confused, frustrated, depleted, empty, fearful. When there was a "night feeling" of the spirit, it was time to call on a spiritual heritage harbored in her heart: "When I fall on my knees with my face to the rising sun, Lord, have mercy, if you please." Clarie Harvey went on to say:

As the sunrise is the daily token of God's faithfulness, Church Women United will face the Rising Sun of our new day begun by becoming an organized opportunity to overcome fear with faith; by discovering in unity the wholeness of life; by serving as a channel for God's grace and the expression of Christ consciousness.

In a profound way, she was touching hands with her nine predecessors, for the national presidents had always kept their eyes on the goals ahead. The dreams which Clarie Collins Harvey expressed for the national movement consumed the time of the full executive committee as it met in historic Stony Point, New York. The national observance was planned for December. The executive committee wanted so much to talk person-to-person with all their counterparts in local communities so they decided to make a recording which reflected their own dreaming and planning. This record was mailed later to every local president, as a 30th anniversary greeting. One woman in the deep south wrote that she had sat up all night playing the record over and over again. Hope is generated when you live in the present with your eyes to the future!

The national celebration of the 30th anniversary took place in early December at the Women's Congressional Club in Washington, D.C., with the vice president, Abigail McCarthy, acting as hostess. There were one hundred women present, about half of whom were prominent persons in the national government community.

It being the Advent Season, the theme of the program was *Star the Dark.* On this day we wished to honor, and in a sense to symbolize, millions of creative women whose names we did not know, but whose endeavors still star the dark of suffering, of misunderstanding, and of want.

All but one of the national presidents were present. Their testimonies were a thrilling summary of the ways in which church women had worked together to "star the dark" in the last thirty years. Young women, all but one of whom was on the national board, responded to the message of each president with her dream for CWU in the next thirty years. Just because the future may go that way, let us make record here of some key sentences which expressed the hope within the young women of that time.

From Gabrielle Beard, Assistant Professor of Sociology of the University of Mississippi:

> There are women who are still separated from us and who are kept on the fringes of society by artificial boundaries. We are conscious now of new voices, new demands upon our concept of community, and we are witnessing a breakthrough as we are attempting to come to terms with the very complex, pluralistic society. We are listening to these new liberating voices and we must continue to do so until the boundaries become bonds of love . . .

> As church women we must dare to "Priest" to one another—to reach across national, racial, ethnic and class divisions. As we make steps—some tentative and some bold—toward the future, let us not attempt to do it alone. Survival requires that we reach out for the hand of one another and another and another . . . We can be grateful that life is so arranged that we need not move through days on a calendar but move through forces that link life and life . . . women to other women, and Stars in the Dark to even brighter stars.

From Helga Day, born in Germany, a graduate theology student:

In the 1940's, Germany brought on herself darkness and evil; she had been defeated, destroyed, separated. Into the midst of the spiritual and physical hunger and despair, came signs of love that went beyond expectation. Some of you came to our country then; money, food and clothing was sent as a sign of reconciliation across hostile boundaries to enable us to reenter the community of Christians and nations . . . There will be no peace without social justice and there is no justice as long as there are people in our midst who live at a disadvantage on the fringe of society.

From Sally Cunneen, A Roman Catholic editor:

If we are going to have further significant advances in the ecumenical sphere they will be non-official; they will be made by lay people, and it seems to me, most especially by women . . . Since we are the ones who will often hear voices in the particular situation we are in, we will have to serve as interpreters to those in our church bodies who will listen. Because we are all responding to the human aspirations of this one world in which we live, all of our activities will converge and will have spiritual significance . . . But, by our attempts to share in pain and to relieve some of the unfulfilled ambitions of men and women everywhere, we can share, also, in the great task of helping bring this world to the spiritual unity for which it was made.

From Helen Chupco, Director of an Indian Center in Oklahoma:

People do not really understand our Indian culture or our Indian ways. American Indian culture is unique in this nation today because it has endured almost five hundred years of exposure to the predominantly Euro-American culture and has resisted to some degree all the philosophic, social-economic pressures to conform to white middle class American standards. Today the American Indians find themselves in a society based on an economy calling for a highly competitive ability with ultimate goals being financial success and upward nobility . . . There is a great deal of frustration among our people. We, as American Indian women, are seeking a chance. We need an opportunity. This is a path that is still unfinished for the church women.

From Charlene Piper, a reading specialist in a Roman Catholic School and in the Public Schools of Parsons, Kansas:

Children and adults need a context in which they can more easily express deep emotional experiences. With whom does one do this? Well, with a family, of course, and maybe, occasionally, with friends. But with whom does one cry for Vietnam, for hungry children and for unjust action; and where does one go to express her own complicity in the acts that disturb her? Where does one express outrage, today? Where else but in the church or in a movement as significant as Church Women United? Where does one express joy and inspiration and in what context does she dream her dreams?

The future of Church Women United may depend on the capacity to welcome human emotion—share it, focus it and unleash it as a humanizing power in this world. Not many churches are equipped to accept, channel and heighten the longing for emotional expression that is beginning to soften our divided culture . . . Women are finding freedom to express this gift of emotion which in the past has been confined to the home. These sensitivities must invade the business and educational world. Please, God, may we put it all together?

From Virginia Baron, a writer from Chappaqua, New York:

The swords haven't turned into plowshares as we all know too well. We live in a world community where few plan, and many witness power and repression. People have forgotten that we are all part of the human family .. and that everything is interrelated.

At the United Nations there is a lot of talk about development. What I think is marvelous is that we have now begun to question who is developed, and we have come to realize that the important thing is that we all keep developing in whichever way. Action is the way that we come to new kinds of understanding, maybe new kinds of thinking and new kinds of doing in the world.

From Lilia Clemente, Director of Investment Research of a large foundation, born in the Philippines:

Instead of the omniscience we once hoped for from science and technology, we have wound up with a big sense of physical powerlessness and insurgency . . . We are searching for organizational philosophies within this country to meet the fractures that wound this nation today. Ultimately we shall have to extend our organizational thinking to a world view.

We must call for unfolders! Unfolders value the individual, the universal, the creative. They are self-reliant, highly integrated, democratic, in touch with themselves. In our society we are neglecting the development of the full human being. The result is a vast short-fall in terms of happiness, well-being and beauty. What we need is education for unfolding . . . housing for unfolding . . . institutions for unfolding.

There is no reason why such a society would not work or why Church Women United cannot survive if we believe in it enough. We would have to believe that learning is more than facts, that truth is more than measurement, that reality is more than things. We would have to feel that our abilities to fulfill our objectives in the full are the very heart of our continuity. The upward swing requires maintenance of our faith and the serious, yet challenging responsibility we have in the use of larger resources for our basic, larger programs . . . The horizon is happy and it is difficult to guess what is behind the clouds. Let us unfold and break through to the year 2001!

BecLee Wilson, who was a toddler in 1941, led the worship service which climaxed the celebration. She had listened to the expectations of her contemporaries. Women as priests to one another in a pluralistic society—visible signs across hostile boundaries—the rise of a global ecumenism stemming from human aspirations—a hospitable homing place to express the full range of human emotions—peace building with new kinds of thinking, new kinds of doing—a value system with church women as unfolders of the full human being in the whole society.

She lighted the "Christ-candle" in the center of the Advent wreath and, on behalf of all church women, made a commitment to follow the light of this "Day-Star on High" into all the years to come.

Church Women United was now well past the midpoint of her birth and the year 2001, about which the futurists talked so much. The tempo of life was reaching tornado proportion, sweeping the lives of many women into the debris of a mobile population. Would CWU congeal into a hardcore organization trying to save itself? Or would we live out our Spirit-driven faith beyond anything we could think or imagine?

For over thirty years church women have worked together across racial and denominational lines, glad for a friendly company with whom they could spend themselves in finding and doing the will of God.

From them I have learned of the ways and work of women in groups. Yet I was uneasy about these learnings as I thought of the future. Things were not so simple anymore.

What seemed to be required were some actual places where our mobile constituency could find itself. Two suggestions were proposed to local units, namely the development of

Discovery Centers, aimed at developing the capacity of church women to cope with the possibilities and problems facing them, and the setting up of *Listening Rooms* designed to provide a neutral place for individual and group reflection. Although it is too early to predict whether these proposals will have any widespread appeal, we shall set down for the record how they were initiated.

LISTENING Ellen Klemperer has lived many years on a farm
ROOMS south of Richmond, Indiana. She is a member of
Clear Creek Meeting of Friends and has degrees from Wellesley College, and the University of Chicago. Her greatest fulfillment is through people—all kinds of people. Her passion is finding ways of discovering that area of life where all are literally one—or rather, ways in which that area can discover itself. This has led her to work in international relations and to spend many years in Richmond's interracial center. She finds joy in children and grandchildren, farm life, loneliness and tragedy, flowers, the over-busy schedule, friends, giving and music.

She found peace in an interracial interdenominational prayer group because she was 'sick of the bleakness of the segregated church.' She was a member of the Committee of 100 United Church Women—where I first met her in Berea, Kentucky in 1966.

Ellen never bothered you unless it was important and then you might as well stop and listen. The first time was a telephone call offering to set up at the 1967 Assembly in Purdue the magnificent Ames mural where scenes depicting black history were carved in mahogany.

Then there was a postcard in January, 1974, offering the tapes and books of Dr. Thurman as a means of reconciliation in Asia. The Causeway teams were already on their way to San Francisco, but Ellen saw to it that Dr. Thurman delivered them to the hotel. And, of course, where the tapes went from there was beyond our imaginings.

Then she called to see if I wouldn't stop by her farm on a week-end ahead of a state meeting. I quickly agreed as I wanted to see a room off the kitchen of her home, called a

Listening Room where anyone whose need leads there, is welcome to *listen* to herself in meditation, to the birds outside the window, to the silent speech of pictures, to meditation tapes, and perhaps even to God.

We asked her to create such a room at the annual Board meeting at Nazareth, Kentucky in April, 1974. There, in the heart of tornado devastation with communication disrupted and women trying to reassure faroff families, the Listening Room offered to the many who visited it a place of quiet and peace. When I wrote to ask about the origins of the Listening Room, she answered:

> As you know, the original Listening Room is simply a room off the kitchen of my home. On Christmas morning, 1972, I was told, quite literally and specifically, in my heart, that the room should come into being. The need which prompted it was my own. It still is.

> There are four essentials for such a room: the tapes and books of Dr. Howard Thurman as well as other devotional materials, a place of quiet and comfort, a tape recorder, and a caring heart. It doesn't matter how many "helps" you have, nothing takes the place of a person who is simply there, caring about those who come. About this central core, one can play, literally play, with all sorts of things: the choice devotional books, pictures, and prints ever changing, fabrics, a record player with the best of music, soft, colorful pillows, and a couch. Each room is itself, and that is good, so long as the central pulse beat remains the same.

> This is the room as you found it, Margaret, when you came to visit me in the spring of '74. Then you asked me to transport it to Memphis for the Ecumenical Assembly of Church Women United!

> Memphis could be a story in itself: driving from Indiana there with my friend, Elizabeth Kelley, the car

loaded with essentials from my Listening Room: setting up the Memphis room with the devoted help of Church Women in Memphis and being there as hundreds of women found their way to that place. It was unforgettable.

"As I listened to women who used the listening room for reflection," observed Ellen Klemperer, "I noted a certain ripeness for growth . . . a terrible hunger to get at what was wrong, both individually and in the world, and to find the courage to do something about it . . . a concern that the person should not be lost with the enormity of the need." She has said:

Since that time, and partly because of that experience some forty Listening Rooms have come into existence. CWU's own Clarie Harvey, for instance, has established such a room in her home as well as three Listening Rooms in Black institutions of learning. Graced by her touch, they include artifacts from her wide travels, inviting the minds and spirits of those who come there to touch hearts with others around the world. Several such rooms have been created abroad.

As I write, I wonder at all this. Certainly it is not any of *our* doing. I see it more as a leap of life from the source, looking to us to let it sparkle.

DISCOVERY CENTERS The suggestion of the Discovery Center came during the consultation for the People's Platform for a Global Society. Dr. Jean Houston proposed that our best preparation could be in established "Discovery Centers" in each community. She again offered to prepare the Spark Kit for the development of women's potential in areas of creative thinking. Later she called and introduced us to some schools for children built on these models. Although we modified the idea somewhat, Jean would have been pleased as she heard BecLee Wilson present the idea to the Board through "imagining the future." It went something like this:

idea somewhat, Jean would have been pleased as she heard BecLee Wilson present the idea to the Board through "imagining the future." It went something like this:

• Imagine that it is 1977 and that "Discovery Centers" have been created by Church Women United in communities all around the country. Now, imagine that women from around the nation have come together to compare notes about the results. "Where it is possible for these small spontaneous groups to spring up," one woman is saying, "there is the seedbed for our future."

• In one city, there's a small room in a downtown church near a busy department store. CWU volunteers have created an environment for both planned and impromptu gatherings of women. They have set up a large research library filled with government publications on everything from nutrition and gardening to child care and aids to establishing day care centers. Other books deal with child nurturing, parenting, life crises such as divorce and death; and there is, of course, a wide range of scriptural materials. Professional women with careers in law, medicine, specialists in gardening and sewing are often visitors at the Discovery Center; there is a child psychologist volunteer to hold seminars at lunch time for women in business who may wish to have a 'bag lunch' and spend the time this way. Or perhaps the noon seminar includes women shoppers who want an alternative to the store tea rooms and consider a thought-provoking session an added bonus.

• In the largest hospital in a rural area, a small room near the chapel has been set aside for a Discovery Center. Particularly, it emphasizes the need of the women employed in the hospital. It was furnished under the direction of Church Women United through special gifts from former women patients. There is a "quiet area" with records and head phones for relaxation to music. There are special resource materials dealing with health questions. Life and death are part of a hospital day, and therefore materials to offer spiritual strength as well as factual knowledge are provided. Volunteers are present during some hours of the day; other periods are known as "solitude times."

• The largest insurance company in the Southwest has just moved to the suburbs of a city. This firm employs so many women that Church Women United requested permission to provide a Discovery Center. Again, there are resource and meditation materials and this one functions in conjunction with the company's new employee's day care center.

• On a college campus a Discovery Center, sponsored by Church Women United, especially emphasizes the gathering together of international and American women of the university and the community.

• All of these situations, through the vision of Church Women United throughout the nation, are all perfectly possible projects! In fact, all of them are actually based in reality. In our kind of time, when there is such a need for each other in coping with problems, when newcomers often find it difficult to discover CWU, when there is a universal need for just plain "human encounter," a Discovery Center has great possibilities.

• Although there would be local variation, the general design would hinge around a library and other facilities for planning and conversation groups; creative sessions in art, weaving, play reading or group discussion; a table-and-chairs area for two or three; a browsing chair for one. There might be a team to manage the Discovery Center, with a volunteer hostess on hand during certain hours; a bulletin board for leaving notices or circulating needs which CWU wished to share. All kinds of locations are possible—a room in a church or shopping center or an empty store . . .

locations are possible—a room in a church or shopping center or an empty store . . .

- If you like the idea of a Discovery Center, why not try it! Then share your experiences with the national office, and it will try to channel these experiences so that all of us know what is going on.

CHURCH WOMEN TOMORROW The present melds into the future only if the hand of one generation touches the hand of the next. The continuing dynamics of any movement require that there are a sufficient number of persons who are committed to its purpose, see possibilities in its way of work, articulate their aspirations to close associates, display an openness toward the ideas of others, and have a vision for the society they want to live in.

The movement flourishes as natural leaders are recognized in our midst, particularly if these leaders are sensitive to the longings of the wider circle of participants and can sharpen their objectives, clear the path for their progress, and take the brunt of criticism when they go astray!

The Search Committee, appointed to seek a new general director, was fortunate to find a person with these capacities of leadership in a related field. She was a person young enough to take the time required to gather loyalties in a national movement. Martha Edens came from twenty years of professional experience in the Mental Health Association, working during various periods in its local, regional, and national offices. Active in the United Methodist Church, she had undertaken special assignments for CWU, the goals and spirit of which she was happily atune.

Many a long termer in Church Women United can testify that its great variety of roles and activities provide a special incentive to renewed endeavor. I had a foretaste of the experience of changing roles at a celebration of the Greek Orthodox Easter on May 1, 1975. A seminar planned for International Women's Year was to open the following Monday. Those who came on the previous weekend had the opportunity to share in the midnight service, which highlights Easter for the Greek

Orthodox. The liturgy was to be led by Archbishop Iacovacs in the Greek Orthodox Cathedral of the Holy Trinity in New York City.

Among those who took advantage of this privilege were Martha and Maurice Edens of Pasadena, California. Our group was placed in the front central section, and Martha Edens was seated on the central aisle, while I was at the opposite end of the pew in front of her. We lived through the dramatic parts of the liturgy, the dark hours when Jesus was a "guest in the tomb," the mourning of the women, and the acts of contrition and expectation which anticipated the remembrance of the resurrection itself. The climax was timed to come just after the midnight hour. The Archbishop entered the inner sanctum, changed an outer robe, and emerged carrying high the double candelabra of blazing candles. He proceeded down the aisle to go out the main door of the church where he was to proclaim in five languages from an outdoor pulpit, "Christ is risen!"

The congregation stood reverently as the processional went down the aisle. Wondering about Martha Edens' reaction, I looked toward her. She was facing the aisle as the Archbishop passed her place, the lights from the candelabra illuminating her face, rapt in radiant ecstasy. As long as she reflects with such beauty the power of the resurrection, I thought, Church Women United will be in constant renewal.

The congregation followed the priests into the dark streets, lighting the tapers in their hands as they went out the door. By the time I emerged, the whole block was alive with men, women, and children. Although the candelabras were very effective in symbolizing the Good News of the risen Christ within the Church, it took a thousand tiny tapers in the hands of many different persons to light the dark city block! I was glad mine was one light among many!

The vibrant voice of Archbishop Iacovacs sounded over the crowd: "CHRIST IS RISEN! Christ is risen—in deed and in word!" Suddenly I was aware of the buzz of human voices all around me: a young couple making a date, a husband calling to his wife temporarily separated by the crowd, a group of men chuckling over some joke, a worried mother looking for a child. Here we were together—human beings living in the present world. Yet, each had light enough. Christ alive in us, the hope of glory!

The Archbishop led the faithful back into the Church where the Easter communion would be celebrated. I noticed that the Edens were returning under the friendly guidance of Terry Kocas, who handles the public relations for the Archdiocese.

Most of the crowd with their candles started down the street toward their homes. My friend and I entered the church briefly but then decided that we would rather be among the people. We drove the seventy blocks to our apartment house, carrying our lighted candles all the way. At the traffic signals, as we came alongside a taxi taking night celebrants home from the party, I lifted my candle slightly to greet them with the glad news: CHRIST IS RISEN!

In our Kansas home, we light a candle each meal and celebrate the holy seasons with a full complement of two burning candelabra. We share in the neighborhood crisis, we enjoy small triumphs, and receive gladly the offer of friends to cut wood, clear snow . . . or type manuscripts! As the gloom of today's vast disorders encircle us, candles of human kindness light the path ahead.

GLOSSARY

ABE	Adult Basic Education
ACWC	Asian Church Women's Conference
AP	Associated Press
CCA	Council of Churches in Asia (known earlier as East Asia Christian Conference)
CCUN	Church Center for the United Nations
CHART	
CIMADE	A French relief organization
CWHM	Council of Women for Home Missions
CCW	Council of Church Women (same thing as an organized "unit" of CWU)
CWS	Church World Service
CWU	Church Women United
CWW-FMC	Committee on Women's Work of the Foreign Missions Conference
EACC	East Asia Christian Conference (later called Council of Churches in Asia)
ERA	Equal Rights Amendment
FAO	Food and Agricultural Organization (United Nations)
FLC	Fellowship of the Least Coin
GDUCW	General Department of United Church Women
HOPE	Help Our Public Education
ICRE	International Council of Religious Education
ICWDP	International Committee for World Day of Prayer
IWY	International Women's Year
JAIL	Jail Alternatives and Involvement League

JSAC	Joint Strategy and Action Committee
LLL	Lessons Learned from Life
NCCC	National Council of Churches of Christ
NCCW	National Council of Church Women
NCFCW	National Council of Federated Church Women
NCW	National Commission of Women
NGO	Non-governmental Organization (related to the UN)
NCNW	National Council of Negro Women
NAE	National Association of Evangelicals
OASIS	Organization to Assist Schools in September
Unit	a term used after 1965 for the local organization or council
UCCW	United Council of Church Women (see UCW)
UCW	United Church Women
UNICEF	United Nations International Children's Emergency Fund
UNESCO	United Nations Educational, Scientific, and Cultural Organization
UNRRA	United Nations
UN	United Nations
SNCC	Student Non-violent Coordinating Committee
SCLC	Southern Christian Leadership Conference
WCC	World Council of Churches
WCFMC	Women's Committee of the Foreign Missions Conference
WILPF	Women's International League for Peace and Freedom
WACS	Women's Army Corps (Women's branch of the U.S. Army)

| WAVES | Women Appointed for Voluntary Emergency Service (Women's branch of the U.S. Navy) |
| WUCWO | World Union of Catholic Women's Organizations |

APPENDIX A

OFFICERS

1941 - 1942:

President:	Miss Amy Ogden Welcher	Hartford, Conn.
Vice Presidents:	Mrs. Robert McLean (Mary)	Santa Barbara, Cal.
	Mrs. C.E. Smith (Christine)	Detroit, Mich.
Vice Presidents at Large:	Mrs. I.J. Ayers	El Paso, Texas
	Mrs. Andrew Dale	Columbia, Tenn.
	Mrs. E.L. Eggers	Hammond, Ind.
	Mrs. E.H. Gebert	Longview, Wash.
	Mrs. Virgil Sease	New Brunswick, N.J.
	Miss Mary C. Smith	Minneapolis, Minn.
Recording Secretary:	Mrs. Fred H. White (Bernice)	Buffalo, N.Y.
Treasurer:	Miss Henrietta Gibson	Albany, N.Y.

1942 - 1944:

President:	Miss Amy Ogden Welcher	Hartford, Conn.

Vice Presidents:	Mrs. Abram LeGrand (Mabelle Rae)	Beaver Dam, Wis.
	Mrs. Robert S. McLean (Mary)	Yakima, Wash.
	Mrs. C.E. Smith (Christine)	Detroit, Mich.
Area Vice Presidents:	Mrs. I.J. Ayers	El Paso, Texas
	Mrs. Andrew Dale	Nashville, Tenn.
	Mrs. E.L. Eggers	Hammond, Ind.
	Mrs. E.H. Gebert	Longview, Wash.
	Mrs. Emory Ross	New York, N.Y.
	Miss Mary C. Smith	Minneapolis, Minn.
Recording Secretary:	Mrs. Fred H. White (Bernice)	Buffalo, N.Y.
Treasurer:	Miss Henrietta Gibson	Albany, N.Y.

1944 – 1946:

President:	Mrs. Harper Sibley (Georgiana)	Rochester, N.Y.
Vice Presidents:	Miss Mabel Head	Cleveland, Ohio
	Mrs. Robert S. McLean (Mary)	Yakima, Wash.
	Mrs. David D. Jones	Greensboro, N.C.
Area Vice Presidents:	Mrs. I.J. Ayers	El Paso, Texas
	Mrs. George Nace	Portland, Ore.
	Mrs. Charles H. Seymour	Knoxville, Tenn.

	Mrs. J.R. Smiley	Indianapolis, Ind.
	Mrs. E.S. Wegner	Lincoln, Neb.
	Miss Amy Ogden Welcher	Hartford, Conn.
Recording Secretary:	Mrs. Fred H. White (Bernice)	Buffalo, N.Y.
Treasurer:	Miss Henrietta Gibson	New York, N.Y.

1946 - 1948:

President:	Mrs. Harper Sibley (Georgiana)	Rochester, N.Y.
Vice Presidents:	Mrs. David D. Jones	Greensboro, N.C.
	Mrs. Charles Gilkey	Chicago, Ill.
	Mrs. Wilson Compton	Pullman, Wash.
	Mrs. M.M. Dozier	Pasadena, Cal.
	Mrs. J. Quinter Miller	Tuckahoe, N.Y.
	Mrs. A.H. Sterne	Atlanta, Ga.
Recording Secretary:	Mrs. Virgil Sly	Indianapolis, Ind.
Treasurer:	Miss Gertrude Vint	New York, N.Y.

1948 - 1950:

President:	Mrs. Harper Sibley (Georgiana)	Rochester, N.Y.

Vice Presidents:	Mrs. Wilson Compton	Pullman, Wash.
	Mrs. Charles Gilkey	S. Yarmouth, Mass.
	Mrs. John M. Hanna	Dallas, Texas
	Mrs. David D. Jones	Greensboro, N.C.
	Mrs. David Jorgenson	Altadena, Cal.
	Mrs. J. Quinter Miller	Tuckahoe, N.Y.
	Mrs. A.H. Sterne	Atlanta, Ga.
Recording Secretary:	Mrs. Abbie Clement Jackson	Louisville, Ky.
Treasurers:	Miss Gertrude Vint	New York, N.Y.
	Mrs. B.W. Hamilton	New York, N.Y.

1950 - 1953:

President:	Mrs. James D. Wyker (Mossie)•	Columbia, Mo.
Vice Presidents:	Mrs. J. Lewis Gillies	Los Angeles, Cal.
	Mrs. R. Thompson Hollis	Spencer, Okla.
	Mrs. William Sale Terrill	W. Hartford, Conn.
Recording Secretary:	Mrs. H.M. Patrick	Bernardsville, N.J.
Corresponding Secretary:	Mrs. F.R. Crawford	Farmville, Va.
Treasurer:	Mrs. Norman Vincent Peale (Ruth)	New York, N.Y.

1953 - 1955:

President:	Mrs. James D. Wyker (Mossie)	Columbia, Mo.
Vice Presidents:	Mrs. J. Birdsall Calkins (Gladys)	Arlington, Va.
	Mrs. Howard G. Colwell	Loveland, Colo.
	Mrs. Charles S. Johnson	Nashville, Tenn.
Recording Secretary:	Mrs. Norvell E. Wicker	Louisville, Ky.
Corresponding Secretary:	Mrs. E.L. Hillman	Durham, N.C.
Treasurer:	Mrs. Norman Vincent Peale (Ruth)	New York, N.Y.

1955 - 1958:

President:	Mrs. Theodore O. Wedel (Cynthia)	Washington, D.C.
Vice Presidents:	Mrs. Spann W. Milner (Ida)	Atlanta, Ga.
	Mrs. Samuel J. Walker	Whittier, Cal.
	Mrs. Rosa Page Welch	Chicago, Ill.
Recording Secretary:	Mrs. Edwin B. Zeller	Cedar Rapids, Iowa
Corresponding Secretary:	Mrs. Anne E. Heath	Washington, D.C.
Treasurer:	Mrs. E. Roy Corman	Wilkinsburg, Pa.

1958 - 1961:

President:	Mrs. William Sale Terrill (Marjorie S.)	W. Hartford, Conn.
Vice Presidents:	Mrs. Jesse Jai McNeil (Pearl)	Detroit, Mich.
	Mrs. Wallace N. Streeter	Washington, D.C.
	Mrs. Theodore F. Wallace (Louise)	Kansas City, Kan.
Recording Secretary:	Mrs. C. Newton Kidd (Irma)	Baltimore, Md.
Corresponding Secretary:	Mrs. Fred H. White (Bernice H.)	Buffalo, N.Y.
Treasurer:	Mrs. Stuart E. Sinclair (Edna)	Greenfield, Mass.

1961 - 1964:

President:	Mrs. Theodore F. Wallace (Louise)	Kansas City, Kan.
Vice Presidents:	Mrs. D.R. Kellum	Indianapolis, Ind.
	Mrs. Hugo Ringstrom	Seattle, Wash.
	Mrs. Stuart E. Sinclair	Greenfield, Mass.
Recording Secretary:	Mrs. Emile M. O'Bee (Ernestine)	Milwaukee, Wis.
Corresponding Secretary:	Mrs. H.C. Bleckschmidt	St. Louis, Mo.
Treasurer:	Mrs. Ernest H. Hoeldtke (Catherine)	Buffalo, N.Y.

1964 - 1967:

President:	Mrs. Stuart E. Sinclair (Edna)	Greenfield, Mass.
Vice Presidents:	Mrs. J. Russell Henderson (Ernestine)	Little Rock, Ark.
	Mrs. George B. Martin (Mabel)	Summit, N.J.
	Mrs. Mary O. Ross	Detroit, Mich.
Recording Secretary:	Mrs. James Clapp (Edna)	Rapid City, S.D.
Corresponding Secretary:	Mrs. J. Paul Gruver (Alberta)	Dayton, Va.
Treasurer:	Mrs. Percy Rex (Ruth)	Wilmington, Del.

1967 - 1971:

President:	Mrs. James M. Dolbey (Dorothy N.)	Cincinnati, Ohio
Vice Presidents:	Mrs. Kyle Haselden (Elizabeth L.)	Chicago, Ill.
	Mrs. Leo Marsh (Bessie M.)	Montclair, N.J.
	Mrs. J.W. Sonnenday (Margaret L.)	St. Louis, Mo.
Secretary:	Miss Clara Nickolson	Allston, Mass.
Treasurer:	Miss Dorothy Nossett	New York, N.Y.

1971 - 1974:

President:	Clarie Collins Harvey (Mrs. Martin L., Jr.)	Jackson, Miss.
Vice Presidents:	Julia L. Piper (Mrs. James C.)	Parsons, Kan.
	Abigail Q. McCarthy (Mrs. Eugene)	Washington, D.C.
	Margaret L. Sonnenday (Mrs. J.W.)	St. Louis, Mo.
Secretary:	Georgia Gayden (Mrs.) (d. 1971)	Brooklyn, N.Y.
	Nobuko Haworth (Mrs. Robert)	New York, N.Y.
Treasurer:	Opal W. Sherman (Mrs. Dallas B.)	New York, N.Y.
Vice Presidents for Interpretation and Cultivation:	Ruth Aurelius (Mrs. Marcus)	Des Moines, Iowa
	Helen L. Chupco (Mrs. Lee)	Jenks, Okla.
	Louise B. Davidson (Mrs. Raymond B.)	Boonton, N.J.
Vice Presidents for Interpretation and Cultivation (cont.):	Maxine Drinkard (Mrs. Clifton B.)	Austin, Texas
	Norma Eby (Mrs. John E.)	Auburn, Wash.
	Dorothy D. France (Mrs. Carl G.)	Pulaski, Va.
	Jessie A. Pratt (Mrs. Robert B.)	Philadelphia, Pa.
	Nomi H. Smith (Mrs. David T.)	Tucson, Ariz.
	Sister Mary Luke Tobin, S.L.	Lakewood, Colo.
	Elnora B. Walcott (Mrs. LeRoy V.)	Grand Rapids, Mich.

1974 - 1977:

President:	Margaret L. Sonnenday (Mrs. J.W.)	St. Louis, Mo.
Vice Presidents:	Mary Louise Rowand (Mrs. E.C. Jr.)	Dallas, Texas
	Miriam Phillips (Mrs. Oscar G.)	West Medford, Mass.
	Ruth Segerhammar (Mrs. Carl W.)	Los Angeles, Cal.
	Beclee N. Wilson (Mrs. John O.)	Piedmont, Cal.
Secretary:	Nobuko Haworth (Mrs. Robert)	New York, N.Y.
Treasurer:	Margaret W. Driscoll (Mrs. Walter B.)	Sante Fe, N.M.

APPENDIX B

Professional Staff

1942-1976

Baker, Helen (Mrs. David D.)	Editor, *The Church Woman*, Assoc. General Director	1952-1964
Baron, Virginia	Program Materials	1973-1975
Bidwell, Leslie S.	Public Relations	1958-1964
Booth, Katie	Urban Programs	1972-
Boswell, Nina	Administration/Finance	1966-
Byrd, Fannie	Publications	1957-1961
Cushing, Frances (Mrs. S.T.)	Christian Social Relations	1946-1950
Dail, Hilda (Mrs. Roderick)	Financial Development	1971-1973
Dow, Dorothe	WICS Liaison	1971-1976
Edens, Martha (Mrs. R. Maurice)	General Director	1975-
Ellison, Virginia H. (Mrs. James W.)	Publications	1961-1964

Evans, Miriam Libby (Mrs. James)	Christian World Missions	1949–1960
French, Eleanor	Christian Social Relations	1959–1966
Gates, Janet (Mrs. C.M.)	Financial Development	1969–1970
Groner, Edith L.	Finance/Associate General Director; Associate General Director	1949–1957
Harper, Elsie D.	Christian World Relations	1953–1956
Haselden, Elizabeth L. (Mrs. Kyle)	Urban Programs	1969–
Head, Mabel	Christian World Relations	1946–1950
Hyde, Dr. Floy S. (Mrs. L. Eldred)	Leadership Education	1952–1957
Hymer, Esther W. (Mrs. Howard)	Christian World Relations	1957–1964
Johns, R. Elizabeth	Citizen Action	1968–1971
Jones, Elsie (Mrs. Caspar)	State Cultivation	1965–1970
LeGrand, Mabelle (Mrs. Abram)	Editor, *The Church Woman*	1943–1952
Leppert, Alice M. (Mrs. Walter)	Community Services	1968–1976
MacLeod, Dorothy (Mrs. W. Murdoch)	General Director	1948–1965
McCallion, Edna (Mrs. Harry J.)	UN Program	1976–
Meares, Carrie E.	Assignment Race	1961–1964

Naylor, Gladys (Mrs. Kurtis)	International Community	1968-1973
Nossett, Dorothy	Finance/Assoc. General Director	1957-1970
	Assoc. General Director	
Pfuetze, Louise (Mrs. Paul)	WICS Liaison	1967-1968
Randall, Claire	Christian World Missions	1962-1973
	National Program Development	
Rowland, Wilmina M.	Leadership Training	1954-1955
Reckmeyer, Luella	Christian World Relations	1949-1953
Roberts, Nina	Assoc. Secretary - Christian Social Relations	1946-1948
Ross, Myrta P. (Mrs. Emory)	Public Relations Christian World Missions	1943-1957
Shannon, Margaret	Executive Director	1966-1975
Stachurski, Betty	Finance/Personnel	1971-1973
Stamats, Esther	Christian Social Relations	1951-1958
Strong, Katherine (Mrs. Robbins)	Christian World Relations	1964-1967
Subramanya, Shireen	Public Relations/Publications	1970-
Tilghman, Maza	Public Relations	1965-1970
Tobin, Sister Mary Luke	Citizen Action	1973-

Turnbull, Helen.B.	Leadership Training	1959–1969
Verdesi, Elizabeth (Mrs. Ariel)	State Cultivation	1971–
VanderRoest, Elizabeth (Mrs. John)	Finance/Personnel	1970–1972
Wagner, Dorothy	International Community	1974–
Weber, Ruth	Editor, *The Church Woman*	1965–
Woodcock, Ruth (Mrs.)	Associate General Director	1975–
Worrell, Ruth Mougey (Mrs.)	Executive Secretary	1942–1948
Wyker, Mossie (Mrs. James D.)	Special Staff Representative	1960–1967

APPENDIX C

CELEBRATION THEMES

	WORLD DAY OF PRAYER	MAY FELLOWSHIP DAY	WORLD COMMUNITY DAY
1920	The World to Christ We Bring		
1921	God's Word and Work for the World		
1922	A Service of Prayer and Praise ("More things are wrought by prayer than this world dreams of." —Tennyson)		
1923	Ye Are the Light of the World		
1924	The Spirit of Power		
1925	Even as Thou Wilt		
1926	In Everything by Prayer		
1927	Pray Ye Therefore		
1928	Breaking Down Barriers		
1929	That They All May Be One		

1930	That Jesus May Be Lifted Up	
1932	Hold Fast in Prayer	
1933	Follow Thou Me	Dedication Day
1934	Pray for the Peace of Jerusalem	Dedication Day
1935	Bear Ye One Another's Burdens	Dedication Day
1936	On Earth, Peace, Goodwill Toward Men	Dedication Day
1937	Thou Art the Christ, the Son of the Living God	Dedication Day
1938	The Church—A World Fellowship	May Luncheons: Unity in Christian Service
1939	Let Us Put Our Love Into Deeds—and Make It Real	Women's May Luncheon: Can Christians Bind the World Together?
1940	In Quietness and In Confidence Shall Be Your Strength	Nationwide May Luncheons: What-Why-Where-How Do Ye More Than Others?
1941	Thy Kingdom Come	Thy Kingdom Come—Through the Work United Hearts Can Do

Year			
1942	I Am The Way	With Malice Toward None; With Charity For All	
1943	Father, I Pray That They May All Be One	Christian Family Life	The Price of An Enduring Peace
1944	And the Lord Wondered That There Was No Intercessor	May Fellowship Day: Children and Youth—Leaders of Tomorrow!	The Price of Enduring Peace—The Economic Price
1945	That Ye Should Show Forth the Praises of Him Who Hath Called You Out of Darkness into His Marvelous Light	Our Town	Price of Peace
1946	The Things That Make for Our Peace	Our Families—Challenges to Church, Home, Families, Community, Rediscover—the Home, Family, God, Unity	One World
1947	But We Will Give Ourselves Continually to Prayer and to the Ministry of the Word	The Fabric of Fellowship	The World Is My Community
1948	The World at Prayer	Every Child Is My Child—In The Fabric of Fellowship	Peace Is My Responsibility

Year			
1949	The Lord Is Thy Keeper	Freedom's Foundation—The Christian Home	Peace IS Possible
1950	Faith For Our Time	Our Daily Bread	Love Thy Neighbor
1951	Perfect Love Casteth Out Fear	Thank God For Work	Live Thy Faith!
1952	Christ, Our Hope	Spiritual Security for Today's Families	Building Lasting Peace
1953	Walk As Children Of Light	Citizenship—Our Christian Concern	Building Lasting Peace—What Do Ye More Than Others?
1954	That They May Have Life	The Christian Women's Trusteeship	Building Lasting Peace—Let The Children Come To Me
1955	Abide In Me	The Responsible Christian Family	Give Us This Day Our Daily Bread
1956	One Flock, One Shepherd	Who Forms Your Opinions?	Human Rights—For The Sake Of My Brethren, My Kinsmen
1957	Who Shall Separate Us . . . ?	Free Schools In A Free America	Bread, Freedom, Dignity
1958	The Bread Of Life	A Place To Live	Exchange: Goods, Ideas, People
1959	Lord, I Believe	How Much Is Enough?	Full Partners For Peace
1960	Labourers Together With God	Citizenship—Free and Responsible	Christian Action For Freedom

1961	Forward Through The Ages (WDP 75th Anniversary)	The Churches—Free and Responsible	Freedom To Know
1962	For God So Loved The World	One Family Under God: Who Is My Family?	Deepen The Channels
1963	More Than Conquerors	One Family Under God: Genuine And Full Participation	Nation Building and the UN
1964	Let Us Pray	One Family Under God: Freedom Of Residence And Job Opportunity	Nations In Community
1965	What Doth The Lord Require?	People, Poverty, Plenty	Laity's Mission in World Affairs
1966	You Are My Witness	People, Poverty, Plenty—Discover, Plan, ACT	Laity—Rights, Resources, Responsibilities
1967	Of His Kingdom There Shall Be No End	People, Poverty, Plenty—How Can ALL Share?	Who Shall Separate Us?
1968	Bear Ye One Another's Burdens	Human Values In A Technological Society	New World A'Coming
1969	Growing Together In Christ	Beginning Anew	Community Development and Nation Building
1970	Take Courage!	Dissolve The Distance Between	Use A Key For Tomorrow: Education

Year			
1971	New Life Awaits	Focus On The Family In A New Era: Enlarge The Place Of Your Tent	Build A New Earth
1972	All Joy Be Yours	Behold The Woman	Coming Of Age
1973	Alert In Our Time	As Hand Touches Hand	Where In The World Is My Neighbor?
1974	Make Us Builders Of Peace	Explore New Paths	Discover The Aspiring Majority
1975	Become Perfectly One	Open To Live Fully	One Community Under God
1976	Education FOR ALL OF LIFE	1776 * Valiant Women * 1976	Into The Third Century—Unafraid
1977	Love In Action	Gifts To Claim	Heart Change—Global Change

APPENDIX D

ASSEMBLIES

SECTION 1

UNITED COUNCIL OF CHURCH WOMEN

December 11-13, 1941	UCCW Constituting Convention	Atlantic City, New Jersey
December 5-10, 1942	First National Assembly "Church Women on the Alert"	Cleveland, Ohio
November 14-16, 1944	Second National Assembly "Our Responsibility in Our World-Wide Christian Fellowship"	Columbus, Ohio
November 11-15, 1946	Third National Assembly "Until We All Attain to the Unity of Faith"	Grand Rapids, Michigan
November 15-18, 1948	Fourth National Assembly "Thy Kingdom Come"	Milwaukee, Wisconsin

November 13-16, 1950 — Fifth National Assembly "Thy Word—On Earth" — Cincinnati, Ohio

SECTION 2

UNITED CHURCH WOMEN

October 5-8, 1953 — Sixth National Assembly "Christ Calls to Mission and Unity" — Atlantic City, New Jersey

November 7-10, 1955 — Seventh National Assembly "The Working of His Power" — Cleveland, Ohio

October 27-30, 1958 — Eighth National Assembly "Christianity and Freedom" — Denver, Colorado

October 9-12, 1961 — Ninth National Assembly "The Church Ecumenical" — Miami Beach, Florida

October 5-9, 1964 — Tenth National Assembly "Laity in Mission" — Kansas City, Missouri

CHURCH WOMEN UNITED IN THE U.S.A.

July 13–16, 1967	Eleventh Ecumenical Assembly "New Dimensions"	Purdue University West Lafayette, Indiana
April 22–25, 1971	Twelfth Ecumenical Assembly "Breakthru"	Wichita, Kansas
October 10–13, 1974	Thirteenth Ecumenical Assembly "Journey to Wholeness"	Memphis, Tennessee
July 7–10, 1977	Fourteenth Ecumenical Assembly "Signatures of Faith"	Purdue University West Lafayette, Indiana

INDEX for *"Just Because"*

This index is limited to a cross reference of topics developed in several chapters and to leaders involved with new policy or program. No attempt is made to list the many volunteers or professional staff related to the programs identified in the Table of Contents.

continued ▶